LOYOLA
HTS
WELCOME TO
ORIOLE PARK AT CAMDEN YARDS

The Baltimore Orioles

◆

Forty Years of Magic from 33rd Street to Camden Yards

TED PATTERSON

TAYLOR PUBLISHING COMPANY
DALLAS, TEXAS

Published by
Taylor Publishing Company
1550 West Mockingbird Lane
Dallas, Texas 75235

Contributing photographers: Kevin Allen, Louis Berney, John Cummings. Dick Darcey, Brian D. Dziuba, Rick Lippenholz, Rich Riggins, Morton Tadder, Jerry Wachter, and Stu Zolotorow

Designed by David Timmons

Library of Congress Cataloging-in-Publication Data

Patterson, Ted.
The Baltimore Orioles : 40 Years of Magic from 33rd Street to Camden Yards / by Ted Patterson
p. cm.
Includes index.
ISBN 0-87833-865-9
1. The Baltimore Orioles (Baseball team)—History. I. Title.
GV875.B2P36 1994
796.357'64'097526—dc 20 94-21570
CIP

Printed in the United States of America

10 9 8 7 6 5 4 3 2 1

This book is dedicated to all the players, coaches and managers
who ever slipped on a uniform and took the field as a member of the Baltimore Orioles.
Yours is a special fraternity, one of class and distinction,
and all of you should be proud, regardless of your contributions.

RIPKEN
8
HOILES
23

Contents

Acknowledgments

Certainly, compiling a volume that encompasses well over 100 years of baseball history is far from a one-man job. Finding words to thank all the people who have aided in this project is difficult and there is always the fear of leaving deserving people out.

Former public relations director Bob Brown, who currently edits the *Oriole Gazette,* heads my thank you list. Long before the age of computers, Bob was compiling detailed statistical information on the Orioles over a long period, as well as chronicling the Orioles from year-to-year in the annual press guide and yearbook.

Thanks to Bob's successor Rick Vaughn and his staff, with special thanks to Stephanie Parrilo for her help in photo research. Also thanks to Public Affairs head Charles Steinberg, and to retired Sunpapers writer Jim Bready, who authored the most complete history of Baltimore baseball in his book, *The Home Team.*

My appreciation to Greg Schwalenberg, curator of the Babe Ruth Museum in Baltimore, who made available photos of the old Orioles and the Negroe Leagues.

Thanks to photographer Rick Lippenholz for his painstaking work in photographing Oriole memorabilia, and also thanks to photographers Mort Tadder, Louis Berney, Kevin Allen, Harry McLaughlin, John Cummings, Dick Darcey, Rich Riggins, Jerry Wachter, and Stu Zolotorow for their help. Thanks to collectors Blair Jett, Phil Wood, and Ron Menchine for their loan of Oriole memorabilia. And thanks to The Babe Ruth Museum.

The new Oriole ownership deserves my appreciation for approving the backing of this history of Oriole baseball. I'd especially like to single out minority owner Steve Geppi, who has keen recollections of his youth rooting for the Orioles and had realized a lifelong dream to be part of the ownership of his hometown team.

Special thanks go to computer genius Will Fastie for his guidance and expertise, and to Mike Patterson for his computer troubleshooting. Also to editor-proofer Louis Berney for his efforts in correcting the text and to Oriole historian Dave Howell. Finally, thanks to Michael Emmerich and the folks at Taylor Publishing who believed in this project from the beginning and put together such a quality book.

Foreword

BY BROOKS ROBINSON

It's hard for me to comprehend, but of the 40 years the Orioles have been in business, I've been involved in 39 of them as a player and broadcaster. That's over two-thirds of my life.

I never dreamed when I signed that Oriole contract in May of 1955 after my high school graduation, hoping for a shot at the big leagues, that I'd play 23 years with one club. I was just hoping I'd be good enough to play a couple of years.

After my playing days came broadcasting and I've enjoyed that end of it, too. It's been fun playing and watching as the Orioles developed into one of the premier franchises in baseball. And who could have ever predicted the attendance levels? When I played the Colts were more popular than the Orioles in Baltimore. In those years we were fighting to draw a million fans, but that changed just as I was nearing the end of my career. Today's attendance figures, however, are staggering. Three-and-one-half million people is a real tribute to the Orioles—and especially their fans.

Yet those years I played were so special. Money hadn't become the factor it is now. There was more togetherness and a love of the game. From the front office to the grounds crew, the Orioles were a family. The players and their families hung around together. That doesn't seem to be the case as much today. No question the game has changed, but everything has. Baseball just reflects the times we live in.

To have played my entire twenty-three-year career with one team is something that means a great deal to me. Even in those rocky early days, when I was trying to get a foothold in the major leagues, the Baltimore fans were something special. They were patient with me and they took their lumps right along with me. As I mentioned earlier, they didn't come out in huge numbers, but they were dyed-in-the-wool fans who knew and loved the game. If they weren't at the park, they were listening on radio or watching on television.

I had great early teachers in Baltimore. Paul Richards saw my raw ability and refused to listen to the people that didn't think I'd ever hit in the big leagues. The man I replaced at third base, George Kell, taught me all he know about playing third. He also taught me how to conduct myself as a big leaguer, to be a role model, and someone kids and all fans could look up to. George and I hailed from the state of Arkansas and the two of us went arm and arm into the Hall of Fame in 1983. That Cooperstown induction ceremony made me even more proud to call Baltimore my home. There was a sea of orange and black colors in the crowd that day, a crowd that broke all previous induction records. For the ultimate in thrills, that day rivaled the day the club gave me in 1977 when I bowed out as a player.

I think of the players I played with, several of whom have gone on to the Hall of Fame, but so many others who were solid ballplayers who contributed to the development of the Orioles. In the early years, there was Willy Miranda, Ronnie Hansen, Billy Gardner, Gene Woodling, Gus Triandos, Bob Nieman and Skinny Brown. Then came Jim Gentile, Boog Powell, Dave McNally, Paul Blair, and Jim Palmer. By the time I retired in 1977 only Palmer remained from the first World Series teams, but I was playing with a new group of kids, Eddie Murray, Doug DeCinces, Mike Flanagan, Scott McGregor, Ken Singleton, Dennis Martinez, and Rick Dempsey, to name a few, who would carry the Orioles back to the World Series in 1979 and 1983.

All the managers I played for were different. Richards was like a father figure. Billy Hitchcock was a southern gentleman who sat back and expected the players to motivate themselves. Unfortunately, not all of them could. Hank Bauer kicked a few behinds but was a player's manager who took little credit for managing our 1966 team to the championship. Earl Weaver was intense and just insecure enough to have us playing all out all the time. Hopefully Earl will one day join Frank Robinson, Jim Palmer, and me in the Hall of Fame.

Now for the first time, the entire 40 years of Oriole baseball is pulled together in one volume. Ted Patterson, a friend for over 20 years, has assembled one of the greatest collections of Oriole memorabilia I've seen. He shares it with all of us here. I'm sure you'll enjoy reliving 40 years of Oriole memories as much as I did.

Brooks Robinson
September 1994

Preface

Years ending in four have played a significant role in Baltimore baseball history. In 1894, the "old Orioles" of Ned Hanlon, John McGraw, Wee Willie Keeler, Hughie Jennings, Wilbert Robinson and company were winning their first of three straight National League championships.

In 1914 the Baltimore Terrapins were beginning their first of two seasons as a major-league team in the ill-fated Federal League.

In 1924 Jack Dunn's International League Orioles were winning their sixth of seven consecutive International League crowns, an unprecedented feat in any professional baseball league.

In the war year of 1944, Tommy Thomas guided the Orioles to their last International League championship and a win over Louisville in the Junior World Series. It was also the year in which Oriole Park burned down and the short trek up Greenmount Avenue was made from 29th to 33rd Street, a trek that would eventually lead to the big leagues.

Ten years later, 1954 signaled the rebirth of major-league baseball in Baltimore after a 52-year hiatus, (excluding the truncated Federal League). In 1964 the Orioles mounted their first serious run at the pennant, finishing just two games behind the Yankees. The Birds won the American League East in 1974, their last with vintage names like Robinson, Powell, McNally, Blair, and Cuellar. Jim Palmer, the O's greatest pitcher, retired in 1984. Now, in 1994, the Orioles have reached another milestone, their 40th anniversary. Not many franchises can boast of a legacy comparable to the Orioles, a legacy even more impressive given that they started from the bottom in 1954. Thanks to such luminaries as Paul Richards, Lee MacPhail, Harry Dalton, Hank Bauer, Earl Weaver, Frank Cashen, Jerry Hoffberger, Hank Peters, Edward Bennett Williams, Frank Robinson, and Roland Hemond, the Orioles made a quick ascent from the American League cellar, the regular home of their St. Louis predecessor, and established themselves as one of the best franchises in baseball. And one of the primary reasons is the Orioles' ability to swiftly rebound from the game's inevitable down cycles—an Oriole earmark for years.

I've covered the Orioles for more than half of their 40 years, coming to Baltimore in 1973. Those great Oriole teams of Brooks, Boog, McNally, Cuellar, Blair, and Belanger would soon give way to a new flock of Birds named Murray, Flanagan, McGregor, Singleton, Dempsey, Bumbry, Dauer, and a kid named Ripken. Like Brooks, Jim Palmer seemed to stay forever and transcend the eras, the only pitcher to win World Series games in three different decades.

This 40-year anniversary volume pays tribute to the Baltimore Orioles through words, pictures, and memorabilia. It's the story of a love affair between a city and its baseball team, a bond that grows stronger every year. Happy anniversary Orioles and here's to many happy returns.

THE BALTIMORE ORIOLES

ROWLAN

BALTIMORE 1894-5-6
FAYETTE
City Steam Bottling House
CHALLENGE GINGER ALE
OFFICIAL SCORE CARD
BALTIMORE BASEBALL CLUB
A HOME MANUFACTURE
GEORGE BREHM'S BEER
ONE GRADE ONLY
George Brehm's BEER
FAMILIES PROMPTLY SUPPLIED

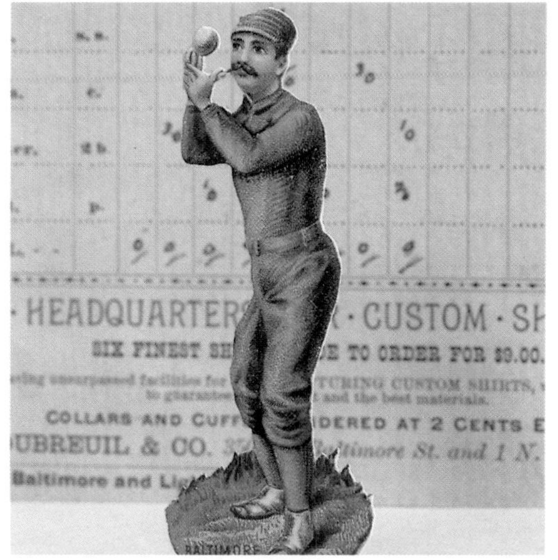
HEADQUARTERS
CUSTOM
COLLARS AND CUFFS
DUBREUIL & CO.
Baltimore and Ligh

ALL-AMERICA
BASE BALL
BALTIMORE
1897
OFFICIAL SCORE CARD
1896

Before the Dawn

Baltimore's entry into major-league baseball did not begin in 1954. It just resumed—after a 52-year separation. Sixty years before, in 1894, the old Orioles of John J. McGraw won their first National League pennant. The game's beginnings in Baltimore, in fact, trace back ever farther than the McGraw era, all the way to 1859 when a team named the Baltimore Excelsiors made their debut.

Uncle Wilbert Robinson played longer for the Orioles than anybody until another Robinson named Brooks.

The game didn't exactly flourish here during the Civil War years, as it did in military camps and some other parts of the country, but Baltimore did field a team. Sporting players from both the North and South, its team was known as the Pastimes. The players wore blue caps with white visors, white shirts with a large blue "P" on the front, and blue pants. They also wore neckties. The Pastimes hit their peak in 1867 when they triumphed over the New York Mutuals, the self-proclaimed champions of the United States, 47-31.

Standing only 5-4 1/2 and weighing 140 pounds, Willie Keeler "hit 'em where they ain't" for 19 big league seasons, banging out 2,962 hits and compiling a .345 lifetime average, fifth on the all-time list. In his first season in Baltimore in 1894 he hit .371 and followed it with .391, .392, and .432 averages, dropping down to .379 in 1898.

Before 1869 baseball had been considered an amateur sport. Reports circulated that players were paid, and the hat was always passed to meet expenses, but it wasn't until the Wright brothers of Cincinnati, Harry and George, formed the famed Red Stockings in 1869 that the game turned professional. They barnstormed throughout the East and Midwest and made a stop in Baltimore, embarrassing the Maryland Baseball Club 47-7. The Red Stocking juggernaut won 92 straight, with one tie, before they lost a game.

That 47-7 shellacking was a dramatic illustration of the benefits of paying players, so in 1870 Baltimore fielded its first professional team. The game in those years following the Civil War bore little resemblance to the one of today. Gloves were mostly skin tight and not worn by everyone. Pitchers stayed in the entire game, a more reasonable expectation because overhand pitches were illegal and the distance between the mound and home plate was only 45 feet. Not surprisingly no pitcher changed speeds so scores often topped 40 runs a game—per team. In 1884 the overhand pitch was finally legalized and in 1893 the mound was moved to its traditional 60 feet six inches from home plate.

John J. McGraw, who swung from the left side, and compiled a .334 lifetime average. The brash third baseman became the Orioles player-manager at the age of 26. His fiery play and leadership helped them win three straight National League pennants. He would later win 10 pennants in his 30 years as manager of the New York Giants.

The first major league (the National Association) was formed in 1871, and even though the Baltimore team had been a power for years, it wasn't included in the 10-city circuit. The Maryland nine had toured the Midwest the summer before and made a stop in Fort Wayne, Indiana, where they were offered salaries to represent that city. So they stayed, formed the Fort Wayne Kekiongas, and joined the National Association with Philadelphia, Boston, Chicago, Cleveland, and New York. Some 113 years later, another Indiana town spirited away Baltimore's beloved football Colts in the middle of a snowy March night. Little did anyone know that precedent had been set in 1871.

In May of 1871 the Baltimore-turned-Fort Wayne club played the first ever major-league game, beating the Cleveland Forest Citys 2-0. The players were almost all from Maryland, including the Baltimore boy who pitched and won the game, little Bobby Mathews, who weighed a scant 120 pounds. Because of the benign nature of pitching in those days, teams carried only one pitcher, meaning Mathews hurled every inning of every game. When he retired at the age of 36 he had amassed 298 wins, including 42 in one season.

The Fort Wayne team folded before the end of 1871 due to pitiful play and attendance. When the Kekiongas, named after an Indian tribe, disbanded, many of their players returned to Baltimore where they joined the city's first major-league franchise in 1872. They were called the Lord Baltimores, and behind the pitching of Cherokee Fisher beat the vaunted New York Mutuals 14-8. The Lord Baltimores played at long-gone Newington Park on Pennsylvania Avenue. They won 35 and lost 19 that first year, good for second place, with Bobby Mathews winning 26 of them. Boston, behind the pitching of A.G. Spalding, won the pennant the first five years. Spalding's record in 1875 was an awesome 56-5.

The National League was formed in 1875—without a team from Baltimore. The Lord Baltimores dissolved the year before, and except for isolated games the city was without professional baseball until 1882 when the American Association was born. Baltimore and Philadelphia were the only Eastern cities in the six-team loop. In 1883, the team moved into a new ballpark at the corner of Greenmount and 25th, and even more significantly, changed its nickname to Orioles. In honor of the new nickname the field was called Oriole Park.

Hughie Jennings, a peppery shortstop whose famed "Ee-yah" cry rallied his teammates. Altogether, Jennings played or managed with 12 big-league pennant winners, including in his first three years as manager in Detroit.

By 1884 12 teams were in the American Association. Baltimore also had a professional club in the Union Association and the Eastern League, the minor-league forerunner of the International League of today.

The Orioles, though, grabbed the public's fancy, especially a pitcher named Matt Kilroy who became a local hero. In 1886 Kilroy struck out 505 batters; in 1887 he won 46 games. Pitching from a distance of fifty feet, the young left-handed fireballer overmatched batters. In 1886 he tossed the first no-hitter for a Baltimore big-league team against the Alleghenies in their Pittsburgh park. He threw another two no-hitters that year to become the toast of the town; gifts were bestowed on the young phenom and a nickel cigar called "The Kilroy" was manufactured by Aug. Mencken & Brothers.

The Orioles' popularity continued to climb the next year. The largest single-game crowd to that point in baseball history, 15,000, turned out for the first tilt of a key four-game series in June against, ironically, the first-place St. Louis Browns. Kilroy pitched the second-place Orioles to victory in that game. After a tie in game two, St. Louis won the final two and went on to win the pennant. The Orioles finished third. Needless to say, those were not the Browns of last-place fame we remember in the American League.

From 1886 through 1889, Kilroy won 119 games, an average of almost 30 a season, but the heavy number of innings exacted a tremendous toll. By 1890, when he joined the new and ill-fated Players' League, Kilroy's arm had gone dead. He returned to his native Philadelphia where he operated a saloon across from Shibe Park until his death in 1940.

Ballplayers were rough-and-tumble characters in those days; none was rougher than hard-drinking Oriole first baseman Tommy Tucker, who despite his off-the-field antics led the Association in hitting in 1889 with a .372 average. Men like Tucker reinforced the late 19th-century image of ballplayers as a dissapated bunch who were probably incapable of holding any other job. Certainly, mothers did not want their sons to grow up to play baseball.

The Gay '90s began without a Baltimore team in any of the three major leagues. The exodus to the new Player's League saw to that. The Orioles shifted to Brooklyn where they again had to contend with competition from

Four baseball immortals who brought greatness to the old Orioles. Joe Kelley, a .319 lifetime hitter, and Hughie Jennings, .311 in 17 seasons, are in front. Wee Willie Keeler with a .345 lifetime average and John McGraw are in back.

The National League champions of 1895. That's John McGraw and Willie Keeler reclining in front. Kid Gleason, who would manage the infamous 1919 Black Sox, sits at the left of row two, next to Joe Kelley. Two more Hall of Famers are sitting in the second row. Uncle Wilbert Robinson, third from the right, and Hughie Jennings on the far right.

two other teams. The club limped back to Baltimore the next year where colorful local favorite Billy Barnie took over as manager and finished last. They called Barnie "the Bald-Headed Eagle of the Chesapeake"

"Bald Billy" had come down from his native New York City where he caught and was team leader of the minor-league Brooklyn Atlantics. He first appeared in Baltimore in 1883 as a 30-year-old player-manager for the American Association team. The feisty Barnie, who stood only 5-7 and weighed 157 pounds, brought in several ex-Brooklyn teammates and newcomers Bob Emslie, who won 32 games in 1884, and pitcher Hardie Henderson. He soon added the aforementioned Tucker and Kilroy, but in nine years with the Orioles he could muster only one third-place finish. It was in 1890 that the Orioles left for Brooklyn and then returned to Baltimore to play 34 games and finish up the season. It was an amazing era of teams jumping leagues and towns at the drop of a hat.

Beer and baseball have been synonymous for more than a century in baseball. Long before local favorites National Boh and Gunther there was the Eagle brewery, one of 40 in the Baltimore area, owned by John H. von der Horst and his sons, who became the principal owners of the Orioles in 1883 and held control until 1900. The brewery titan built three ballparks in those 17 years. It also built a powerhouse, bringing in legendary players like Wee Willie Keeler, John McGraw, Wilbert Robinson, and Hughie Jennings.

The old Orioles, National League pennant winners from 1894-'96. They sported as many as six Hall of Famers in the same lineup. In the back row, left to right: Joe Quinn, Sadie McMahon, Charley Esper, George Henning, Frank Bowerman, William Clarke and James Donnelly. Second row, left to right: Steve Brodie, Bill Hoffer, Joe Kelley, Manager Ned Hanlon, Wilbert Robinson, Hughie Jennings, Henry Reitz. In the front row, left to right, are: Jack Doyle, John J. McGraw, Willie Keeler and Arlie Pond.

Baltimore joined the National League in 1892 as one of four expansion teams that swelled the league to 12. Belying their future greatness the Orioles lost 101 games that first season. The only moment worth preserving from '92 happened June 10. On that historic day, Wilbert Robinson banged out seven hits in seven trips to the plate against St. Louis, a feat not equalled until 1975 when Rennie Stennett of Pittsburgh did it against the Cubs.

Brought on to manage late in 1892 was Ed Hanlon, who played and served as captain of the Detroit Nationals for years. He dislocated a knee while chasing a fly ball with Pittsburgh on opening day in 1892, ending his playing career. Nicknamed "Ned," Hanlon was only 34 when he took over as manager; his presence was felt immediately. He soon became president as well as manager and put everyone on alert: those just going through the motions would be gone. Hanlon stressed conditioning, and in keeping with this ethos, he took his 1893 Orioles south to train for the first time. Florida at that time was basically unsettled, so Hanlon based his spring camps in Georgia towns like Augusta and Macon.

The most rigid of conditioning regiments, however, couldn't solve Hanlon's most persistent problem: pitching. He went through more than 30 pitchers in his seven years at the helm and only Sadie McMahon lasted

more than four. Teaming with his old batterymate in Philadelphia, Wilbert Robinson, McMahon won 34 games in '91 to lead the league and was 25-8 in '94. McMahon boasted that he was never battered from the box nor lifted from a game.

If pitching was a problem, Hanlon's expertise in offense more than compensated for it. Hanlon experimented constantly; for instance, he was the first manager to use as strategy a left-handed batter against a right-handed pitcher and vice versa. Moreover, he was the pioneer of scientific or "inside" baseball: the hit-and-run, double-steal, squeeze play, sacrifice bunt. His Orioles scratched out runs with every means possible and played with a daring that flaunted the rules of the game, and none was paid more than $2,400 for their efforts. (That was certainly a sizable sum of money compared to annual wages of the average worker but not close to what their abilities commanded. The pay for the players, who were prisoners of the reserve clause that bound them to the same team, was static—even though the owners enjoyed handsome profits.) He picked fiery, tobacco-spitting players who loved the game. An early move was to trade a .363-hitting regular shortstop, Voiceless Tim O'Rourke, to Louisville for a kid who had hit .222 the year before and was hitting only .136 at the time of the trade. The kid, Hughie Jennings, would rather play baseball than do anything else in the world. He'd battle you 24 hours a day—just the kind of attitude Hanlon coveted. "Ee-Yah" Jennings they called him because Hughie loved to shout "Ee-Yah" to fire up his teammates. Jennings went on to hit .386 in '95, .398 in '96 and .355 in '97. He entered the Hall of Fame in 1945.

Scorecards were rich with color and ornate designs in the gay '90s, befitting the Victorian era breweries that tended to dominate the advertisers. The Diamond was the combination tavern, pool hall and bowling alley co-owned by John McGraw and Wilbert Robinson.

Late in the 1892 season, Hanlon sent former player-manager George Van Haltren, a .316 lifetime hitter over 17 seasons, to Pittsburgh for a rookie outfielder named Joe Kelley, who was hitting all of .239. Kelley soon blossomed into one of the greatest players in the game. From 1894 though 1898 Kelley didn't miss a game, averaged .360, and drove in 100 runs plus every year. He was inducted into baseball's Hall of Fame in 1971. McGraw showed up as an 18-year-old, 121-pound shortstop in 1891, and by '94 was playing third base, hitting cleanup, and batting .340.

In January of 1894 Hanlon made a deal that befuddled many fans, trading his regular third baseman, Billy Shindle, and outfielder George Treadway, to Brooklyn for Big Dan Brouthers, a thirty-five-year old first baseman, and a diminutive 5-4½, 140-pound wisp of a player named William H. Keeler. Wee Willie, who "hit 'em where they ain't," became a .432 hitter in 1897 and one of the most scientific sluggers the game has ever known. For five straight seasons as an Oriole Wee Willie averaged 220 hits, 50 steals and 150 runs scored. He finished with 2,962 hits in 19 years and a .345 lifetime average, fifth all-time. Getting Keeler was the final stroke in Ned Hanlon's masterpiece which now included six eventual Hall of Famers in one lineup.

Using the hit-and-run and other elements of surprise, Hanlon's Orioles won 24 of their last 25 games to win the 1894 pennant with an 89-39 record. They

Union Park, home of the 1890s three-time pennant winners. It seated 12,000 but more than 30,000 turned out on September 27, 1897, to watch Kid Nichols and Boston beat the Orioles for the pennant. The park operated from 1891 through 1900.

clinched in Cleveland and returned by train to Camden Station. A huge parade, numbering 200 floats and 10,000 people, escorted the team to the 5th Regiment Armory for a celebration.

Still to be played was the Temple Cup Series, the forerunner of the World Series, against the league runner-up, in this case the New York Giants. The cup was a no-win situation for the Orioles who had already won the pennant. As it turned out, the Orioles celebrated prematurely as the Giants swept the Birds four straight in the best of seven. Their team batting average that season was an astounding .343. Muggsy McGraw hit .340 and gets much of the credit for raising Jennings' average from .241 in 1893 to .332 in '94. McGraw observed that Jennings often bailed out at the plate, especially on curve balls, so he changed Hughie's stance and pitched to him for hours until he overcame the fault. Cleanup hitter Joe Kelley hit .393, Wilbert Robinson .353, Brouthers .347 in his lone Baltimore season, and Keeler .361. Using a 31-½ inch bat, the shortest in big-league history, and choking up so high that only about half was usable, Keeler was a magician at the plate. Five- and six-man infields were used against him, yet he still collected his hits, sometimes fouling off numerous balls until he got one he could drive.

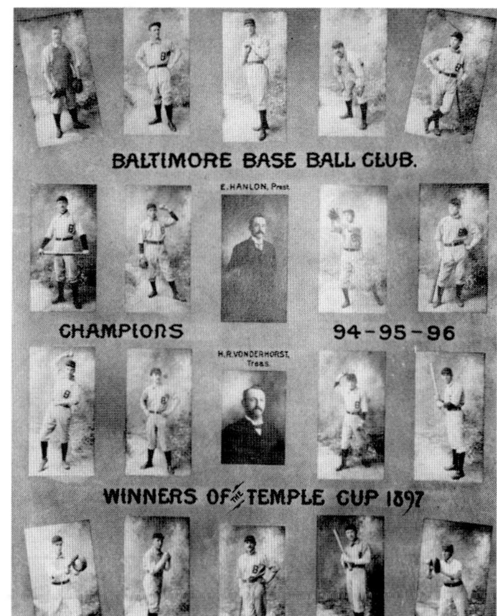

Although their streak of pennants was snapped by Boston in 1897, the Orioles bounced the Beaneaters in the Temple Cup, wining four of five games. Robinson is at the top left and Keeler at the top right. Jennings and McGraw are at the bottom right.

These upstart Orioles repeated in '95 (87-43) and '96 (90-39), losing the Temple Cup to Cleveland in '95 as Cy Young beat them three times, but with Uncle Wilbert Robinson batting .354 and Jennings an awesome .397 they rolled to the Temple Cup championship in '96 over the same Cleveland Spiders. This Oriole team, which was so dominant for a three-year period, shared something with the 1969-70-71 Orioles besides stunning on-the-field success: fans who grew so accustomed to winning they became blasé, which in turn hurt attendance. Their paths diverged, however, in one significant way: Hanlon's Orioles moved out of town; Weaver's moved, but only across town.

The Orioles finished second in '97 (90-40), buoyed by Keeler's remarkable .424 batting average and 44-game hitting streak, a National League record that was tied by Pete Rose in 1978. Keeler had 243 hits in a 130-game schedule and missed by two percentage points tying Hugh Duffy's record .434 average set in 1894. The Orioles were tied with Boston late in the season when 30,000 fans squeezed into Union Park, which seated 10,000, for the rubber game of a three-game series against their co-leader. In a slugfest, the Beaneaters prevailed 19-10 and went on to win the pennant.

In the fourth and last Temple Cup series in 1897 the Orioles lost to Boston 13-12 in the opener but won the next four to capture the Cup. Only 1,600 fans watched the final two games at Union Park. Over the next two years the Orioles discarded stars to save money. Only McGraw and Robinson survived the trimming. Most of the Orioles' best players, plus Hanlon, ended up in Brooklyn. After the 1899 season, despite outdrawing Brooklyn in attendance for some poetic justice, the league shrunk from twelve to eight teams. Baltimore was one of the casualties. Thus ended one of the great eras in baseball history, one that produced such innovations as the squeeze play, the hit-and-run,

Gone were Jennings, Keeler, and Kelley but McGraw and Robinson were still on board in 1899. McGraw hit an astounding .391 in 399 at-bats while Iron Man Joe McGinnity, a 28-year-old rookie, won 28. The Orioles finished fourth. Brooklyn, with Hanlon managing and Keeler, Kelley, and Jennings in the lineup, finished with a pennant-winning 101-47 record.

Signed as a pitcher, Babe Ruth didn't hit a home run as an Oriole. His pitching record of 13-6 was good enough to get him sold to the Red Sox in July, 1914, for the meager sum of $2,900.

the Baltimore chop, and "Hit 'em where they ain't."

As the new century dawned, Baltimore found itself without a major-league team. But only for one year. In 1901 a new major league was born, the American League, the brainchild of former Cincinnati sportswriter Ban Johnson. McGraw helped secure an ownership group for Baltimore and a new park was built farther out York Road at Greenmount and 29th.

Managed by McGraw, the 1901 Orioles finished in fourth place with a 68-65 record. McGraw played third base and hit .349 while another old Oriole, Steve Brodie, hit .310. Behind the plate was Roger Bresnahan, who was embarking on a catching career that would take him to the Hall of Fame, and on the mound, was pitching great Iron Man Joe McGinnity, who won 26 games. Midway through the 1902 season, McGraw abruptly left the Orioles to manage the National League Giants. He departed under a cloud of controversy. McGraw had lent the club $7,000 a while back. In exchange for releasing him from his contract, the manager waived the team's debt. His feud with American League president Ban Johnson, who had suspended McGraw for arguing with an umpire, was behind his desire to escape the American League. McGraw had been secretly negotiating with the National League Giants and on July 1 he signed a contract to manage them. It proved the death knell of major-league baseball in Baltimore. Wilbert Robinson finished the season with a 22-54 record as the Orioles stumbled into last place. It was Baltimore's last major-league season for 52 years.

McGraw took many of his top Baltimore players with him to New York, including his brilliant battery of Joe McGinnity and Roger Bresnahan. McGraw would manage 30 seasons and win a record 10 pennants in New York. He didn't return to Baltimore until his death in 1934. He was buried in New Cathedral Cemetery, resting alongside several old Orioles, including Hanlon, Joe Kelley, and Robinson, who died just six months after McGraw in 1934.

Baltimore deserved a better fate. Robinson had to finish out the 1902 season with players loaned from other clubs. After the 1902 season the league shifted the Oriole franchise to New York where it was called the Highlanders, later to become known as the New York Yankees.

The 1914 Orioles with 19-year-old Babe Ruth squatting fifth from the left in the front row. Right behind him with arms folded is Jack Dunn, who signed Ruth to his first professional contract.

Professional baseball continued in Baltimore in a minor-league capacity after the Orioles abandoned town. The minor-league Orioles joined the Eastern League, which in 1920 became the International League. A former Oriole utility man who went with McGraw to New York, Jack Dunn, returned as manager in 1907. Dunn, a .245 lifetime hitter in eight big-league seasons with four teams (he also pitched a little, winning 64 games, 23 in one year), almost single-handedly kept baseball alive in Baltimore from his first day as a manager in 1907 to his sudden death in October

The Federal League opener at Terrapin Park, Monday, April 13, 1914. More than 30,000 watched Baltimore beat Buffalo 3-2. Built at the corner of Greenmount Avenue and 29th Street, the park was purchased by Jack Dunn in 1916 and renamed Oriole Park.

Jack Dunn (fifth from the left, rear) smiles confidently as his 1923 Orioles win another league championship. Twenty-three-year-old Lefty Grove (second from right, rear), then called Groves, had come out of the small Western Maryland town of Lonaconing to begin his Hall of Fame career. Rube Parnham (rear, left) won 33 games. Other notables: Jack Ogden (rear, right) and Max Bishop (bottom, right).

of 1928. Like so many players who spent more time riding the bench than playing, Dunn learned and listened from his managers, Hanlon and McGraw.

Pitching became his forte. Despite being a minor-league team, the Orioles went first class thanks to Dunn. Players oftentimes refused promotion to the big leagues to remain in Baltimore and play for him. Dunn turned down at least one opportunity to manage in the majors. He was team president, general manager, and manager and after his death at the age of 56 it took three people to replace him. Unfortunately his son Jack Jr. never got the chance. Young Jack was only 27 and heading the Orioles business office when he died from pneumonia before opening day in 1923. It would have pleased Dunn to know that his grandson, Jack Dunn III, would spend his life as an Oriole executive on both the minor- and then major-league level.

Dunn experienced both the good times and the bad in 1914. That year he discovered a youngster from the wrong side of the tracks right under his nose, Baltimore-native George Herman Ruth. He also had to confront competition from a new major league, the Federal League.

Baltimore's entry, the Terrapins, were indeed a threat. An overflow crowd of more than 30,000 fans packed their way into their new park, which was built right across the street from Oriole Park. Ironically, old Ned Hanlon owned the property and became one of the Terrapins' directors. Jack Quinn, who would win 26 games in 1914, pitched the Terrapins to a 3-2 win over Buffalo in the opener. Besides Quinn, several other players were lured away from existing major-league teams to play in Baltimore, including manager Otto Knabe, pitcher Chief Bender, and shortstop Mickey Doolan. Baltimore finished third behind the Indianapolis Hoosiers in 1914, just four games back.

The Federal League challenged the American and National League pennant winners to a playoff to determine a true champion, but its challenge fell on deaf ears. Not wanting to aid an upstart and rival, the existing leagues went on with their own series, which the Miracle Braves swept in four games against the Athletics. The Chicago Whales, led by player-manager Joe Tinker and pitcher Mordecai Brown, won the 1915 Federal League pennant by .001 percentage points over St. Louis. Baltimore collapsed, winning 47 and losing

Lefty Grove won 26 games for the 1924 pennant winners. Twitchy Dick Porter (middle, third from right) led the league with a .364 average. Trainer Eddie Weidner (rear, fourth from left) had begun his 45-year career as trainer a few years before. He finally retired after the 1966 championship.

(From left) Jack Dunn, Baseball Commissioner Landis, and John McGraw in the 20s.

107, finishing 40 games behind Chicago and 25 behind eighth-place Brooklyn.

The Federal League folded after the 1915 season, leaving Baltimore once again without a major-league team (although many had doubted the major-league status of the Federal League). The Terrapins did leave Baltimore with more than just memories. Their two-year-old ballpark became the new home of Jack Dunn's minor-league Orioles. The Orioles barely scraped by in 1914 despite having one of the best teams. With former big-leaguers Freddy Parent and Neal Ball, and future big-league stars Dave Danforth and Ernie Shore, Dunn's Orioles beat in exhibitions both the Philadelphia A's and New York Giants, the pennant winners from the year before. There was also that youngster named Ruth, who pitched a six-hit shutout in his debut before all of 200 people. Ruth went on to win 10 straight games in 1914.

Poor attendance forced Dunn to sell his best players, including Ruth for $2,900, and move the team to Richmond in 1915, events that broke his heart, especially the sale of his young sensation, the Babe. (Ruth's famous nickname was pinned on him as an Oriole. In spring training in 1914 Ruth pitched and beat the champion Athletics, as well as the Dodgers and Phillies. The story goes that a sportswriter in wonderment asked "Who's that?" Oriole coach Henry Steinman quickly replied, "That? That's Jack's new baby." Baby became "Babe" and a legend was born.)

Jack Dunn would eventually smile again. He sold the Richmond team and bought Jersey City in 1916, moving the franchise to his beloved Baltimore that same year and into the new park. Following the World War I interruption, when all but the major leagues and International League were shut down, Dunn's Orioles embarked on a string of championships that would never be duplicated in organized baseball. Beginning in 1919, the Orioles reeled off seven straight pennants.

Led by roly-poly Fritz Maisel, an ex-big-leaguer who would play nine years at third base for the Orioles and work for the club for the better part of the next 50 years, and youngsters like Max Bishop, Merwin Jacobson, Joe Boley, and the kid from western Maryland, Robert Moses Grove (not yet called Lefty), the Orioles developed the prowess—and swagger—of a big-league club . In 1920 Jacobson hit .404, the league's first .400 hitter in 25 years.

In 1930 Joe Hauser (rear, second player from right) belted 63 homers to set a new one-season professional record. General Manager George Weiss (standing at far right) was the general manager for three years. He later ran the New York Yankees and was inducted into baseball's Hall of Fame.

The Orioles won their last 25 games and cruised past American Association winner St. Paul in the Junior World Series, winning five of six games. Even the mighty Yankees, who sported a blossoming Babe Ruth and his record-breaking 54 homers, couldn't beat the 1920 Orioles. The Yankees stopped over for a late-season exhibition and lost 1-0, the Babe striking out twice.

Future Oriole manager Tommy Thomas came out of City College and won 24 games for the 1921 Orioles. Grove topped him by one; Jack Ogden, however, was the ace, posting a 31-8 record. Jack Bentley hit .412, leading the International League in singles, doubles, homers, hits, and total bases. The Birds won 119 games in a 168-game schedule, including 27 straight.

Oriole Park was the home of the Orioles from 1916 until it burned to the ground on the night of July 4, 1944. It was the home of Jack Dunn's seven-time pennant winners from 1919-1925.

The major leagues were taking notice of Dunn's Dynasty and came calling for players. John McGraw, who bore a grudge against Dunn for not selling him Babe Ruth in 1914, spent $72,500 to acquire Bentley.

Alphonse "Tommy" Thomas (shown with the 1928 White Sox) came out of Baltimore's City College high school, winning 24 games for the 1921 Orioles. He went on to win 117 games in the big leagues and came back and managed the 1944 Orioles to the Junior World Series championship.

Still, the Orioles made it four pennants in a row in '22 and beat St. Paul again in the Junior World Series. In 1923, grieving over the loss of his son, Dunn managed to focus enough on the field to pilot his team to a fifth straight pennant. Rube Parnham won his last 20 in a row and finished with a 33-7 record. Lefty Grove fanned a league record 330 batters.

The Orioles won again in 1924 with Grove sporting a 26-6 record. By now Grove had the majors drooling—to the tune of $100,600, the sum Connie Mack and the Athletics paid for his services. Mack's money was well spent because Grove went on to win an even 300 games in the major leagues. Big right-hander George Earnshaw came aboard in 1925 and won 29 games—second to Thomas' 32. Dunn and his machine capped the dynasty by knocking off Louisville that year in the Junior World Series. The Orioles didn't relinquish their crown quietly. In 1926, they won 101 games but finished in second place.

The next 18 years were lean ones in Baltimore: nine second-division finishes and a parade of managers that would make George Steinbrenner envious. Fritz Maisel replaced the stricken Dunn as manager in 1929 and did a respectable job for four seasons. One of his best moves was to write Joe Hauser's name in the lineup. The left-handed belter smacked 63 home runs in a 167-game season, driving in 175. Later for Minneapolis Hauser would hit 69 homers, but his 63 in Baltimore remains the best in International League history.

When Hauser tailed off to 31 homers and was sold, Buzz Arlett replaced him as the hometown hero, socking 54 home runs and collecting 144 RBI in 1932. Twice Arlett, who spent only one season in the majors, hit four homers in one game. Buzz's heroics weren't enough to keep the Orioles afloat, however, and they began a tumble into the second division. In 1935 George Puccinelli won MVP honors, leading the league with a .359 average and in hits, homers, runs, RBI, doubles, and total bases.

Frank McGowan, Joe Judge, Guy Sturdy, and Bucky Crouse led the parade of skippers, culminating in 1939 with the signing of the immortal Rogers Hornsby as player-manager. Hornsby was too unyielding and hard-driving as a manager and lasted just one sixth-place season. He was succeeded by his third base coach, Tommy Thomas, the same Thomas who pitched in the 1920s and went on to carve a 12-year career in the big leagues with five clubs, winning 117 games, including 19 with the 1927 White Sox.

The last great Oriole era of minor-league baseball was beginning under Thomas, an era that included an International League championship in 1944. Players were tough to come by in both the majors and the minors during the war years, but the Orioles unearthed a couple of gems: a slugger from North Carolina named Howie Moss, who banged out 27 homers and had a

The International League and Junior World Series champs of 1944. Managed by Tommy Thomas and led by Howie Moss, Frank Skaff, Sherm Lollar, and Bob Latshaw, the Orioles survived the burning of Oriole Park and the adjustment to Municipal Stadium to beat American Association champ Louisville in the Junior World Series.

cup of coffee with the Giants, Reds, and Indians in the majors, and a future major-league catcher named Sherm Lollar. Second baseman Blas Monaco walked an amazing 167 times, and 18-year-old shortstop Kenny Braun became an idol of the bobbysoxers despite hitting only .176. Solid pros like Bob Latshaw,

Baltimore Elite Giants catcher Roy Campanella, on right, was only 17 years old when he joined the team in 1939. He followed Jackie Robinson to the Dodgers in 1948 and three times was named National League Most Valuable Player. Nicknamed "Pootchie," Campy hit .350 for the 1944 Elites.

Frankie Skaff, Stan Benjamin, and Red Embree added to the mix.

The fireworks came early to Greenmount and 29th in July of 1944. Hours after an 11-4 10-inning loss to Syracuse a fire engulfed the all-wood Oriole Park. Nothing was spared, as the grandstand, offices, clubhouses, and even the field were completely destroyed. Irreplaceable photographs, trophies, and other historic items from Baltimore's baseball archives were lost forever. Only 25 road uniforms sent out to be cleaned survived.

With their home of almost 30 years reduced to ashes the Orioles' only alternative was to move a few blocks north to 33rd Street and play in Municipal Stadium, a horseshoe-shaped park better suited for football.

Baltimore and Afro-American Baseball

Throughout the Orioles' proud minor-league history, the black leagues thrived in Baltimore but mostly in obscurity. As far back as 1887 a team calling itself the Lord Baltimores was renting Oriole Park and playing in a league that included Philadelphia, New York, and Boston. John McGraw tried to sign an early Negro star, Charley Grant, in 1901, billing him as a Cherokee Indian. Noted baseball bigot Cap Anson of the Chicago White Stockings raised a furor and the plan was squelched.

The Baltimore Black Sox played in the Negro Eastern League in the 1920s and eventually won a championship in 1929 before the league collapsed in the 1930s. The Black Sox team of 1929 sported such greats as Jud Wilson, Dick Lundy, and Laymon Yokely. In 1938 the Elite Giant franchise shifted from Washington and won a pennant in 1939 in the eastern Negro National League. Bill Wright hit .488 and won league batting honors and lefty Jonas Gaines led the pitchers, who were caught by a young 17 year old named Roy Campanella. The Negro National League's heyday was during World War II and the Elites, playing at Bugle Field, featured a powerful lineup, led by Campanella behind the plate, Peewee Butts at shortstop, Henry Kimbro in the outfield, and Bill Byrd pitching. The 1949 Elites won the pennant and swept the Chicago American Giants in four straight to win the Negro World Series. Spitballing Bill Byrd at 41 years old and in his 16th season with the club in 1949 still finished 13-3. Leon Day, one of the greatest hurlers in Negro League history, also pitched on the 1949 team, as did future major-league pitcher Joe Black. Another future Dodger, Jim "Junior" Gilliam played the infield for the Elites from 1945 to 1950.

Negro League baseball left Baltimore for good after 1950. For that last season, owner Dick Powell shifted the team to Westport Stadium. With the color line broken in 1947, the Negro Leagues faded away in the early 1950s. Many of its top players were being signed by major-league teams.

Satchel Paige, who had pitched for the 1930 Baltimore Black Sox, almost became an Oriole in 1954. Paige pitched with the Browns in 1953 but the new Oriole ownership released him. Thus the distinction of becoming the first Oriole black player went to pitcher Jehosie Heard, who had pitched with the Birmingham Black Barons. Other Orioles who began their professional careers in the old Negro Leagues included Bob Boyd, Connie Johnson, Al Smith, and Joe Taylor.

Navy regularly played Notre Dame there (it hosted the first meeting in 1927 between the old rivals), and other big games, including the Army-Navy game later that same year of 1944, which drew 70,000 fans. Business manager Herb Armstrong supervised the conversion of the stadium to a ballpark. The third-base dugout was a wooden shed sitting by itself next to a light pole, more than 100 feet from the stands.

Forced to cancel the remainder of a homestand and go on the road for two weeks, the Orioles dropped to fourth place before climbing back into contention. A crowd of 12,999 watched the Orioles sweep a doubleheader from the Jersey City Giants in the Birds' first games at Municipal Stadium. Catcher Sherm Lollar hit the first home run at the 33rd Street site. Municipal Stadium was a forerunner of the L.A. Coliseum, with its short home run distance to left and wide-open spaces to right. Howitzer Howie Moss, a fearsome right-handed hitter, took advantage of the 290-foot distance to left field and began hitting homers in clumps over the short fence. Because of the vast territory in center and right, five triples were hit in the first two games. A couple of nights later in the first night game at the stadium, pitcher Stan West tossed a no-hitter at Jersey City before 9,000 fans, the first no-hitter by an Oriole pitcher since 1907. They won 18 of their first 19 at their new home, sweeping Montreal in four doubleheaders in four successive days. The Orioles lost their last game of the season, splitting a doubleheader with Jersey City, but backed into the pennant when Newark dropped a doubleheader to the last-place Syracuse Chiefs.

Joe Black came off the Morgan State College campus and joined the Elite Giants in 1943 and stayed through 1950. Black burst on the scene with the Brooklyn Dodgers in 1952, posting a 15-4 record with 15 saves and a 2.15 ERA.

The Orioles won by the tiniest of margins, .0007 percentage points. They then eliminated Buffalo and Newark in the International League playoffs, both in seven games, before meeting Louisville in the 1944 Junior World Series. The cinderella Birds prevailed with Lollar batting .423 with a grand slam and Embree pitching two shutouts. An impressive crowd of 52,833 watched the Orioles play the first game in Baltimore after they took two of the first three in Louisville. The Colonels won 5-4 in that game, but the crowd received national attention because on the same day the sixth game of the World Series in St. Louis drew only 31,630.

The 1949 Elite Giants, paced by future Dodgers Junior Gilliam and Joe Black and the all-around brilliance of Leon Day, beat the Chicago American Giants for the Negro League championship.

The Orioles took the next two games to win the series, drawing more than 95,000 for the three games. Baltimore might have been minor league in name, but it proved it was major league in enthusiasm and support. One of the more colorful figures from that era

Hard-throwing Bob Turley, nicknamed "Bullet," won only two games for the Browns in 1953. The next year he won 14 for the Orioles, including the home opener against the White Sox.

was Bill Dyer, who broadcast the Oriole games from the grandstand of the team's new home while sitting on a little red chair and, when circumstances required, circling around it to bring the Orioles luck. He re-created the away games from a Western Union ticker and talked excitedly about how he was walking around his red chair to help ignite an Oriole rally. Invariably the Orioles would rally or score runs. But Dyer was no clairvoyant, because he had already received the play-by-play from the ticker and knew what was happening.

Don Larsen would one day reach greatness with the New York Yankees. In 1953 with the Browns he was a 24-year-old with oodles of potential–and a 7-12 record.

Instead of contending for the pennant in those years after the war, the Orioles struggled to make the first division, managing it just three times in the ensuing nine years. Some great individual achievements brightened the era, however, such as Lollar winning the 1945 batting title with a .364 average and Howitzer Howie Moss and Eddie Robinson hitting 38 and 34 homers respectively in 1946. Moss, Lollar, and Robinson won successive MVP awards from 1944 through 1946. Baseball attendance was booming after the war and the Orioles drew more than 600,000 in 1946, despite a third-place finish. Moss bashed 53 homers in 1947, but the Birds finished one game out of the cellar. They finished last in 1948, and when Thomas resigned as manager in May of 1949, callow Jack Dunn III took over as manager. The younger Dunn couldn't conjure up memories of his legendary grandfather, however, and the Orioles settled in seventh place. Still though there were notable players for the fans to cheer: Al "Yogi" Cihocki, Bobby Young, Ray Poat, Don Heffner, Eddie Pellagrini, and Joe Melendick.

In 1950 former major-league outfielder Nick Cullop was named manager. A managerial success at Columbus of the American Association, Cullop led the Orioles to a surprising third in 1950 and beat Montreal and then pennant-winning Rochester in the playoffs. Cullop's old team, the Columbus Red Birds, won the Junior World Series, however, beating the Orioles 4-1. That 1950 season was the Orioles' last hurrah in the minor leagues. Two sixth-place finishes followed and then, with stadium reconstruction happening around them in 1953, a fourth-place finish under Don Heffner and a near upset of Rochester in the playoffs. Baltimore baseball fans weren't downcast long, however. Just one week after the 1953 playoffs big-league baseball returned—for good!

A Major Bloom in Baltimore

The Orioles were actually the third professional sports team to arrive in Baltimore. The Bullets joined the old B.A.A., the forerunner of the N.B.A., in 1947, and the Colts debuted the same year in the All-America Football Conference. Neither team's arrival came close to matching the delirium set off by the return of big-league baseball to Baltimore, which ended a 52-year wait.

April 15, 1954. A huge downtown parade welcomed the Orioles back. In the car (from left): Vern Stephens, Vinicio Garcia, and Billy Hunter.

Jimmie Dykes, veteran player and manager, was the Orioles' first skipper in 1954. The animated Dykes played more than 20 years and managed the White Sox and Athletics before leading the Orioles to a 54-100 record that first year.

Efforts to bring major-league baseball back to Baltimore first surfaced in the 1920s in the wake of Jack Dunn's seven straight pennant winners. A committee, headed by spice magnate W.M. McCormick, was formed by then mayor William F. Broening to lure either the Philadelphia Athletics or the Washington Senators to Baltimore. Both bids failed. Another attempt came in 1935 when the Boston Braves, despite Babe Ruth's final appearance as an active player, couldn't pay their bills. Baltimore insurance executive Harry Goldman spearheaded an effort to bring the Braves to Baltimore but was rebuffed as new backers kept the Braves in Boston. In 1947 Baltimore Colts president Robert Rodenberg courted the St. Louis Browns, but Richard Muckerman, the majority stockholder of the Browns, set a deliberately high price tag, deflating Rodenberg's interest. When the DeWitts, Bill and Charles, gained control of the Browns in 1950, they talked about moving to Baltimore, even visiting the city and stadium, which by 1950 was being modernized and converted to a dual-purpose facility. Commissioner Happy Chandler ordered the DeWitts to desist, but they kept the rumors alive until 1951 when Bill Veeck bought the team. Veeck, a man with a million ideas, insisted he was going to keep the Browns in St. Louis and duplicate his amazing success story in Cleveland, where the Indians drew 2,620,000 in 1948. But Veeck's non-stop promotional stunts couldn't overcome the Browns perennial last-place finishes. Soon he was looking at greener pastures. Those pastures were on the shores of the Chesapeake Bay.

The story of how the ragtag Browns finally became the Baltimore Orioles began in March of 1953 when Veeck proposed to move his team to Baltimore immediately.

In 52 seasons the Browns had finished in the first division just 13 times, winning only one pennant (in the war year 1944, the same year the minor-league Orioles won the Junior World Series). Sharing Sportsman's Park with the more successful and popular Cardinals of the NL, Browns' attendance ranged from a low of 80,922 in 1935 to a high of 713,000 in 1922 when George Sisler, the franchise's best player all-time, was in his heyday. Instead of pennants, the Browns were better known for their anomalies: They were the team that had a one-armed outfielder, Pete Gray, in 1945, a 50-plus-year-old pitcher in Satchel Paige in 1953, and, in one of Veeck's most irreverent stunts, a midget pinch-hitter named Eddie Gaedel in 1951. It was after a crowd total of 293,790 in 1951 that Veeck realized the attendance problem was irreversible.

Many felt the move was a mere formality when the owners voted on March 17, 1953, especially because only six of eight votes were required for the move. Instead, the vote went against the transfer six to two, with only the Browns and White Sox assenting. Powerful Washington Senators owner Clark Griffith led the opposition, the short 35-mile distance between the two cities the primary reason. In addition, there was a universal dislike of the maverick Veeck and his methods. Said Senators vice-president Calvin Griffith, "Veeck was not a good candidate to own the Baltimore team because he's in debt. The people of Baltimore

Winning pitcher Bob Turley (middle) hugs home run heroes Clint Courtney (right) and Vern Stephens after the Orioles beat the White Sox 3-1 in their first home opener on April 15, 1954.

Clint "Scrap Iron" Courtney was a fan favorite in Baltimore because of his all-out hustle and colorful personality. The American League Rookie of the Year in 1952 with the Browns, Courtney hit .270 with the 1954 Orioles, striking out just seven times in 437 at-bats, still a club record.

don't know it, but we did them a favor." That's not how the vote was viewed in Baltimore, which was sent reeling by the unexpected turn of events.

Just two days after the American League denied Veeck's request, the Boston Braves were allowed to move to Milwaukee, the first franchise shift in major-league baseball since Baltimore moved to New York in 1902. Meanwhile, the Cardinals had been sold to beer baron August Busch, whose family controlled the Anheuser-Busch fortune. Veeck now was desperate. He knew his mom-and-pop operation could certainly not survive competing against the deep-pocketed Busch. It was either sell or move. He ended up doing both. Refusing to entertain offers from St. Louis, Veeck concentrated all of his efforts on Baltimore.

Despite his cash crunch, Veeck still made valiant attempts to improve the club on the field for the lame-duck season of 1953, sending $90,000 along with pitcher Bob Mahoney, infielder Stan Rojek, and outfielder Ray Coleman to the Dodgers for infielder Billy Hunter, who would serve the Orioles as their first shortstop and for 15 years as their best-ever third base coach. Hunter and the ageless Satchel Paige were the Browns' representatives in the 1953 All-Star game in Cincinnati.

Veeck had promised Baltimore mayor Thomas D'Alesandro that he would try again to move after the 1953 season. To that end, he sold Sportsman's Park for $300,00 to Busch. (Imagine, an entire ballpark for $300,000!) The park was renamed Busch Stadium.

In May of 1953 the *Baltimore Sun* reported that the Philadelphia Athletics, also hurting at the gate and a perennial second-division club, approached the city about moving there. D'Alesandro admitted talking to Philadelphia, but he declared that his focus was still on the Browns. "We're engaged to the Browns," said the mayor, "and we can't go with two girls and marry them both."

By July other suitors were lining up. Los Angeles, San Francisco, Kansas City, Toronto, and Montreal all joined the hunt for the Browns. Veeck began telling the Los Angeles papers that if L.A. officials could purchase Wrigley Field, home of the Pacific Coast League Angels, he would consider heading west. He also chatted with San Francisco officials about moving to Seals Stadium. By expanding his discussions, Veeck was stirring up a hornet's nest—deliberately.

On August 20, 1953, he brought the Browns to Baltimore to play an exhibition game against the minor-league Orioles. He wanted to test the waters. A crowd of 10,681 turned out to see the Browns, behind the pitching of Don Larsen, win 8-2. By September efforts accelerated to once again move the Browns to Baltimore. Eastern Shore attorney Clarence W. Miles, a familiar figure in Baltimore political, civic, and business circles, emerged at the forefront of a local group that numbered nearly 100 investors. Miles' plan was to buy the Browns from Veeck, thus assuring the team would not be moved again and also ridding the league of the owner all other owners despised.

On September 16, 1953, a special American League committee studying the Browns financial status recommended the franchise be transferred to another city. On September 26, in the next-to-last game of their history, only 1,937 turned out to watch the White Sox beat the Browns 6-3. Billy Hunter hit his only home run of the season—the last home run in Browns history.

On September 27, 1953, the American League

Gil Coan was obtained from the Senators before the 1954 season for Roy Sievers, a deal that proved more fruitful for Washington than Baltimore. Gil hit .279 in 98 games for the '54 Orioles but slumped the next season and was traded. Sievers, meanwhile, became one of the majors' top home run threats for years.

Pat Dobson

Dick Hall

Luis Aparicio

Mike Cuellar

Boog Powell

Paul Blair

Dave McNally

1958 All-Star Game, Memorial Stadium

Mickey Mantle, New York Yankees

Ted Williams, Boston Red Sox

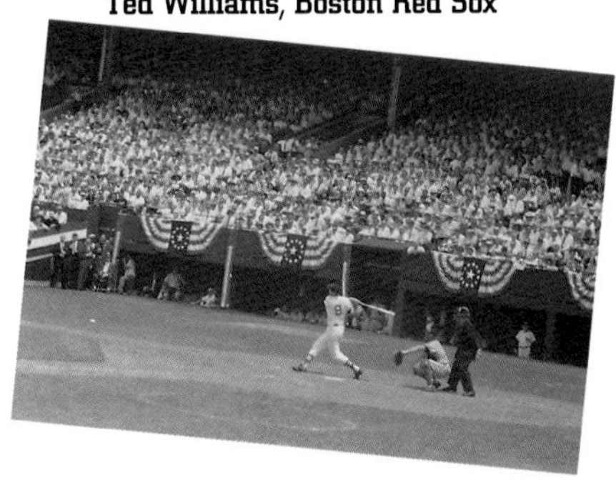

Nellie Fox, Chicago White Sox

Stan Musial, St Louis Cardinals

Jackie Jensen, Boston Red Sox

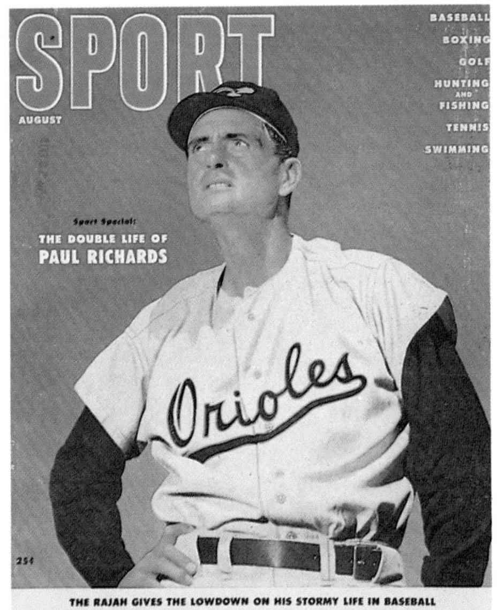
SPORT
BASEBALL
BOXING
GOLF
HUNTING AND FISHING
TENNIS
SWIMMING
AUGUST
Sport Special:
THE DOUBLE LIFE OF
PAUL RICHARDS
Orioles
25¢
THE RAJAH GIVES THE LOWDOWN ON HIS STORMY LIFE IN BASEBALL
I ALWAYS KEPT MY BAGS PACKED! By ROGERS HORNSBY

Sports Illustrated
THE HOTSHOT KIDS
BALTIMORE'S ANDY ETCHEBARREN

GREEN BAY—THE ROAD BACK
Sports Illustrated
Thunder and Lightning in Baltimore
Frank Robinson
Boog Powell

TEXAS BIDS FOR NO. 1
THE WORLD SERIES
Sports Illustrated
Oriole Brooks Robinson
Challenges the Mets

THIRTY-FIVE CENTS
SEPTEMBER 11, 1964
BASEBALL: The Year They Made a Game of I
TIME
BALTIMORE
MANAGER
BAUER
VOL. 84 NO. 11

BALTIMORE'S HEROES
Sports Illustrated
MANAGER HANK BAUER
WITH BROOKS AND FRANK ROBINSON

SPORT
JUNE 60¢
Hank Aaron: "I Say Baseball Has Become Too Specialized!"
Bill Hartack's Blast: Few People In Horse Racing Want Honesty
An Expert Probes The Pro Football Draft: Team By Team, Player By Player Ratings
Indy 500 Preview
Why Everyone Loves Brooks Robinson
BROOKS ROBINSON

The Sporting News
Price: 60 Cents
SPRING TRAINING OPENS
MARCH 4, 1972

Sports Illustrated
WORLD SERIES

The Sporting News
Oriole Aces
JULY 8, 1978
ONE DOLLAR

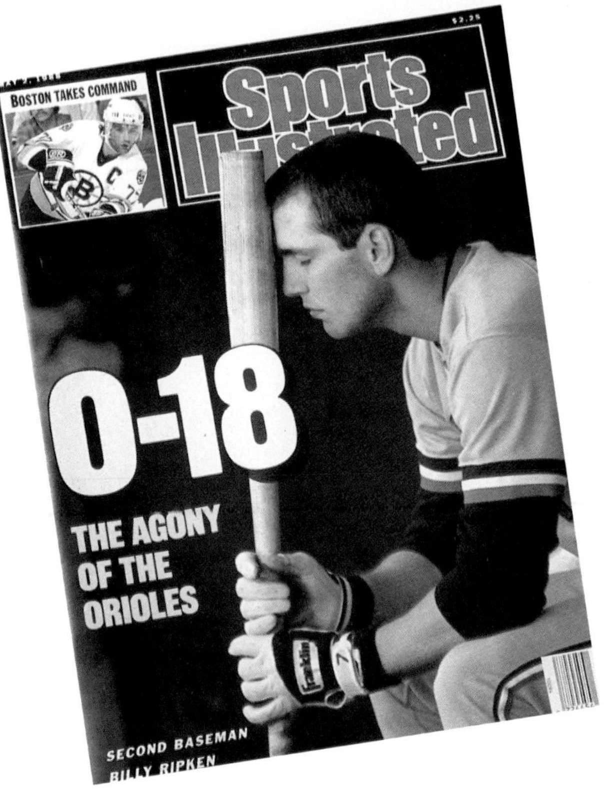
$2.25
BOSTON TAKES COMMAND
Sports Illustrated
0-18
THE AGONY OF THE ORIOLES
SECOND BASEMAN
BILLY RIPKEN

Sports Illustrated
OCTOBER 24, 1983 $1.75
THE HERO!
Rick Dempsey:
Baltimore's World Series MVP

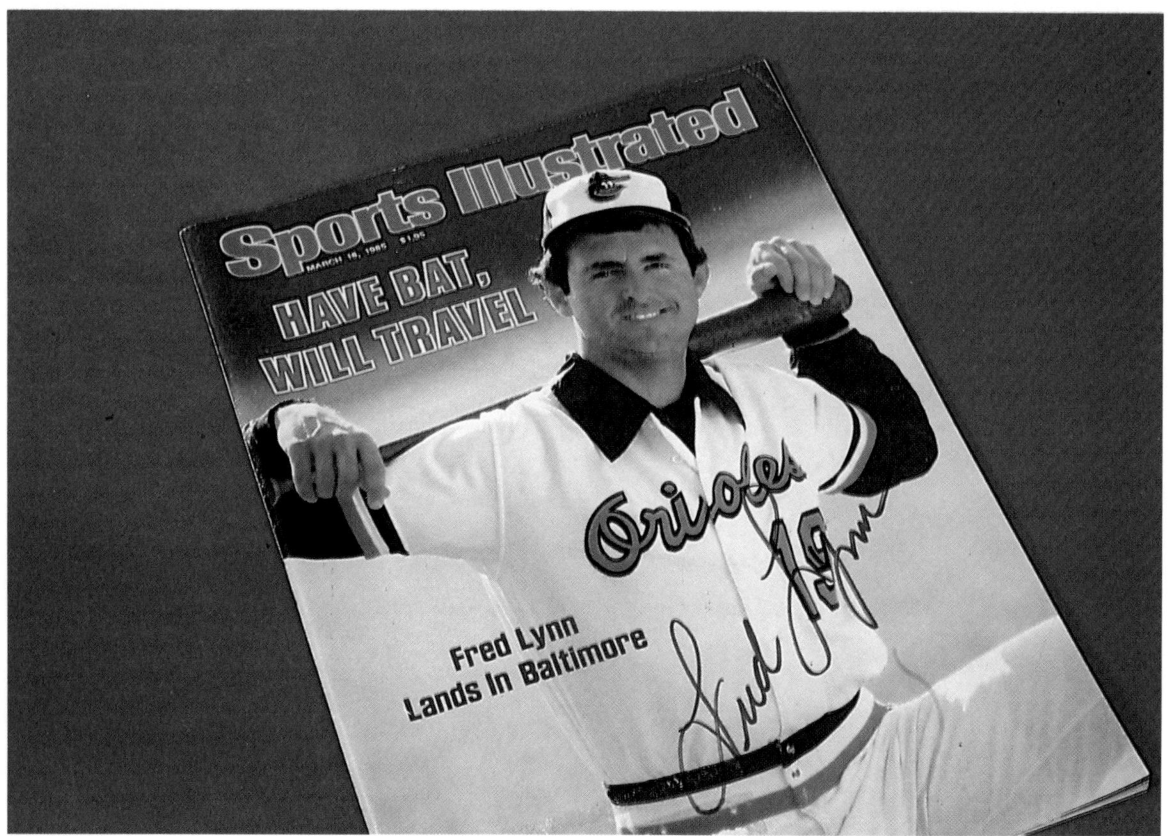
Sports Illustrated
MARCH 18, 1985 $1.95
HAVE BAT, WILL TRAVEL
Orioles
Fred Lynn
Lands In Baltimore

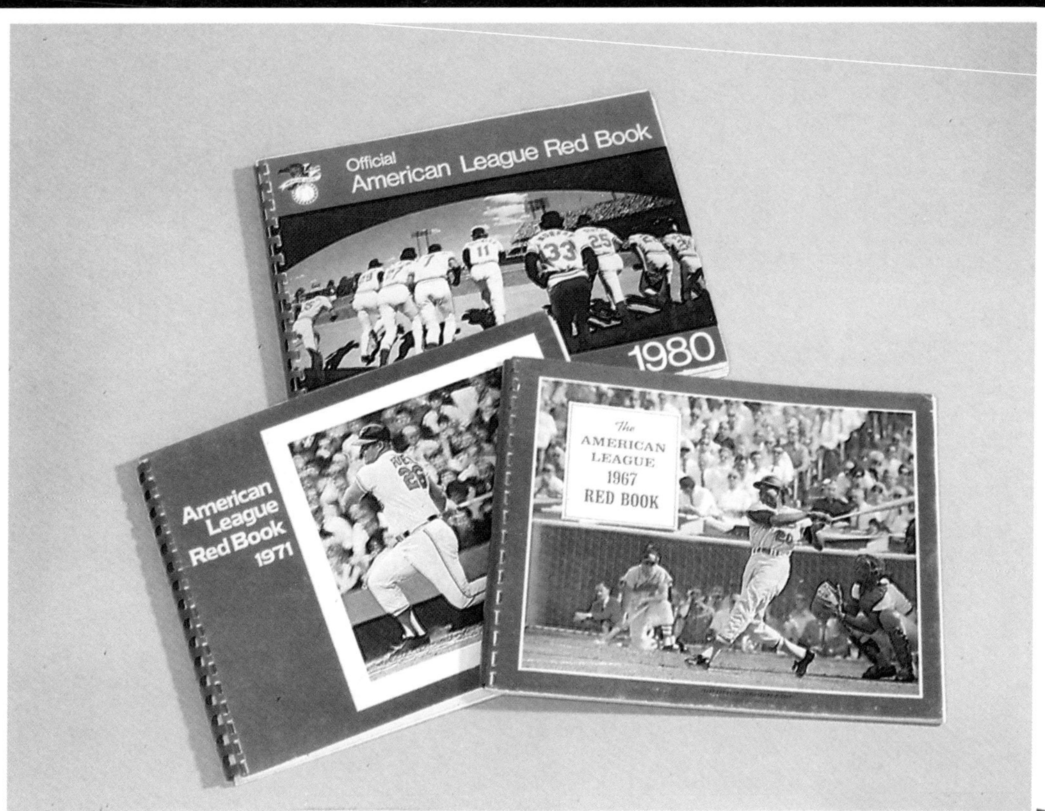
Official
American League Red Book
1980
American League Red Book 1971
The AMERICAN LEAGUE 1967 RED BOOK

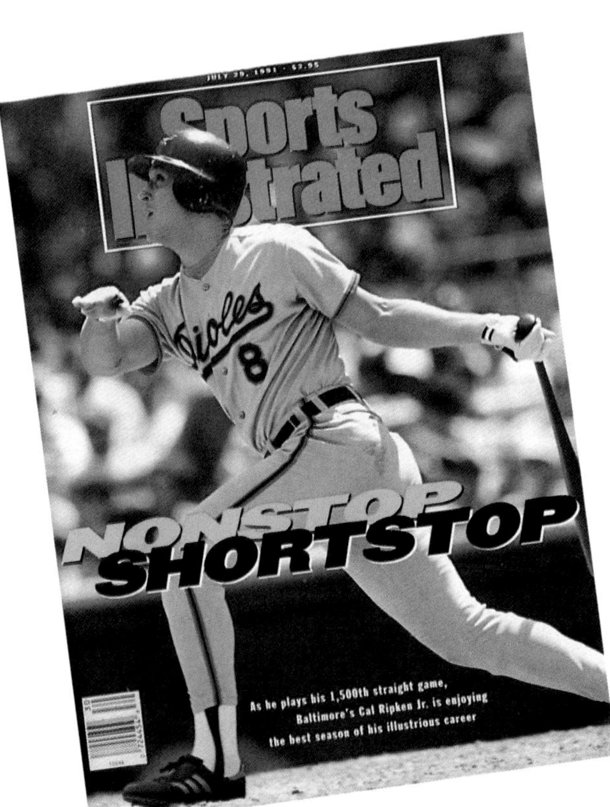
Sports Illustrated
NONSTOP SHORTSTOP
As he plays his 1,500th straight game, Baltimore's Cal Ripken Jr. is enjoying the best season of his illustrious career

Sports Illustrated for KIDS
MR. EVERYTHING
CAL RIPKEN TELLS YOU HOW TO IMPROVE ALL YOUR BASEBALL SKILLS

Hank Bauer (left) and coaches

Frank Robinson

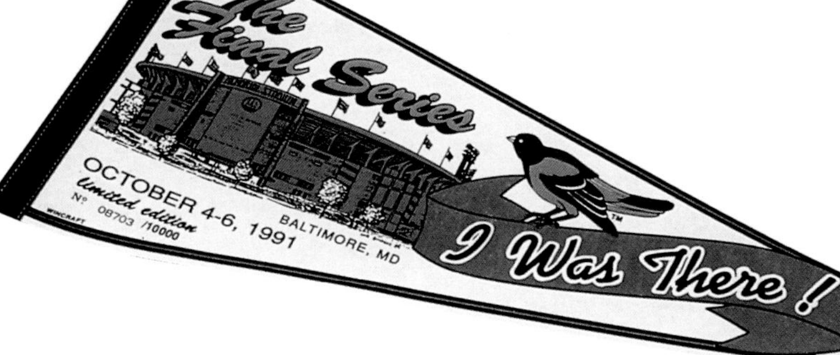

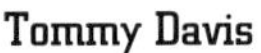
Tommy Davis

Orioles

500
home
runs
20

500
20
20th Anniversary 1971-1991
500th Home Run, September 13, 1971
Orioles '91
A Season To Remember
Frank
Robinson
THE ONE BOOK

Mark Belanger

Brooks Robinson,
1970 World Series
against the Reds

Supreme Bench Denies
Bias In Rape Cases: C 20

40 Pages 10 Cents

THE SUN

BALTIMORE, FRIDAY, SEPTEMBER 23, 1966

The Weather

BIRDS WIN AMERICAN LEAGUE PENNANT

Palmer Pitches Clincher, Beating Kansas City, 6-1

Frank Robinson Raps
Three Hits And Bats
Two Runs Home

MAIL ONLY
REQUESTS
ACCEPTED

$17 Checks Or Money
Orders Required
For Ducats

Wild Scene Follows
Birds' Flag-Clinching

THE Morning After

GENERAL MOTORS
INCREASES COSTS

'BIRDLAND' HAILS
ITS GREATEST DAY

Trading Cards

Memorial Stadium

Willy Miranda
ORIOLES
LEE MAY
STEVE STONE
Dennis Martinez
MARK BELANGER

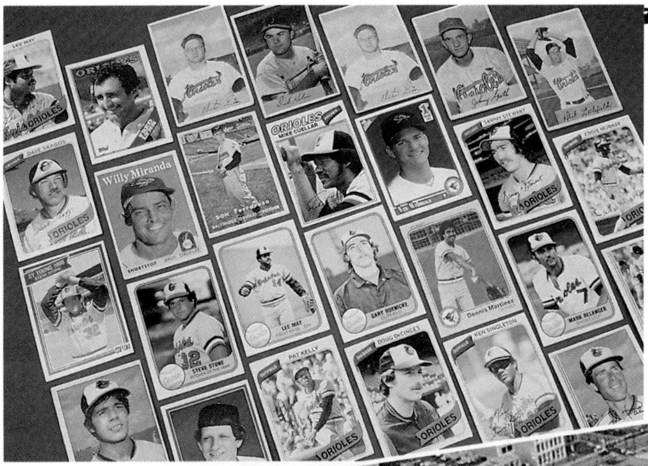

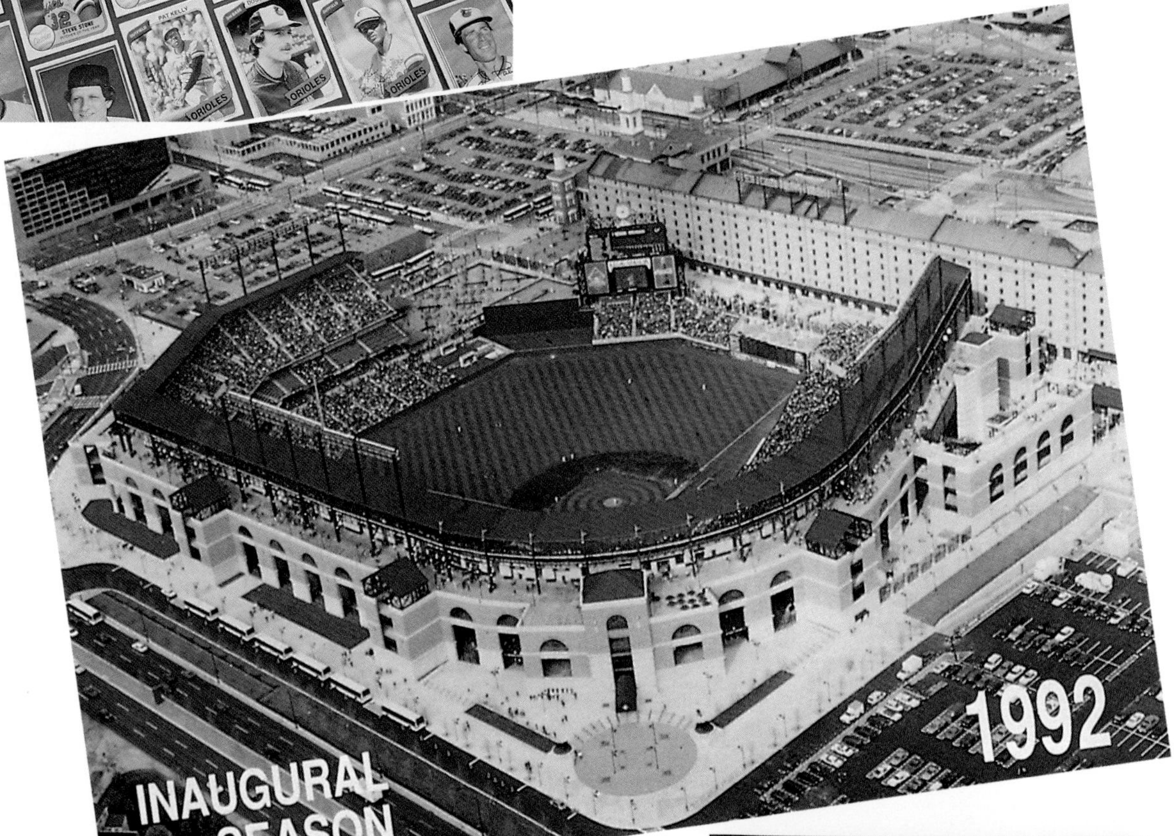

INAUGURAL SEASON
1992

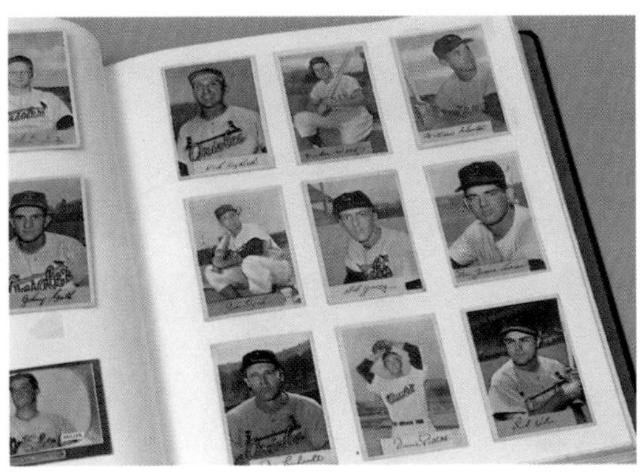

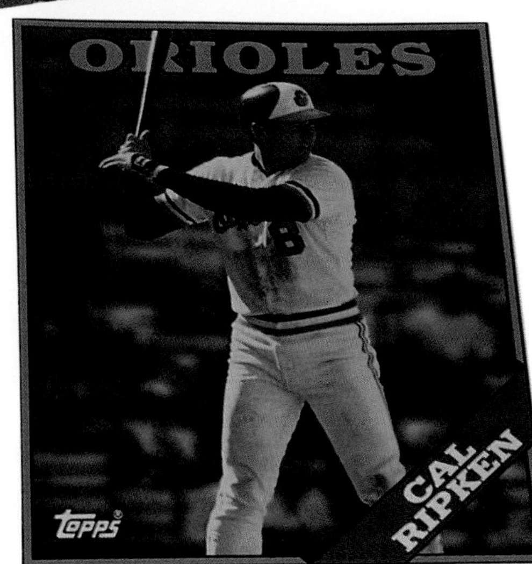

ORIOLES
topps
CAL RIPKEN

VERN STEPHENS
third base BALTIMORE ORIOLES

Willy Miranda
ORIOLES

INAUGURAL SEASON
1992

MEMORIAL STADIUM

Lee May

Frank Robinson, 1971 ALCS against Oakland

Brooks with his 16 Gold Gloves

owners convened at the Hotel Commodore in New York to vote on the transfer. It ended in a tie. New York, Philadelphia, Boston, and Cleveland voted no. Washington, not wanting to alienate its Maryland fans, voted this time for the move to Baltimore. Yankee owner Del Webb had such contempt for Veeck he wanted to keep him in St. Louis, where he would be forced to declare bankruptcy. After exacting that revenge, Webb figured the AL could then decide where to dump the Browns.

Centerfielder Chuck Diering was named "Most Valuable Oriole" in 1954, not so much for his .258 batting average, but for his sensational play in center field.

On September 27, the Browns lost their final game of the year, 2-1 in 11 innings to Chicago. It was loss 100 and, mercifully, the last in franchise history. Duane Pillette, who would win the first game in Oriole history in April of the next season, went all the way in defeat. A crowd of 3,174 showed up for the funeral. The owners convened again the next day at the Commodore, and this time Miles put an offer of $2,475,000 on the table for control of Veeck's 79 percent of the Browns stock. Veeck accepted. With the grand promoter now out of the picture, the league approved the transfer unanimously. The Orioles were back in the big leagues.

Over the winter, the new owners mounted a mammoth preseason ticket campaign. They also cleaned house at the top, hiring former Philadelphia A's executive Arthur Ehlers as the first general manager. Although many of the Browns made the switch to Baltimore, manager Marty Marion did not, even though he had another year on his contract. Baltimore might have many of the same players who lost 100 games in St. Louis, but management wanted to create a new feeling on the field and that started with the skipper.

Don Larsen accompanied the Browns to Baltimore and was counted on heavily to win big. Instead, he established a club record for futility that still stands, losing 21 games against just three wins.

Hired instead was a colorful former infielder who spent 22 seasons as a player with the A's and White Sox, Jimmie Dykes. The 57-year-old Dykes had begun his playing career in 1918, retiring in 1939. One of the game's characters, he became famous for his ability to spin a baseball yarn and for knowing the rule book better than any umpire. Dykes banged out 2,256 hits, playing on Connie Mack's powerful Philadelphia pennant winners in 1929, 1930, and 1931. He had two hits in the first All-Star game in 1933 and began managing the White Sox a year later in 1934 as a player-manager. He lasted for 12 seasons, finishing in the first division six times.

In 1946 Dykes managed the Hollywood Stars in the Pacific Coast League and in 1949 returned to Philadelphia as a coach under his old mentor, Connie Mack. The next year when Mack stepped down after 50 years at the helm, Dykes was picked to succeed him. With Ehlers making some favorable player moves, Dykes overcame a miserable start in 1951 to close on a modest high, escaping the basement with a sixth-place finish. In 1952 the Athletics finished in the first division behind the pitching of little Bobby Shantz, who won 24 games, and the hitting of Ferris Fain, whose .327 average led the league. Injuries sent the Athletics plummeting to seventh place in 1953.

So tackling the challenge of a last-place club was known territory for Jimmie. But known did not equal stale. The Baltimore job renewed Dykes' passion for the game. He surrounded himself with a veteran coaching staff in Rebel Tom Oliver, former Oriole minor-league star Frank Skaff, and pitching coach Harry "The Cat" Brecheen, who won three games in the 1946 World Series with the St. Louis Cardinals.

When the pitchers and catchers reported to the Orioles' first spring camp in Yuma, Arizona, on February 22, 1954, a hodgepodge of veterans and youngsters greeted Dykes and his staff. The same held true when the rest of the squad reported on March 1. Nineteen pitchers, 11 infielders, 12 outfielders and three catchers made up the spring roster. Of 45 players

20 had seen action with the Browns the year before. One of those, first baseman Roy Sievers, was traded just before spring training to Washington for outfielder Gil Coan. The Baltimore brass' first trade was one they would just as soon forget. Sievers, the American League's Rookie of the Year in 1949 with the Browns, blossomed in Washington, emerging as one of the top sluggers in the league. Four times he drove in more than 100 runs with the Nats, plus he connected for 42 homers in 1957 and 39 the following year. The Coan story was less uplifting. In the early '50s he had enjoyed a pair of .300 seasons, but by 1953 he slipped to .196 due to a string of major injuries, including a broken ankle in a preseason exhibition. Coan would hit .279 for the 1954 Orioles with just two home runs. After a slow start in '55 he was sold to the White Sox after 61 games for the $20,000 waiver price.

Bill Veeck, fresh from selling his St. Louis Browns to Baltimore interests, visits with a pair of his old Brown infielders, Bobby Young (left) and Billy Hunter. Longtime Oriole minor and major league executive Jack Dun III is on the right.

The pitching staff had veterans Vern Bickford, Mike Blyzka, Joe Coleman, Duane Pillette, and Marlin Stuart, plus Don Larsen and promising rookie Bob Turley. One holdover from the 1953 minor-league Orioles, right-hander Howie Fox, appeared in 38 games in 1954 but was released in 1955. Fox was killed later that year, stabbed by three youths in a fight in his San Antonio tavern. He was 34.

Another notable name on the 1954 staff was Jehosie Heard, a 29-year-old left-hander from Memphis who had toiled for years in the old Negro Leagues. Standing all of 5-7 and weighing 147 pounds, Jehosie appeared in just two games without a decision in '54 and was peddled in a trade after the season, never to appear again in the majors. Jehosie Heard was the first black player in modern Orioles history. Joe Durham, called up late in the season, was the first black player to hit a homer in an Oriole uniform.

Clint "Scrap Iron" Courtney was Dykes' choice to start behind the plate, with Les Moss and Darrell Johnson backing up. Veteran Philadelphia Athletic Ray Murray was picked up just two weeks before the season as a backup. The Deacon would appear in just 22 games in what turned out to be his last big-league season.

The infield sported a crackerjack double-play combo in shortstop Billy Hunter and second baseman and former minor-league Oriole Bobby Young. In a season of firsts, Young's story was dearest to the hearts of the Bird faithful: he was the first native Baltimorean to play on the Orioles. Long-time, power-hitting shortstop Vern "Junior" Stephens moved over to play third base. Former Phillies "Whiz Kid" Eddie Waitkus, a solid all-around player best remembered for being shot by a deranged woman in a Chicago hotel room in 1949, was obtained in spring training to provide insurance at first base. It turned out to be a prophetic move because on the very day Art Ehlers acquired Waitkus, first baseman Dick Kryhoski broke his left wrist in a spring game. Six players in all were used at first base in that maiden season.

Roaming the outfield were a couple of fleet fly-chasers, Chuck Diering and Coan. They would need their track shoes to combat the wide-open spaces of the Memorial Stadium outfield. The alleys in left- and right-center were 446 feet away from home plate; home plate to the scoreboard in deep center measured 450 feet. The third outfield spot was shared among veterans Sam Mele, Vic Wertz, Jim Fridley, Don Lenhardt, and Jim Dyck. Dyck was traded just a few days after the season began to Cleveland for 12-year veteran third baseman Bob Kennedy. National League outfield veteran Cal Abrams was picked up from Pittsburgh six weeks into the sea-

Former Negro League left-hander Jehosie "Jay" Heard was the Orioles' first black player. The diminutive 5-7 1/2, 147-pounder appeared in just two games in 1954 without a decision.

son and went on to lead the team in hitting with a .293 average, the highest average of his eight-year career.

Desiring to sever all links with their St. Louis heritage, the Orioles' first press guide, a primitive 12-page effort, made no mention of the Browns records. Starting in 1872, year-by-year standings of each Baltimore entry in the American Association, National League, Eastern League, and International League were recounted, as were the exploits of Matt Kilroy, Joe Kelley, Joe McGinnity, and Wee Willie Keeler. A special American League records section listed only the 1901 and 1902 seasons, the two years before the Orioles became the New York Highlanders. The uniform colors were orange and black (the colors dated back to the 1890s), with "Orioles" appearing on both the home and road jerseys. The cap was all black with a true-to-life Baltimore Oriole on the front. Sunpapers cartoonist Jim Hartzell had begun his long association with the club by creating a laughing cartoon Oriole. For years Hartzell's Bird appeared in the Sun newspaper, pronouncing a win or a loss from the day before, with a capsule on the game. In the early days the Bird was frowning much more than he was laughing.

A special team–the first.

An 18-13 spring training record raised hopes. Don Lenhardt hit .591. "Fearless" Jim Fridley slugged seven homers and hit a gaudy .500. "Scrap Iron" Courtney wowed 'em with a .438 mark. "With good pitching, we could beat out three other clubs," Dykes predicted. "No, I won't name them and get them mad."

The days-long train trip from Yuma to Detroit, for the season's first regular-season game on April 13, was a symbolic one. From the barren fields of the desert to the verdant pastures of the the Great Lakes area, the Orioles' long journey back to the major leagues was complete. Don Larsen gained the honor of starting the first game in modern Oriole history but the Tigers, behind Steve Gromek, blanked the Birds 3-0. Twenty more losses followed for Larsen that year, against just three wins. (Two years later with the Yankees, Larsen pitched a perfect game in the 1956 World Series, rubbing out the memory of those 21 losses.) Dykes came back with lanky right-hander Duane "Dee" Pillette the next day and Pillette pitched the Orioles to their first win, 3-2 over the Tigers at Briggs Stadium.

The following day, Thursday April 15, 1954, was one of the most glorious in the history of Baltimore baseball, the home-opener against Paul Richards' Chicago White Sox. The day dawned gray, with the threat of rain lasting throughout, but a few gray skies couldn't dampen the enthusiasm of the fans who had waited decades for the return of major-league baseball. The team arrived from Detroit in the morning, wearing their uniforms when they disembarked at Camden Station. A parade loaded with floats and 12 marching bands waited. The entire team was put in individual convertibles and escorted down Charles, Madison, Howard, and Baltimore Streets. A holiday atmosphere seized the town, as city schools and many businesses closed for the day. The *Evening Sun* estimated that 350,000 fans braved the damp 58-degree day to welcome the Birds home. Several baseball dignitaries were in the parade, including the venerable Connie Mack and Clark Griffith—the same Griffith who the year before led the opposition against the Browns' move to Baltimore. Commissioner Ford Frick was also on hand.

The players tossed some 10,000 styrofoam baseballs into the crowd along the parade route, which wound its way through 56 city blocks. It ended at City Hall, where the players were whisked up Calvert Street to Memorial Stadium, which was still under construction when the sellout crowd began arriving; bricks were being laid that morning to the 6.5-million dollar structure.

Several of the Orioles players had played in Memorial Stadium during their minor-league days but few had seen the park's new configuration. "We just stared at it," remembered Gil Coan years later. "The outfield especially was so vast, we needed five outfielders, not three. Our long-ball hitters, Vic Wertz, Vern Stephens, Sam Mele and Clint Courtney, couldn't reach the fences. You had to dead pull-hit or forget it."

Orioles skipper Paul Richards peers into the crystal ball and grins over what he hopes are brighter days to come for the Birds. Thanks to Richards, those brighter days arrived in the early 1960s.

Approximate seating capacity was 46,000; a few more than that showed up for the opener: 46,354. Vice-President Richard M. Nixon threw out the first ball. The plate umpire was Eddie Rommel, a Baltimore native who once won 27 games for Connie Mack's Philadelphia Athletics. Dykes selected 23-year-old fastballer Bob Turley to start. The first batter he faced, Chico Carrasquel, rapped a single but was stranded. Another fireballer, Virgil "Fire" Trucks started for Chicago. His catcher was one of the Orioles' 1944 heroes, Sherman Lollar. Bobby Young was the first Oriole to bat and he flied out. Coan, batting third, drew a walk and became the first Oriole to reach base in Baltimore.

The Orioles broke through in the third inning for their first run, a homer that landed in the right-field bleachers off the bat of Clint Courtney. Vern Stephens followed in the fourth inning with a 340-foot homer into the left-field bleachers. The Orioles' third run came in the seventh when Waitkus scored on a Vic Wertz single. Baltimore won the game 3-1. Turley struck out nine and surrendered seven hits. Waitkus led the nine-hit Oriole attack with three hits. The two home runs were not exactly trend setting because the Orioles would hit just 17 more homers in their cavernous ballpark all season. "The 1954 opener was the biggest thing to hit Baltimore since the end of World War II," said historian Jim Bready, who attended the game. "It was strange, though, because the fans didn't know how to act. This was all something new. We knew something big was happening, but fans then weren't nearly as rambunctious and uninhibited as they are today. We cheered and booed at the right times but nothing like today."

The home opener finished in the nick of time. The light towers still hadn't been hooked up and were without power. Six days later, with the lights aglow for Memorial Stadium's first night game, the Orioles squared off against Cleveland in a contest almost as memorable as the opener. The Indians, who were on their way to snapping the Yankees' five-year stranglehold on the American League pennant, owned the Orioles and just about everyone else in 1954 as they went on to win a record 111 games (in a 154-game schedule). More than 43,000 were on hand to watch opening-day pitcher Bob Turley take a no-hitter and a 1-0 lead into the ninth. Consecutive first-inning singles by Gil Coan, Vic Wertz, and Don Lenhardt off Bob Lemon accounted for the lone tally. With one out in the top of the ninth, Al Rosen singled to break up the no-hitter and Larry Doby followed with a two-run homer that made Turley the hard-luck loser in a 14-strikeout performance. Cleveland would win 19 of the 22 games played against the Orioles in 1954. The nadir occurred in a July game when the Tribe scored 11 runs in the first inning off Joe Coleman, who left without retiring a batter as Cleveland sent 16 men to the plate.

The Orioles finished 57 games behind the Indians with a 54-100 record, enough to nose out the Athletics for seventh place. More discouraging than the seventh-place finish was that their record was the same one notched the year before by the hapless Browns. But in many ways these were the old Browns—18 of the 38 players listed in Orioles' box scores in 1954 were former Brownies.

Some other highlights: a five-game win streak in June (this was countered by a 14-game losing streak in August). Turley's 185 strikeouts in 247 innings led the league. He finished with a 14-15 record. Joe Coleman won 13 games, including a one-hitter over the Yankees on September 9. Enos Slaughter's bad-hop single over Bobby Young's head in the eighth inning deprived Coleman of the no-hitter, but he won the game 1-0, the first one-hitter in Oriole history. Dick Kryhoski's 19-game hitting streak was tops in the league. Courtney was one of four hitters in the league to hit safely five times in one game.

On May 28, the Orioles set an American League record by using eight pinch-hitters in an 11-6 loss to

At a time when the Orioles were struggling for victories, Willy Miranda electrified the fans with his play at shortstop. Blessed with a strong throwing arm, Willy could range deep in the hole and throw batters out. He played five seasons in Baltimore, coming over in the big trade with the Yankees. He was a .221 lifetime hitter.

Chicago. Collectively they went one for seven with a walk as the Orioles left 16 on base. In that game Cass Michaels of the White Sox socked the first grand slam at Memorial Stadium.

On June 27, Dick Kryhoski, who hit a solid .260 for the season in 300 at-bats, delivered two "sudden death" game-winning RBI singles to give the Orioles a doubleheader sweep of the Philadelphia A's.

Vern Stephens hit the first inside-the-park homer in stadium history on July 3 in a 5-3 win over Detroit. Stephens led the team with eight homers and 46 RBI. In 154 games the Orioles mustered just 52 homers. They were shut out 14 times and lost 30 one-run games. Turley was the victim of several of those one-run losses, bravely calling them "moral victories." On July 30 against the Yankees Bob Kennedy drove in six runs, hitting the first grand slam in Oriole history, as Larsen snapped an eight-game losing streak by blanking the Yankees 10-0, spoiling Casey Stengel's 65th birthday. Two of Larsen's three wins were against the Yankees, which didn't go unnoticed by Casey. The next season Larsen was wearing Yankee pinstripes.

Larsen was a regular patron at several Baltimore nightspots, and it didn't endear him to his manager. Admonished once by Dykes for arriving late for a Sunday doubleheader, Larsen retorted: "But Jimmie, you got me down to pitch the second game."

Clint Courtney quickly became a fan favorite, hitting .270 in 1954 and impressing the fans with his all-out hustle. In 437 plate appearances in that first year, "Scraps" set a club record by striking out only seven times. One of those seven strikeouts occurred against the White Sox with two outs and the bases loaded in the bottom of the ninth. With the count 3-2, a thunderstorm struck, resulting in a two-hour rain delay. When play resumed old Scraps gamely returned to the plate—only to take the first pitch from Harry Dorish for a called third strike to end the game. Dykes wondered afterward how Courtney could take the third strike. Replied Courtney, "I don't know now, ask me tomorrow. I always told you I was a tough man to strike out. It took them two hours to do it."

Courtney was traded after the '54 season to the White Sox but came back to Baltimore before the 1960 season in a deal with Washington that sent Billy Gardner to the Nats. Hampered by injuries, he played in only 83 games but proved very capable of catching Hoyt Wilhelm's elusive knuckle-ball offerings. Scraps was traded to Kansas City the following January in a multi-player deal that sent Bob Boyd, Al Pilarcik, and Wayne Causey to the A's for Russ Snyder, Whitey Herzog, and a player to be named later. On April 15, 1961, the player-to-be-named was finally named: Clint Courtney, who came back for his third tour of duty as an Oriole. Plagued by a sore throwing arm, Clint was released in June of 1961; he retired after that at 34. He became a minor-league manager and was piloting the Richmond Braves when stricken with a fatal heart attack while playing ping-pong in 1975 in Rochester. He was 47.

George Kell finished his Hall of Fame career in Baltimore, playing most of the '56 season and all of '57. Brooks Robinson modeled himself after the classy Kell.

Vic Wertz, counted on to provide long-ball punch in 1954, instead had a short stay in Baltimore. Frustrated by his inability to reach the seats at Memorial Stadium (he hit only one home run), Wertz was traded to Cleveland on June 1 for pitcher Bob Chakales. Vic was hitting only .202 as an Oriole. He turned things around in Cleveland hitting .275 with 14 homers and went eight for 16 in the World Series, robbed of a possible inside-the-park home run by the famous Willie Mays, over-the-head catch in the

Tragedy struck the Orioles on September 20, 1956, when promising young catcher Tom Gastall was killed when his light plane crashed into the Chesapeake Bay. He was 23.

first game of the 1954 fall classic at the Polo Grounds.

The Most Valuable Oriole award in 1954 went to center fielder Chuck Diering, who hit only .258 but electrified the crowd often with his sensational grabs in patrolling the center field expanse of Memorial Stadium.

Fan support was better than run support. The Orioles drew 1,060,910 paid customers in 67 home dates. The largest crowd, 46,796, jammed their way into Memorial Stadium for a May 16 Sunday doubleheader with the Yankees, the Bronx Bombers' first appearance in Baltimore (in a scheduling oddity they were in town only that day). The two teams split the twin bill. New York won the first game 2-0, but Don Larsen took the second 6-2. That Sunday crowd topped the all-time best of six National League clubs up to that point. Even though the league was happy with the transition from St. Louis to Baltimore, the Oriole owners, although pleased with the attendance, were not happy with the results on the field. They started making changes before the season even ended.

On September 14, 1954, the Orioles' brass announced they had hired White Sox manager Paul Richards to be both manager and general manager of the team, replacing Dykes and Ehlers. Dykes finished out the 1954 season and then went on to manage in Cincinnati, Detroit, and Cleveland. Bizarre circumstances surrounded his managerial shift from Detroit to Cleveland. In 1960 he was traded for Indians manager Joe Gordon in mid-season, the only such swap in major-league history. Ironically, Marty Marion, who did not accompany the Browns to Baltimore after managing in St. Louis in 1953, became a coach for Richards in Chicago. When Richards resigned to come to Baltimore, Marion was signed to manage the White Sox where he finished in third place for two seasons before leaving after the 1956 campaign.

Known as the "Wizard of Waxahachie" after his Texas hometown, Richards was 45 years old when he assumed control of the Orioles. An astute catcher for eight big-league seasons primarily with the Giants and Tigers, Richards was a patient man who possessed great teaching skills—just what Baltimore needed to build a winning foundation.

Armed with a three-year contract, Richards believed the more players he could shake out of the tree the better the chances to find a few acorns. He would go with veterans for the short run while rebuilding the farm system, which would include uniform player instruction at every level and expanded scouting. Richards also set in motion an Oriole tradition by stressing pitching and defense, the cornerstones of future Oriole success. "Pitching and defense keeps you in games, and if you have a chance to win the fans will keep interested and have hope." With his droll wit, Richards told the press early on: "Someday, boys, maybe in four or five years from now, Baltimore will have a fine young team on the field. When the day finally comes and a pennant is hoisted on the Stadium flagpole, all I ask is that you observe a moment of respectful silence in memory of old number 12."

Richards didn't waste time in making moves, and his first one was a doozy. On November 18, 1954, the Orioles and Yankees swung the biggest trade in baseball history, a 17-player extravaganza that took a couple of weeks to complete. When the smoke cleared, the Orioles had parted with their best young pitcher, Bob Turley,

George Zuverink, who pitched for the Orioles from 1955 to 1959, was the club's steadiest relief pitcher over most of that period. His 4-3 record in 1955 was the only mark above .500 out of 23 Oriole pitchers. He led the league in appearances in 1956 and 1957 and posted a 10 6 record and 2.47 ERA in 1957, his best year in eight big league seasons.

along with Don Larsen, Mike Blyzka, Dick Kryhoski, Billy Hunter, Darrell Johnson, Jim Fridley, and Ted del Guerico. Coming to Baltimore were catchers Gus Triandos and Hal Smith, outfielder Gene Woodling, shortstop Willy Miranda, infielders Don Leppert and Kal Segrist, and pitchers Harry Byrd, Jim McDonald, and Bill Miller. Turley of course went on to have several All-Star seasons in New York, and Larsen developed a no-windup delivery that helped him make history in the 1956 World Series. The two keys for Baltimore were Triandos, who became an All-Star catcher, and Miranda, who developed into a fielding whiz at shortstop. "Willy couldn't hit a lick," remembered Richards several years later. "The only switch hitter I knew who bailed out from both sides of the plate. But boy could he go into the hole and gun people out with that arm. He was an acrobat in the field and helped us bridge the gap until some of our youngsters developed."

Hal "Skinny" Brown, using guile and grit, won more than 60 games in his seven seasons in an Oriole uniform. Brown joined the Birds in 1955 and got better with age, posting a 12-5 record in 1960, walking only 22 batters in 155 innings. The following year he pitched 36 consecutive scoreless innings.

The next season was a cattle call for the Orioles with Richards as the trail boss. Altogether, 54 players appeared in Oriole box scores, just two less than the big-league record. Third base was the busiest, where ten men played at least once, including a youngster named Brooks Robinson who manned the hot corner for six games near the end of the season. Twenty-three pitchers saw action, and only one, George Zuverink, managed a winning record at 4-3. Jim Wilson led the pitchers with a 12-18 record. "Old Blue" Ray Moore won 10 and lost 10. Even the team presidency changed, with home builder James Keelty Jr. replacing Miles as club president. Among the coaches, only pitching coach Harry Brecheen remained. Richards unofficially was the co-pitching coach. He loved working with young pitchers and teaching old pitchers new tricks that might prolong their careers. The new coaches were Luman Harris and Al Vincent, who had coached in Detroit in 1945 when Richards was still catching.

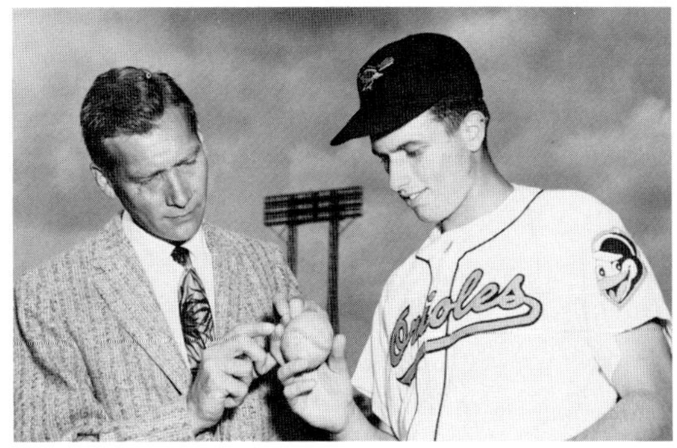

Hall of Fame left-hander Hal Newhouser scouted and signed young Detroit prospect Milt Pappas for the Orioles. Pappas was pitching for the Birds when he was 18 years old.

The trend for the season was set on opening day when Red Sox third baseman Ted Lepcio became the first player to hit two home runs in a game at Memorial Stadium. He homered off Joe Coleman in the second inning and added another off Lou Kretlow in the sixth as Boston won 7-1 before 38,085. The Orioles lost their first six games and, like the year before, rallied in September to climb out of the cellar by winning 15 of their last 20, wresting seventh place from the Senators. The Orioles improved three games, finishing 57-97, 39 games behind the front-running Yankees. Richards later said he managed harder that year than in any season of his career because he didn't want to lose 100 games like the year before. Attendance slipped to a little over 850,000 in 62 dates.

The Orioles were last in team batting average, slugging percentage, and fielding percentage in the American League. As a team they hit only 54 home runs for the season. Woodling, expected to provide a big boost in run production, was a flop at the plate, hitting only .221 in 47 games before being traded to Cleveland in mid-June. "Paul liked me from my minor-league days and insisted I be included in that big deal," remembers Woodling. "I left the top with the Yankees to go to the bottom with the Orioles. As it turned out I got about one base hit a week and got booed out of town." Woodling was to return to the Orioles three years later and erase all the bad memories of 1955.

The 1955 Orioles couldn't even beat their own minor-league teams. Their Class B farm team in York, Pennsylvania, smacked them 13-1 in a June exhibition. Bob Hale was promoted from that York club and hit an amazing .357 in 182 at-bats. Dave Philley was acquired from Cleveland and hit .299 in 83 games and was voted Most Valuable Oriole. So many players were coming and going that the same nine players started and finished a game just three times all year. Miranda, who led the league's shortstops in putouts, assists and double plays while batting .255, said the clubhouse resembled a train station. "Every day I seemed to be introducing myself to somebody new at the next locker."

A capacity crowd of 48,829 watched the American League edge the National League 4-3 in the annual All-Star game on July 8, 1958. It was the only All-Star game in Baltimore until 1993.

Memorable moments were scarce in 1955. On May 27 centerfielder Chuck Diering made one of the greatest catches in Oriole history, hauling in Mickey Mantle's deep drive with his back to the plate, then crashing into the hedge some 440 feet from home plate and only 10 feet shy of the scoreboard. The catch completed a pretty fair day for Diering who homered in the second and singled in the sixth, two of only five hits allowed by Whitey Ford as the Yankees won 6-2.

Paul Richards specialized in rejuvenating the careers of fading pitchers; one of his first projects in Baltimore was Hal "Skinny" Brown. After a 1-8 record with the Red Sox in 1954, the 31-year-old right hander found himself in the minor leagues pitching for the Oakland Oaks. Richards bought his contract in July, 1955, and in the next seven years Brown would win 62 games while losing 48, a percentage much better than the team's. He was the winningest Oriole pitcher of the 1950s. The ageless Brown was effective into his late 30s, hurling a club record 36 consecutive scoreless innings in 1961. He was eventually inducted into the Orioles Hall of Fame.

But in 1955 Brown was a hard-luck 0-4. An August game with Cleveland typified his season. Bill Wight started for Baltimore but gave up five runs in the first inning before recording an out. Brown relieved and held the Tribe hitless the rest of the game, striking out 10. Herb Score and the Indians won 5-1.

Certainly one of the most important events in Oriole history occurred on May 30, 1955. More than a thousand miles away from Baltimore, far from any big-league ballpark, Brooks Calbert Robinson, two weeks past his 18th birthday, signed his first professional contract in his Little Rock, Arkansas, home with his parents looking on. Lindsey Deal, teammate of Richards in Atlanta, had watched Brooks play in high school and legion ball. He wrote the Oriole skipper saying, "He's no speed demon, but neither is he a truck horse. Brooks has a lot of power, baseball savvy, and is always cool when the chips are down." Art Ehlers, then an assistant to Richards, offered $4,000 and Brooks accepted, feeling he could reach the majors quicker in Baltimore.

The Brooks Robinson saga from the Little Rock sandlots to the Hall of Fame began humbly. "Hitting was his problem at the beginning," recalled Richards years later. "But my how he could field. Because we needed hitting, I threatened to take him out of the lineup, but our pitchers wouldn't stand for it. They didn't care if he hit. They just wanted his glove in there."

After he signed his contract he joined the team on a trip to Cleveland, just to get a feel for life in the big leagues. Playing second base during a pregame workout, Brooks dazzled with his fielding skills. After awhile, Richards leaned over to club vice-president Jack Dunn III and said, "That boy just might become the greatest third baseman who ever lived." Richards saw in Brooks what few did at first: excellent quickness and instincts, great hands, and an accurate throwing arm. "I thought Paul was kidding when he had me watch the kid work out one day," remembers Woodling. "He couldn't hit, he couldn't run and his arm wasn't that strong. It shows you how much I know."

Brooks was sent to Class B York, Pennsylvania, in the Piedmont League where George Staller became his first professional manager. Staller had played on the minor-league Orioles and later coached for Earl Weaver on the big-league level. Brooks hit a lusty .331 in 354 at-bats at York and was promoted to the Orioles late in the season. He made his first start on September 17 against Washington, going two for four in a win over the Senators. His first hit came off right-hander Chuck Stobbs. The 18-year-old was so thrilled with his hitting that he called home to Little Rock. "I thought the major leagues were a piece of cake," said Brooks. "But then reality set in when I went 0 for 18 the rest of the way and finished at .091."

The climb to respectability began for the Orioles in 1956. They improved their record by a dozen games from the year before, finishing at 69-85, jumping a notch in the standings to sixth, 28 games behind the Yankees. After 30 games the Orioles stood 15-15 before slipping under .500. Once again attendance failed to reach the million mark as they drew a hair above 900,000. But they did post their first winning record at home, 41-36.

Veteran George Kell became the first Oriole to play in the All-Star game when he started the '56 classic at Griffith Stadium in Washington. Bob Turley had been selected in 1954 but never appeared in the game in Cleveland. The same was true for pitcher Jim Wilson in 1955 in Milwaukee.

Kell had come over from Chicago on May 21 in what turned out to be one of the best trades in the Paul Richards era. Besides former batting champion Kell, the Orioles acquired .300-hitting outfielder Bob Nieman and pitchers Connie Johnson and Mike Fornieles. Heading to the White Sox were Wilson and outfielder Dave Philley. Except for bonus babies Billy O'Dell, Wayne Causey, and Jim Pyburn, the 1956 Orioles were a veteran bunch, led by Nieman, Kell, Bob Boyd, Gus Triandos, and Billy Gardner.

The team's best pitcher was 30-year old Ray Moore, a native of Upper Marlboro, Maryland, who won 12 and lost seven. Skinny Brown was 9-7. Wight, who finished 9-12, allowed only seven home runs in the 175 innings he worked, the best percentage in the league. New York's Mickey Mantle socked 52 homers in 1956 en route to the Triple Crown, but he failed to connect in 11 games in Baltimore. Mantle hit only .219 (7-for-32) in Memorial Stadium, 134 points below his league-leading mark of .353.

Gus Triandos slides into second base trying to break up a double play as Ernie Banks fires to first in the '58 mid-summer classic.

Behind Gus Triandos' 21 homers, up from 12 the year before, the Orioles slugged 91 home runs in 1956, a big improvement from the 54 they hit the year before. The number of players who saw action was still amazingly high; 48 passed through at one time or another, but the mainstays had quality seasons, Nieman in particular. Nieman had always hit. As a St. Louis Browns rookie in September 1951, he became the only player in history to homer his first two times up in the major leagues, connecting both times off Red Sox lefty Mickey McDermott. Traded to the Tigers in 1953 and then to the White Sox in 1955, Nieman blossomed in 1956, hitting .322 in 114 games in Baltimore. From August 17 through September 7, he hit in a club record 20 straight games. His one-season average of .325 in 1958 remained tops until 1977 when Ken Singleton hit .328. In four Oriole seasons, Neiman, who died in 1985 at the age of 58, compiled a .303 lifetime average, still tops on the Orioles' all-time list.

Kell had been obtained for a couple of reasons. Richards wanted an old hand to help break in young Brooks Robinson. Plus, he viewed George as his eventual replacement when his contract was up the following year. "I had played with Paul in Detroit and under him with the White Sox," remembers Kell, who is in his 33rd season as a broadcaster with the Tigers. "Paul had said he was going to take me to Baltimore so the trade didn't surprise me. What did surprise me was that the Oriole brass extended Paul's contract to manage. I couldn't blame them as Paul was an outstanding manager." Kell batted .261 in 102 games in 1956, far below his lifetime average of .306. He went one for four in the All-Star game, won by the National League, 7-3. The next year, his last as an active player, Kell bounced back to hit .297 in 99 games, and once again started in the All-Star game. Kell said this about Richards' ability to get the most out of older players. "He never let us play ourselves out. He'd play me two

Billy O'Dell accepts congratulations from Yankee first baseman Bill Skowron and Yankee catcher Yogi Berra after retiring all nine National Leaguers he faced in the 1958 All-Star game.

weeks, give me three days off, and I'd come right back strong and ready to go."

Ironically, Kell hailed from Arkansas, just like his heir apparent, Brooks Robinson. Another irony: the two were inducted into baseball's Hall of Fame in the same year, 1983. As for helping Brooks break into the big leagues, Kell declines credit. "I didn't help him do anything except teach him how to act like a big leaguer," said George. "Since he wasn't married, my wife Charlene and I took him under our wing. If I helped him at all it was to show him how a big-league player was expected to conduct himself." As a hitter, Brooks fooled Kell. "When I first saw him, he swung at everything from the letters up, the high stuff. In the field of course he needed no teaching. He was quick, had great instincts and a soft pair of hands." To be inducted into Cooperstown with Brooks was one of Kell's great thrills. "It was unbelievable that two kids raised just 90 miles apart, and with the same church-going backgrounds and the same ideals, would go into the Hall of Fame the same day. You couldn't write the script any better." Kell also said the script on his 14-year career, in which he hit over .300 for eight straight seasons, ended on a high note in Baltimore. "Baltimore was a great place for me to finish my career. The people were so good to me. We didn't have a good ball club but I was a bear-down player and I tried hard. I gave the fans 100 percent and they gave their appreciation right back to me from the stands. I could just hear 'em." Baltimore adored Kell, not only for his effort on the field but his comportment off it. Kell exuded class, a class he passed on to young Brooks, who collected 44 at-bats in 1956 at the tail end of the season. He hit .227 and cracked his first big-league homer on September 29 in Washington against the Senators' Evelio Hernandez.

First baseman-outfielder Bob Boyd turned in another solid season. Batting .357 in his first Baltimore season, he broke his left elbow throwing the ball in from the outfield and missed 10 weeks. He wound up with a .311 average in 70 games, including a 19-game hitting streak.

Starting in 1967, Dick Williams managed three different teams in three different decades into the World Series. In 1956, however, he was struggling to get there as a player. In 87 games with the Orioles Williams hit a solid .286. He tied Clint Courtney for most tours of duty with the club, three, coming over from Cleveland in 1958 and then over from Kansas City in 1961. "Paul Richards was my savior as far as staying in the majors," says Williams, now 66 years old and living in Las Vegas. "I loved the guy and I learned so much from him that I took with me as a manager, like the way he'd talk to his pitcher after each inning, about the inning just past and the hitters coming up." Richards liked Williams' versatility. "One time I played six different positions in a doubleheader against Detroit. Evidently he liked my bat. Paul could be brazen and sharp but he gave me my major-league career and for that I'll always be grateful."

The 1956 season produced a couple of notable moments. On May 12, young lefty Don Ferrarese pitched a brilliant two-hit shutout to beat the Yankees 1-0 for his first major-league victory. Ferrarese took a no-hitter into the ninth but singles by Andy Carey and Hank Bauer broke it up.

Then on June 21 the Orioles and White Sox tied an American League

Bob Nieman hit .320 in his first Oriole season in 1956 and .325 in 1958. In four seasons in Baltimore he hit a combined .303, still the top career mark in Oriole history.

record in Chicago by combining for just two total hits in a game. Each side collected one hit but Nellie Fox's double followed a walk and drove in the game's only run. Connie Johnson and George Zuverink pitched for Baltimore with Connie going seven innings; Jack Harshman went the route to win for Chicago.

Manager Paul Richards (center) congratulates pitcher Hoyt Wilhelm (right) moments after the knuckleballer tosses the first no-hitter in modern Oriole history. The date was Sept. 20, 1958, as Wilhelm blanked the Yankees 1-0 at Memorial Stadium. Gus Triandos provided the only run of the game with his 30th home run of the season.

On September 24 rookie right-hander Charlie Beamon made his major-league debut and beat Whitey Ford and the champion Yankees 1-0 on a four-hitter. The loss denied Ford the victory he needed for his first 20-win season.

Just four days before Beamon's gem, on the off-day of September 20, tragedy struck when promising catcher Tom Gastall, a bonus baby signed out of Boston University in 1955, was killed when the light plane he was piloting crashed into the Chesapeake Bay. The 23-year-old Gastall's body was never found.

By 1957, 105 different players had seen action in an Oriole uniform in Richards' two years at the helm. Except for Billy O'Dell not a single player remained from the inaugural season just three years before. The Baltimore brass hoped bonus babies O'Dell, Wayne Causey, Bob Nelson, and Jim Pyburn would emerge after a couple of years in the majors, and they were counting on others like Brooks Robinson, Ron Hansen, Marv Breeding, and Willie Tasby to start jelling.

Richards was occasionally criticized for his "buckshot" way of spending money on young players. The story of a young pitcher named Bruce Swango illustrates what bothered some. The day the scout arrived to watch Swango pitch his game was rained out. Richards instructed the scout to warm him up in a gymnasium. Under these controlled circumstances, the youngster was impressive. Richards rashly signed him—adding a big bonus to the deal. What Richards didn't know was that Swango froze up in front of crowds. Unable to suppress this problem, he bounced around the minors for several years, never reaching the majors. Then there was Bob Nelson, the last of Richards' big bonus signings in June of 1955. An impressive physical specimen at 6-3, 220 pounds, Nelson was nicknamed "the Babe Ruth of Dallas" for his high school exploits. As a senior he hurled five straight shutouts, hit .375, and slammed seven homers in 14 games. The Orioles outbid 13 other teams to sign him. The bottom line on his 79-game, three-year stay in the big leagues: a .205 batting average and no home runs in 122 at-bats. The Babe was a bust.

The veterans again saved the day in 1957, helping the club reach a milestone: their first .500 season. Finishing in fifth place, 21 games behind the champion Yankees, the Orioles won 76 and lost 76. They managed to beat New York in nine of 22 games, including a Labor Day twin bill sweep. Second baseman Billy Gardner won Most Valuable Oriole honors. He played in all 154 games, hitting .262 behind a club record 169 hits, including 36 doubles.

Gardner was one of many who turned in banner years. First baseman Bob Boyd, nicknamed "The Rope" because the sharp line drives that came off his bat resembled frozen ropes, hit .318 in 141 games, finishing fourth in the American League batting race. Triandos slugged 19 of the club total 87 homers, no easy feat considering Memorial Stadium was still a pitcher's paradise. Gus also led in RBI with 72.

Pitching was the big surprise in '57, with 35-year-old right hander Connie Johnson leading the way with a 14-11 record and 3.20 ERA. (He victimized Kansas City five times alone without a loss.) Johnson threw hard, modeling himself after his idol Satchel Paige, his old Kansas City Monarch teammate in the Negro Leagues. Connie's biggest thrill in the majors was striking out 14 Yankees in a 6-1 win in early September 1957. "Eight struck out on a changeup that Paul Richards taught me. It took me two years to master the pitch. I finally learned how to pitch under Paul. I just wish it had come 10 years sooner."

Bob Boyd, nicknamed "The Rope" because of the line drives that seemed to jump off his bat, had several .300 plus seasons in his five years in Baltimore. The veteran of the Negro Leagues hit .301 as an Oriole.

Johnson was also involved in a memorable stretch in late June when four pitchers pitched shutouts in consecutive days. Skinny Brown started it with a 6-0 whitewash of the Tigers. In a two-game series against the A's, Billy Loes won 5-0, then the next day Johnson duplicated the feat by the same score. Ray Moore completed the string of goose eggs with a 6-0 win over Cleveland.

Ray Moore achieved something in 1957 that is incomprehensible in this day and age. Against Detroit on May 20, "Old Blue" pitched 15 innings, at the time an Oriole record (Jerry Walker went 16 innings two years later), but didn't get the decision as the Orioles lost 2-1 to the Tigers in 16 innings. Moore's homer in the third off Jim Bunning accounted for the only Oriole run of the game. Mike Fornieles pitched the 16th and took the loss. Bunning went 13 innings for Detroit.

Loes, who had several respectable seasons with the Dodgers, had a solid 1957 season in Baltimore, winning 12 and losing 7 with a 3.24 ERA. He never won more than 14 games, prompting him to utter that now-famous baseball axiom, "Never win 20 because they'll expect you to do it every year." Loes won seven straight at one point for the '57 Birds and allowed only eight home runs in 155 innings. Picked for the All-Star game in St. Louis along with Kell and Triandos, Loes pitched three scoreless innings in the 6-5 American League win.

Brooks Robinson, shown here in 1959, was establishing himself as the premier third baseman in the league by the end of the decade. In 1960 he began a long string of All-Star appearances that saw him play in 18 mid-summer classics and start 11.

Kell wound up his career in '57, despite the urgings of Richards to keep playing. George was only 35. In June of 1957, he delivered his 2,000th major-league hit in a 9-7 win over Kansas City.

One of the most bizarre games in Oriole history happened on May 18, 1957. A 10:20 P.M. curfew was set for that evening's game in Baltimore against the White Sox because the Pale Hose needed to catch a train later that night. The curfew meant that all play would stop at exactly 10:20 P.M. Chicago held a 4-3 lead in the bottom of the ninth with just seconds to go before the bewitching hour. Dick Williams hastily came to the plate to lead off the inning. Sox pitcher Paul LaPalme only had to kick the dirt a few times and hold the ball. Instead he pitched to Williams. "The first pitch he threw me was a high knuckleball and I hit it foul," remembers Williams as if it happened yesterday. "Then came another knuckler high and outside. LaPalme just had to bend over to tie his shoe and the game would have ended. Manager Al Lopez even came out to talk over the options. Al had barely returned to the bench when LaPalme, with about 20 seconds remaining before the curfew, threw me another knuckler and I hit it out of the park for my first home run of the year." The score was tied and the game stopped. The home run meant the contest had to be made up later in the season. La Palme's promptness cost his team a victory, as the Birds went on to win the make-up.

The fans rewarded the Birds first .500 effort by exceeding the million mark for the first time since 1954. They drew 1,029,581, including 45,276 for a night game in July with the Yankees. They played 10 double-headers at home in 1957. (In 1994 none were scheduled.)

The Orioles fell below .500 in

1958, finishing with a 74-79 record but they were only 17½ games behind the first-place Yankees. The home run total swelled to 108, finally topping the century mark. For almost a third of the season they hovered in fourth place or better and were tied for second in late July when an 11-game losing streak bumped them from contention and into sixth place.

Gus Triandos was named Most Valuable Oriole, slugging 30 home runs to tie an American League record for most homers by a catcher, set originally by Yogi Berra. It was the fourth straight season that Triandos, who was establishing himself as one of the top players in the league, led the Orioles in both home runs and RBI.

Triandos was a high-strung player prone to excessive self-criticism; the vast dimensions of Memorial Stadium only heightened this problem. "I was a player of limited ability and the thing I could do best was hit with power, but the park was too big for me." Gus' 30th home run in 1958 was the most memorable of his career because it provided the only run of the game in Hoyt Wilhelm's no-hitter against the Yankees, the first no-hitter in modern Orioles history. The homer sailed over the 410-foot sign in dead center field and came off reliever Bobby Shantz in the seventh inning.

Wilhelm was 35 years old when he joined Baltimore in late August from Cleveland. He was 0-3 as an Oriole when he made that historic Saturday afternoon start against the Yankees. It came on September 20, the day after the Birds had rallied from a 4-0 ninth-inning deficit to win 5-4, the tying and winning run scoring on Gene Woodling's single. Wilhelm's famed knuckleball worked to perfection that day, aided by a heavy mist that surrounded the stadium. The 10,941 paying customers and 7,251 knotholers began to sense history in the making when "Ol Sarge" retired nine straight Yankees in the fifth, sixth, and seventh. A nationwide television audience was watching and listening to Lindsey Nelson and Leo Durocher describe the action. Ernie Harwell and Herb Carneal were in the home radio booth. Dick Williams remembers that no-hitter because he was playing third base. "Bob Nieman, not much of an outfielder, was playing left," recalls Williams. "I hadn't gotten one ground ball hit to me all day and neither had Nieman had a chance in left. At the end of the seventh, Richards moved me to left and put in young Brooks Robinson to play third. The kid handled three

The Oriole Way

The Orioles have long had the reputation of being a feeding ground for other major-league franchises, both in the front office and on the field. Currently, former Oriole catching prospect Kevin Kennedy manages the Texas Rangers while former Oriole farmhand Lou Piniella pilots the Seattle Mariners. Davey Johnson manages in Cincinatti and Don Baylor is at the helm of the expansion Colorado Rockies. Johnny Oates, the current Orioles skipper, came up through the Baltimore farm system.

Whitey Herzog, who once played the outfield in Baltimore, managed the Cardinals to a World Championship and recently retired as general manager of the California Angels. Coaches Billy Hunter, George Bamberger, Jim Frey, and Ray Miller all left the Orioles to manage other clubs. Miller is now pitching coach in Pittsburgh. Frey managed the Royals to a 1980 World Series berth against the Phillies and took the Cubs to the 1984 National League East title.

Toronto's highly successful general manager Pat Gillick signed with the Orioles and pitched in the Birds' minor-league system from 1959 through 1963, including three seasons under Earl Weaver, before retiring with a sore arm. Gillick's first base coach in Toronto, Bob Bailor, came up with the Orioles and is the heir apparent to current manager Cito Gaston.

Baltimore native John Schuerholz started in the Oriole farm department and ended up building the Kansas City Royals into a pennant contender before taking the ragtag Atlanta Braves to new heights in the National League. Add in Frank Cashen and Al Harazin, who spent years with the Mets, Lou Gorman in Boston, Joe McIlvaine in San Diego, John Hart in Cleveland, Jerry Walker in Detroit, Larry Himes with the Cubs, Herk Robinson in Kansas City, and Harry Dalton in Milwaukee and you've got an impressive array of front office talent who cut their teeth in Baltimore with the Orioles.

tough chances on topped balls and made the outs all three times." With one out in the ninth, Hall of Fame outfielder Enos Slaughter lined a drive to right-center but Willie Tasby ran it down. Hank Bauer followed with a bunt attempt. It rolled foul. Bauer swung away on the next pitch and popped to short right near the line. Second baseman Billy Gardner, who had robbed Norm Seibern of a hit in the eighth, raced over and caught it for the final out. A no-hitter. Hoyt struck out eight and walked only two. Triandos committed one passed ball. The game took only one hour and 48 minutes. Afterward Hoyt, the toast of the baseball world, returned to the Southern Hotel, called his wife in North Carolina (it was their wedding anniversary), sipped a cup of coffee, and went to bed.

Knuckleballer and Hall of Famer Hoyt Wilhelm, nicknamed "ol' Sarge," spent just over four of his 21 years in Baltimore, but they were memorable seasons. Wilhelm's career was rejuvenated in Baltimore as he switched to starter, pitched a no-hitter, and won 15 games in 1959.

Brooks Robinson played his first full season in 1958, hitting .238 in 145 games. On April 17, 1958, Brooks hit his first Memorial Stadium home run, off Washington's Russ Kemmerer—his fourth career homer, all off Senators pitching.

After hitting .321 the year before in Cleveland, Gene Woodling returned for his second tour in Baltimore. This time the marriage clicked. Gene hit a solid .276 with 15 homers and 65 RBI. Nieman had his best year as an Oriole, hitting .325 with 16 homers and 60 RBI. Bob Boyd eclipsed .300 for the third straight year, finishing with a .309 mark. His .367 average at night was tops in the league.

Some of the pitchers fell off from the previous year but others filled the breach. Left-hander Jack Harshman had come over from the White Sox and tossed 17 complete games. He finished with a 12-15 record and sported a 2.90 ERA, tops in Oriole history to that point. Harshman had begun his career as a first baseman and could help his cause at the plate. He hit two home runs in one game including a three-run shot against Chicago, driving in four in a 6-5 win. For the season Harshman belted six round-trippers.

Arnie Portocarrero, with a career record of 18-37 in four seasons with the Athletics, was obtained a few days before the '58 season. He epitomized the great success of the Richards-Brecheen pitching-makeover team. Arnie became the Orioles' first 15-game winner, (against 11 losses). His favorite target was Boston, which he defeated five out of six times.

Nineteen-year-old Milt Pappas, after appearing in just three minor-league games in 1957, catapulted to the big club in 1958 and launched his long Oriole pitching career with a respectable 10-10 record. Then there was Billy O'Dell. Forced to join the major-league club out of Clemson because of the bonus rule, Billy was deprived of minor-league instruction and seasoning. He sat on the bench most of his first three seasons, and lost another to the U.S. Army. Between 1954 and 1957, O'Dell won a total of five games and lost 11. His first win came late in 1954 against Richards' White Sox when he thwarted Virgil Trucks' last attempt that season at winning 20. The outing impressed Richards and when he came to Baltimore he kept an eye on O'Dell. In 1958 his chance came and he thrived, going 14-11 with a gaudy 2.97 ERA. "I got to pitch while in the Army and that served as the minor-league experience I never got in pro ball," says O'Dell. "Plus I learned from the many veterans we had." For his efforts he was picked to pitch in the mid-summer classic, before the hometown fans.

The 1958 All-Star Game was played in Baltimore's Memorial Stadium. Unlike the previous two years when the fans stuffed the ballot boxes in Cincinnati in an effort to elect the entire Reds' team as All-Star starters, the voting for the 1958 game was conducted by the players, managers, and coaches. Gus Triandos won the catching job over Yogi Berra and O'Dell was picked by Casey Stengel as the other Oriole representative. Memorial Stadium seated 47,778 but an eager crowd of 48,829 crammed their way into the park on July 8 to watch the game's silver anniversary edition. Usually the players bus from their hotel to the game, but for the first time in All-Star history, the players

Journeyman catcher Joe Ginsberg spent five seasons with the Orioles, backing up Gus Triandos. His batting average crested at .274 in 1957. Joe had a hand in a dubious record (along with Triandos): most passed balls in an inning, three, and a game, four, while catching for Hoyt Wilhelm.

traveled from their downtown hotel, the Emerson, by motorcade. In a parade similar to the 1954 opener, the players sat in open-air convertibles with fans lining the streets.

The lineups represented a veritable who's who of baseball greats: Mickey Mantle, Henry Aaron, Willie Mays, Ernie Banks, Ted Williams, and Stan Musial. Yet for the first and only time in All-Star history, there were no extra-base hits. The American League out-singled the Nationals 9-4. Triandos collected one of them, and then, before his second at bat, was lifted to a chorus of boos by Stengel, who sent Berra up to pinch-hit for the Baltimore favorite.

The American League had forged ahead on that overcast day with a run in the sixth as Yankee Gil McDougald singled in Boston's Frank Malzone to make the score 4-3. Former Oriole Bob Turley had given up all three National League runs in less than two innings, but Ray Narleski of Cleveland had come in and limited the N.L. to one hit over the next 3⅓. Early Wynn pitched a scoreless sixth. Still available in the bullpen were Yankee great Whitey Ford, White Sox mainstay Billy Pierce, fastballing Yankee reliever Ryne Duren, and the Orioles' O'Dell. To the surprise of everyone including Billy, Casey summoned the Oriole lefty.

"I was shocked," remembers Billy. "I thought sure he'd pick Ford or Pierce. Maybe he wanted to get back in the good graces of the crowd for taking out Gus." So the 25-year-old lefty with a 13-20 career record came in and sparkled. Nine up and nine down. Four future Hall of Famers were among the nine. Only the first, Johnny Logan, hit the ball out of the infield, lining to left. "I had great stuff, using just a fastball and slider. I broke Willie Mays' bat on a ground out to short and got Stan Musial on another broken bat grounder." He struck out Ernie Banks to end the eighth. In the ninth he induced Frank Thomas to foul to the catcher, struck out Bill Mazeroski, and got Milwaukee catcher Del Crandall to pop to Nellie Fox at second to end the game. "There really wasn't a tough out in the bunch," quipped Digger on his 27-pitch effort. He was voted the Most Valuable Player of the game.

In the hubbub of the postgame celebration, O'Dell never had a chance to thank Stengel for using him, and vice versa. Finally, four years later when Billy was with the Giants and Casey was managing the Mets the two met again. "He walked over to me while I was warming up," said Billy, "and said, 'Mr. O'Dell, I never had the opportunity to thank you for the way you pitched for me in that '58 All-Star Game.' To hear Casey say that was one of my biggest thrills. Other than the thrill of pitching in my first big league game in 1954, the All-Star Game was my career high moment."

The era of two All-Star Games in one season began the next year in 1959 and carried through the 1962 season. Although cities like Cleveland, Pittsburgh, and even Washington hosted two All-Star Games after 1958, Baltimore had to wait until 1993 to host another mid-summer classic, 35 years and 38 games after their first one, the only All-Star Game at Memorial Stadium.

For the first time since 1954, a team other than New York won the American League pennant in 1959. The Chicago White Sox out-pitched the Cleveland Indians to win by five games. In Baltimore, the Orioles finished ahead of Kansas City and Washington for sixth place with a 74-80 record, 20 games behind Chicago. For more than half the season the Birds hovered in the lofty region of third place. As late as August 11, they were a game over .500 at 56-55, and on August 27 they still clung to third place—their highest point in the standings this late in the season. The Orioles played the pennant-winning White Sox tougher than anybody, the only team in the league to break even with them (11-11). Nine innings was usually not enough to settle their games, as the two played an 18-inning tie, two 17-inning, one 16-inning, and two 10-inning games.

The twin Ws, Woodling and Wilhelm, were the story in 1959. In what he called the best season of his 17-year career, the 37-year-old Woodling led the Orioles in hitting (.300), RBI (77), doubles (22), total bases (200), and walks (78). As a pinch-hitter he went 10-18 (.556) and drove in eight runs. He also hit 14 home runs. In one late July stretch he drove in all nine Oriole runs in back-to-back games, hit his first major-league grand slam, moved to the top of the American League batting race with a .344 average, and was named to the All-Star team for the first time in his career. The "Old Pro," with his unorthodox batting stance and all-out competitive desire, played in a career-high 140 games. "The season was like magic" remembers Woodling, who played on five straight World Series winners with the Yankees. "Every time I came up with men on base, I seemed to drive them in."

On June 10, 1959, Cleveland's Rocky Colavito hit four consecutive home runs at Memorial Stadium.

The fans so appreciated Woodling's efforts they feted him before a night game in September, presenting the Most Valuable Oriole with, among other gifts, a new car and a prize heifer cow. Gene told the crowd that coming back to Baltimore and doing well after failing the first time was the proudest achievement of his baseball career. Later he said that playing left field behind a great young third baseman like Brooks Robinson added a few extra years to his career.

Besides Woodling, the Orioles placed four other players on the All-Star roster, O'Dell, Triandos, young Jerry Walker, and the ageless knuckleballer, Wilhelm. At 36, Hoyt became the first pitcher in history to win ERA titles in both major leagues. His 2.19 figure easily outdistanced Chicago's Bob Shaw (2.65). As a 29-year-old rookie with the 1952 New York Giants, Wilhelm led the National League with a 2.43 ERA. After a 3-10 record and 10 starts including the no-hitter the year before, Wilhelm, a relief pitcher his entire career, started 27 games and completed 13 in 1959, winning a career high 15 against 11 losses. He also led the league in strikeouts and innings pitched, winning his first nine decisions while shaving his ERA to a microscopic 0.996 for 90-plus innings. Hoyt didn't lose until June 15, when he allowed his first home run in 115 innings.

Many of Wilhelm's wins were spectacular and for a time it was difficult to pick up a national magazine, read a newspaper, or turn on a radio or television set without being reminded of his exploits. He even overcame a swarm of gnats at Comiskey Park to beat the White Sox 3-2 for his eighth straight. In the first inning Hoyt was attacked by gnats that made pitching not only uncomfortable, but almost impossible. The White Sox grounds crew did their best to disperse the gnats to no avail. The umpires tried to scare them off with spray cans but that method, too, was unsuccessful. The bugs were finally "blasted" off the mound by fireworks that owner Bill Veeck was saving for the post-game display. Nothing could stop Wilhelm in 1959. *Life* magazine even took him to Aberdeen Proving Ground so the baffling course of his elusive knuckleball could be plotted on a special missile tracking device. Of his knuckler, one harassed umpire said, "If the hitters can't hit it and the catchers can't catch it, how in blazes do they expect me to call it?"

During his blistering start, Hoyt pitched eight complete games and three shutouts, including back-to-backers against the Yankees in late May in which he tossed a one-hitter and a four-hitter. In six starts against New York dating back to the no-hitter the year before, Wilhelm had gone 5-0 with five complete games, allowing the Bronx Bombers only three earned runs in 52 innings.

Only opposing batters shuddered more than the Oriole catchers at the sight of Hoyt on the mound. Having to catch Wilhem's dancing knuckler every fourth day, Triandos and his backup, Joe Ginsberg, set a new league record for passed balls with 49. Gus committed 28 passed balls, 24 with Wilhelm pitching,

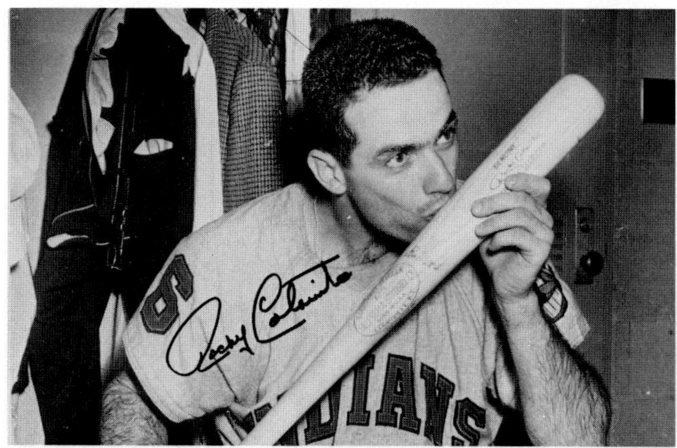

Afterward he kissed the bat that brought him instant immortality.

Brooks with Baltimore native and future Hall of Famer Al Kaline of Detroit. Kaline collected his 3000th career hit at Memorial Stadium in 1974.

Brooks

Doug DeCinces

Wild Bill Hagy

Jim Palmer

Eddie Murray

Mike Flanagan

Dennis Martinez

Earl Weaver

Sunday
MAGAZINE
THE SUN
BALTIMORE, MD.
Wilhelm's Knuckleball
Story on Pages 8-9

Sunday
MAGAZINE
THE SUN
Henry A. Bauer
with TV WEEK

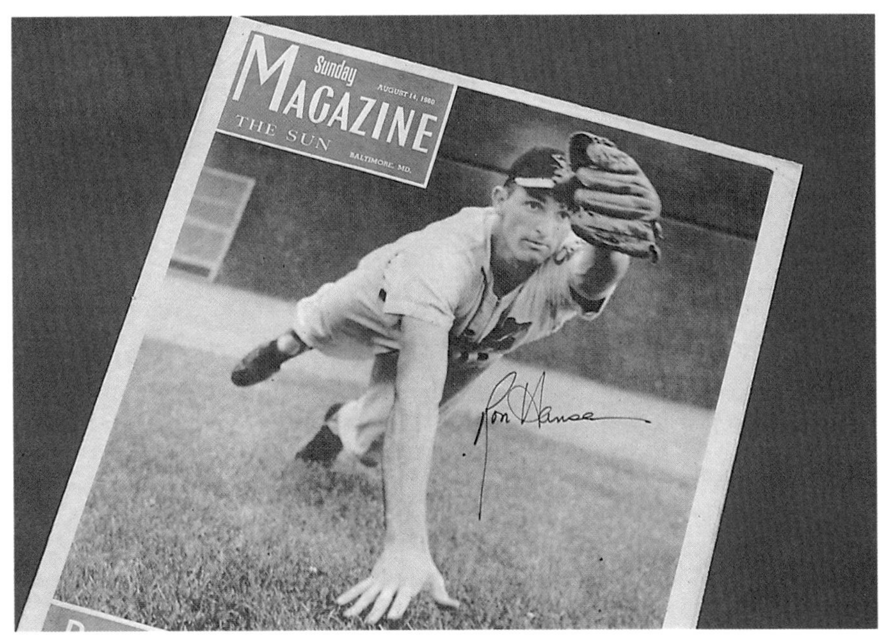
Sunday
MAGAZINE
THE SUN
BALTIMORE, MD.

SILVER JUBILEE PROGRAM
BALTIMORE THE NEWS-POST
Monday, July 7, 1958
SILVER JUBILEE PROGRAM
25th Silver Jubilee...
1958
All Star GAME
MEMORIAL STADIUM

MAGAZINE
THE SUN
ALL STAR GAME
JULY 6, 1958
BALTIMORE, MD.
NATIONAL
AMERICAN

SILVER JUBILEE PROGRAM
BALTIMORE THE NEWS-POST
Monday, July 7, 1958
SILVER JUBILEE PROGRAM
25th Silver Jubilee...
1958
All Star GAME
MEMORIAL STADIUM

BEN McDONALD
POSTER PAGE
THURSDAY, MAY 19
COLLECT ALL TEN!
THE BALTIMORE SUN
In 5/17 Out 5/19

ORIOLES
ORIOLES
ORIOLES
ENTERED AS SECOND-CLASS MATTER AT BALTIMORE POST OFFICE
THE EVENING SUN SOUVENIR BASEBALL EDITION
NAME
ADDRESS
CITY

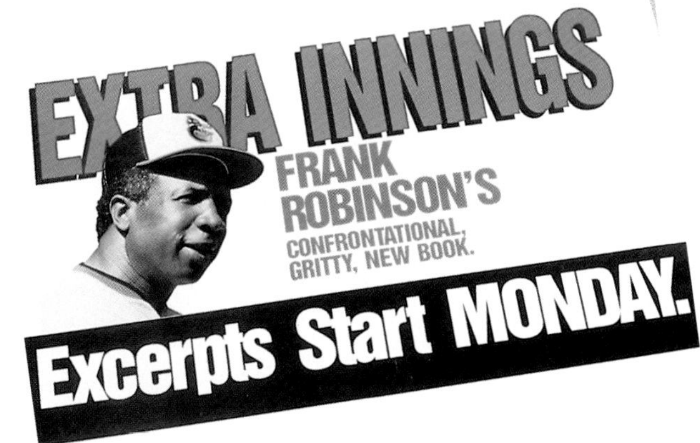
EXTRA INNINGS
FRANK
ROBINSON'S
CONFRONTATIONAL,
GRITTY, NEW BOOK.
Excerpts Start MONDAY.

ALL STAR LATEST SPORTS

	1	2	3	4	5	6	7	8	9		R	H	E
Chicago..	0	0	0	0	0	0	1	0	0	--	1	7	0
Orioles...	0	0	1	1	0	0	0	1	x	--	3	9	1

THE EVENING SUN

Vol. 88—No. 153 · PAID CIRCULATION IN MARCH · 388,883 SUNDAY 317,902 · BALTIMORE, THURSDAY, APRIL 15, 1954 · 86 Pages

FINAL · CLOSING STOCKS

ORIOLES TOP WHITE SOX, 3-1

Courtney, Stephens Homer For Birds In Opener Here

By James Ellis

A pair of home runs by Clint Courtney and Vern Stephens sparked the Orioles to 3-1 win over the Chicago White Sox in the opening American League game at Memorial Stadium here today.

and Waitkus later scored on a single by Wertz.

The White Sox also tallied in the seventh, Carrasquel scoring after the Sox got three singles

THE SUN

Special Section

Baseball '87

SECTION E

THURSDAY APRIL 2, 1987

RIP

REST IN PEACE, '86; NEW LIFE FOR ORIOLES WITH CAL RIPKEN SR.

THE SUN

Sunday MAGAZINE

BALTIMORE, MD. JULY 2, 1961

The Baltimore Orioles' big man with the bat is 6-foot, 4-inch Jim Gentile. He made baseball history in April by hitting two grand-slam home runs in successive times at bat. Story inside.

'Diamond Jim'

Orioles '89 SEASON OF DREAMS

SUN MAGAZINE
FEBRUARY 27, 1983
Joe Altobelli:
Can he keep that 'Orioles Magic' alive?
Orioles
26

THE EVENING SUN
SPECIAL ORIOLES SECTION
We Know You'll Make Your Grandpa Proud
Manager Dykes Ranks Yankees On Top Again
Orioles Back In Major Loop

SOUVENIER
Oriole EDITION
HOME NEWS
Vol. 20, No. 13
BALTIMORE, THURSDAY, APRIL 15, 1954
5c COPY
"WE'RE IN THE MAJORS NOW!"
LOOK WHAT THE BUNNY BRUNG US!
Dykes Selects Bob Turley For Opening Combat
Today's lineup

Orioles Baseball 1991
THE BALTIMORE SUN
THURSDAY, APRIL 4, 1991
The Last Hurrah
NEWS-POST

Baseball Extra
THE EVENING SUN
THURSDAY, APRIL 2, 1987
C1
RIP COMES TO THE RESCUE
Cal Ripken Sr. operates to take Birds off critical list
— Page 2

THE SUN
Special Section
Baseball '86
E

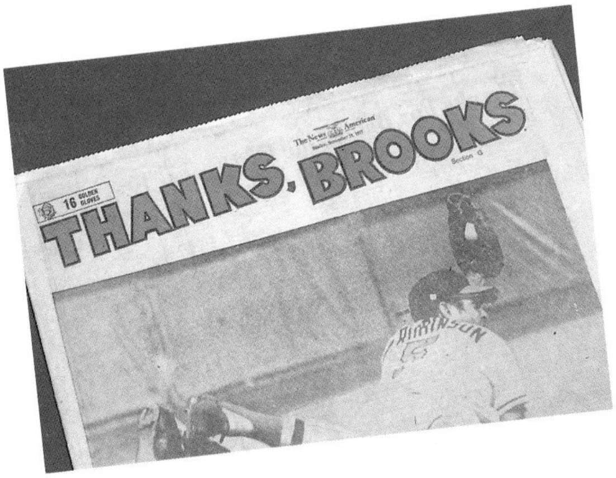

The News American
THANKS, BROOKS
16 GOLDEN GLOVES
Section

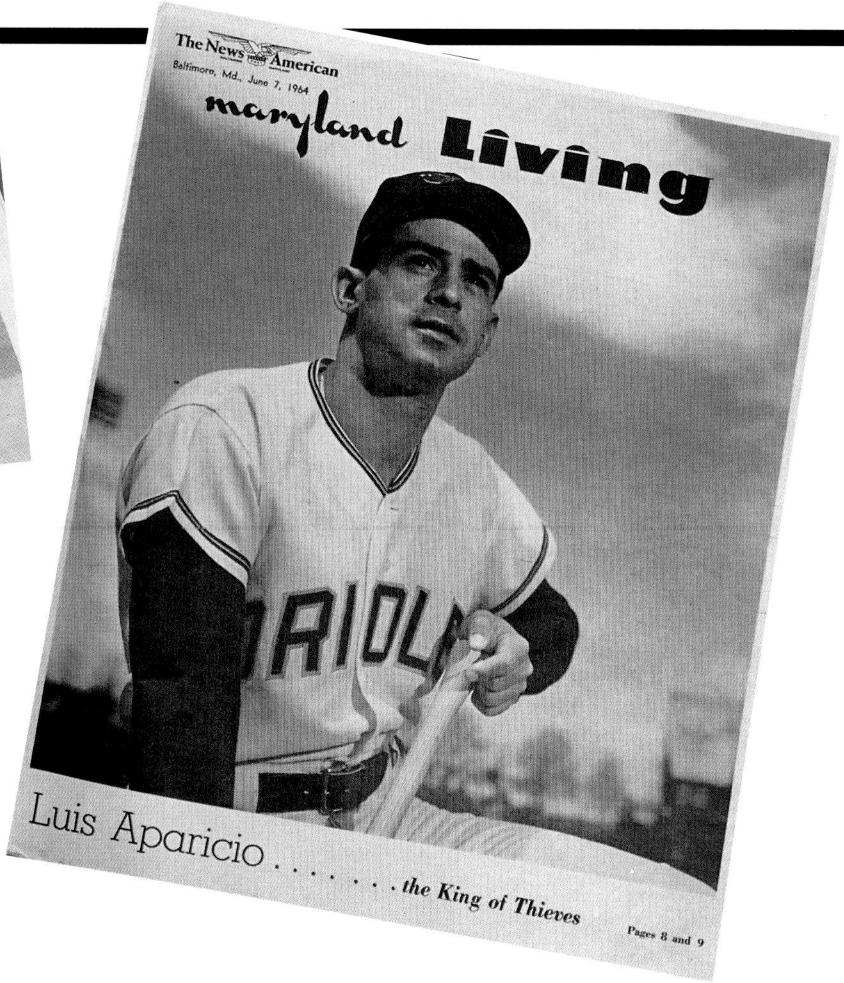

The News American
Baltimore, Md., June 7, 1964
maryland Living
Luis Aparicio . . . . the King of Thieves
Pages 8 and 9

The News American
ORIOLES '77
SOUVENIR ISSUE
SECTION C
Thursday, April 7, 1977
John F. Steadman
SPORTS EDITOR SAYS:
Will Weaver Alter Managing Style?
This will, without question, be the most challenging year Earl Weaver has had as manager since the Baltimore Orioles decided they had a future together.
The Orioles have, out of necessity, been reshaped with new faces and a third of the roster will be rookies. Virtually all the pre-season surveys peg the club to finish fourth in the Eastern Division of the American League.
If that happens it'll be their lowest showing since 1967. So anything higher than that would figure to be pleasing.
The driving hand of Weaver will be important. He's an intense leader and extracts the maximum out of a
So the burden will be much heavier on May, whose 25 home runs and 109 runs-batted-in a year ago made him the team's most valuable player.
The pitching is the one aspect that could save the Orioles from embarrassment. There's not going to be much run-making in their behalf so the pitchers are going to have to perform in a way that will keep the rivals from scoring if the Orioles are going to be "in" games.
Outfield defense isn't what it was with the departure of Paul Blair, who could run down pitching mistakes. The infield, with Mark Belanger at shortstop, will be solid and, no doubt, continue to be a feature of the club.
Palmer Key
New Look Generates Interest
By JIM HENNEMAN
Most observers agree that the 1977 season will be one of the more interesting in the Orioles' 24 year history.
Those with optimistic leanings prefer to use the word exciting to describe the club's "new look," but it will take at least a month, maybe longer, to make such an appraisal.
For sure, the season figures to be interesting — if only to see how the Orioles fare after having been stripped of three top performers. For the most part they will attempt to replace Reggie Jackson, Bobby Grich and Wayne Garland with kids loaded with potential, but untested in the major leagues.

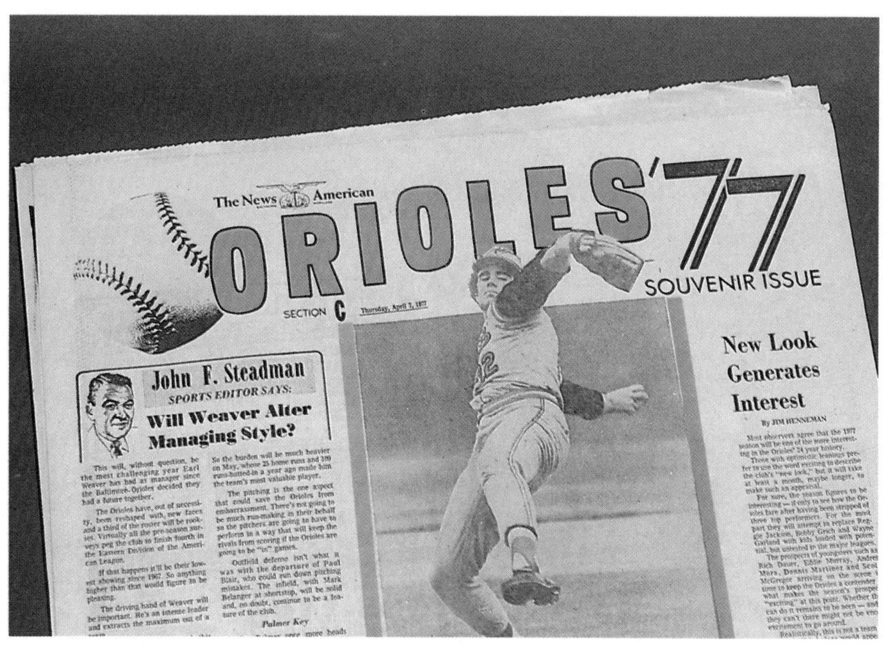

EDDIE!
EDDIE!

1985 free agents
(from left) Lee Lacy,
Don Aase, Fred Lynn

The Birds celebrate a dinger

Brooks with other 1983 Hall of Fame inductees Walter Alston (represented by grandson Robin Ogle, far left), George Kell (center left), and Juan Marichal.

Ken Singleton

Mark Belanger forces Jim Rice at second

1983 World Series victory parade

Tippy Martinez

Rick Dempsey

breaking the record of 25 set in 1911. Twice Triandos and Ginsberg were charged with four passed balls in the same game. Catching the knuckler also took its toll on Gus' hands. "I was having an excellent season in '59," recalls Triandos, "with 20 homers and 50 RBI at the first All-Star break, but a foul tip off the bat of my old teammate, Jack Harshman, put me out of action for 17 days. I had to miss the second All-Star game in Los Angeles." Gus did bounce back a few weeks later to hit two home runs, including a grand slam, and drive in seven runs in an 11-0 rout of Detroit. Playing with the injured hand, Triandos hit only five homers over the second half with a batting average of .148. His 25 homers still led the club, four more than Neiman's career high 21.

A converted first baseman, Jack Harshman pitched for the Orioles in 1958 and 1959. In '58 his 2.90 ERA was third best in the league, although his record was a subpar 12-15. He never forgot how to hit, blasting six home runs in 1958, picking up two in one game twice at Memorial Stadium.

The next year, to combat the passed balls, the innovative Richards devised "the big mitt," an oversized catcher's glove more than twice the size of a regular catcher's mitt. "It worked pretty well in catching the knuckler," remembers Ginsberg. "The problem was trying to get the ball out of the glove when someone was stealing a base. It was hard to find the ball in the glove." Before the "mitt debut" Wilhelm had pitched 28 innings and been charged with four wild pitches while his catchers had been charged with 11 passed balls. His ERA was 5.96. With his catchers wearing the mitt, Wilhelm pitched 118 innings and was charged with just two wild pitches; and his catchers had just three passed balls. His ERA was 2.66.

Richards pioneered another strategy that involved his battery: having the pitcher back up the catcher in case of an overthrow on a play at the plate. "Paul wanted the pitcher to flip me his glove as he ran by and I would use it like an infielder," says Ginsberg, smiling at the recollection. "Either I could catch a short hop or a high throw and still tag out the runner. It seemed like a pretty good idea and we worked on it in the spring. On the third day of the season we tried it in Cleveland. Larry Doby tried to score from second on a hit up the middle. Here comes the pitcher and he tosses me his glove and I threw the catchers mitt at him. Trouble was, the pitcher was Bill Wight, a left-hander. Here I was trying to get Bill's glove on backwards, catch the ball, and make a tag. That, needless to say, was the end of the glove-switch play."

Richards said young Brooks Robinson was the best player in the league over the last six weeks of the 1959 season. Reporting to the club late in the spring upon his discharge from the army, Brooks was only five for 25 in 13 games and was optioned to Vancouver of the Pacific Coast League. There he hit .331 in 42 games with the Mounties and on July 9 was recalled to the big leagues for good. Over the last six weeks of the season Brooks hit safely in 29 of 35 games and went 52 for 141, a .369 average that raised his season total to .284—an impressive mark for the kid some thought would never hit.

In 1959 the Oriole farm system finally began bearing fruit, not only Robinson but young pitchers Milt Pappas, Jack Fisher, and Jerry Walker. Twice the trio of 20-year-olds participated in double shutout wins. In July,

In September 1959 outfielder Gene Woodling was feted at Memorial Stadium. Here receiving a portrait of himself as an Oriole, Gene also received a new car and a heifer cow for his farm in Ohio. Woodling hit .300 with 77 RBI in 1959. He played in his first All-Star game in '59 and belted his first career grand slam.

The Knotholers

Souvenirs from the first couple of seasons are coveted by collectors, none more than the Esskay hotdog cards from 1954 and '55. The cards were spawned from the popular pregame television show sponsored by Esskay called "Bobo Newsom's Knothole Gang" seen on both WAAM and WMAR-TV. The colorful Newsom had concluded his long major-league career (which began in Brooklyn in 1929) by going 2-1 with the Philadelphia A's at the age of 46. In between he pitched on 16 big-league clubs including the Senators five different times, the Brown three different times and the Dodgers and A's twice. His best year was with Detroit in the pennant year of 1940 when he went 21-5. With a rubber arm that enabled him to throw over 3,700 innings, Bobo became one of the few pitchers with more than 200 games (211) who lost more than he won (222). Spending most of your career with second division teams can have that effect.

How he popped up in Baltimore in 1954 isn't clear. The Esskay cards were issued in color, two to a box, on the bottoms of the hot dog cartons. Fans had to cut them out to save them. There were 34 different cards in 1954 and 26 in 1955, 52 different players in all, including Bobo in an Oriole Uniform. Finding the cards in panel form is almost impossible. Individually they are still extremely rare. Complete sets in mint condition sell for a couple of thousand dollars. Only one Oriole wasn't included in the Esskay series, third baseman Vern Stephens. It seemed Junior signed with rival Wilson Wiener for that company's set of cards, causing, frankly, a conflict of interest. Bobo was never one to stay in one place too long, however, so it's not surprising that the show disappeared after the next season. Bobo passed away seven years later in Orlando at 55.

Pappas, who didn't turn 20 until May 11, had a remarkable year, winning 15 games and losing but nine. Four of his 15 complete games were shutouts, and he allowed only eight gopher balls in 209 innings. Despite his tender age, Pappas wasn't intimidated about pitching in the majors. "I was cocky enough to realize that I was in the big leagues for a reason and that I had to produce to stay." Milt admitted his youth caused some friction with his teammates. "It took five and six years for most of them to make the big leagues. Here I was an 18-year-old kid out of high school. There was one player who took me under his wing and gave me confidence. Willy Miranda was like a second father and I owe a lot to him."

The year also produced its share of bizarre events. Willie Tasby, a gifted outfielder who made circus catches and bullet throws, gained more permanent fame because he played a rainy-day game in his stocking feet. His reason: he feared his metal cleats would attract a bolt of lightning. O'Dell, who compiled a brilliant 2.94 ERA in 199 innings, helped his own cause in

Pappas and Walker blanked the Senators, 8-0 and 5-0. Then, in September, Fisher blanked Chicago 3-0 on a three-hitter, followed by Walker's magnificent 16-inning effort against the White Sox that saw the Orioles win 1-0 on Brooks Robinson's RBI single in the 16th. In recalling the game, Walker said both Brecheen and Richards were keeping close tabs on him. "They asked me after each inning how I felt. I only threw around 170 pitches so it wasn't that taxing. I didn't have any major jams to pitch out of and I didn't strike out too many people." Walker was the starting and winning pitcher for the American League in the second All-Star game in Los Angeles in 1959, allowing one run over three innings in a 5-3 American League win.

a game against the White Sox at Memorial Stadium on May 19. Locked in a pitchers' duel with lefty Billy Pierce, O'Dell won his own game with a 120-foot two-run homer. "The foul lines were made of wood in those days and I blooped a ball over first base with a man on. The ball hit the line and bounced to the right and beyond the charging rightfielder Al Smith. The ball kept bouncing and I kept running for an inside-the-park homer that won the game 2-1."

Perhaps the most impressive achievement in the first six seasons at Memorial Stadium was turned in by an opposing player, Cleveland's Rocky Colavito, on the night of June 10, 1959. Colavito became just the eighth player in big-league history to hit four home runs in one game and just the third to do it in four consecutive at-bats. Lou Gehrig accomplished it last in 1932. His feat was even more amazing because Memorial Stadium was no friend of long-ball hitters. It was 382 feet to the alleys in left- and right-center and 410 feet to dead center. Since baseball's return to Baltimore no player had hit more than two homers in a game and no team more than three at the stadium.

Colavito had been struggling with only four hits in his previous 30 at-bats entering the game. In the first inning off Walker, Rocky walked and Minnie Minoso homered for a 2-0 lead. "In the bottom of the inning I ran down little Albie Pearson's line drive into the right-field corner and a fan poured a cup of beer right in my face," remembers Rocky, who still seethes when recalling the episode. "I was furious and challenged the fan to meet me after the game. He said he would and I said 'you better be there.'" The next time up Rocky homered to left off Walker. In his second official at-bat against reliever Arnold Portocarrero, Colavito socked a slider over the fence in left-center for a 400-foot homer. "When I went out to right field after the second homer the fans in the immediate area gave me a nice hand, even though I was a visiting player. I had always been treated well in Baltimore. In my third official trip up I homered again off Portocarrero, this one landing some 420 feet away. There was louder applause when I went out to right after the third homer." In his final at-bat in the ninth against Baltimore's top reliever, Ernie Johnson, Colavito etched his name in the record books. "Johnson hadn't given up a homer all year," says Rocky, who almost 30 years after retirement still keeps himself in playing shape. "The first pitch he threw me was under my chin, a brush back pitch. The next pitch I got out in front of and hit harder than the other three, 425 feet into the left center field bleachers. You'd have thought I was a hometown player as they gave me a standing ovation. It was heartwarming. Even the guy who poured beer on me was cheering and waving at me. Suddenly I wasn't mad anymore. I don't know whether that night endeared me to Baltimore or not, but they always treated me great after that." Cleveland won the game that night 11-8, and the Tribe's total of six homers (Minoso and Billy Martin hit the others) established a one-game record at Memorial Stadium.

Diamond Jim, the Kiddie Korps, and a Whole Lot More

The Orioles have generated several "Miracles on 33rd Street" over the years. The first was in 1960. That's the year Baltimore, comprised of seven rookies, 10 players still in their 20s, and a nucleus of hardened veterans, made the first legitimate pennant charge in modern

Milt Pappas was a member of the O's famed Kiddie Korps pitching staff.

Oriole history. In early September they held first place for seven straight days, leading by two games after sweeping the Yankees three straight. In August they had set a club record with an eight-game win streak.

The three-game sweep of the Yankees in early September, the most exciting series to that point in the Orioles' seven-year history, drew more than 114,000 fans. In May they had also swept three from New York in Baltimore with Skinny Brown hurling a one-hitter in the middle game, but this sweep was special. It occurred in September—with the O's in a pennant race. In the series the two leaders of the peach-fuzz Kiddie Korps pitching staff, Milt Pappas and Jack Fisher, led off with shutouts over Whitey Ford and Art Ditmar. Twenty-two-year-old rookie right-hander Chuck Estrada pitched 6⅔ hitless innings in the third game with Hoyt Wilhelm finishing up.

The two premier fielding third basemen in baseball from the late 1950s to the mid 1960s, Brooks Robinson and Clete Boyer of the Yankees. Boyer played in Brooks' shadow, never making the All-Star team or winning a Gold Glove.

The Yankees got even a few weeks later at Yankee Stadium. The two teams were virtually tied for first place when the Birds arrived in the Bronx. Three days later they left town four games out, having been swept four straight. The Birds still managed to nest in the dizzying position of second place, eight games behind the Yankees. Richards was named Manager of the Year by both the A.P. and U.P.I. The Orioles beat Boston 16 times in 22 tries in 1960 and were a part of history on September 28 at Fenway Park when Ted Williams made his final home appearance. He had gone 0-3 including a long drive caught by Al Pilarcik against the fence in right-center on his third trip. Then in his final at-bat in the eighth inning, the 42-year-old legend socked his 521st career home run off Jack Fisher. The crowd cheered uncontrollably, bringing the game to a temporary halt. Despite the fans' show of affection, Williams never came out of the dugout to salute them. Nor did he wave after Carroll Hardy replaced him in right field in the top of the ninth as he dashed to the dugout amid thunderous applause.

The seven Oriole rookies in 1960 all made contributions, especially Jim Gentile, Rookie of the Year Ron Hansen, Marv Breeding, Chuck Estrada, and Steve Barber. Walker and Fisher were in their second year and Pappas his third. The Kiddie Korps of five pitchers all 22 years old or younger (Estrada, Barber, Pappas, Fisher, and Walker) combined for 58 of the Birds' 85 wins. Estrada led the way with 18, a modern Oriole record to that point. Estrada won Pitcher of the Year honors from *The Sporting News*. "It was unheard of to have so many kids pitching in the big leagues at the same time," says Pappas. "We broke that barrier and I think we revolutionized the game."

Every season has its share of oddities and bizarre occurrences; one of the strangest in Oriole history took place August 28 in Baltimore. Pappas, who finished 15-11, was shutting out the White Sox going into the eighth inning. But then the Sox punched one run across and had runners on first and second when muscular Ted Kluszewski pinch-hit for Minnie Minoso. Klu promptly hit Pappas' second pitch into the seats for a dramatic three-run homer. Or so it appeared. Third base umpire Ed Hurley nullified the play, saying he'd called time-out right before the pitch. Hurley called time because a couple of White Sox were warming up outside the bullpen area (they were preparing to enter in the bottom of the inning for defensive purposes). After a bitter argument, Klu lined to center to end the inning. Wilhelm pitched the ninth for the save, preserving the victory umpire Hurley made possible. Chicago filed a lengthy seven-paragraph protest that was disallowed by league president Joe Cronin.

There were heroes galore in 1960 as attendance reached 1,187,848, a new club high. Lefty Steve Barber jumped all the way from Class D ball to win 10 games including a one-hit shutout of the A's. In his three previous years in Class D, Barber won 22 and lost 32. He was 10-7 with the 1960 Orioles. The Takoma Park, Maryland, native earned the title "fastest pitcher in baseball" when in a series of tests his fastball was

Gus Triandos became an early folk hero in Baltimore because he was the club's first authentic power hitter. His 30 homers in 1958 tied Yogi Berra's American League record for most homers by a catcher in one season. Gus's feat was doubly impressive because of Memorial Stadium's long fences; Yogi enjoyed the short porch in right field at Yankee Stadium.

Gus Triandos

It's not that Gus Triandos didn't like playing in Baltimore. He did. It's just that he never felt he was as good as his numbers bore out. Until his production waned in the early 1960s because of injuries, Gus was as solid as any catcher in the league. "Playing for me just wasn't that much fun," says Gus. "It was a struggle for me to get the most out of what I had." There were also the psychological scars of trying to catch the fluttering knuckleballs of Hoyt Wilhelm, which led to new records for passed balls.

The Baltimore fans had a love-hate relationship with Gus. Some elevated him to hero status, even naming a road in Baltimore County after him that stands today as a lasting tribute to the big backstop. Others booed their catcher every chance they got, feeling Gus rarely delivered in the clutch, even though Paul Richards had statistics saying Triandos was the team's top clutch hitter. "They always boo the big guys," says Gus, who stood 6-3 and weighed 215 pounds. "Fellows my size look like we should murder the ball every time. When we don't, the fans get on us."

If it hadn't been for his trade to Baltimore after the 1954 season in that huge multi-player deal with the Yankees, Gus might not have had much of a career at all in the big leagues. He was playing behind Yogi Berra in New York and Yogi was the premier catcher in the league. In his memorable 1958 season, Gus banged out 30 home runs to tie his old Yankee teammate for the most home runs by an American League catcher in one season.

In those days Memorial Stadium was cavernous. Yet Gus belted 142 career homers as an Oriole, still the most ever by a Baltimore catcher.

Life after baseball has not been that kind to Gus, who has had numerous physical afflictions, many brought on by two serious car crashes. Still, he's battled back from them, showing the same courage and perseverance that he exhibited on the baseball field.

Whether he realizes it or not, Gus Triandos was a hero in Baltimore. He was the first star the Orioles had, and his contributions in those struggling early years have placed him near the top of the list as one of the most important players in Oriole history. Every year you could expect over 20 home runs and 80 RBI from Gus. "The funny thing," he said during his playing days, "is I know the fans like me. They really aren't my enemies. They always treat me just fine off the field."

clocked at 95.55 miles an hour. Don Drysdale's was timed at 95.31 and former Oriole-turned-Yankee Ryne Duren's at 91.16 miles an hour.

Skinny Brown kept rolling along like Old Man River, establishing a personal high for wins with 12 against just five losses. On June 1 Brown pitched a one-hitter to beat the Yankees, allowing only a Mickey Mantle first inning solo homer.

Jack Fisher won six straight decisions, pitching three consecutive shutouts en route to a 12-11 record. "Fat Jack" pitched 29 ⅓ scoreless innings during that stretch.

The Orioles cornered all 24 votes for "Rookie of the Year," with Ron Hansen earning 22 and Jim Gentile and Chuck Estrada one each. Hansen, the 6-4 shortstop from Nebraska, socked 22 homers and drove in 86 runs. Playing in both All-Star games, Ronnie went 3-6. His roomie, Brooks Robinson, also played in the first of his 16 All-Star games.

At the start of the 1960 season Boston's Frank Malzone was considered the best third baseman in the

Desperately wanting to hit .300 to top off his magical season in 1961, Jim Gentile struck out twice against Chicago's Herb Score in the final game of the season before pulling himself out to freeze his batting average at .302.

American League. By mid-season it was a toss-up and by the end there was no contest. Brooks Robinson had come of age. Voted Most Valuable Oriole, he finished third in league MVP voting behind Roger Maris and Mickey Mantle in a close ballot. Playing 152 games, Robby hit a sparkling .294 and cracked 14 homers while driving in 88 runs. He even led the club in triples with nine and hit his first grand slam off Cleveland's Gary Bell. On July 15 he went 5-5 against the White Sox, hitting for the cycle. He also led American League third basemen in fielding. Even though this was Brooks' sixth season, he was still only 23. The future was glistening.

The new Oriole infield had a brilliant first season in 1960. Breeding, the fleet second baseman, played in 152 of 154 games, hit a solid .267, and participated in the lion's share of the record-breaking 172 double plays reeled off by the Oriole infield. Breeding was a fun-loving southerner from Decatur, Alabama, who had a tough time meshing with his all-business manager, Richards. "He was a tough man to get to know as he never talked directly to you. It was always through a coach even if he was sitting four feet from you in the dugout," said Breeding. Marv's starting role was short-lived as Jerry Adair replaced him in 1961.

Gentile, purchased from the Dodger organization after the 1959 season, was a big, strapping, first baseman with matinee idol looks. Nicknamed "Diamond Jim," Gentile had bounced around the Dodger chain for eight years, playing for 11 different clubs, including four games in Brooklyn in 1957 and 12 in Los Angeles in 1958. He sported impressive minor-league numbers (34 homers at class A Pueblo in 1953, and 40 homers and 104 RBI with Fort Worth—Double A—in 1956) but never earned a permanent promotion to the big leagues because the Dodgers had perennial All-Star Gil Hodges entrenched at first. With the reserve clause strangling a player's ability to shift organizations, Gentile was buried.

Gentile was underrated as a first baseman. For his size he was extremely nimble and could stretch for low throws as well or better than any first baseman in the game.

Despite a miserable spring in 1960, Richards penciled in the 26-year-old Gentile as his starting first baseman. He went on to drive in a club record 98 runs and smash 21 round trippers, many of them tape measure shots, including a 475-foot blast in Washington. Chosen by Casey Stengel for the All-Star team, Gentile went 1-2 in the Kansas City dream game. His biggest day of the year was in Kansas City on June 26 when he went 3-5 with a grand slam and a three-run homer off Dick Hall. As it turned out, Gentile's homer heroics were just a prelude to what would lie ahead in 1961.

Gentile was the Orioles marquee player of the early 1960s. Here he is appearing on Curt Cowdy's Red Sox television pregame show at Boston's Fenway Park.

A couple of old pros wound up their Oriole careers in 1960. Gene Woodling, despite turning 38, played in 140 games and hit .283, including a 17-game hitting streak in late August. Said Gene about his three years in Baltimore: "It isn't always batting average and stats that prove a player. You have some players who hit 30 home runs and drive in 100 but only nine of the homers win games. Like magic, for three years in a row, it seemed like every time I had men on base, I got a base hit."

Bob Boyd's listed age

was 33 but the veteran of the old Negro Leagues was probably much older than that. As the Orioles' principal pinch-hitter in 1960, the Rope hit .317 and over five seasons in Baltimore hit a combined .301. The secret to his success: "I hit balls to all fields and didn't try and pull. Most of the time I hit balls rather than strikes. I actually could hit balls out of the strike zone for a base hit as well as I could hit strikes."

"It Can Be Done in '61" was the adopted slogan for the expansion year of 1961. The old Washington Senators had moved to Minnesota and a new team began play in D.C. The Los Angeles Angels also debuted to increase the league to 10 teams. As major-league baseball expanded so did Memorial Stadium, which underwent its first face-lift since 1954. Field box seats were installed down each line, eliminating the eight-foot wall that had distanced the fans and made the foul ground the most expansive in baseball.

With the help of the new 162-game schedule the Orioles eclipsed 90 wins for the first time, finishing an impressive 95-67. Unfortunately, the Yankees set a torrid pace with a fearsome lineup including Roger Maris, who hit 61 homers to break Babe Ruth's single-season mark, and Mickey Mantle, who clouted 54. The Birds' 95 wins was good for only third place, 14 behind New York. Detroit won 101 games yet still finished eight back.

Home runs were hit at a record clip in the American League; the Orioles set a club record with 149. Gentile emerged as a full-fledged folk hero in Baltimore, setting 11 team records. He tied a major-league record by hitting five grand slams and set a big-league record by becoming the first player in baseball history to hit grand-slam homers on successive

Jim Gentile

"Diamond Jim" Gentile owes his baseball career to Paul Richards. Richards "rescued" Gentile from the Dodger organization where he had spent eight seasons in the minor leagues. The Dodgers had Gil Hodges at first base and Gentile was buried in the farm system. Like so many players who were bound to one team because of the reserve clause, it looked as though Jim Gentile would experience an unfulfilled baseball career.

Richards bought Gentile from the Dodgers' St. Paul Triple A club but when Gentile arrived for spring training in 1960 he did little to justify Paul's faith in him. "I didn't do a thing all spring," says Gentile, now retired and living in Oklahoma. "My batting average was under .200 and I was all thumbs in the field. I was nervous and all wound up about not trying to muff my last big chance to make the major leagues. I don't know why to this day that Paul brought me north with the team. He had Bob Boyd and Walt Dropo at first, both of whom were proven big leaguers, and a 19-year old kid name Boog Powell who played better than any of us."

To the surprise of many, Richards told Gentile on opening day in 1960 that he was his first baseman. "He told me it was up to me and gave me 30 days to prove myself," said Gentile, still strikingly handsome at the age of 60. "He said no one could look as bad as I looked in spring training."

Platooning with Dropo, Gentile hit .292, belting 21 homers and driving in a club-record 98 runs. That was just a prelude to his magical season in 1961 in which he hit .302, walloping 46 homers, and driving in 141 runs, still a club record. Amazingly none of these accomplishments were enough to lead the league since Roger Maris blasted 61 homers and drove in 142 runs. Gentile became the people's choice though in Baltimore, ranking with Johnny Unitas in popularity.

Unfortunately, Gentile's star dimmed quickly because of his intense desire for perfection. "I wanted to get a hit every time I went up there," he says, "and when I'd pop up or strike out, I just couldn't handle it. I broke many a bat deliberately in frustration. I'd watch Brooks Robinson's even-keeled approach to the game and just marvel at how nothing got him down."

Failure wore on Diamond Jim and by 1964 he was on his way to Kansas City. Now, years after his playing days, he says his personality has taken a 180-degree turn. "I'm just a big pussycat now. It took me half a century to mature and realize you can't be perfect at everything." For one special season in 1961, Jim Gentile was as close to perfection as anyone could be.

trips to the plate. Jim clubbed 46 home runs, which tied Harmon Killebrew for third in the league, and his 141 RBI was one behind Maris. He led the club in batting with a .302 average. "Every journeyman player has that one good year, the one you look back on as your best. That year for me was 1961," says Gentile. "In 1960 I drove in 98 runs in only 384 at-bats so the momentum was with me in '61. It seemed that every ball I hit either fell in or left the park." Amazingly Gentile had only seven more hits than RBI in his monster season.

Chuck Estrada burst on the scene as a 22-year-old rookie in 1960 with 18 wins and was named *The Sporting News'* American League "Pitcher of the Year." Estrada won 15 games in 1961 before arm troubles shortened his career. Chuck, oddly, was the Orioles pitcher when Jim Gentile hit each of his six grand slams in 1960 and '61.

Diamond Jim's double grand slam night happened in Minnesota on May 9. "In the first inning, Jackie Brandt had reached on an error to load the bases and Pedro Ramos got two quick strikes on me," remembers Gentile. "I said to myself, 'Oh boy, don't hit it on the ground. Make him get the ball up. Don't go after a low fastball.' So he gives me a high fastball and I just wanted to get it to the outfield. Instead it went out of the park." The next inning lightning struck twice. The same three batters, Whitey Herzog, Brooks Robinson, and Brandt, safe on another error, were on base, only this time reliever Paul Giel was pitching. "I was looking for a good fastball and he threw it right down the pipe. He told me later it was a screwball that didn't screw. I wasn't trying to overpower it and just met the ball. When I came back to the dugout Richards slapped me on the behind and said, 'Son I don't think that's ever been done.'" Paul was right. It hadn't. Frank Robinson of the Orioles and Jim Northrup of the Tigers duplicated the feat several years later, but Diamond Jim was the first. Gentile added a sacrifice fly for nine RBI in the 13-5 Oriole win.

Part of the Orioles "Kiddie Korps" staff of 1960 that saw five pitchers under the age of 22 pick up 58 of the club's 85 wins, Jack Fisher won 12 games that season, fashioning three-straight shutouts. He also served up Ted Williams 521st homer, which came on his final big league at-bat, at Fenway Park on September 28.

Gentile hit three more grand slams that year, setting an American League mark and tying Ernie Banks' major-league record for most in one season. His top Memorial Stadium thrill was grand slam number four on July 7. He did it as a sixth-inning pinch hitter in a 2-2 game against the Athletics. "I had jammed my thumb a few days before while tagging a runner. I hit the grand slam off my old Dodger minor-league teammate Ed Rakow," recalled Gentile.

Ron Hansen won Rookie of the Year honors in 1960 when he hit 22 homers and drove in 86 runs. His career with the Orioles fizzled two years later, and he was dealt to the White Sox.

Hitting in the clutch brought out his best. He drove in the tying, winning, or lead run 48 times during the season. For his efforts he finished a solid third in the MVP balloting behind Maris and Mantle. An excellent first baseman who used his 6-4 frame to stretch and dig out low throws, Gentile was voted second to Cleveland's Vic Power as the best fielding first baseman in the league by a vote of American League

One of the few players to jump from Class D ball to the majors, fastballing Steve Barber became the Orioles first 20-game winner in 1963. In six-plus seasons he won 95 games in Baltimore, posting a 10-5 record in the pennant year of 1966.

One of seven rookies on the Orioles 1960 25-man roster, second baseman Marv Breeding turned in a solid rookie season at second base. He hit .268 in 152 games and led the club with 10 steals. Unfortunately Breeding's career was shortlived as the next year Jerry Adair took over at second and Marv faded from the scene.

players. His exploits earned him Oriole MVP and a night in his honor in which he received a Corvette.

The Baby Birds of 1961 seemed to feed off Gentile as several had outstanding years. Brooks Robinson played in 163 games and banged out a club record 192 hits with a .287 batting average, mostly as the lead-off hitter. He was elected by the league's players

Billy Hitchcock, a southern gentleman with an easy manner, managed the Orioles in 1962 and 1963 with disappointing results. They finished in seventh place in '62 and improved to fourth in 1963 with an 86-76 record, but an 8-22 June dropped them from the race. Billy was replaced by Hank Bauer at season's end.

to start in both All-Star games and won his second Gold Glove.

Jackie Brandt, obtained from the Giants for Billy O'Dell and Billy Loes before the 1960 season, hit safely in the first 12 games of the season and never stopped hitting, finishing with a .297 average and 72 RBI, second to Gentile in both categories. Nicknamed "Flakey," Brandt was a free spirit who many felt failed to fulfill his potential. "I was told throughout my whole career that I was supposed to do better than I did," says Jackie. "But to me 100 percent is 100 percent. I didn't know how to give 105 percent or 110 percent. They said I was too nonchalant, that I could have run faster and hit harder, but I gave it all I had and it looked easy, but it wasn't." Paul Richards of course was all business and grew tired of what he perceived as Brandt's lack of enthusiasm. "He should show some life. He goes around as if this were just another job. It makes you wonder." Yet Brandt was picked on the All-Star team in 1961 and hit 19 homers and drove in 75 runs in 1962. About his "Flakey" nickname: "Flakey is not the name I like to describe myself. Different is okay and unexpected is better. I played for the fans that way and in the clubhouse and on the planes and buses." Once after a heart-to-heart talk with his manager, Brandt was asked whether the conversation helped motivate him. "Well, I'm trying to make myself think I'm trying harder," replied Jackie. "But when you're capable of making things look easy, it's hard to do the same things and make them look hard."

Whitey Herzog hit .280 in 212 games as a part time outfielder with the Orioles in 1961 and 1962. He began his managing career in 1973 in Texas and went on to pilot the Royals to three division crowns and the Cardinals to a pennant and World Championship in 1982.

Even though he lives 1,100 miles away in Omaha, Jackie Brandt still comes back to Baltimore at least once a year, just to drive around town and watch a ballgame. "You can't put a price tag on a place like Baltimore and its people," says Brandt with affection. Back in September 1977, on the day Brooks Robinson was honored at Memorial Stadium, a former teammate still sporting a crewcut and still looking in playing condition sat high in the upper deck to watch the ceremonies. He had driven west from Nebraska, bought a ticket, and informed nobody. That's the kind of guy Jackie Brandt was—and still is.

Although not overtly clashing

Boog Powell was only 20 when he made his Oriole debut in 1961 as a leftfielder. The next year he was hitting 15 home runs and launching one of the great careers in Oriole history.

with Richards like Brandt, outfielder Whitey Herzog didn't agree with his manager's philosophy. Obtained with Russ Snyder from Kansas City for Bob Boyd, Al Pilarcik, Clint Courtney, Wayne Causey, and Jim Archer before the '61 season, Whitey hit .291 in 1961 as a reserve outfielder. "Paul was a defensive manager," says Herzog, who managed St. Louis to the 1982 World Series title over Milwaukee. "He liked to see green paint on the outfielders' backs and didn't like attempts at shoestring catches. I don't think he opened it up enough. He thought three runs would win every game. He didn't want a triple or a double to go over our heads. I think you need to gamble sometimes."

Through hard work and a load of heart, Dave McNally won 181 games as an Oriole, ranking second to Jim Palmer on the club's all-time list. McNally was only 21 years old when this photo was snapped in 1963. Mac went on to post four straight 20-win seasons and become the ace of a strong pitching staff in the late '60s, early '70s.

At 36, Hal Brown yielded nothing to his advancing age, pitching three shutouts and reeling off a club record 36 consecutive scoreless innings. With a couple of relief stints thrown in Skinny went five weeks without giving up a run. "I wasn't flashy and didn't have many great years but I had eight good years," says Brown, who won 62 and lost 48 in an Oriole uniform. "To win in the majors I needed another pitch since I wasn't overpowering, so I perfected a knuckleball that I could control and it became a good pitch for me."

Altogether, Bird pitchers led the majors in shutouts with 21. Steve Barber became the first major-league pitcher to throw eight since 1954 when Washington's Bob Porterfield tossed nine. Barber led with 18 wins while Chuck Estrada went 15-9. Wilhelm returned to the bullpen and notched nine wins and 16 saves, second only to Luis Arroyo's 19 saves with the Yankees.

Throughout the 1961 season rumors persisted that Paul Richards would leave the Orioles at season's end to assume command of the new Houston National League franchise, slated to begin play in 1962. Because he was in the first year of a three-year contract in Baltimore, the Orioles demanded an answer by September 1. On August 29, Richards announced his resignation and managed his last game the next day. Tall Paul went out with a bang as the Orioles walloped five homers and beat the Angels 11-4. Third base coach Luman Harris stepped in as manager for the rest of the season and then joined Richards in Houston.

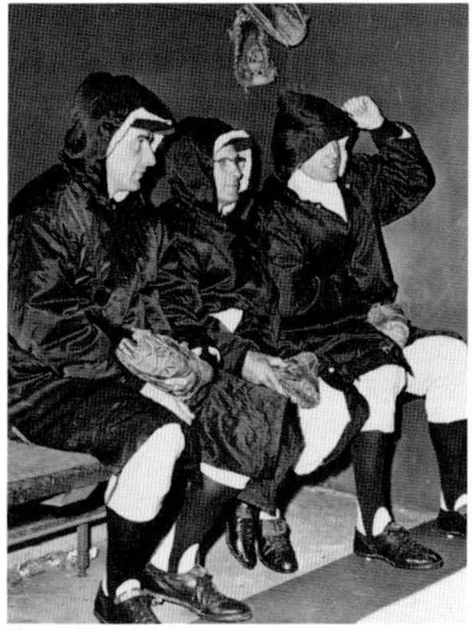

Early April in Baltimore oftentimes means frigid conditions. In this 1963 game, (from left) pitcher Dean Stone, pitching coach Harry Brecheen and pitcher Dick Hall are taking no chances, dressing warmly for the occasion.

Richards built a solid foundation in his nearly seven years as manager. His record, 517-539 with a second- and third-place finish, was not glittering, but the Birds showed steady improvement. Paul's greatest legacy was a farm system that produced a flow of young talent that began taking hold in the late 1950s. Thanks to Richards the Orioles established the standard for constructing an organization from top to bottom. His vision helped the Birds record the best record over the next quarter century. After coming out of retirement to manage Bill Veeck's Chicago White Sox in the mid-1970s, Richards returned to Waxahachie where he passed away in May of 1986 at the age of 77.

Nicknamed "Flakey," Jackie Brandt carved a permanent niche in Oriole history with his offbeat personality and unorthodox style of play. Blessed with enormous talent, Jackie's career went largely unfullfilled, although he did hit .297 in 1961.

Former journeyman infielder Billy Hitchcock, a southern gentleman from Alabama who played for six American League clubs in the 1940s and early '50s was named to succeed Richards. The 1962 Orioles suffered a major relapse from the year before, tumbling to seventh place and a 77-85 record. Against Detroit they were a miserable 2-16, but against the pennant-winning Yankees they were 11-7. The home attendance sank to 790,254, a nine-year low as several mainstay players suffered off years. Injuries and military call-ups also took their toll. Steve Barber, along with Ron Hansen, was called up by the Army reserve and when the lefty returned at mid-season he contracted mononucleosis. When Hansen returned he broke a bone in his right hand and was lost for the season. Nine front-line players at one time or another were out with injuries.

Hall of Famer Luke Appling, a .310 lifetime hitter in 20 seasons with the White Sox, spent one season as the Orioles third base coach in 1963. "Old Aches and Pains" coached under Billy Hitchcock.

Milt Pappas led the pitching staff with 12 wins. The only other pitcher in double figures was Robin Roberts, the venerable former Phillie who had been released by the Yankees in May. The 35-year-old Roberts' record had fallen to 1-10 in 1961 with the Phillies, but he rebounded to 10-9 in 1962 with a 2.78 ERA, second lowest in the league.

Roberts' first win in more than a year was a notable one. At Yankee Stadium on June 11 Robin and the Orioles led 3-0 in the fourth when Yankee pitcher Bud Daley beaned Oriole rookie John "Boog" Powell. Powell was taken away on a stretcher. The following inning Roberts dusted first-batter Roger Maris with several inside pitches and both benches emptied. Robin and the rest of the Birds hung on to win 5-3. Roberts, who later beat Whitey Ford 2-1 to cap a five-game sweep of the Yankees in late August, was voted "Comeback Player of the Year" by *The Sporting News*.

Gentile helped win that August game with a homer. Before the round tripper, Jim was 2-for-27 lifetime against Ford, including three consecutive strikeouts prior to the home run. Although he belted 33 homers, pulling him to 100 as an Oriole, and drove in 87, Diamond's batting average dropped to .251. "I thought I would hit between .250 and .275 and that's what I did," says Gentile. "I wasn't fast enough to hit .300." He was also having a tough time meshing with Hitchcock. "Jim was such a proud fellow and very demanding," said Billy. "He demanded so much of himself and when he didn't get a hit, he'd get down on himself."

Phillie great Robin Roberts' career re-started in Baltimore. After a 1-10 season with Philadelphia in 1961, he joined the Orioles in 1962 and won 42 games as a spot starter over three-plus seasons. Robin posted some sparkling ERA's in Baltimore and helped Jim Palmer launch his career by rooming with the rookie in 1965.

Brooks Robinson won Oriole MVP honors for the second time, hitting .303 with 23 home runs, both career highs, and 86 RBI. Brooks played in both All-Star games and collected his third straight Gold Glove. He hit grand slams in consecutive games and in one three-game span had eight consecutive hits. Roberts, who with the Phillies had played with a fine third base-

The Orioles contended for the pennant in Hank Bauer's first year as manager in 1964. Here he is conferring with pitching coach Harry Brecheen.

Until Tippy Martinez and Gregg Olsen, Stu Miller was the premier relief pitcher in Orioles history. Already an 11-year major-league veteran when he joined the Orioles in 1963, Stu appeared in 297 games for the Birds over five seasons, sporting a 38-36 record with 100 saves and a 2.37 ERA. He was voted Most Valuable Oriole in 1963 and 1965.

man in Willie Jones, was stupefied by Brooks' play. "He was quicker than Willie and had the fastest reflexes I've ever seen. In one of my first games I remember Joe Cunningham of the White Sox bunted on a 2-0 pitch. It was a great bunt and I was just going to walk over and pick it up. Suddenly I heard Brooks yelling 'look out' so I quickly fell down and he threw out Cunningham easy. He then patted me on the butt and said 'I'm pretty good on that play old man, so stay out of the way and leave it to me.' I did from then on."

Other 1962 positives: shortstop-second baseman Jerry Adair hit .284 including .407 against the Yankees. Powell, only 1-13 the September before in his initial taste of the majors, became the first player to hit a ball over the hedge in centerfield. Boog's shot off Don Schwall on June 22 traveled 469 feet on the fly and rolled to a stop 508 feet away from home plate. The rookie left-fielder hit 15 homers including a grand slam off 42-year-old right-hander Early Wynn. Twenty-year-old Dave McNally, called up from Elmira on September 21, pitched a brilliant two-hit shutout and blanked the Athletics 3-0 in his first major-league appearance on September 26.

On the down side, Gus Triandos sustained his fourth serious injury in four years, breaking a finger on a foul tip in May. His average plummeted to .159 and his home run production slipped to six homers in 66 games. The man with the most homers and games played in Oriole history was traded after the season to Detroit, thus ending his eight-year career in Baltimore.

Other downers: Bo Belinsky, a former Oriole farmhand, pitched the first ever no-hitter against the Orioles, beating his old minor-league roommate Steve Barber 2-0 on May 5 at Dodger Stadium. "I was just trying to finish my career in the minors until expansion came and the Angels drafted me," recalls Bo. "Then I pitch this no-hitter in the shadow of Hollywood and I'm the toast of baseball. I probably got more out of that no-hitter than anybody in history since I won only 28 games in the majors. I then became the playboy of the western world, dating beautiful women like Mamie Van Doren, living a life other big leaguers dreamed of. I dreamed of winning 200 games and they dreamed about doing the things I did off the field."

Getting in shape in Miami before the 1964 season are shortstop Luis Aparicio and John Wesley "Boog" Powell, then an outfielder and wearing number eight.

On September 12, 1962, another journeyman pitcher, Tom Cheney of Washington, set a major-league record by striking out 21 Orioles in going the route to beat the Birds 2-1 in 16 innings at Memorial Stadium. Ten different players went down on strikes, with Russ Snyder, Gentile, Dave Nicholson, Marv Breeding, and Dick Hall all striking out three times.

A fast start and a decent finish, sandwiched around a June swoon, added up to an 86-76 fourth-

Brooks Robinson introducing his young son Chris (right) to John Powell Jr. at 1964 Father-Son game.

By 1965 Boog Powell was playing more first base than left field. Here he tags Cleveland's Vic Davalillo on a bang-bang play at first base.

place finish in 1963, 18½ games behind the front-running Yankees. Sporting new home uniforms (the "Orioles" on the front was changed to block letters from the old script style) and a more nasty-looking Bird logo on pennants and programs, the Orioles entered June in first place. They had won 10 of 14 in the last two weeks of May, climbing to 30-18 and a 3½ game lead, but when June rolled around they dropped 22 of 30 games and sunk to seventh place. They went 48-39 after the swoon to finish 10 games over the .500 mark.

Gone were Ronnie Hansen and Hoyt Wilhelm, traded to the White Sox before the season as part of a deal to obtain baseball's top shortstop, Luis Aparicio. Luis tied Maury Wills for the major-league lead in steals with 40, a record eighth straight year he led the league in pilfers. Little Looie also led the Orioles in hits and made the 1963 All-Star team. Several front liners suffered off years though. Gentile hit 24 home runs but batted only .248. After a sizzling start Brooks Robinson cooled to only .222 in his last 117 games to finish at .251. He did win his fourth Gold Glove and went 2-2 in the All-Star game in Cleveland. Boog Powell led the club with 25 homers and 82 RBI to go with a .265 average. Boog became the first Oriole to hit three home runs in a game in a 6-5 August 10 loss to the Senators in Washington. Two of Boog's blasts were off Bennie Daniels, and the third was off Steve Ridzik. All were solo clouts.

Second baseman Jerry Adair appears to be taking ground balls in the clubhouse in this 1964 photo. He really showed his stuff on the field in 1964 and 1965, setting four major-league fielding records at second base including highest fielding percentage, fewest errors, and most consecutive errorless games.

Pitching was the name of the game in 1963. Steve Barber became the first 20-game winner in Oriole history. Milt Pappas logged an impressive 16-9 record, pitching four shutouts and tying Barber for the club lead in complete games with 11. Pappas loved pitching in Memorial Stadium. He was 9-2 at home in '63, 16-3 over the last two years, and 22-6 over the last three years. Robin Roberts had jump-started his career in Baltimore, winning 14 games in 1963, including two two-hitters, one three-hitter, and two four-hitters. His two shutouts raised his lifetime total to 37.

Luis Aparicio brought his acrobatic fielding style and Gold Glove play at shortstop to the Orioles in 1963. Over a five-season span he notched two Gold Gloves and set a one-season Baltimore stolen base record with 57 in 1964, a mark that still stands.

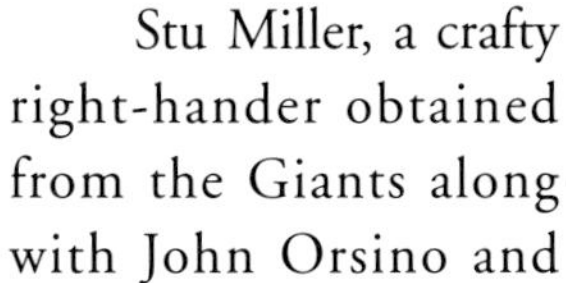

Stu Miller, a crafty right-hander obtained from the Giants along with John Orsino and Mike McCormick for Billy Hoeft, Jack Fisher, and Jim Coker, supplanted Wilhelm in the bullpen in 1963 with a season that would have made Hoyt envious. Miller, best known as the pitcher blown off the mound during the 1961 All-Star game at Candlestick Park, set an American League record for appearances with 71, just three shy of Jim Konstanty's major-league mark established with the 1950 Phillies Whiz Kids. The 35-year-old veteran, who used a head fake and a vast assortment of off-speed pitches that wouldn't break a pane of glass, led the league in saves with 26 and became the first pitcher to be named Most Valuable Oriole. Miller allowed only five home runs in 112 innings, fanned 114 batters in 112 innings, and helped his own cause by batting .313.

The June collapse cost Hitchcock his job, which was given to his third base coach, Hank Bauer. Bauer, an ex-Marine who won a Bronze Star and two Purple Hearts for bravery at Guadalcanal and Okinawa, had played in nine World Series with the Yankees, hitting in a record 17 consecutive World Series games. Oriole general manager Lee MacPhail was looking for a tougher leader than the easy-going Hitchcock and felt he had his man in Bauer, whose face, one writer said, resembled a "clenched fist." Despite his gruff exterior, Hank wasn't all that tough either. "I had a meeting to talk about the dress code and curfew and told the players they wouldn't do anything that I hadn't already done, so they shouldn't think they could put something past me."

Curt Blefary won Rookie of the Year honors with the Orioles in 1965. The outfielder-first baseman and sometime catcher belted 67 homers in his first three seasons as an Oriole and after an off-year in '67, hit 22 more in 1968. Blefary started all four games of the 1966 World Series sweep of the Dodgers.

Davey Johnson has played and managed in the major leagues for more than 30 years. Here he is as a wide-eyed rookie in 1965, a year in which he hit only .170 in 47 at-bats. By the next season he was playing second base like an old pro and helping to lead the Orioles to the World Series.

One of Bauer's first moves was to trade the up-and-down Gentile to Kansas City for Norm Siebern, a power hitter who hit for average. Siebern failed on both counts in 1964, hitting a career low .245 with only 12 home runs. The trade devastated Gentile, who hit 28 homers in Kansas City while driving in 71. "Bauer had told me the day before I was in his plans and then I found out he had made his mind up a month before to trade me. If I could have afforded it, I'd have quit right there. My heart was in Baltimore and to play anywhere else wouldn't be the same."

The disappointing results from the trade were overshadowed by the Baby Birds' pennant run in 1964. The pennant chase triggered a wave of baseball fever in Baltimore. Attendance jumped 350,000 from the year before to 1,116,215 with 138,793 pouring in for a three-game series with the Yankees in mid-August. Capacity at Memorial Stadium was almost 52,000 with the upper decks extended two sections around the horseshoe on each side.

The Orioles battled the Yankees and White Sox down to the wire. As late as September 16, after 149 games, they were in first place. But from that point, the Yankees started streaking, winning 11 in a row to capture the pennant by a game over Chicago and two over the fast-closing Orioles, who won seven of their last eight. The Orioles, not the Yankees, copped most of the individual honors. Brooks Robinson had a magnificent season, playing in 163 games and hitting .317 with 194 hits, 28 homers, and 118 RBI. He was a runaway winner of the American League Most Valuable Player award. The Oriole ironman missed just two innings all year, winning his fifth Gold Glove and playing in his eighth straight All-Star game. Over the last month of the season, in the teeth of pennant pressure, Brooks hit a blistering .464 to raise his average from .294 to .317. Other honorees were Bauer, named Manager of the Year, and 19-year-old Wally Bunker named Rookie

Under the watchful eye of pitching coach Harry Brecheen, 19-year-old Jim Palmer works on his delivery at spring training in Miami. The year was 1965 and Palmer won 5 and lost 4 in his first big league season.

Pitcher of the Year, winning 19 games in just his second pro season. Of his 12 complete games, two were one-hitters, including his first major-league win over Washington in early May. Bunker's ERA was a glittering 2.69.

Boog Powell developed into one of the league's top sluggers, wacking 39 homers and hitting .290, and Pappas rung up seven shutouts to post a 16-7 record with 13 complete games and a 2.96 ERA. Robin Roberts was six games over .500 for the first time since 1955 (13-7) and vaulted past six pitchers including Bob Feller, Burleigh Grimes, and Ted Lyons into 17th on the all time win list with 271 victories. Second baseman Jerry Adair set a major-league fielding record for fewest errors (five) and highest fielding percentage (.995) at second base, accepting 822 chances. His fielding was nearly flawless; in 153 games he had only two fumbled ground balls, two bad throws, and one dropped throw.

Young Paul Blair made his major-league debut in 1964 at the age of 20. By 1966, in his first full season, he was patrolling center field and helping the Orioles win the World Series.

In retrospect, a pivotal moment in Oriole history occurred the night of June 23, 1964. In what became known as "That Yankee Game," New York grabbed a 7-2 lead through 7⅓ innings in the first game of a three-game set. Unbowed, the Orioles rallied for seven runs in the bottom of the eighth. Brooks Robinson provided a key two-run bases-loaded single, and Willie Kirkland also drove in two to pull the Birds close. Then, catcher Charlie Lau, who led off the inning with a pinch-single, followed Jerry Adair's RBI go-ahead single with a double to score Adair, giving the Orioles a lead they never surrendered. In unison the 31,000 fans gave the Birds a standing ovation when they took the field for the top of the ninth. Roger Maris homered in the ninth before Stu Miller shut the door for a 9-8 victory. With a few exceptions, the Orioles have managed to go toe-to-toe with the Yankees and all comers since. Sensing the game's greater significance, local songwriter-ad man Bobby Goodman penned a song about it called "That Yankee Game," which was part of an album about the 1964 season entitled "Pennant Fever."

The Orioles nearly pulled a '64 encore in 1965 but fell just short, winning 94 and losing 68 and finishing a solid third, eight games behind the Twins, who ended the Yankees' five-year reign. Baltimore contributed heavily to the Yankees' demise, beating them 13 out of 18 and 10 of 11 at Yankee Stadium. Brooks Robinson led the hitters with a .297 average and 80 RBI. Brooklyn-born Curt Blefary was elected American League Rookie of the Year by the baseball writers and *The Sporting News.* Blefary slugged 22 homers and hit .260 in 144 games. The Yankees had cut Blefary in 1963 but Harry Dalton, the O's minor-league director, signed him unhesitatingly. Ironically, six of Curt's 22 homers were against the Yankees. Soon-to-be teammate Frank Robinson christened Blefary, not a gazelle in the field, with the nickname "Clank" in tribute to his glove. One time, Robinson, spotting a junkyard through the window of the passing team bus, yelled for the driver to stop so Curt could pick through the rubble for another glove.

Two of the Kiddie Korps pitchers from 1960, Steve Barber and Milt Pappas, were joined by McNally and Bunker to form a solid starting staff. A 19-year-old phenom from Arizona, Jim Palmer, made his debut and logged a 5-4 record, mostly in relief. Palmer remembered some advice from coach Gene Woodling before that 1965 season. "He told Curt Blefary that the fastball is the toughest pitch to hit and he could hit it. Then he turned to me and said, 'You have one of the best fastballs I've ever seen. So why don't you throw it?' I took his advice and made the Hall of Fame." Palmer's first roommate was Robin Roberts. "Jimmy was an outstanding athlete and I wondered if maybe he shouldn't have become an outfielder since he could hit and field so well," said Robin. "But once he got the ball over he became a great pitcher. At 19 he just needed the ball. We lose sight of the fact that maturity is better than another pitch. Once Jimmy matured, he was ready."

The bullpen was a strength again in 1965. Control artist Dick Hall won 11 games and saved eight, and Stu Miller again copped Oriole MVP honors with 21 saves, a 14-7 record, and a brilliant 1.89 ERA. The secret of the 37-year-old Miller's success? "I didn't have a real good fastball although it looked faster after all the off-speed stuff I threw. I always had good control so I'd throw off-speed pitches when I was behind on the count. I didn't have to come in with a fat pitch." In one two-and-a-half month stretch, Miller allowed only three runs in 31 appearances, winning six and saving 12. Said Frank Robinson about Miller, "It was amazing how he could throw the ball so slow and consistently throw it over the plate. As a hitter you couldn't wait long enough for it to get there. You'd say 'wait...wait...wait' and you still couldn't wait long enough. I'd be out in the outfield laughing at the hitters because they'd look silly against Stu. I've never seen anyone quite like him."

Frank Robinson still wore a Cincinnati Red uniform in 1965, but during the off-season he traded in the red and white for the black and orange, moving to the Orioles in a ballyhooed trade that produced instant results for the Birds.

"1966." Bound for Glory

Despite five first-division finishes in six years no pennant flew atop Memorial Stadium; obviously something was missing—and sorely needed—to put the Birds over the hump. That something arrived on December 9, 1965, when the Orioles traded starting pitcher Milt Pappas and a couple of recently acquired throw-ins, Jack Baldschun and Dick Simpson, to Cincinnati for outfielder Frank Robinson. Labeled an "old 30" by Reds

A billboard says it all

general manager Bill DeWitt, the erstwhile Browns boss, Robinson had spent 10 seasons playing in Crosley Field where he slugged 324 homers, drove in more than 1,000 runs, and compiled a .303 lifetime average. Named the National League's Most Valuable Player in 1961 for leading the Reds to the pennant, he was coming off a great season in 1965, which begs the question: what prompted DeWitt's comment and the trade? In any event, Dewitt's erroneous evaluation of his star was of a great benefit to the Orioles, who eagerly took "old" Frank off the Reds' hands. Said a distressed Pappas about the trade: "I didn't want to leave Baltimore. It was Steve Barber who had asked to be traded. I kept my mouth shut and yet I was the one to go." Outgoing general manager Lee MacPhail, who was heading to the commissioner's office, and his replacement, Harry Dalton, engineered the deal.

Paul Blair comes streaking for home, beginning his slide against the Angels with Luis Aparicio imploring him to hit the dirt. Blair hit a solid .277 in 1966 and emerged as one of the top center fielders in the game.

Robinson, one of 11 children, was born in Beaumont, Texas, but moved with his family to Oakland, California, at the age of four. A natural athlete, he played basketball with the legendary Bill Russell at McClymonds High School. Robinson pursued victory implacably, and as a result gained the respect of his young teammates who needed a player they could rally around. After he heard DeWitt's criticism, Robinson became a man on a mission. "Frank was definitely the missing cog," said Hank Bauer. "He had something to prove and took away the pressure on Brooks and Boog. He helped the young players just by talking to them."

When Frank homered in his first at-bat in the exhibition season against Minnesota, several of the players looked at each other and thought the same thing. No words were needed, but universally they felt as though the pennant had already been won.

The first two games of the regular season foreshadowed the events of the rest of the summer, which more or less became the Frank and Brooks show. In his first at-bat in the American League against the Red Sox in Boston, Frank was hit by a pitch. Brooks followed with a two-run homer and the Orioles went on to win 5-4 in 13 innings. The next day Frank and Brooks hit back-to-back first-inning homers and Palmer added a two-run shot in the second en route to an 8-1 win. Frank went on to rack up 49 homers, an Oriole record, and Brooks 23.

Frank Robinson's arrival in 1966 provided the missing ingredient. He won the Triple Crown, leading the American League in batting, homers, RBI, total bases, runs, and slugging percentage. Not surprisingly Frank was a unanimous winner of the 1966 MVP.

The Birds jumped out of the gate by winning nine of their first 10 games—a pace good enough for only second place. The Cleveland Indians, behind pitchers Sam McDowell, Sonny Siebert, and Luis Tiant, started 10-0. With a 12-1 record through May the Birds slipped ahead of the Tribe by a half game. On May 6 the Indians came to town for a four-game series; the Orioles won three of them. The fourth game of the series (the second of a Sunday doubleheader) produced a moment for the ages. In the first inning, facing Tiant, who had reeled off three straight shutouts to start the season, Frank walloped a shot to left that cleared the left-field bleachers. He became the first—and only—player ever to hit a ball completely out of Memorial Stadium. The ball soared 451 feet on the fly over the stands and landed 540 feet from home plate. Boog Powell was on deck: "The thing that amazed me is that Frank hit a good pitch from Tiant totally out of the park. It was a slider that was down and he just tonged it. Over the years I went on to hit a couple of balls in the last few rows. It's some shot because the ball doesn't carry that high." A flag was hoisted soon after that bore the word "Here," indicating the spot where the ball left the park. It flew proudly over the bleachers until the park closed after the 1991 season.

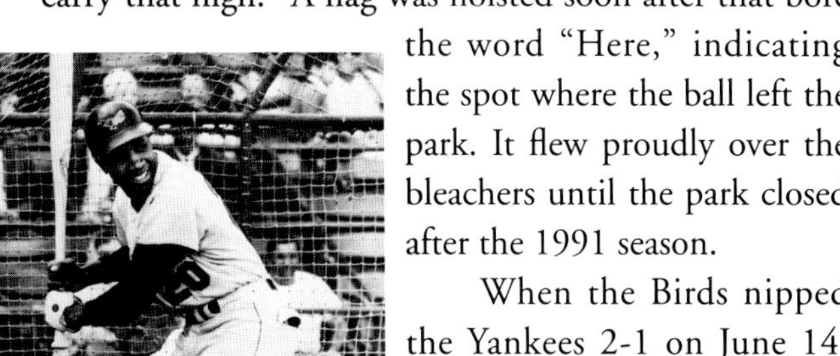

When the Birds nipped the Yankees 2-1 on June 14, they moved into first place to stay. The following day Moe Drabowsky retired 10 straight Senators, upping to 37 the number of batters retired consecutively by the bullpen. Drabowsky was one of several relievers Bauer credited as the key to the pitching staff, especially with starters Barber and Wally Bunker hampered by sore arms. "When we retired the 37 straight," said Moe, "we did it with myself, Dick Hall, Stu Miller, Eddie Watt, and Gene Brabender. Then we traded Jerry Adair to Chicago for Eddie Fisher in June and the first guy Eddie faces gets a base hit to break the streak." Fisher proved his worth, though, by notching 12 saves, second to Miller's 16.

Drabowsky was a practical joker whose pranks on both teammates and opponents became legendary. Snakes were his favorite vehicle for scaring players, with Luis Aparicio and Paul Blair his favorite targets. Moe would stick the serpents in their lockers or their gloves and watch—or hear—them run in fright. Even at old-timer games years later, Luis and Paul kept their distance from Moe.

One of Drabowsky's classic capers occurred in a 1966 game in Kansas City. In the second inning the phone rang in the A's bullpen and coach Bobby Hofman picked it up, thinking it was KC manager Alvin Dark. "Get Krausse hot!" the voice

Jim Palmer

If they were casting for the movie *The Natural* back in the 1960s, Jim Palmer would have won the role hands down. In fact, they could have made the movie about him. He was one of those high school athletes who played everything better than anybody else, including the instruments in the band. At Scottsdale High School in Arizona, he was a three-sport, all-state athlete. As a senior he caught 54 passes as a wide receiver in football, played centerfield and attracted pro scouts who drooled over his hitting and throwing arm, and was offered a basketball scholarship to UCLA by legendary coach John Wooden.

Fortunately for Baltimore Oriole fans, Jim chose baseball. Promoted to replace Milt Pappas in 1966 after just one full year of minor-league seasoning, he won 15 games and beat Sandy Koufax in the World Series. Jim figured prominently in the Orioles' three World Series championships, six pennants, and eight divisional crowns. In almost 20 years of pitching, he had eight 20-win seasons, 12 seasons with 15 or more wins, and three Cy Young awards. His 2.85 ERA ranks fourth in baseball history behind Walter Johnson, Grover Cleveland Alexander, and Whitey Ford. Along the way there was one no-hitter, five one-hitters, and 11 two-hitters.

Overcoming injuries and other adversities, Jim used his fluid, high-kicking, overhand delivery to get hitters out, challenging them with a high fastball that became his trademark. An intense student of the game, Jim had the uncanny ability to remember just about every pitch he ever threw. He questioned his managers and coaches to learn every facet about the game. As Earl Weaver said, "Palmer isn't a pitcher who works every four days. He's in the ballgame nine innings every night, sitting on the bench studying pitchers' motions and watching how other teams hit." He and Weaver had their differences over the years. As Earl puts it, "Jim won 20 percent of my games. I sent him out there 300 times and he'll tell you he'd have won them all if I did my job right."

In 1982, Palmer beat the Rangers, Tigers, Twins, and A's, all for the 20th time in his career. That gave him 20 or more wins against all eleven pre-1977 expansion teams. No pitcher in baseball history owns 20 or more victories against that many teams.

Palmer had opportunities to go to other teams for bigger contracts, especially after free agency, but he just couldn't see himself pitching for another team. "All those years, I never would have won 268 games if it wasn't for the players I played with. They were a select group who not only had talent, but got along well. We knew we had a chance to win every year."

Reaching the end of his career was not easy for Jim. "When you get to the majors at 19 and are still around at 38, you have the tendency to remember how you were at 19," he remarked. By 1984 the rigors of over 3,900 innings pitched had taken their toll. He still misses pitching 10 years later. "Once you've been on the mound and effectively combined the physical and mental aspects to win games, you miss that competition. When one season ended I'd think of the next and it kept me young. I knew that no matter how many 20-win seasons I had, I still had to get ready to do what I'd been doing for 15 years. That's a challenge I miss."

ordered. Hofman shouted to Lew Krausse to warm up. Moments later the phone rang again. "Okay, sit him down," the voice commanded, and Krausse stopped warming. Across the field, in the Oriole bullpen, the players were rocking with laughter. Moe, who had pitched in Kansas City and knew the bullpen number, had made the calls.

Frank Robinson provided another indelible stamp on the 1966 season on June 21 at Yankee Stadium. The Orioles were leading 7-5 in the bottom of the ninth, but the Yankees had two on with two out. Miller relieved Watt and Yankee outfielder Roy White hit a long drive to right. Frank raced to the wall, leaped at the last second, and caught the ball, then tumbled over the fence into the seats. He held on for the final out. Yankee skipper Ralph Houk went berserk but, as always, the umpire's decision stood. The win was the Birds' 12th straight at Yankee Stadium.

On July 6, 1966, Boog Powell enjoyed his greatest day as an Oriole in a twi-night doubleheader against Kansas City. Boog drove in 11 runs, four in the first game win and seven in the nightcap loss, hitting a grand slam and a two-run homer.

Twenty-one-year-old Jim Palmer about to dig into a stack of pancakes during the 1966 season. Palmer said he won seven of eight starts at one point after eating pancakes for breakfast. Thus pancakes became a basic staple for Jim on days he pitched and the nickname "Cakes" still clings to him.

Luis Aparicio streaks around third and heads for home in a game with the Yankees. Yankee third baseman Clete Boyer awaits the ball from the outfield. Little Looie played in 151 games in '66, hitting .276 and scoring 97 runs.

Baseball people were astounded by the Oriole success because they fielded several rookies at key positions. "We had a rookie owner in Jerry Hoffberger, a rookie general manager in Harry Dalton, a rookie second baseman in Davey Johnson, and a rookie center fielder in Paul Blair," said catcher Andy Etchebarren. "And I was a rookie behind the plate." Despite the inexperience up the middle, the Orioles pulled away from the pack and clinched the pennant on September 22 in Kansas City when 20-year-old Jim Palmer tossed his first complete game in two months. Brooks Robinson, who had waited longer than anybody for the first pennant, drove in two runs in the 6-1 win. Russ Snyder's diving catch in center field ended the game, triggering a three-hour celebration. The Orioles finished 97-63, nine games ahead of second-place Minnesota.

Not many gave the Birds a chance against the pitching-rich Dodgers in the World Series. L.A. sported the best lefty-righty combo in baseball: 27-game winner Sandy Koufax and the fearsome Don Drysdale. Fellow 13-game winners Dave McNally and Drysdale faced each other in game one at Dodger Stadium on October 5. The Birds set the tone in the first inning when Frank and Brooks Robinson homered to stake McNally to a 3-0 lead. Wildness, no doubt a product of World Series pressure, seized Mac and he gave back two of the runs. With the Orioles ahead 4-2 in the third inning Bauer decided to go to his bullpen, bringing in Drabowsky. It was a calculated move. "I wasn't in on scout Jim Russo's meeting with the players before the series. It lasted about five hours and I imagine he scared the hell out of the players," said Hank with a grin. "Late in the season I had run into my old minor-league roommate in Kansas City, Harry Craft, who had been a longtime scout. I asked him how you pitch the Dodgers. 'Fastballs,' he told me. So early on I brought in Moe to

Boog Powell

Although Eddie Murray had better stats than Boog Powell at first base in Baltimore, when it came time for the fans to vote on their all-time Oriole first baseman in 1991, Boog was still the people's choice.

Huge but amazingly agile for a man his size, Boog at 6-4 and 250 pounds was a moving mountain of a man who had some monster seasons as an Oriole. In 1966, 1969, and 1970 he bashed over 30 homers and drove in more than 100 runs. His home runs were unmistakable–high and majestic.

An outstanding football and baseball player from Key West, Florida, John Wesley Powell was all baseball as a player. Outside interests and endorsements were something that he didn't involve himself with until after his playing days were over. "I was a baseball player and it was double the fun to get paid for it. I wasn't an investment broker or a businessman. I wanted to play ball and enjoy it for what it was," says Boog, who now operates the popular Boog's barbecue stand at Camden Yards. He returned to Baltimore after a 15-year absence, and his love affair with the fans resumed as though it had never been interrupted.

Boog had some great games as an Oriole, but one of his most memorable happened in the minors, a game that could have been straight out of the baseball novel and movie, *The Natural*. While playing for Earl Weaver and the Fox Cities Foxes of the Three-I-League in 1960, Boog actually stopped time at 7:10 when a Powell line drive in batting practice broke the wire screen protecting the clock, sending clock parts flying everywhere.

How did John Wesley come to be called Boog? When he was a tyke about the age of two, John was always getting into mischief. He'd pull off the tablecloth and knock over dishes. He was constantly active. In the South, a kid who got into mischief was called a "booger." Later the name was changed to "Boog" and it's remained for a lifetime.

see if Harry was right. Throwing nothing but heat Moe mowed them down and we won the game 5-2. Outside of platooning Blair and Snyder in center, that was the only decision I had to make the entire series." Drabowsky set a Series strikeout record by a reliever with 11 and tied another by striking out six straight Dodgers.

The Birds made history in the next three games, reeling off three straight complete game shutouts to sweep the Dodgers. In the second contest, fifteen-game winner Jim Palmer beat Koufax 6-0, in what turned out to be Sandy's last game. (Citing chronic arm pain and an arthritic condition, Koufax retired during the off season). Palmer became the youngest pitcher to throw a World Series shutout. The Birds scored three times in the fifth, thanks to a Series record three errors by Willie Davis in center field. He lost one in the sun, dropped another, and threw wildly past third. The Dodgers, built on pitching and defense, committed six errors in the game.

Games three and four were in Baltimore, and they were more of the same. Twenty-one-year-old Wally Bunker, who had battled a sore arm most of the year in winning 10 games, hooked up in a pitching duel with left-hander Claude Osteen. Claude gave up only three hits, but one was to 22-year-old Paul Blair who sent a blast into the left center field seats 430 feet away in the fifth inning for the only run of the game. Like Palmer the day before it was Wally's first shutout of the year. The following day, October 9, before a crowd of 54,458, McNally and Drysdale met in a rematch of the first game. Both pitchers allowed only four hits, but Frank Robinson made one of the Orioles' hits count, slugging a fourth-inning homer into the left-field seats. McNally tamed the Dodgers all afternoon, not allowing a runner into scoring position until the ninth when he got Willie Davis on a fly to right and Lou Johnson flew to Blair in center to end it. For the second straight game the Orioles were 1-0 winners, and more importantly they were World Champs. Incredibly, the Oriole pitching staff had blanked the Dodgers over the last 33 innings of the series, setting a new series record. In four games the Oriole team ERA was 0.50 and the Dodgers' batting average only .142. They scored two runs to 13 for the Birds. In the 64-year history of the World Series, only two 1-0 games had been decided by

Despite shoulder and elbow problems, Wally Bunker posted a 10-6 record in 1966, blanking the Dodgers 1-0 in the third game of the World Series. By the time he was 21, Wally had won 39 games as an Oriole.

homers. In the 1966 classic, the Orioles did it in back-to-back games. As Baltimore celebrated, the clock at City Hall struck 66 times to pay tribute to the 1966 Orioles, a team that won the city of Baltimore's adoradion as did the World Champion Colts of 1958-1959.

Frank Robinson was crowned World Series MVP, just one of many tributes accorded the league's MVP for his banner season. His regular-season totals were awesome: a .316 batting average, 49 homers, 122 RBI—the first Triple Crown winner in the majors since Mickey Mantle 10 years earlier. Frank, Brooks, and Boog finished 1-2-3 in the league MVP voting. Frank became the first and only player to win the award in both leagues. Bauer was named Manager of the Year and confessed that this World Series win was more special than all he had been involved in as a player with the Yankees. "When I was playing I only had to worry about myself. As a manager I had to worry about all 25. In looking over the season I had an exceptional bullpen (which he used at least once in 137 of 160 games). We went to the bank in October so they must have been pretty good. I came to Baltimore in 1963 as Billy Hitchcock's third base coach, and that's all I wanted to do. Managing wasn't something I sought out." Frank Robinson, the superstar, had no problem getting along with Bauer, the gruff ex-Marine. "Hank's not tough, he just looks that way," said Frank. "He's the most understanding manager I've ever played for. He gives you the sense that you're a professional. But if you don't do your job, you'll hear about it."

For Brooks Robinson, 1966 was the apex of a long hard 11-year climb. "It was the culmination of everything," said Brooks. "You dream about signing a big-league contract. You dream about getting to the majors. And you dream about getting to the World Series. I remember thinking, 'Now if you never win anything else again, at least you've done this.' I felt a lot different after we won."

Each player received a winner's share of $11,683.04 for the series. And for the 12 Orioles who never even played in the four games, it was the easiest paycheck they ever received.

Some other vignettes from 1966 include Palmer revealing in July that he had won seven of his last eight starts after eating pancakes for breakfast. The only game he lost was when he had a muffin and juice as he hurried to catch the team bus. The nickname "Cakes" was placed on Palmer forevermore. Tom Phoebus, a graduate of Mt. St. Joseph's High School in Baltimore, became only the sixth pitcher since 1900 to toss shutouts in his first two major-league starts. He beat the Angels in mid-September, 2-0, on a four-hitter while his mother, brother, and host of relatives watched in the stands. A few days later he beat the Athletics, 4-0. "I always felt it would be a privilege to pitch in my hometown," recalled Phoebus. "All through the minors I wondered how it would be to pitch with the Orioles. In Rochester in 1966 I had pitched seven shutouts including a no-hitter against Buffalo. To throw those shutouts my first two starts with the Orioles convinced me right away that I belonged. I felt like I opened the door."

Both Brooks and Frank started for the American League in the All-Star game in St. Louis. The Nationals won 2-1 in 10 innings on a blistering 106-degree day. Brooks rapped out three of the

Moe Drabowsky was a prankster off the field yet all business on the mound. Moe turned 31 during the 1966 season, making him one of the Oriole greybeards. His 6 2/3 innings of one-hit relief in the first game of the 1966 World Series will never be forgotten. Moe struck out 11 Dodgers, including six straight.

American League's six hits including a triple off Sandy Koufax that accounted for the lone American League run. He won the Arch Ward Memorial Trophy as the game's outstanding player. He also set an All-Star record by handling eight chances at third base. Brooks still remembers the searing heat in the new Busch Stadium. "Busch Stadium was a hot box that day," he said. "Early on our batboy passed out in the dugout and I remember seeing fans in the stands passing out during the game."

Frank Robinson belted a Luis Tiant pitch completely out of Memorial Stadium early in 1966, a feat never before or since accomplished. His 586 career homers rank fourth on the all-time list.

Oriole attendance in 1966 soared to a new high of 1,203,366 and for the next 13 years that number remained the highest attendance mark.

Since the Orioles were such a young team, 1966 was predicted as just the start of more great years to come. But the momentum of '66 did not carry over to 1967. Amazingly they fell to sixth place, 15½ games behind "The Impossible Dream" Red Sox. They tied with the lowly Washington Senators, posting a 76-85 record. Hitting was one of the problems. The team's batting average fell to .240 as Boog Powell slumped to .234 with only 13 homers and 55 RBI. Luis Aparico hit .233 and Andy Etchebarren .215.

Moreover, the pitching staff was plagued by an epidemic of sore arms. Steve Barber had a troubled year and was traded to the Yankees on the 4th of July. Wally Bunker was pitching in pain and ended up in the bullpen. He won only three games all year. Dave McNally had tendonitis in his arm and shoulder and won only seven games. Jim Palmer pitched a one-hitter on May 12 and beat the Yankees 14-0, but shoulder miseries from the year before shelved him for most of the season. He finished only 3-1. Stu Miller, losing eight of his first nine decisions, finished 3-10. Phoebus was the only pitcher in double figures with 14 wins including four shutouts.

The situation was so disastrous in the pitching department that the Birds couldn't win even when they tossed a no-hitter. On April 30 Steve Barber and Stu Miller teamed up to no-hit the Tigers at Memorial Stadium, but lost 2-1. Barber went 8 ⅔ innings, walking 10, hitting two, and throwing a wild pitch. "I joked about it five minutes after the game was over," recalled Barber, "because when you walk that many guys you should get killed. There's no problem in pitching a no-hitter if you walk everybody that can hit you." Barber led 1-0 in the ninth but walked Norm Cash and Ray Oyler. After a walk moved the runners up, Barber got Willie Horton to foul out. Then with a 1-2 count on Mickey Stanley, Steve tossed the wild pitch that brought in the tying run. Another walk brought in Stu Miller, who coaxed a ground ball to short from Don Wert. Aparicio flipped the ball to Mark Belanger who dropped it at second allowing the winning run to score.

The major factor in the collapse of 1967 was the injury to team leader Frank Robinson. Trying to break up a double play in late June, Frank collided with Chicago second baseman Al Weis, and suffered a concussion and double vision when his head hit Weis' knee. Frank missed 28 games while Weis suffered torn knee ligaments and was out for the rest of the year. Despite missing 32 games, Frank still slugged 30 homers and drove in 94 runs with a team high .311 average.

Frank Robinson reached an important milestone on September 9, 1967, when he hit his 400th career home run. He connected off Minnesota lefty Jim Kaat in a game the Twins won 3-2. Said Kaat about Frank:

Despite not turning 23 until June 20, Andy Etchebarren emerged as the Orioles regular catcher in 1966, catching 121 games and belting 11 home runs while driving in 50. Andy was named to the 1966 All-Star team.

"He was so quick with the bat on inside pitches, but if I pitched him outside he'd hit the ball to right. If you got him out with a pitch, he'd eventually hit that pitch, so you had to constantly change your pattern on him."

The celebration begins

One of the few highlights of the 1967 season was the 12-8 thumping of the Red Sox on May 17 at Fenway Park. Seven different Orioles homered to set a major-league record. Brooks and Frank Robinson, Andy Etchebarren, Sam Bowens, Boog Powell, Paul Blair, and Dave Johnson each hit round trippers, four of them coming in the nine-run seventh inning.

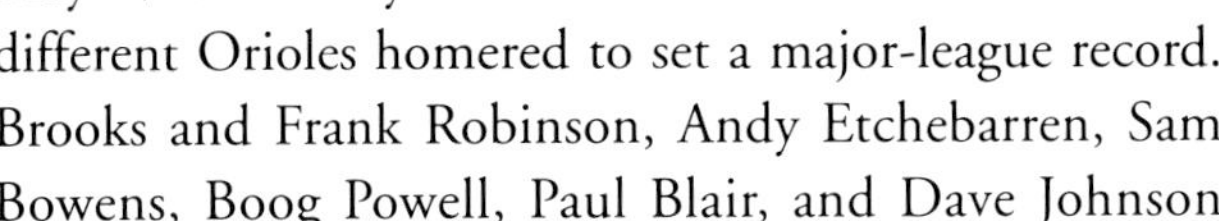

Brooks hit one of the Orioles' four home runs in the 1966 Series, one of three in his World Series career.

Brooks accounted for the only American League run in the All-Star game at Anaheim Stadium, homering in the 2-1, 15-inning loss to the Nationals.

There was plenty of turnover during and after the disappointing 1967 season—10 players were let go or traded, including veteran left-hander Steve Barber. Even Hank Bauer's coaching staff wasn't immune to the changes. Pitching coach Harry Brecheen, an original Oriole since 1954, and coaches Gene Woodling and Sherm Lollar, were let go and replaced by new pitching coach George Bamberger, and coaches Vern Hoscheit, Ray Scarborough, and long-time minor-league manager Earl Weaver. Only Billy Hunter remained off Hank's previous staff. Bauer had a right to feel uneasy.

Bauer's Birds got off to a good start in 1968, leading the league after a month into the season. But they limped into the All-Star break in third place, 10½ games behind the pennant-bound Tigers. Hank paid the price and was fired after 4½ seasons. He was replaced by first base coach Earl Weaver. Said Hank: "In 1966 the players won me manager of the year honors and in 1968 they got me fired. In 1966 the experts called me one of the brightest managers in the game. I got dumb awful quick."

The 37-year-old Weaver had an excellent track record as a minor-league manager but was a virtual unknown on the major-league scene. Standing only 5-8, the bantam Weaver had been signed by the Cardinals as a second baseman in 1948, but the Redbirds had Hall of Fame second baseman Red Schoendienst, and, outside of 1952, when he spent spring training with the Cardinals, Earl never got close to the majors as a player, even though he had been named MVP in three different leagues. Earl was only 26 when he began his managerial career, a career that through persistence and tenacity would one day propel him to the top. He had managed in the Oriole system for 11 years, never finishing out of the first division. His teams won pennants in three leagues, and finished second five times. Many of the 1968 Oriole players had played for him at one time or another in the minors. Of the five managers who had gone before him, none were homegrown. General manager Harry Dalton knew all about Weaver from their days in the farm system, which Dalton headed for years. Dalton called Weaver a "battler" and a "winner." Weaver himself said he'd "rather lose making a move" than by sitting there and doing nothing.

The Birds improved quickly under Weaver, winning their first six games after he took the helm. In late August, after sweeping a doubleheader from Oakland, they had trimmed the Tiger lead to four games. Weaver's burning will to win had spread to his players. That, however,

Frank Robinson connects for a solo home run off Don Drysdale in the fourth inning of game four. The blast accounted for the only run of the game as the Birds clinched their first championship.

The right mix finally came together in 1966: the veteran savvy and potent bat of Frank Robinson; the gritty, clutch play of Brooks Robinson and Luis Aparicio; the rise of a young but wickedly talented pitching staff spearheaded by Jim Palmer and Dave McNally. Four members of the team are enshrined at Cooperstown, both Robinsons, Palmer, and Aparicio.

was as close as the Orioles got to Detroit as they finished with a 91-71 record, 12 games back in second place. They were within six games of the lead on September 1 when they were beaten by Denny McLain, who caught a Boog Powell smash up the middle with two on and a run in, and turned it into a triple play. It was that kind of sensational year for McLain, who went on to win 31 games. The Orioles never recovered from that 7-3 loss. Under Weaver the Birds had gone 48-34.

1968 was the year of the pitcher. Carl Yastrzemski led the league in hitting with only a .301 average. As a team the Orioles hit a dismal .225. Frank Robinson, shackled with a five-week-long arm injury and a case of the mumps, hit only .268, 36 points below his lifetime average. His homer (15) and RBI totals (53) were the lowest of his 21-year career.

One of Weaver's first moves turned out to be one of his best when he installed leftfielder Don Buford in the lead-off spot. Obtained in a deal with the White Sox after the 1967 season that sent Luis Aparicio back to Chicago, Buford had played sparingly the first half of the season. Entering the lineup in July, Buford hit .300 over the second half and led the Birds in hitting with an overall average of .282. He hit 15 homers and stole 27 bases and became instrumental in winning the three straight pennants that would follow.

The highlight of the 1968 season came on the night of April 27 at Memorial Stadium when hometowner Tom Phoebus pitched the third no-hitter in modern Baltimore history, blanking the Red Sox 6-0. Phoebus, who stood only 5-8, didn't fit the mold of the tall, hard throwers and always felt he had to prove himself. He struck out nine Red Sox and retired the last 12 batters he faced. "The toughest chance was handled by Brooks in the eighth," remembers Phoebus. "He speared Rico Petrocelli's ankle-high line drive. Mark Belanger handled the only other tough chance. Everything just clicked for me that night. I felt so strong I could have pitched 13 innings."

What was unique about the Phoebus no-hitter was that Curt Blefary, an outfielder-first baseman, was the catcher. "I remember in spring training that year they used Curt to catch some exhibition games," recalls Phoebus. "He caught everybody but me and when told about it, Bauer said 'Don't worry, he probably won't catch you during the season.' So as it turned out Curt caught the no-hitter and did a good job, although I think he was more nervous than I was. He had a lot of enthusiasm, was aggressive, and always gave his best. We worked really well together." For the season Phoebus finished 15-15 with a 2.61 ERA.

Dave McNally, 8-8 when Weaver took over, finished 22-10 with a 1.95 ERA and completely rewrote the Oriole record book. From July 11 to September 8, McNally won 12 straight games, including three against Detroit. Ten of the 12 wins were complete game wins. Mac tied Moe Drabowsky, who also won 12 straight in the 1966-1967 seasons. McNally became the first Oriole pitcher to crack a grand slam, which he did against Oakland's Chuck Dobson.

For Jim Palmer, 1968 was even worse than 1967. He pitched a total of 37 innings for three different minor-league teams, dropping as low as "A" ball in Miami. He failed to win a game at any level all year as his back and shoulder problems persisted. He did pitch well in winter ball in Puerto Rico, compiling a 6-1 record and tossing a no-hitter. Palmer, thus, was optimistic about 1969. So was Earl Weaver.

As it turned out, Weaver had inherited a club poised for greatness.

1969–1971: "The Best Damn Team in Baseball"

The Oriole dynasty predicted after the 1966 sweep of the Dodgers didn't happen. "You can't anticipate dynasties," said general manager Harry Dalton. "You can only recognize them after they happen." Thanks to the improving health of Jim Palmer and Frank Robinson and a deal or two engineered by Dalton, a dynasty was in the making.

In response to an opponent's comment that the 1970 Orioles weren't supermen, Frank Robinson (left), Paul Blair (middle), and Moe Drabowsky beg to differ.

The year 1969 brought big changes in baseball. Both leagues expanded by two teams, the Kansas City Royals and the ill-fated Seattle Pilots in the American League and the Montreal Expos and San Diego Padres in the National. The leagues were split into two divisions with six teams each, creating a best-of-five playoff system to determine the pennant winner. The Orioles were in the American League East, along with the Red Sox, Tigers, Yankees, Indians, and Washington Senators. The 100th season of professional baseball brought a big departure from tradition.

One of the great infields of all time: Brooks Robinson, Mark Belanger, Davey Johnson, and Boog Powell. Between them they won 27 Gold Gloves. Boog didn't win any, but, perhaps because of his size, he was vastly underrated as a first baseman. This foursome terrorized American League hitters during the 1969-71 pennant years.

The 1969 Orioles opened their season on April 8. By April 16 they were in first place to stay. It was that simple. Dalton had made one major off-season deal, sending Curt Blefary to Houston for Cuban left-hander Mike Cuellar who had won 42 games and lost 41 in the National League and was only 8-11 in 1968 with the Astros. Cuellar might not have had the impact that Frank Robinson did in 1966, but he stabilized the pitching staff.

Earl Weaver, in his first full season as manager, made all the right moves. Besides being an excellent tactical manager, who knew the game inside and out, he was also a master at handling his players. All those years in the minor leagues made him appreciate being in the big leagues. He was determined to bear down every second he was in uniform. He had a burning will to win, and at times seemed impatient and out of control. Yet when times were bad, Earl was the calmest of all. The majority of his tirades were aimed at the umpires, and he had some classic dirt-kicking, cap-throwing confrontations over the years.

Dave McNally, a bulldog left-hander from Billings, Montana, didn't have the great natural ability of a Jim Palmer or Mike Cuellar, but insiders invariably would pick McNally if a game was on the line and they needed one pitcher to win it.

The 1969 season progressed so perfectly and smoothly that Earl's theatrics weren't really needed. The Orioles clinched the pennant on September 13, a full two-and-a-half weeks before the regular season ended. Winning 109 games and losing only 53, they came within two wins of tying Cleveland's 1954 one-season mark of 111. With Kansas City and Seattle entering the league in the first year of the divisional restructuring, the Birds finished 19 games in front of second-place Detroit, the biggest margin of victory since the 1936 Yankees won by 19½ games. Lead-off hitter Don Buford (who hit .291 with 11 homers, 64 RBI and 19 steals) had a good feeling about 1969 from the first day of spring training. "We jelled immediately. There was great camaraderie. We kidded and joked off the field but were all business on it. There were no jealousies or animosities. Weaver instituted some subtle strategies, such as a pickoff at third base that worked more than a few times. He just told me to get on base. Pitchers didn't want to walk me so they threw me a lot of fastballs and I hit some home runs."

It was a season of positives. Palmer shut out the Senators 2-0 on April 13, his first win in two seasons. After missing more than a month of the season with a torn back muscle, Palmer reeled off 11 straight wins, including an 8-0 no-hitter against Oakland on August 13. In pitching the club's third no-hitter in as many years, Palmer walked the bases loaded in the ninth before getting the final three outs. Jim summed up his success this way: "I took George Bamberger's advice and established the outside half of the plate. I had a little hesitation where the hitters wouldn't think the ball was going to be on them as quick as it was. I'd get ahead of the hitters and make them swing at balls out of the strike zone. The high fastball was tantalizing to hitters and I made my living off it." The result was a 16-4 record, including six shutouts and 11 complete games.

On May 15 against the Twins at the Met in Bloomington, Dave McNally was within two outs of a no-hitter when Cesar Tovar broke it up with a single. McNally finished with a one-hit, 5-0 win en route to a sensational 20-7 season. From late September 1968 until July 30 of '69, McNally reeled off 17 straight victories to tie an American League record. His 15 wins to start the season also tied a record. Yet McNally's 20 victories were only good for second place on the staff. Mike Cuellar won 23 with 18 complete games and a stubborn 2.38 ERA. He won 13 of 15 after the All-Star break, including seven in a row. Mike, nicknamed "Crazy Horse" by his teammates, shared the Cy Young Award with Denny McLain. Like McNally, Cuellar had a no-hitter broken up by Cesar Tovar, this time leading off the ninth. Mike then retired the side and finished with a 2-0 one-hitter.

Although Brooks Robinson fell off to a .234 average with 23 homers and 84 RBI, the rest of the lineup had eye-popping years. Shortstop Mark Belanger, winning his first Gold Glove, added 79 points on his average from the year before, hitting .287. Sportswriter and ESPN commentator Peter Gammons is not alone in thinking that Belanger was the best shortstop of the last 40 or 50 years. "They can talk all they want about Ozzie Smith. Belanger didn't have to dive for balls like Smith. He got them with his quickness." Former Yankee shortstop and long-time broadcaster Tony Kubek said, "Belanger was the best defensive shortstop I've ever seen, and I've seen some good ones, beginning with Cincinnati's Roy McMillan. Ozzie Smith is brilliant but for defense only, there's never been a shortstop like Mark Belanger."

Davey Johnson won three Gold Gloves before being dealt to Atlanta after the 1972 season.

In center field Paul Blair rebounded from a .211 average in '68 to hit a solid .285 and play in his first All-Star game. He also snagged his second Gold Glove for his fielding prowess. More than once Weaver said to Blair, "Paul you're playing too shallow." To which Blair would reply, "Earl, when you see a ball go over my head and it doesn't leave the ballpark and I don't catch it, then I'll back up." There's no question Blair played the shallowest center field in the majors, but he rarely got burned. Blair was uncanny in tracking fly balls. Just the sound of the bat hitting the ball would tell him where the ball was headed. Once in practice he turned his back to home plate and on every hit predicted where the ball was going. He was right every time, including the one coming right at him, which he quickly turned and caught.

Boog Powell bounced back from two off seasons to crush 37 homers and drive in 121 runs. Named Most Valuable Oriole, Boog hit .304 and finished second to Harmon Killebrew for American League MVP honors. "I didn't realize I was getting pitched around until we got Frank," said Boog. "Then all of a sudden I started seeing pitches I never saw before. You couldn't walk Frank to get to me or vice versa."

Billy Martin's Minnesota Twins who had won the Western Division pennant with a 97-65 record, nine games ahead of Oakland, flew to Baltimore to play the first American League Championship Series. Games one and two ended up as nail-biting, extra-inning thrillers. The October 4 first game was knotted up 3-3 going into the bottom of the 13th. Boog Powell had forced extra innings with a lead-off homer off Jim Perry in the ninth. Frank Robinson and Mark Belanger, who hit only two homers all year, had homered earlier. Ron Perranoski had relieved Jim Perry in the ninth and was

Tom Phoebus came out of Mt. St. Joseph's High School in Baltimore to spin shutouts in his first two major league starts in 1966. In 1967 he tossed three straight shutouts and in 1968 he no-hit the Red Sox. He won a game in the 1970 World Series in his swan-song as an Oriole.

still pitching in the bottom of the 13th with two outs and Belanger on third, when Oriole Paul Blair dropped a perfect bunt down the third-baseline to score the game winner. Dick Hall won in relief.

Dave McNally and Baltimore native Dave Boswell faced each other in a classic pitchers' duel the following day. The game was scoreless going into the bottom of the 11th. Then, with two on and two outs Perranoski relieved Boswell. Pinch-hitter Curt Motton greeted the portly left-hander with a line single to right, scoring Boog Powell from second for the only run of the game.

Boog Powell put together two monster seasons in 1969 and 1970, winning the MVP in 1970 when he hit .304 with 37 homers and 121 RBI. He and Frank Robinson became a feared one-two power punch.

The Orioles swept the best-of-five-game playoffs the next day in Minnesota. The Birds clobbered the Twins 11-2 as Paul Blair had five hits including a homer and five RBI. Jim Palmer cruised to victory on a 10-hitter.

Next up was the World Series. Just like the Colts of a few months before in Super Bowl III, the Orioles were huge favorites against a New York team. Joe Namath and the Jets upset the Colts for the first AFL win in Super Bowl history. Now a Baltimore team was taking on the other tenant of Shea Stadium, the upstart Mets, but history couldn't repeat itself—could it?

The Series certainly started well for the Orioles. Don Buford homered to lead off the bottom of the first and Mike Cuellar outpitched Tom Seaver to win game one, 4-1. The strength of the Mets was in their pitching, and it began to assert itself the following day. Jerry Koosman tossed a two-hitter to beat Dave McNally 2-1 with Al Weis' two-out single in the ninth scoring Ed Charles and the Mets' winning run.

When the Series moved to Shea Stadium the Mets blanked the Birds 5-0 behind the pitching of Gary Gentry and Nolan Ryan. Tommy Agee homered off loser Jim Palmer in the first and made two sensational catches robbing the Orioles of at least five runs, including a bases-loaded drive by Paul Blair off Ryan in the seventh that would have cleared the bases. The Mets led the Series 2-1.

In the second inning of game four, plate umpire Shag Crawford tossed Weaver out of the game, after Donn Clendenon homered off Mike Cuellar, the first managerial ejection in a World Series since 1935. Weaver had been complaining about Crawford's ball and strike calls and after Shag walked over to the Orioles dugout and pointed a finger in Earl's direction, the spark was lit. Weaver, frustrated at dropping two of the first three in the series, came bouncing out of the dugout in the direction of Crawford, who immediately tossed Earl out of the game. Tom Seaver led 1-0 in the ninth with one out when Frank Robinson and Boog Powell singled to put runners on the corners. Brooks Robinson followed with a line drive to right that appeared to be a hit, but rightfielder Ron Swoboda, a Baltimore native, made a headlong, backhanded, diving catch inches off the grass that ranks among the top defensive plays in Series history. Frank tagged and scored from third, but the Mets would win it in the 10th on a controversial play. With Dick Hall pitching, Jerry Grote doubled and Weis was walked intentionally. Then, with Pete Richert in relief, Met pinch hitter J.C. Martin dropped a bunt toward first. Richert fielded the ball but hit Martin in the back with the throw, allowing the game-winning run to cross the plate. Replays clearly showed Martin was running out of the baseline but plate umpire Crawford didn't concur.

The Mets wrapped up the Series the following day at Shea Stadium. Homers by McNally and Frank Robinson gave the Birds a 3-0 lead until the bottom of the sixth, when another controversy

In his first four seasons in Baltimore, Don Buford compiled a .400 on base percentage and became the best leadoff man in Oriole history. He hit .291, .272, and .290 in the 1969-71 era, averaging just under 100 walks and scoring 99 runs in each year.

erupted. Mets outfielder Cleon Jones claimed a McNally pitch had grazed him on the foot. Plate ump Lou DiMuro, who disallowed a Frank Robinson claim of being hit in the top of the inning, disagreed. Met manager Gil Hodges burst out of the dugout with a ball that he said had a black scuff mark from Jones' shoe. DiMuro relented and awarded first base to Jones, whereupon Clendenon followed with a two-run homer. Al Weis then hit his first ever Shea Stadium homer to tie the game in the seventh. The end came when New York scored two off Eddie Watt in the eighth, including a Swoboda double to drive in the game-winner in the 5-3 victory. The Miracle Mets had taken four straight from the best team in baseball, leaving the Orioles stunned. "I've thought about it to this day," says Boog Powell, "and I still can't figure what happened. I remember Buford hitting the homer in game one and then it went downhill. We just went south."

A familiar scene over the six-season Frank Robinson era in Baltimore: Robby rounding third and accepting a congratulatory handshake from third-base coach Billy Hunter.

When the Orioles arrived back at Friendship Airport (now BWI), more than ten thousand fans were waiting for the team. Many of the players had tears in their eyes to see such an outpouring of loyalty after losing the Series in five games. Harry Dalton later said, "I think that's when we won the 1970 World Series. It gave the club so much resolve."

In many ways the 1970 regular season was a carbon copy of the year before. This time it took just three weeks for the Birds to establish a permanent hold on first place. In July the lead had shrunk to only three games over Detroit, but by August 19 Baltimore was back on top by 11. Yet despite clinching on September 17, there was no letdown. In fact the Birds reeled off 11 straight wins to close out the regular season, finishing with a 108-54 record, 15 games in front of second-place New York. Their two-year win total of 217 wins set a new American League record.

Cleveland's Tony Horton slides hard into Oriole catcher Andy Etchebarren during the 1969 season. Etch hung on to the ball for the out.

Jim Palmer rebounded from serious arm troubles in 1967 and 1968 to post a 16-4 record in 1969, including a no-hitter over Oakland. That season proved a stepping stone for Jim, who won 20 or more the next four years as the Orioles became the most powerful club in baseball.

There were highlights galore in 1970, including a whopping 23-game win streak over Kansas City that had carried over from the year before. They won 40 one-run games and dropped only 15 and the pitching staff notched a club record 60 complete games. Eight players made the American League All-Star team that lost 5-4 to the National League in 12 innings in Cincinnati. Earl Weaver managed the team. Frank Robinson and Boog Powell were elected starters by the voting fans. Brooks Robinson relieved starter Harmon Killebrew at third and banged out two hits, including a two-run triple. Dave Johnson started at second when Rod Carew was scratched with an injury. Jim Palmer was Weaver's choice to start and pitched three shutout innings, giving up only one hit. Dave McNally and Mike Cuellar, also selected, didn't see action.

Paul Blair didn't make the All-Star team but had an All-Star game against Chicago in late April. At Comiskey Park, a tough home-run park, Blair joined Boog Powell and Curt Blefary in the Oriole record books by slugging three home runs. On May 31, Paulie survived a scary moment when he was hit by a pitch from California's Ken Tatum. The pitch injured his left eye and broke his nose in several places. Paul was carried off the field on a stretcher and underwent surgery, missing the next three weeks. Despite the beaning, he went on to hit .304 after the All-Star break and won his third Gold Glove award. Many felt, however, that Blair developed a fear at the plate after the beaning and was never the same. After his average dropped to .233 with eight home runs in 1972, Paul saw a hypnotist, Dr. Jacob Conn in June 1973 and bounced back to hit .280. He dropped to .218 in 1975 and was traded to the Yankees in 1976.

Top row, left to right–"Boog" Powell, Marcelino Lopez, Dick Hall, Brooks Robinson, Andy Etchebarren, Frank Robinson, Bobby Floyd, Pete Richert, Curt Motton, Paul Blair. Middle row, left to right–Clay Reid (equipment manager), Don Buford, Jim Palmer, Dave Johnson, Dave McNally, Elrod Hendricks, Mark Belanger, Mike Cuellar, Merv Rettenmund, Dave May, Clay Dalrymple, Ralph Salvon (trainer). Front row, left to right–Eddie Watt, Charlie Lau, George Staller, Billy Hunter, Earl Hunter, Earl Weaver, George Bamberger, Tom Phoebus, Jim Hardin, "Chico" Salmon. Seated in front–Jay Mazzone (Bat Boy). Absent: Dave Leonard.

Brooks Robinson was beaned by Boston's Mike Nagy in the fourth inning of a game in Baltimore, but he stayed in the game and delivered a 10th-inning game-winning home run off Sparky Lyle. Brooks, who drove in 94 runs and slugged 18 homers in 1970, was starting to pile up milestones. On June 20 he banged out his 2,000th career hit—a three-run homer off Washington's Joe Coleman Jr. to break a 2-2 tie and give the Birds a 5-4 win at Memorial Stadium. Later in the season, again facing Coleman, Brooks drove in his 1,000th run, a sacrifice fly. In May, he had clouted his 200th career homer off Chicago's Tommy John.

Frank Robinson again hit over .300 (.306), while hitting 25 homers and driving in 78. Frank's leadership was never more evident than in a game at Fenway Park on June 25. The Orioles had trailed 7-0 in the fifth but came back to tie it in the ninth. They won it in the 14th inning with a six-run explosion. They wouldn't have won, however, if it hadn't been for Frank. Writer-commentator Peter Gammons was covering the game that night. "Frank made a game-saving catch in the 13th, robbing Reggie Smith of a home run with the bases loaded. But he cracked a rib on the fence railing and couldn't swing the bat properly. Without tipping off the Red Sox fielders in the top of the 14th, he crossed up everybody by laying down a bunt with a runner on third and beating it out, driving in a run. He couldn't swing a bat so he found another way to win." It was Frank's first bunt in 12 years.

Earl Weaver

To keep the team loose and further deepen team harmony, Frank instituted a

Weaver, Dick Hall, and Andy Etchbarren engaged in a confab during the first game of the '69 ALCS against Minnesota, won by the Birds in three straight. Dick Hall was the "Old Reliable" of the Oriole relief corps. When Earl Weaver handed him the ball he knew Dick would throw strikes and challenge the batters. Standing 6-6, Hall had a tricky delivery that confused hitters. In nine seasons in Baltimore he posted a 2.76 ERA and pitched on the Birds first four World Series teams.

BALTIMORE
1954
ORIOLES
HARTZELL
50c
OPENING-YEAR OFFICIAL SOUVENIR SKETCHBOOK

BALTIMORE
Orioles
1955
HARTZELL
SKETCH BOOK 50¢

BALTIMORE
Orioles
DAYTONA BEACH
HARTZELL
1955
SPRING TRAINING
ROSTER

BALTIMORE
Orioles
1956
OFFICIAL
PHOTO PROFILE
AND RECORD BOOK
50c

BALTIMORE
Orioles
FIRST DIVISION EXPRESS
Official
1958
YEAR
BOOK
50c
HARTZ

BALTIMORE
Orioles
1957
HARTZELL
OFFICIAL
PROFILE, PHOTO
AND RECORD BOOK
50c

FOR Satisfying Flavor
National Bohemian
1956
Official
Orioles
SCORE CARD
AND
REVIEW
LET'S GO!
WELCOME
15c
Oh boy,
what a beer!

BALTIMORE
Orioles
50¢
PROGRESS
REPORT
GAMES BEHIND LEADER
1954
1955
1956
1957
1958
17½
21
28
39
57
Official
1959
YEAR BOOK

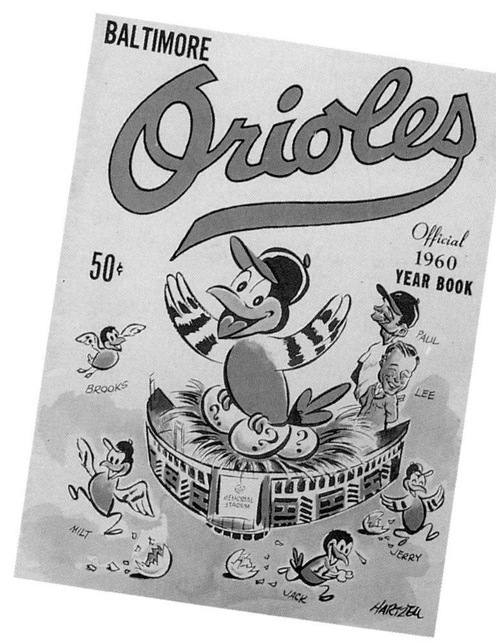
BALTIMORE
Orioles
50¢
Official
1960
YEAR BOOK
PAUL
BROOKS
LEE
MILT
JERRY
JACK

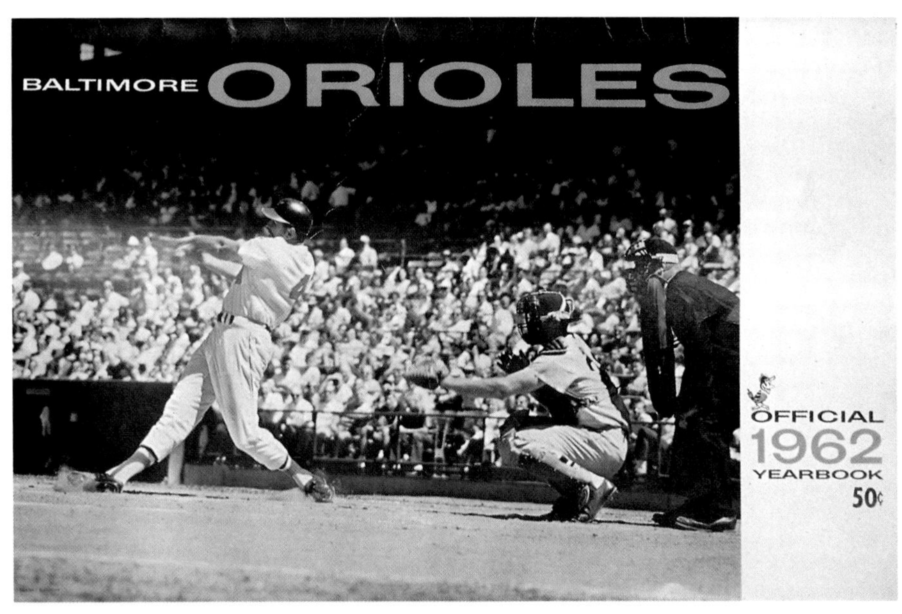
BALTIMORE ORIOLES
OFFICIAL
1962
YEARBOOK
50¢

50¢
BALTIMORE
ORIOLES
64 OFFICIAL YEARBOOK

BALTIMORE
ORIOLES
50¢
2nd Edition
1963 OFFICIAL YEARBOOK

ROOKIE PITCHER OF THE YEAR
MANAGER OF THE YEAR
MOST VALUABLE PLAYER
1965
YEARBOOK 50¢
BALTIMORE
ORIOLES

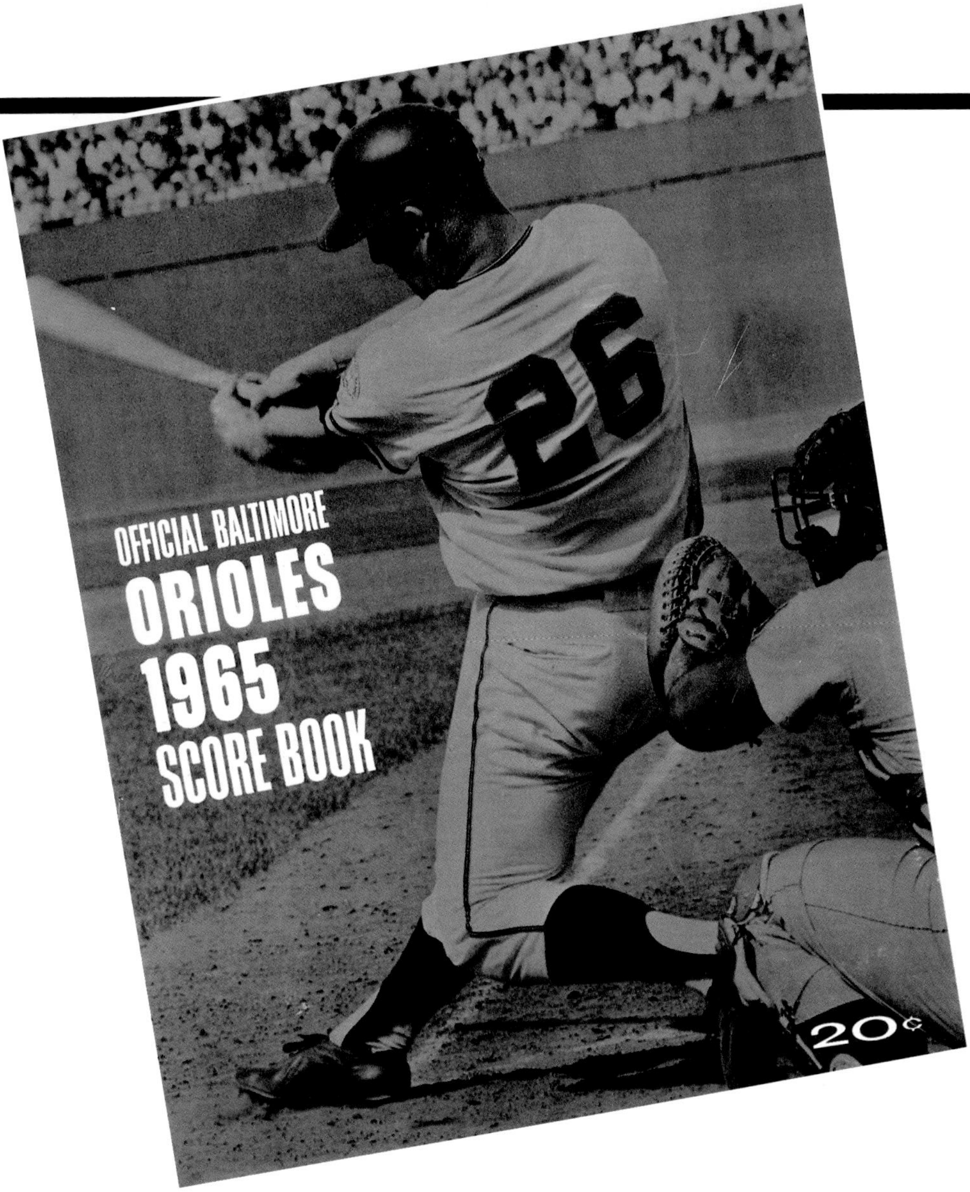
OFFICIAL BALTIMORE
ORIOLES
1965
SCORE BOOK
20¢

1967
BALTIMORE
Orioles
YEARBOOK

1966 Baltimore
Orioles
YEARBOOK 50¢
Spirit of '66

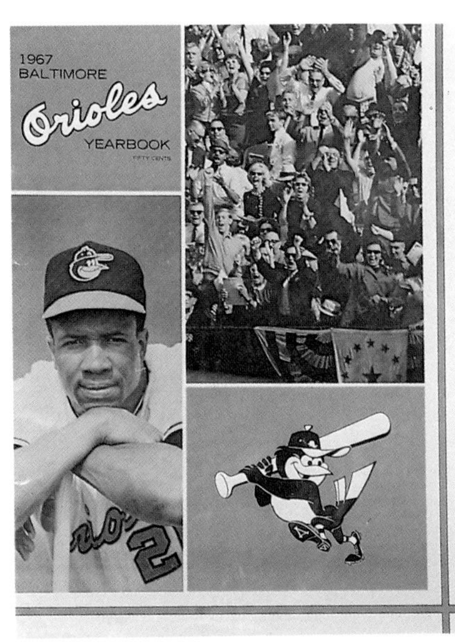

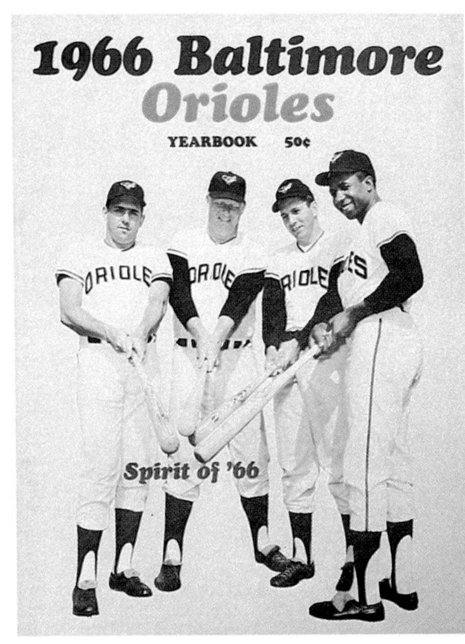

BALTIMORE
orioles
OFFICIAL YEARBOOK·75c

Baltimore Orioles
Official Scorebook
1968...
Year of the Bird
25¢

1869-1969 BASEBALL'S 100TH ANNIVERSARY
Baltimore's First Franchise
It's a brand new ball game.
Baltimore Orioles 1969
Baltimore Orioles Official Scorebook 25¢

B. ROBINSON
5
IT'S A BRAND NEW BALL GAME
Baltimore Orioles Official Scorebook
25¢

BALTIMORE ORIOLES
1970 YEARBOOK

THE MANY FACES OF FRANK*
* 12th on All-Time Home Run List
* Only home run ever hit completely out of Memorial Stadium
* 2,500 Major League Hits
* Outstanding Player—1966 World Series
* Lifetime batting average of .303
* Triple Crown Winner in 1966
* Orioles have won three pennants in his five Baltimore seasons
World Champion
BALTIMORE ORIOLES

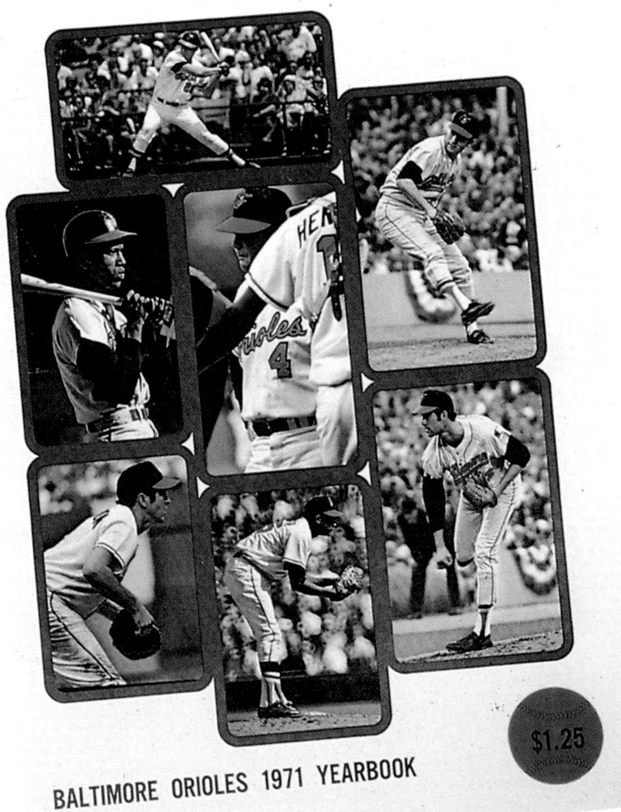
$1.25
BALTIMORE ORIOLES 1971 YEARBOOK

$1.25
BALTIMORE ORIOLES 1972 YEARBOOK

ORIOLES
20th Anniversary Yearbook
GREATEST HITS
BROOKS ROBINSON
DAVE MCNALLY
FRANK ROBINSON
JIM PALMER
BOOG POWELL
DAVE JOHNSON
JIM GENTILE
JERRY ADAIR
MARK BELANGER
PAUL BLAIR
LUIS APARICIO
GENE WOODLING
GUS TRIANDOS
MIKE CUELLAR
DON BUFORD
HOYT WILHELM
STU MILLER
TOMMY DAVIS
STEVE BARBER
ANDY ETCHEBARREN
G H J K
8 9 10
1974 Special Edition $2.00

SCORECARD
BALTIMORE
ORIOLES
35¢
75

Orioles
BALTIMORE
73
FOR EXCITING BASEBALL ACTION • FLIP THE PAGES FROM BACK TO FRONT
OFFICIAL YEARBOOK

CHAMPIONS OF THE 70's
THE TEAM OF THE 80's
$2.00
OFFICIAL
YEARBOOK
1980
BALTIMORE
Orioles

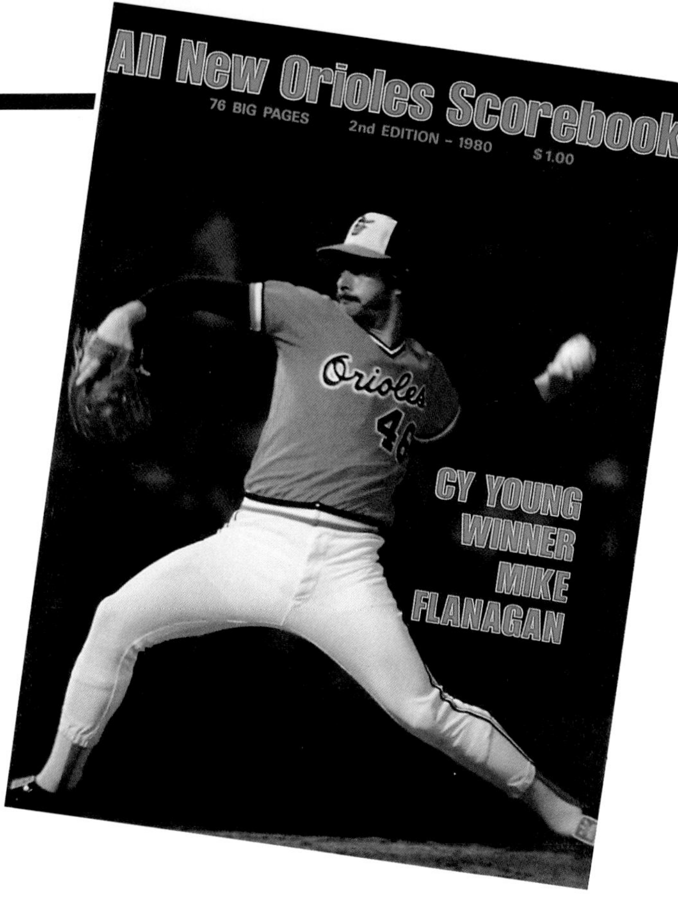
All New Orioles Scorebook
76 BIG PAGES
2nd EDITION - 1980
$1.00
CY YOUNG
WINNER
MIKE
FLANAGAN

All New Orioles Scorebook
6th EDITION - 1980
$1.00
SWEET
SWINGING
KENNY
SINGLETON

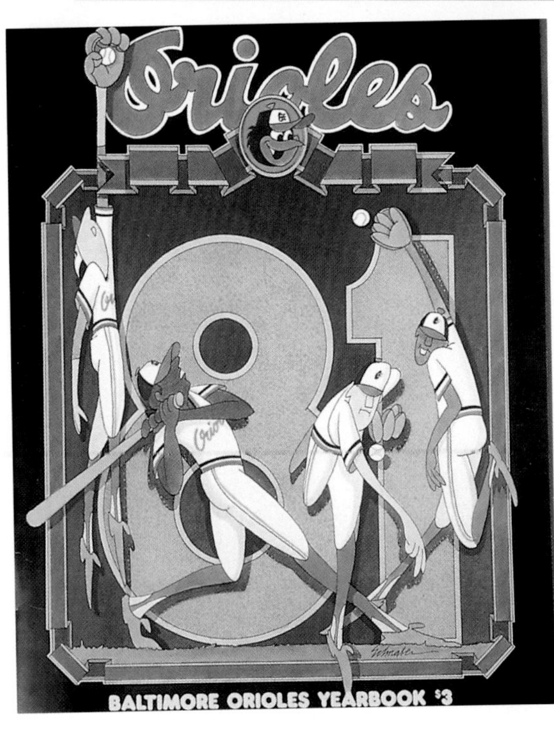
Orioles
BALTIMORE ORIOLES YEARBOOK $3

BALTIMORE ORIOLES
WORLD CHAMPIONS
Orioles
Orioles' Official '82 Yearbook $3

HALL OF FAME
Orioles
1983 MEDIA GUIDE

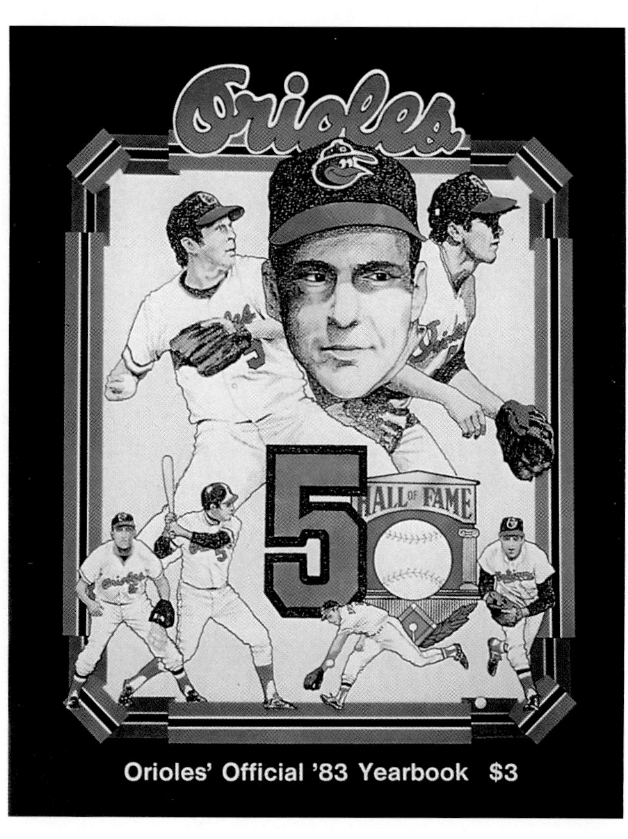
Orioles
HALL OF FAME
Orioles' Official '83 Yearbook $3

1954
1983 WORLD CHAMPIONS
1954 1984
30th ANNIVERSARY
Orioles
1984
30th ANNIVERSARY YEARBOOK
$4.00

SCOREBOOK
1984
1983 WORLD CHAMPIONS
1954 1984
A TRADITION OF EXCELLENCE
30th ANNIVERSARY
Orioles
$1.25

SCOREBOOK
1983
Orioles
$1.25

SCOREBOOK
1984
1983 WORLD CHAMPIONS
1954 1984
Orioles
$1.25

Orioles
MAGAZINE
$2.00
JUNE 1987
THE
PEP BOYS
Bulk Rate
U.S. Postage
PAID
Norfolk, VA
Permit NO. 510

MURRAY
33
8
ORIOLES
MEDIA
GUIDE
'86

BACK TO THE FUTURE
1966
1986
1986 ORIOLES YEARBOOK $4.50

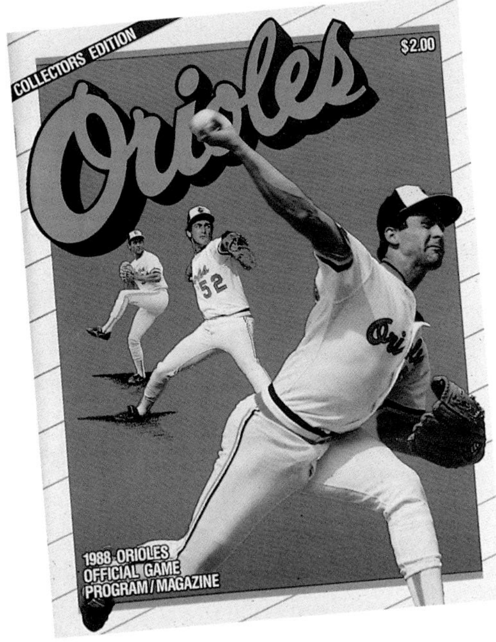
COLLECTORS EDITION
Orioles
$2.00
52
1988 ORIOLES
OFFICIAL GAME
PROGRAM/MAGAZINE

Iron Man
with Soft Hands
Cal Ripken, Jr. #8
Orioles
1990 OFFICIAL
GAME PROGRAM/
SCORECARD
$2.00

THE LAST GAME
FINAL SALUTE TO MEMORIAL STADIUM
Orioles

ETCHEBARREN
McNALLY
19
RIPKEN
47
ROBINSON
20
MEMORIAL STADIUM
Orioles
1991 OFFICIAL
Game Program/Scorecard
2ND EDITION
$2.00
JEFF WILKINSON

2ND EDITION
Orioles
1991 OFFICIAL
Game Program/Scorecard
FIREPOWER
DWIGHT EVANS
RANDY MILLIGAN
CAL RIPKEN, JR.
GLENN DAVIS

Orioles
1991 OFFICIAL
Game Program/Scorecard
$2.00 · 2ND EDITION
Manager
John Oates

THE FIRST GAME - FRIDAY APRIL 3, 1992
THE DAWN OF A NEW ERA
The Baltimore Orioles vs The New York Mets

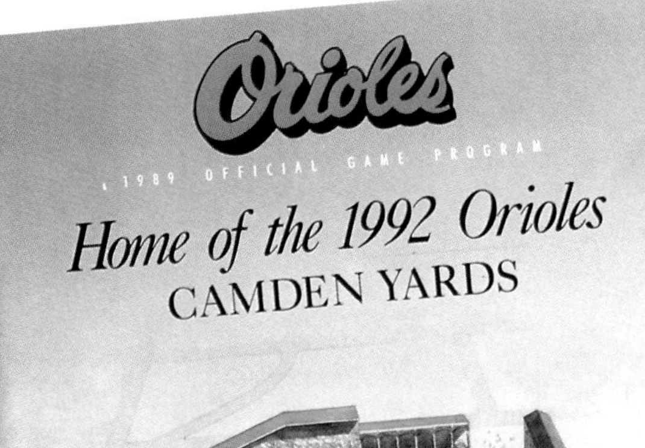
Orioles
1989 OFFICIAL GAME PROGRAM
Home of the 1992 Orioles
CAMDEN YARDS

ORIOLE PARK AT CAMDEN YARDS
THE FIRST OPENING DAY
APRIL 6, 1992

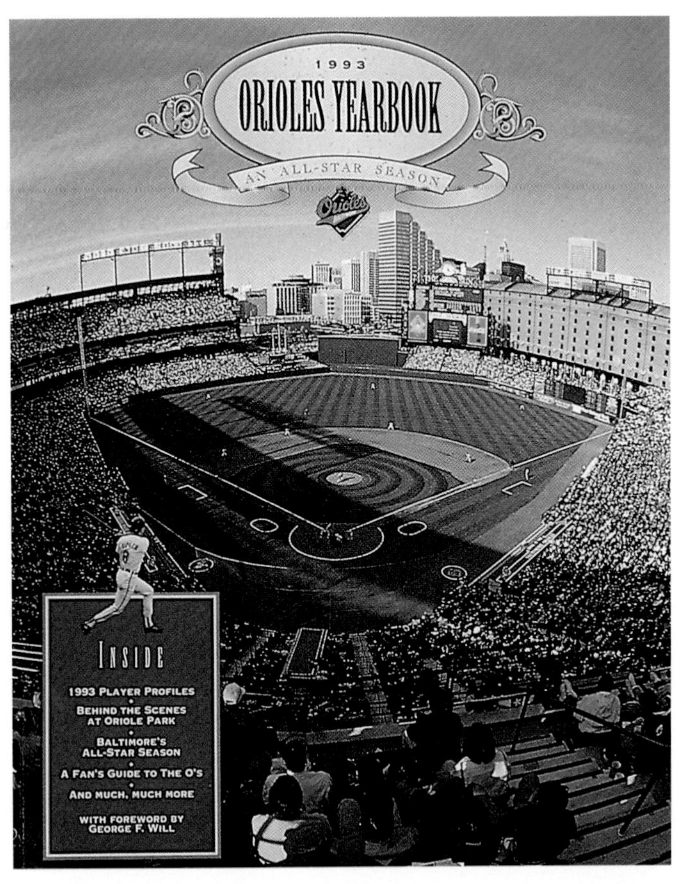
1993
ORIOLES YEARBOOK
AN ALL-STAR SEASON
INSIDE
1993 PLAYER PROFILES
BEHIND THE SCENES AT ORIOLE PARK
BALTIMORE'S ALL-STAR SEASON
A FAN'S GUIDE TO THE O'S
AND MUCH, MUCH MORE
WITH FOREWORD BY GEORGE F. WILL

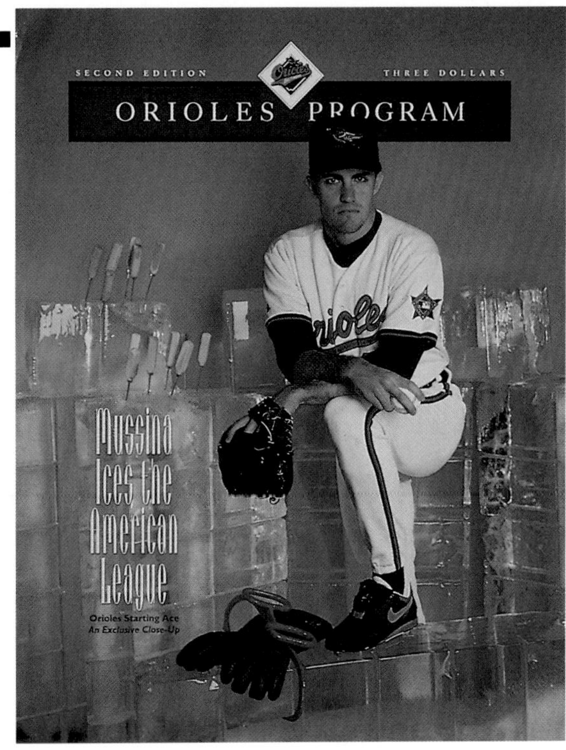
SECOND EDITION
THREE DOLLARS
ORIOLES PROGRAM
Mussina Ices the American League
Orioles Starting Ace
An Exclusive Close-Up

Baltimore
Orioles
1956
SCOTTSDALE ARIZ.
1956
Press · Radio · TV
GUIDE

Elrod Hendricks comes racing home to score on a Mark Belanger single in the fourth inning to lift the Birds to a 4–0 lead in game one of the 1969 World Series. They held on to win 4–1, their only victory of the Series.

"Kangaroo Court" for which he was "da Judge." Fines in the one-dollar range were slapped on players for criminal acts ranging from being late for the team bus to not abiding by the club dress code to acts of omission on the field. As one player put it, "It was a way for Frank to get his point across while keeping the mood light. But if you missed the cutoff man, you heard about it from Frank. If you missed a sign, you heard about it." Frank wore a robe and an old rag mop on his head when court was in session. He was the only player who could get away with saying, "Stand up Earl. Oh, you are standing," in referring to the diminutive Weaver.

Paul Blair scored the Orioles only run in game two of the 1969 World Series, coming home on a Brooks Robinson single in the seventh. The Birds fell 2-1.

Frank's competitive nature was a quality everyone respected. On June 26, at R.F.K. Stadium in Washington, the night after he injured himself in Boston, he became the seventh player in big-league history to hit two grand slams in one game. Like Jim Gentile in 1961, he performed the feat on consecutive trips to the plate, first against Joe Coleman Jr. in the fifth and then against Joe Grzenda in the sixth. The Orioles won the game, 12-2.

Even Frank had to move over for Boog Powell in 1970. The 6-4, 250-pound slugger was voted the league's Most Valuable Player by a wide margin, hitting 35 homers and driving in 114 runs to accompany a .297 batting average. Powell had emerged as one of the leading all-around offensive threats in baseball.

The Orioles sported three 20-game winners in 1970. Dave McNally's 24-9 mark gave him three straight 20-plus-win seasons. Cuellar's screwball was dazzling in 1970 as he won 24 and lost 8 with a club record 21 complete games. Jim Palmer led the staff in innings pitched with 305 and in ERA at 2.71. His 20-10 record included five shutouts. It was the first of eight 20-win seasons for Palmer as an Oriole.

Dick Hall, who had returned to Baltimore two years before after being released by the Phillies, celebrated his 40th birthday in 1970 with one of his best years. It cost the Orioles a plane ticket to spring training in 1969 to reacquire him. He proved he could still pitch, with 15 wins and nine saves in his first two seasons back in Baltimore, including a 10-5 record in 1970. Frank Robinson declared that he was happy to be playing with and not against Hall. "He was all arms and legs and he gave you everything but the baseball. He didn't give you the down and away and up and in pitches. He threw the ball over the plate and made you hit it. He didn't look like he had much," continued Frank. "You'd walk back to the dugout saying 'how'd he get me out?'"

What Hall did have with that herky-jerky motion off his 6-6 frame was amazing control. A converted outfielder-third baseman, he won 44 and lost 27 with 41 saves in his first tour of duty with the Orioles from 1961 through 1966. In his last seven seasons in the majors, the pitcher nicknamed "Turkey" issued only 23 unintentional walks in 462 innings, an average of less than half a walk per nine innings. Dick wound up his 19-year big-league career in 1971 and was inducted into the Orioles Hall of Fame in 1989. He posted a 60-38 record in an Oriole uniform, with 51 saves and a 2.76 ERA.

Earl Weaver was tossed out of game four of the '69 Series, the first manager to get the heave-ho since 1935.

After winning 11 straight to end the regular

Brooks Robinson gloves Johnny Bench's line drive, stealing a base hit from the Reds All-Star catcher in the 1970 World Series. Lee May dubbed Brooks the human vacuum cleaner for his brilliant fielding during the series.

season, the Orioles didn't let up in the 1970 playoffs. They swept the Twins in three straight for the second straight year. On October 3, Mike Cuellar hit his way to a win, connecting for a wind-blown grand slam homer to give the Birds a 10-6 victory in Minnesota. The anticipated pitchers' duel between 24-game winners Cuellar and Cy Young winner Jim Perry never materialized as Don Buford and Boog Powell also homered for Baltimore. After Cuellar gave up a 437-foot homer to Harmon Killebrew and a two-run single to George Mitterwald in the fifth, Weaver summoned Hall who allowed only one hit over the last 4⅔ innings.

Game two the following day was a nail-biter into the ninth with McNally and the Orioles clinging to a 4-3 lead. They then repeated their second seven-run inning in two days to roll, 11-3. The victim once again was reliever Ron Perranoski, who had been caught the inning before with an illegal substance on his pitching hand by plate ump Bill Haller. Haller ordered Perranoski into the clubhouse to remove the substance. When he returned the Orioles jumped on him in the ninth with Boog delivering a two-run single and Merv Rettenmund an RBI hit. Dave Johnson capped the inning with a three-run homer off Luis Tiant.

Back in Baltimore the next day, the Orioles dispatched the Twins, 6-1, behind Jim Palmer's stellar 12-strikeout performance. It was the third time Palmer had gone the distance to clinch a pennant.

Sparky Anderson's fabled "Big Red Machine" of Johnny Bench, Lee May, Tony Perez, Pete Rose, Bobby Tolan, and Joe Morgan, loomed in Cincinnati. The Reds streaked to 102 regular-season victories and swept Pittsburgh in the playoffs for their first pennant since 1961. Bench had slugged 40 homers and driven in 125 runs. May, the big bopper from Birmingham, drove in 98 runs on 29 homers, and Perez had 90 RBI and 21 homers. The Reds' vulnerability was in their pitching. Only one starter had won as many as 15 games, Gary Nolan at 15-5.

Riverfront Stadium, which had opened during the season, now hosted the first game of the 1970 World Series on October 10. It would be the first Series played on artificial turf, with the Reds installed as favorites. Jim Palmer was Earl Weaver's choice to face Nolan in the opener. Lee May's third-inning two-run homer helped the Reds to a 3-0 lead. Brooks Robinson's first fielding chance came in the second inning when Woody Woodward's soft bouncer glanced off Brooks' glove for an error. This was an inauspicious start to what would turn out to be one of the greatest fielding exhibitions in World Series history.

Along with his heroics in the field, Brooks Robinson hit .429 during the 1970 World Series, including two home runs.

The Orioles got on the board in the fourth inning when Powell unloaded a monster two-run homer. Catcher Elrod Hendricks tied the game with a solo shot in the fifth. May, already 2-2, opened the sixth with a smash over the third base bag, destined for extra bases. Brooks instinctively lunged for the ball, gloving it with his backhand and throwing without setting

Boog Powell lunges for the throw to first to nail Bobby Tolan as umpire John Flaherty makes the call in the '70 Series.

Dick Hall, the fifth Oriole pitcher, greeted by teammates after notching the save in the Orioles 6-5 win in game two of the 1970 World Series in Cincinnati.

himself to first. Boog stretched and grabbed the one hopper to nip May by an eyelash. Then came the controversy. Later in the inning, with two on and one out, pinch-hitter Ty Cline hit a "Baltimore chop" in front of the plate. Ellie Hendricks sprang out to catch the ball, which bounced 30 feet into the air. Bernie Carbo was bearing down the line from third trying to score. Palmer alerted Ellie that Carbo was coming so Hendricks lunged at the runner after grabbing the ball. Carbo plowed into plate umpire Ken Burkhart as all three converged at the plate. Burkhart righted himself, saw that Hendricks had the ball, and called Carbo out. Replays later showed Carbo missed the plate and Ellie did tag him before he slid by, but the ball wasn't in Hendricks' glove when he applied the tag. It was in his bare hand instead. Sparky Anderson went wild. Carbo went back and touched home. But Burkhart stuck with his call. The play was reshown for days and has become part of World Series lore. Brooks won the game in the seventh with a solo homer off Nolan and the Orioles took game one, 4-3.

In game two Cincinnati once again jumped out to a lead, this time 4-0 off Mike Cuellar, scoring three unearned runs in the first inning. Tolan hit a solo homer in the third. The Reds would have scored more but for another great play by Brooks. With Tom Phoebus in relief and a runner on first with one down, May hit a laser shot down the line at third. Brooks dove and gloved it on the line, whirled and threw to second to start an inning-ending double play. Another possible big inning was snuffed out by Brooks' magic glove. The Orioles then mounted a comeback. Boog homered off Reds starter Jim McGlothlin in the fourth. In the fifth, Weaver pinch-hit seldom-used Chico Salmon for Phoebus and the Panamanian delivered a single to right to ignite a five-run inning. Hendricks' two-run opposite-field double was the key blow in the eventual 6-5 win. Old reliable Dick Hall retired the Reds in order in the eighth and ninth to preserve the game for Phoebus as Paul Blair hauled down Jimmy Stewart's long drive to deep center to end the game. Now it was on to Baltimore, with the Orioles up 2-0 in games.

The vaunted Big Red Machine, out of sync with a couple of malfunctioning cylinders, sputtered into Baltimore wondering what they had to do to get a ball past Brooks Robinson, and wondering how they could stop the Orioles from scoring. A crowd of 51,773 squeezed into Memorial Stadium to watch Dave McNally face Tony Cloninger in game three. There was no doubting that the fans were after revenge for the Mets' fiasco the year before. This time the Orioles jumped to a lead. Brooks Robinson doubled home two first-inning runs. Frank Robinson socked a solo homer in the third and Don Buford connected for a solo shot in the fifth.

Brooks, besides his two doubles and two RBI, made another rally-killing stop in the sixth. Johnny Bench was the victim. With the Reds trailing 4-1, Bench sent a rifle shot to Brooks' left toward the shortstop hole. Brooks reacted swiftly, appearing to make his move even before Bench connected. Diving for the ball, he gloved it about six inches off the ground. The frustrated Bench said he would knock the next one over Brooks' head. He tried in game five, but the greatest fielding third baseman the game has ever seen leaped and gloved the line drive.

In the bottom of the sixth, the Orioles put together a Blair single and a Brooks double with one out. To create a force and set up a double play the Reds deliberately walked Dave Johnson to load the bases. Reliever Wayne Granger struck out Andy Etchebarren for the second out. Hopes rested with

Mike Cuellar, top, receives congratulations from Don Buford after winning game three.

Moe Drabowsky

Even at the age of 58, Moe Drabowsky still has a childish glint in his eye, as if he's up to some kind of mischief. And even at age 58, he usually is. Moe was the "Clown Prince" of the Orioles. He was 30 years old when he joined the club before the 1966 season. That was his listed age, but in reality, he was more like a teenaged prankster. Boog Powell summed Drabowsky up best when he said, "Obviously, Moe's parents never let him have toys when he was little, so he had a lot of catching up to do. He sat around and dreamed up things. He was unbelievable."

Moe was born in Poland, and his family moved to Connecticut when he was a youngster. His ability to think up pranks is legendary, but he was also smart enough to earn an economics degree from Trinity College in Hartford. That degree proved valuable after his baseball days when he spent several years in the business world. As a player though, he was more interested in elevating clownish pranks to an art form. "Moe would do things other guys got punched in the nose for," remembered third base coach Billy Hunter. "And he got away with them. He was incredible."

There were the rubber snakes he'd hang in players' uniforms before games. Then came real snakes that forced Luis Aparicio and Paul Blair to dress in the hallway outside the clubhouse. Hotfoots were another Drabowsky specialty. He'd light from one match to as many as 20 in one shoe, and the flames would rise like a bonfire, once even catching an unsuspecting reporter's pants on fire.

Moe didn't discriminate among his targets. In the aftermath of the 1970 World Series celebration, he gave then-commissioner Bowie Kuhn a hotfoot. Later came smoke bombs and cherry bombs as his repertoire widened.

There was a method to Moe's madness. His antics eased the pressure of being a relief pitcher. "If you thought about pitching in tight jams, you'd go crazy. So this was kind of a release for me. We had several free spirits on the Orioles who I could play off of."

Back in 1966 Moe received a postcard from an 11-year-old youngster who wrote, "Baseball needs more nuts like you." That statement holds true today. There just aren't any more Moe Drabowskys around. He was indeed one of a kind.

McNally who had driven in only six runs in 105 at-bats in the regular season. With two strikes Granger came in with a waist-high fastball and Mac was ready, clubbing the ball 360 feet into the left-field bleachers. It was the first grand slam home run by a pitcher in World Series history. The improbable blast had given McNally an 8-1 cushion as he went the distance to win, 9-3.

The Birds were now smelling sweep. By this time their winning streak was up to 17, comprising the end of the regular season, the playoffs, and the World Series. In game four, before 53,007, Jim Palmer faced Gary Nolan in a first-game rematch. Brooks continued his series magic with a long home run in the bottom of the second to tie the score 1-1. It was the first of four hits for Brooks that day. After Lee May's RBI single in the Cincinnati third, the Birds scored three times with Frank, Brooks, and Hendricks delivering RBI hits. They might have scored more but Pete Rose threw out Brooks as he was trying to score. Still, the Orioles led, 4-2. Rose got one back with a fifth-inning homer. The Orioles countered with another in the sixth to lead 5-3 and were nine outs away from a sweep.

In the Cincinnati eighth, Palmer walked Perez and Bench singled. Weaver summoned reliever Eddie Watt, known for his competitive nature and grit, who had amassed 51 saves in five years. Future Oriole Lee May bashed Watt's first pitch over 400 feet into the left-field bleachers to give the Reds a 6-5 victory. "I finally found a way to get the ball by Brooks," said a smiling May in the clubhouse. I just hit it over him." It was May who dubbed Robinson "Hoover, the Human Vacuum Cleaner." Watt was never able to shed the goat horns for giving up that home run. He was booed more than cheered every time he took the mound until his departure after the 1973 season. To his credit, Eddie never complained about his treatment by Oriole fans. He posted ERAs of 1.80 and 2.15 in 1971 and 1972. Over a five-year span from 1968 through 1972 he surrendered only 10 home runs in 295 innings pitched. It was that one to Lee May in the 1970 series that lived in infamy.

Game five on October 15 was played in damp, rainy weather before only 45,341. Former Red Mike Cuellar started for the Orioles against fellow lefty Jim Merritt. Hal McRae's two-run double (one of three in the inning) was the key hit in a three-run Cincinnati first inning. After that, Cuellar retired 24 of the next 27 batters he faced, giving up only two seventh-inning singles and a walk. Frank Robinson's two-run homer in the bottom of the first cut the score to 3-2. The Birds scored two more in the second and two in the third to suddenly lead, 6-3. Merv Rettenmund, who led the Orioles in hitting in 1970 with a .322 average, hom-ered in the sixth and the Birds scored two more runs in the eighth to make it 9-3. When Brooks was called out on strikes in the eighth, he walked back to the dugout with his head bowed. The fans rose as one and gave him a standing ovation for his dream series. An Oriole since he was 18 and a fixture at the age of 21, the 33-year-old third baseman had the world as his audience for the 1970 World Series. And the reviews were sensational. He brought the curtain down in the ninth inning by spearing Bench's scorching line drive. It was foul by the time it reached third but Brooks dove and gloved the ball, giving the fans one last memory for posterity. With two outs, Pat Corrales fittingly sent a soft bouncer to third and Brooks threw him out to end the game as he leaped into Cuellar's arms to ignite the celebration. The glove Brooks used in the series, which had originally been owned by former Oriole Dave May, was on its way to Cooperstown immediately, only to be borrowed back by Brooks during the 1971 season when he couldn't find a suitable replacement.

Dave McNally is greeted by a flock of jubilant Birds after hitting his grand slam in game three – the only grand slam a pitcher has ever hit in the World Series.

Boog Powell summed up the feelings of Oriole fans everywhere after the series when he said about Brooks' performance: "What we saw in the World Series was spectacular, but we saw that on a daily basis. It would take a .22 caliber rifle aimed in just the right way to get one past him. Brooks worked hard even though the game came so easily to him. He'd drive in the big run. He was a champion at it. You wanted him up there in the late innings. I'd rather have him up there instead of me."

Besides his obvious efforts in the field, Brooks hit .429 in the five-game series, with nine hits, two homers, and six RBI. He also scored five runs. About his great series, Brooks said, "Sometimes I'd go a week and only have one or two balls hit to me in routine fashion. Yet in this one five-game stretch, I had one tough chance after another and fortunately made the plays. It was uncanny. Almost like it was destined." It's safe to say that in the previous 66 World Series, no player had an effect on the outcome as much as Brooks Robinson did in 1970. The bulk of his 24 fielding chances came at key moments. Needless to say he was voted series MVP, receiving a new Dodge Charger. It prompted Pete Rose to say in admiration, "If we knew he wanted a car so bad, we'd have bought one for him ourselves." "I'll bet it has an over-sized glove compartment," added Bench.

After putting on one of the greatest one-man shows in World Series history, Brooks Robinson runs to embrace winning pitcher Mike Cuellar after the Orioles 9-3 win in game five against the vaunted Big Red Machine to clinch the Series four games to one.

As a team the Orioles hit .292 in the series, with Paul Blair's .474 average leading the way. The Cincinnati side of the ledger was bleak. Perez got one single in five games. Bench had four hits and a .211 average. Only Lee May, with two homers and eight RBI in to go with a .389 average, excelled, and he was robbed several times by Brooks. The Reds' team ERA was a whopping 6.70.

With 217 wins in his first two full seasons as manager, Earl Weaver set an American League record for most wins in two straight seasons, surpassing the 211 racked up by Miller Huggins' famed Yankees of 1927–28. The disappointment after the loss to the

Images from the 1970 post-Series victory celebration.

Mets the year before hadn't been completely forgotten, but the sting was eased considerably by winning it all in 1970.

Pitching and defense had long been the emphasis of the Orioles' philosophy and general manager Harry Dalton swung another deal at the 1970 winter meetings that brought the Orioles yet another 20-game winner. Dalton traded Tom Phoebus, who had become a spot starter in 1970, to San Diego for curve ball artist Pat Dobson and reliever Tom Dukes. Pitchers Al Severinson and Fred Beene and infielder Enzo Hernandez also went to the Padres.

The next season was a bit more difficult than the previous two. A nine-game win streak that began in late May propelled the Orioles into first place by June 5 where they stayed, finishing over the century mark in wins for the third straight year, something accomplished only twice in baseball history before then. They won 101 games and lost 57, winning by 12 games over runner-up Detroit.

It was a season of incredible achievements, headed by a staggering four 20-game winners. Only the 1920 Chicago White Sox foursome of Urban "Red" Faber, Ed Cicotte, Lefty Williams, and Dickie Kerr had ever sported four 20-game winners. Now that post-Black Sox team had company as Dave McNally finished 21-5, Mike Cuellar 20-9, Jim Palmer 20-9, and newcomer Pat Dobson 20-8. Until 1971, Dobson had logged a subpar 25-35 record in three seasons in Detroit and one in San Diego. "I wasn't the kind of guy who struck many hitters out. We had that great defense in 1971 and I just put the ball in play and took advantage," said Dobson. Known as "the Snake," Dobson owned one of the great curve balls in baseball. By mid-June, though, Dobson was only 3-4 and thoughts of 20 wins were nothing but pipe dreams. Then followed a 12-game win streak that encompassed almost two months and featured an impressive 12 complete games. From 3-4 to 15-4 and suddenly 20 wins were in reach.

Cuellar won 11 straight in one early stretch and

bolted to a 13-1 start. McNally, who got the most out of his talent and who never backed down from any challenge, won 13 straight over a three-month-plus period despite a sore elbow that sidelined him for over a month. Like the year before, the Orioles closed the regular season in high-flying style, winning their last 11 regular-season games, and 16 straight counting the post season. All four starters won their 20th within a six-day stretch. McNally began it with a 5-0 shutout of the Yankees on September 21. It was Mac's fourth straight year of 20 or more wins. "Cuellar and I both won our 20th on the same day in Cleveland," remembers Dobson, who called the two years he spent in Baltimore his most enjoyable in baseball. "Mike won the first game of a twi-night doubleheader and we clinched the pennant in the process. I hid the champagne because I didn't want any celebrating until after I won my 20th. I shut out the Indians 7-0 in the nightcap. Then we celebrated." Just two days later, on a Sunday afternoon, Palmer pitched a three-hit shutout to win his 20th. Dobson believes that the accomplishments of the Oriole iron-man foursome in 1971 will never be matched again. "First of all everybody's gone to a five-man rotation and pitching is a lot more diluted now than it was then. All four of us went out there every fourth day and we stayed healthy. When we gave up one run, we'd score two and if we gave up none, we'd score one. Other days we'd give up four or five and we'd score seven or eight."

Dave McNally

If there was one big game to be won, Dave McNally was the pitcher everybody wanted out there. "He has a lot of stomach," said Earl Weaver. He wasn't that big or that fast. Yet when Ted Williams saw him for the first time he said, "That guy has to be the best pitcher in the American League."

Dave McNally was a Whitey Ford pitch-alike. A left-handed finesse pitcher who got hitters out with guile and an assortment of off-speed stuff, he once won 17 straight. Another time 13. He posted four straight 20-win seasons. "McNally has everything," said Tiger star Al Kaline. "He moves the ball around and sets you up real good. He has no one pitch. You can't look for a particular pitch if you get behind in the count. He gets you off balance and makes you hit what he wants to throw you."

In 1971, at the prime age of 28, his arm began to hurt during a 21-win season. He would win 46 games in his last three seasons as an Oriole but was out of the game at the age of 32. His 181 wins are second only to Jim Palmer in Oriole history.

His top thrill was winning it all in 1966. "The Dodgers had been there before and we had a bunch of kids who had never been there," he said. "Our starting pitching was so young. I expected to be the underdog." After faltering on the steep Dodger Stadium mound in the first game, McNally came back to pitch a complete game shutout and complete the four-game sweep in Baltimore. Smart, gutsy, fearless, and with a bushel of talent, Dave McNally was the total package.

There were many milestones in 1971. Frank Robinson delivered the 2,500th hit of his stellar career on July 8 at Memorial Stadium against Washington, a three-run homer off Horatio Pina in a 7-3 win that saw Cuellar win his 11th straight game. On August 10 in Minnesota, Cuellar gave up Harmon Killebrew's 500th and 501st home runs and still won 4-3 in extra innings. On September 13, in the first of two at Memorial Stadium, Frank Robinson socked his 499th career homer off of Detroit's Mike Kilkenny. In the nightcap he connected for number 500 off Fred Scherman to become the 11th player to join the 500-homer club. Unfortunately Frank's historic homer came at 11:47 P.M. and there was hardly anybody in the stands to see it. In another memorable game, a walk-up crowd of 31,626 came out to see young sensation Vida Blue face Jim Palmer on May 9. A total of 43,307 watched Blue win 2-1. For Vida, who struck out nine, it was his eighth straight win to start the season. For Palmer, who struck out 11 in seven innings, it was his first loss of the season after five straight wins.

Hitting stars in 1971 included Don Buford who capped a three-year run as the best lead-off hitter in Oriole history by batting .290 with 19 homers and 99 runs scored. Dave Johnson hit .282 with 18 homers. Merv Rettenmund led the club with a .318 average and

11 home runs. While Brooks hit .272 with 20 homers and 92 RBI, Boog and Frank both dropped below their usual standards. Frank hit .281, far under his lifetime average, with 28 homers and 99 RBI. Boog, hampered by a hairline fracture in his right wrist, slumped to .256 with 22 homers and 92 RBI.

Top row, left to right- Marcelino Lopez, Jim Palmer, Moe Drabowsky, Frank Robinson, Mike Cuellar, Dick Hall, Bobby Grich, Curt Motton, Terry Crowley, Paul Blair. Middle row, left to right- Clay Reid (equipment manager), Andy Etchebarren, "Boog" Powell, Pete Richert, Mark Belanger, Dave Leonhard, Brooks Robinson, Elrod Hendricks, Merv Rettenmund, Dave Johnson, Eddie Watt, Ralph Salvon (trainer). Front row, left to right- Ton Phoebus, Don Buford, Jim Frey, Bill Hunter, Earl Weaver, George Bamberger, George Staller, Dave McNally, "Chico" Salmon. Seated in front- Jay Mazzone (Bat Boy). Absent: Clay Dalrymple and Jim Hardin.

Five Orioles along with manager Earl Weaver helped the American League All-Stars beat the Nationals for the first time since 1962 in a 6-4 battle of homers. It was to be the only American League victory over a 20-year span. Jim Palmer and Mike Cuellar combined to pitch four shutout innings and Brooks Robinson added a single and another magical defensive play against Johnny Bench, who must have had nightmares for a year about Brooks. Although Reggie Jackson clouted a 520-foot homer off a light tower at Tiger Stadium, it was Frank Robinson's two-run blast off Dock Ellis that put the American League in the lead, 4-3. Frank thus became the first player to hit All-Star homers in both leagues. For his efforts he won the Arch Ward Trophy as All-Star MVP. Chicago sportswriter Dave Nightengale wrote after the game: "If nothing else, the 42nd All-Star renewal proved one thing—the World Champion Baltimore Orioles can still beat the National League."

Brooks had a series to both remember and forget against Oakland in July. He belted a grand slam for a 7-3 win on July 18, then unloaded a two-run homer with two outs in the ninth against Rollie Fingers to give the Birds a 6-4 win on July 27. The next night, however, was his worst game ever in the field. Unbelievably, Brooks committed three errors in one inning against Oakland and hit into two double plays. Still, the Orioles won 3-2, as Frank Robinson homered off Fingers in the ninth.

Merv Rettenmund played on four Eastern Division champions and three pennant winners in his five full seasons in Baltimore. He played in eight playoff and 10 World Series games and led the team in hitting in 1970 and '71.

The best of five American League playoffs began on October 3 in Baltimore. This time the opponent was the Oakland Athletics, who ran away with the West with 101 wins as they "nipped" Kansas City by 16 games. The Orioles faced 24-game winner Vida Blue and trailed 3-1 in the seventh when, with one run in, Curt Motton, batting for Dave McNally, stroked a pinch double that tied the game. Paul Blair followed with a two-run double that lifted the Orioles to a 5-3 win.

The following day, four home runs accounted for all five Oriole runs. Two came off the bat of Boog Powell, while Brooks Robinson and Ellie Hendricks each homered to make Mike Cuellar a 5-1 winner over Jim "Catfish" Hunter.

The Orioles made it nine for nine in the American League playoffs by sweeping Oakland in three. Once again it was Jim Palmer, just as in 1966, 1969, and 1970, who pitched the clincher. Going all the way, Palmer beat Diego Segui 5-3. Reggie Jackson touched Palmer for two home runs but Jim finished with a flourish, striking out the side in the ninth to give Baltimore its fourth pennant in six years.

In the National League Pittsburgh beat the Giants in four games to capture the pennant and they arrived in Baltimore primed for their first World Series since the epic 1960 autumn classic. The Pirates took an early 3-0 lead against Dave McNally, but the Birds came back with a solo Frank Robinson homer and a three-run shot by Merv Rettenmund, both off loser Dock Ellis. McNally settled down and retired 21 of the last 22 batters he faced, including 19 straight. The Orioles won game one, 5-3.

Rain had washed out 14 regular-season games involving the Orioles and rain washed out game two. The series resumed the next day and the Orioles clobbered the Bucs 11-3 on 14 singles. Brooks Robinson reached base five straight times on three hits and two walks. The Orioles scored six runs in the fifth to break it open. Merv Rettenmund tied a series record with two hits in one inning. Jim Palmer struck out 10, but lost his shutout in the eighth when Richie Hebner cracked a three-run homer. But the day belonged to Baltimore, now up 2-0 in the series.

The confident Orioles moved into Three Rivers Stadium the next day and were beaten 5-1. Pirate pitcher Steve Blass went the route on a three-hitter to beat Mike Cuellar. The Bucs were now in the Series.

The following night saw history in the making—the first World Series night game ever. A record Pittsburgh crowd of 51,378 was on hand. The Orioles jumped out to a 3-0 first-inning lead. Then 21-year-old Bruce Kison relieved starter Luke Walker in the first

Pitching coach George Bamberger, here conferring with Mike Cuellar and catcher Ellie Hendricks, did not win a game in his brief stint with the Orioles in 1959. However, in 10 years as the club's pitching coach, he helped produce 18 20-game winners.

Frank Robinson

The Orioles stole Frank Robinson from Cincinnati in one of the most lopsided deals in history, and thanks to him they stole four pennants and two World Championships in six years. Frank Robinson was the missing ingredient, the spark the Orioles needed for winning after a couple of near misses. "To leave Cincinnati was a shock," said Frank. "My mind went blank when the trade was announced. But when I thought about it, I changed my thinking. The change of scenery would do me good. I did not feel I had anything to prove, yet I wanted to prove to Bill DeWitt that I was not done at the age of 30."

What Frank Robinson did in 1966 was ignite the Orioles to the pennant and a World Series sweep of the Dodgers. He hit .316, socked 49 homers, drove in 122 runs, and won both the Triple Crown and American League MVP honors. "What motivated me was the trade itself. My new teammates would scrutinize me and wonder about me as a player and a person. All I did was come to Baltimore and play like I always played. All out, every day."

One of Frank's great assets was his baseball instincts. He didn't have great speed but would get a great jump on the ball and was a champion base runner and base stealer. At the plate, with men on base, he could go to right field better than anybody.

Early in the 1966 season, Frank became the only batter to hit a ball completely out of Memorial Stadium. Batting against Cleveland's Luis Tiant, he rocketed the ball 451 feet on the fly from home plate. It rolled another 89 feet before a fan chased the ball down in the parking lot. "I knew it was gone, but I didn't know it went out," said Frank, "until I got back to the dugout. When they told me it went out, I found it hard to believe."

More than one player said that that home run was the turning point of the 1966 season. "Sometimes you point to one moment as the key," said reliever Moe Drabowsky. "To me, Frank's homer galvanized the team. It was like, 'We're going to be tough to beat this year.' "

Frank stood right over the plate, defying pitchers to hit him. He ran the bases with abandon and crashed into fences in the field. He was a leader both on and off the field and the team needed his kind of leadership. His aggressiveness was beyond what normal players were capable of demonstrating. He played with a fierceness that made losing hard to stomach. The Orioles rarely lost with him out there.

Pat Dobson, nicknamed "The Snake" because of his devastating curve ball, had never experienced a winning season in four years in Detroit and San Diego. He blossomed into a 20-game winner in 1971 in Baltimore, joining Dave McNally, Jim Palmer and Mike Cuellar in the 20-win circle.

and proceeded to pitch six and one-third innings of one-hit ball. The Bucs came back against Pat Dobson, who hadn't pitched in three weeks, to scratch out a 4-3 victory and square the series at two apiece.

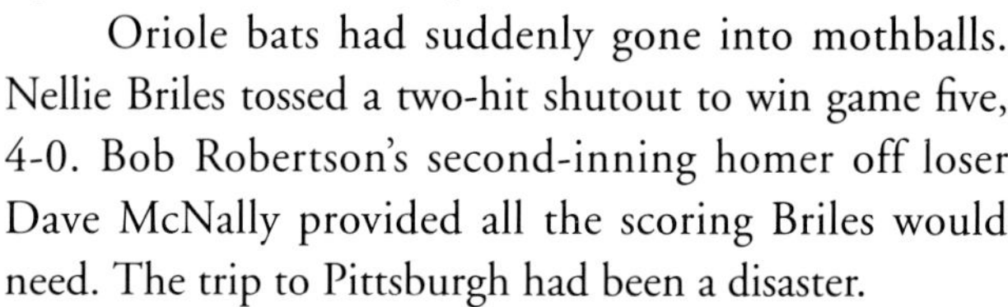

Oriole bats had suddenly gone into mothballs. Nellie Briles tossed a two-hit shutout to win game five, 4-0. Bob Robertson's second-inning homer off loser Dave McNally provided all the scoring Briles would need. The trip to Pittsburgh had been a disaster.

So after going up 2-0 in games, the Orioles were suddenly on the brink of elimination and desperately needed a victory. The Series returned to Baltimore for the October 16 pairing of Jim Palmer and Bob Moose. The Pirates scored two early runs, one on a Roberto Clemente homer, to take a 2-0 lead into the bottom of the sixth. Up to then the Birds had gone 22 straight innings without a run. Incredible as it seems, the team had managed only four hits over the previous 21 innings. Don Buford's sixth-inning home run broke the drought. In the seventh Davey Johnson tied the game with an RBI single. It remained tied through nine innings. In the top of the 10th Dave McNally made a rare relief appearance, walking Willie Stargell and getting Al Oliver to fly out to center.

The stage was set for a dramatic bottom of the 10th. Frank Robinson, playing on aching legs, drew a one-out walk against reliever Bob Miller. Merv Rettenmund grounded a single to center and Frank, with a strained achilles tendon, legged it into third base, dove to avoid the tag, and pulled a muscle in his left thigh. The next batter flew out to short center and Frank, with pain in both legs, tagged up and, racing to beat Vic Davalillo's throw, slid safely across the plate for the winning run. The Series was tied again.

The stage was now set for the decisive seventh game. Mike Cuellar and third-game winner Steve Blass hooked up in a classic pitchers' duel. Cuellar retired the first 11 batters he faced until Roberto Clemente tagged him for a solo home run. In the Pirate eighth, Stargell singled, then scored off Jose Pagan's hit-and-run double. The Orioles answered with a run in the bottom of the eighth and threatened with a man on third, but Blass retired Johnson to strand the runner and douse the Oriole threat. Blass would one day lose his control at the age of 31. But in the pivotal ninth inning he would retire Boog Powell, Frank Robinson, and Merv Rettenmund, giving the Pirates the World Series championship—the fourth in their long history. Series MVP Roberto Clemente (who would die a year later in a tragic plane crash in Puerto Rico on New Year's Eve, 1972), hit .414 in the series with two homers, one triple, two doubles, and seven singles, plus four RBI. The Orioles batted .205 in the series, used 19 pitchers, and committed nine errors.

With 318 wins in three years and one World Championship in three tries, the Birds were in good shape for another run in 1972. If they were going to win, however, it would be without Frank Robinson. This time it was the Oriole management that decided that at 36 Frank was just getting too old to contribute anymore.

Believing that young outfielder Don Baylor was about to blossom and that Rettenmund was an emerging star, new general manager Frank Cashen (Harry Dalton left to join the California Angels) gambled after the 1971 season and traded the one man responsible for four pennants in six years. Of great concern to Cashen too was Frank's salary, which by this time had climbed to $130,000. Frank and pitcher Pete Richert were traded to the Dodgers for four young players: pitchers Doyle Alexander and Bob O'Brien, catcher Sergio Robles, and

Elrod Hendricks, Mark Belanger, and Brooks congratulate Mike Cuellar after he defeats Oakland in game two of the 1971 ALCS.

outfielder Royle Stillman. In six seasons as an Oriole, Frank won a triple crown, was elected MVP, slugged 179 homers, drove in 545 runs, and hit an even .300. His departure signaled the end of a glorious era in Oriole baseball.

The Orioles didn't flop in 1972, but their team batting average plunged from .261 to .229. Only Roric Harrison's homer on the last day of the season gave the club an even 100. With the designated hitter arriving in 1973, Harrison's homer turned out to be the last by an American League pitcher. The team ERA was the lowest in club history, 2.54, and only Palmer, with 21 wins and a 2.04 ERA, and Cuellar with 18 victories, posted winning records. The 80-74 record in the strike-shortened season was good for third place, five-and-one-half games behind Detroit. Yet, as late as September 4, the Birds held first place. The strike left a sour taste in blue-collar Baltimore. Only 11,995 watched the opener against the Yankees after a 13-day delay to the start of the season. Only 655 were on hand for an August make-up date with Chicago.

The high point of the 1972 season came on July 3 in Detroit. Trailing 2-0, the Birds exploded for 15 runs and 17 hits in the final four innings to win 15-3. The 21 Oriole hits set a record for a nine-inning game. But mostly the 1972 season mirrored the 59 one-run games, of which 33 were defeats. Nine games were lost in extra innings. One extra-inning bright spot occurred on June 14 in Oakland when Dave McNally outdueled Catfish Hunter 2-1 on Bobby Grich's 10th-inning homer. McNally fell to a 13-17 record in '72 despite a 2.95 ERA.

Runs were in short supply. Buford slumped to a .206 average. Belanger fell to .186 and Andy Etchebarren to .202. Brooks Robinson and Boog Powell barely hit over .250, but by the standards of 1972, those were blockbuster averages. Rettenmund, who hit well over .300 the two years before, plunged to .233. Baylor reminded no one of Frank Robinson with his 11 home runs and 38 RBI to go with a .253 batting average. From the Robinson deal, only Doyle Alexander made any contribution, winning six games and losing eight. He would go on to win 35 and lose 37 in four and a half seasons as an Oriole. Meanwhile, Frank would go on to have three more solid seasons before becoming baseball's first black manager with the 1975 Cleveland Indians.

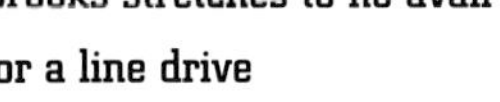

Brooks stretches to no avail for a line drive

Jim Palmer hits the deck against the Pirates during the 1971 World Series at Memorial Stadium. That's shortstop Jackie Hernandez taking the toss from second baseman Dave Cash.

Still, the "best damn team in baseball," as Earl Weaver dubbed them in the 1969-1970-1971 era, was not finished. In 1973 the Orioles' emphasis went from power to speed. For the second straight year there was an ill-fated trade. This time general manager Frank Cashen sent 16-game winner Pat Dobson, regular second baseman Dave Johnson, pitcher Roric Harrison, and backup catcher Johnny Oates to the Atlanta Braves

Gold Gloves

Since 1957, when the Gold Glove Awards were begun by Rawlings, the Orioles have won 50, second only to the Cardinals, who lead with 57½. They had gone six seasons without a winner until Cal Ripken won in 1991 and 1992. During an 11-year span from 1969 through 1979 the Orioles won 33 Gold Gloves. A total of nine Orioles won more than one Gold Glove, headed by Brooks Robinson's 16 (which tied Jim Kaat for most all-time). Paul Blair and Mark Belanger won eight each, Jim Palmer and Bobby Grich four each, and Davey Johnson and Eddie Murray three each. Cal Ripken and Luis Aparicio each won two.

for catcher Earl Williams. During the previous two seasons, Williams had slugged 61 homers and driven in 174 runs. Williams was slow-moving and outspoken and didn't hide his dislike for catching. He clashed repeatedly with Weaver and only lasted two seasons in Baltimore, hitting 34 homers. Still, the Orioles would win the division both years, even without Davey Johnson, who clouted a record 43 homers for a second baseman as a Brave in 1973.

A new rule, the designated hitter, debuted in 1973; the Orioles found themselves one of the best in former National League batting champ Tommy Davis. Davis, who had played with nine teams since leaving the Dodgers after the 1966 season, hit .306 with 89 RBI in his first season as the Oriole DH. He had finally found a home.

Young Don Baylor, the heir apparent to Frank Robinson, was platooned in his early years by Earl Weaver. After socking 21 homers and hitting .282 in 1975, Baylor was dealt to Oakland as part of the trade to acquire Reggie Jackson. Baylor posted outstanding seasons with the Angels and Yankees and was named manager of the expansion Colorado Rockies.

As a club, the Orioles hit .266 in 1973 and had their trademark pitching and defense rolling in high gear. But it was something else that sparked the 1973 Orioles to a 97-65 record and eight-game advantage over second-place Boston. That something was speed. The Birds led the league with a club record 146 steals, 32 by Don Baylor. A couple of rookie speedsters, "Super Bee" Al Bumbry and Rich Coggins, competed against each other for Rookie of the Year honors. Bumbry, a Vietnam veteran, hit a lusty .337 and stole 23 bases. The "Bee" also pounded out 11 triples including three in one game in Milwaukee, the day that the Birds clinched the pennant. The 22-year-old Coggins hit .319, drove in 41 runs, and stole 17 bases.

Frank Robinson, hobbled by a torn achilles tendon, nonetheless scored the winning run on a Brooks Robinson sac fly in the bottom of the 10th of game six of the '71 World Series. The win extended the Series to a seventh game, which the Pirates took 2-1 to capture the Series.

The Birds stayed near the top for several months before reeling off a 14-game winning streak in August. Jim Palmer had another sensational year, winning 22 games with a 2.40 ERA. For his efforts he won his first Cy Young Award. Bumbry won Rookie of the Year honors. Brooks Robinson, Paul Blair, Mark Belanger, and Bobby Grich all won Gold Gloves for fielding excellence—it was Brooks' 14th straight. Grich became the best second baseman in the league, setting a major-league record in committing only five errors while handling 945 chances, a .995 fielding percentage. Weaver, overlooked for the great Orioles' success of 1969-1970-1971, was finally voted Manager of the Year in 1973. Even Earl had admitted rather humbly during the glory days, "My best game plan is to sit on the bench and call out specific instructions like, 'C'mon, Boog,' 'Get hold of one, Frank,' or 'Let's go, Brooks.'"

It was a year filled with highlights. McNally, who would finish with a 17-17 record, won the opener on April 6 with a three-hit shutout over the Brewers. Brooks Robinson hit two homers and drove in four while Baylor homered, tripled, and doubled twice in the 10-0 win. Six days later, McNally gave up only one hit through nine innings to win 1-0 over the Tigers in 10 innings. On August 15 McNally pitched a two-hitter, beating the Rangers 5-1. It was McNally's 17th straight win over the Senators-turned-Rangers, giving him a lifetime 27-4 record against the franchise. On June 16, Palmer, feeling under the weather, took the mound against the Texas Rangers and retired the first 25 batters he faced before Ken Suarez broke up the perfect game with a one-out ninth-inning single. Palmer wound up with a two-hit, 9-1 win. He had another no-hitter going on July 27 against the Indians when

George Hendrick singled in the eighth. Palmer finished with a one-hitter, winning 9-0.

The Oriole defense, still the best in baseball, turned in two triple plays in '73. Blair showed no signs of slipping in center as he batted .280. During the 14-game win streak, Paulie hit a rare inside-the-park grand slam off Paul Splittorf in the 10-1 Bird victory. Now came the American League Championship Series with Oakland. The World Champs from the year before were heavy favorites to beat the Birds.

Al Bumbry became an instant fan favorite in 1973 when he hit .337 and captured Americn League Rookie of the Year honors. The Vietnam veteran eventually replaced Paul Blair in center field and played on the 1979 and 1983 World Series teams. Probably the fastest player in Oriole history, Al holds the club's stolen base record with 252.

Palmer pitched one of the most unforgettable games of his career, blanking the A's 6-0 in the first game of the 1973 playoffs. The Birds knocked out Vida Blue with a four-run first inning, and Jim went on to fan 12.

In game two Oakland exploded for four home runs, two off the bat of Sal Bando. The A's won 6-3 in squaring the best-of-five.

When the series moved to Oakland Mike Cuellar hurled a gem, giving up just three hits through 11 innings. He struck out 11 but Ken Holtzman matched Mike and won, 2-1, thanks to Bert Campaneris' 11th-inning home run, his second of the playoffs after only four all season.

Another pennant by the A's would establish them as the best team in baseball (or at least the league), a title the Orioles felt still belonged to them, despite last year's stumble. So the stakes were even higher than usual. Oakland scored three off Palmer in the second inning of game four, sending Jim to an early shower. They led 4-0 heading into the seventh behind Blue's two-hit pitching. But in the seventh Andy Etchebarren hit the biggest homer of his career, a three-run shot, and Bobby Grich hit a solo homer off Rollie Fingers in the eighth to lift the Orioles to a dramatic 5-4 win. "I remember being out in the field thinking in the sixth that I'll probably be home raking leaves the next day," remembered Brooks Robinson, who singled in the first Oriole run. "Instead we were playing the next day with a trip to the World Series on the line."

Unfortunately the Orioles were no match for future Hall of Famer Jim "Catfish" Hunter, who pitched a five-hit 3-0 shutout to send the A's to their second straight pennant.

Thus concluded the Orioles' first 20 seasons back in the American League. The log showed 13 seasons with .500 or better records, four American League pennants, five divisional crowns, and two world championships. As they began their third decade, they were an aging team, with a 20-year veteran at third and 10 others over the age of 30. Still, the farm system was continuing to produce new prospects and good days loomed.

The Orioles' 21st year, 1974, turned out to be another near miss and the last hurrah for many Oriole greats. Most of the season's highlights took place in the last five weeks of the regular season. On June 18, however, second baseman Bobby Grich became the first Oriole to slug three home runs in one game at Memorial Stadium. "I hit two sliders my first two times up off Joe Decker. The third homer was off Tom Burgmeier, a junkballer. All three were hit to the same spot in the left field stands." The Orioles won the game, 10-1, behind Ross Grimsley's pitching. Grimsley, obtained in a trade with the Reds that sent Merv Rettenmund to Cincinnati after the 1973 season, became one of the big surprises of 1974. Grimsley took up the slack for the injured Jim Palmer, posting an 18-13 record with 17 complete games. Rettenmund had slipped from back-to-back .322 and .318 seasons to a .233 mark in 1972 and .262 in 1973. Merv made the mistake of listening to Earl Weaver, who wanted him to pull the ball and hit more home runs to fill the void left by Frank Robinson's absence. Rettenmund was a natural line-drive hitter to all fields. He tried to do what Weaver wanted and fouled up his swing in the process.

In late August, the Birds were going nowhere, under .500 and eight games behind the Red Sox. Then miraculously, on August 29 in Texas, a winning

Obtained from Cincinnati before the 1974 season, left-hander Ross Grimsley won 18 games and helped pitch the Orioles to the 1974 Eastern Division pennant.

streak of epic proportions began. First there were 10 straight wins including a doubleheader sweep on Labor Day against the Red Sox that saw Ross Grimsley win 1-0 on a three-hitter and Mike Cuellar follow with another 1-0 win on a two-hitter. Jim Palmer, who would battle elbow problems and fall to a 7-12 record for the first losing season of his career, followed with a three-hit 6-0 win over Boston. In three games, the first-place Red Sox had been held to eight hits, all singles, in 27 scoreless innings. Two days later in Cleveland, the Orioles set an American League record with their fifth straight shutout, blanking the Tribe twice with Dave McNally and Mike Cuellar helping to rewrite history. The next night, September 7, the winning streak reached 10 but the consecutive shutout innings streak was snapped at 54 (a new league record) when Ross Grimsley took a 3-0 lead into the ninth before surrendering a two-run homer to Charlie Spikes.

When the season ended on October 2, the Orioles had won 28 of their last 34 games and nosed out the Yankees by two games and the fading Red Sox by seven.

There were thrills aplenty in the 1974 home stretch. On September 9 in Milwaukee Darrell Porter's ninth-inning grand slam erased a 5-1 Oriole lead, but the Birds scored on a wild pitch in the 11th and Paul Blair saved the day by running down George Scott's deep drive to center with two runners on to end the game. Two days later Boog Powell ended the longest game of the year with a 17th-inning RBI single to beat the Yankees 3-2. On September 17 Paul Blair belted a three-run homer and Jim Palmer blanked the Yankees 4-0 at Shea Stadium. (Yankee Stadium was being renovated). The next day Mike Cuellar joined the 20-win club for the fourth time, beating the Yankees 10-4 and pulling the Orioles within a half game of the lead. McNally pitched a three-hit shutout the following night, winning 7-0 as the Birds moved into first place by a half game. Their team ERA in the 24 previous games was 1.76.

On September 21 the game began at 2:21 and, because of numerous rain delays, ended at 8:48. Thanks to Dwight Evans' three-run ninth-inning homer the Red Sox came back to win 6-5 and drop the Birds one game back. On September 27, in another 17-inning marathon, the Orioles scored the only run on Bob Oliver's swinging bunt for a 1-0 win over Milwaukee. Jim Palmer pitched 12 shutout innings and the Birds led the division by a game.

On October 1 the Orioles stretched their streak to 27-6 by winning their eighth straight with a 7-6 win over the Tigers in the afternoon. That night at County Stadium in Milwaukee, the Brewers scored a 10th-inning run to edge the Yankees and the pennant race was over. Yankee broadcaster Phil Rizzuto was in tears, trying to describe the loss of not only the game but what would have been the first Yankee pennant in 10 years.

Mike Cuellar, the crafty Cuban with a bat-freezing screwball, went from 8-11 in Houston in 1968 to 23-11 in 1969 in Baltimore, good enough to help him earn a share of the Cy Young with Denny McLain. He followed that season with 24 wins in 1970 and 20 in 1971. Few lefties in Oriole history have been better.

At 37, Brooks Robinson enjoyed his last solid season, hitting .288 with 159 hits to put him within reach of the coveted 3,000-hit mark. Paul Blair hit .261 with 17 homers to share Oriole MVP honors with 37-year-old Mike Cuellar. "Crazy Horse" had a magnificent season with 22 wins and 20 complete games, including five shutouts.

In what was to be Dave McNally's last season as an Oriole, the classy lefty posted a 16-10 record with four shutouts. On the night of September 24, Baltimore native

Al Kaline and the Tigers came to town for a brief two-game series. At the start of the first game Kaline was sitting on 2,999 base hits. Facing McNally in the fourth inning as his parents, family members, and friends watched from the stands, Al doubled into the right field corner to become the 12th hitter in history to reach 3,000 hits. "There's a story behind the fact McNally gave up my 3,000th," says Kaline, who entered the Hall of Fame in his first year of eligibility in 1979. "In spring training he called me about setting up a car agency in his hometown of Billings, Montana. He wanted some contacts in Detroit. 'By the way,' he said, 'I had a dream last night that you got your 3,000th hit off of me.' Sure enough, five months later in Baltimore his dream became reality."

Once again the Orioles faced the powerful Oakland A's in the ALCS and like the year before they started fast, winning game one. Brooks Robinson, Paul Blair, and Bobby Grich homered off Catfish Hunter as Mike Cuellar won 6-3 in Oakland. Then the bats went silent. The Birds scored only one run in losing three straight. In the pivotal third game Vida Blue, who had lost his previous two playoff starts against Baltimore, pitched a brilliant two-hitter and won 1-0. Jim Palmer, the hard-luck loser, yielded just four hits, but one was a solo homer to Sal Bando.

More bad luck came to Mike Cuellar and reliever Ross Grimsley who combined to pitch a one-hitter and lost 2-1 as Oakland wrapped up the playoffs in four games. Cuellar's downfall was control, or lack of it. Never had he walked more than six in his Oriole career but in four and two-thirds innings he walked nine, including Gene Tenace with the bases loaded. Reggie Jackson's RBI double off Grimsley in the seventh scored what proved to be the game-winning run. Boog Powell singled in Blair in the ninth off reliever Rollie Fingers in what turned out to be Boog's last hit as an Oriole. Oakland won the game, 2-1, and went on to beat the Dodgers in the World Series for their third straight World Championship.

By the following season, Boog Powell was gone, traded to Cleveland for journeyman catcher Dave Duncan. Boog, with his club-leading 303 career homers, became expendable when the O's acquired Houston's Lee May in a trade for Rob Andrews and Enos Cabell. Gone too was all-time Oriole lefty McNally and his 181 career wins, traded to Montreal for Ken Singleton and Mike Torrez. It was a shrewd deal. Singleton would have 10 solid years in an Oriole uniform and Torrez would become a 20-game winner. Only 32, McNally retired just two months into the 1975 season due to chronic arm trouble. The transition was under way that would bridge the halcyon years of the late 1960s and early 1970s to a new generation of players who would create their own magic by the end of the decade.

1975–1979: Turbulence and Transition

The 1975 season started on a high note. Newcomer Lee May, in his first official at-bat as an Oriole, bashed a three-run homer and Jim Palmer and the Birds clobbered Detroit, 10-0, in the opener. But then a six-game losing streak in late April and a whopper of a slump beginning in mid-May resulted in 11 losses in 12 games.

The inner sanctuary of the 1979 Orioles

The losses put the Orioles in a catch-up situation similar to 1974. This time, however, they couldn't overcome the deficit despite posting the second best record in baseball (73-43) during the last four months of the season. Only pennant-bound Cincinnati did better. No one did better after the All-Star break. Still it wasn't enough as the Red Sox went on to win by four-and-one-half games over the second place Orioles.

Bobby Grich played five full seasons in Baltimore, winning four Gold Gloves for his fielding wizardry at second base. In 1973 he set an all-time major league fielding record by committing only five errors in 945 total chances, fielding percentage of .995. Here he forces Boston's Bernie Carbo before throwing on to first to complete a double play.

All the newcomers contributed. Kenny Singleton hit an even .300 and won Oriole MVP honors. May finished with 20 homers and 99 RBI. Torrez posted his first 20-win season with 17 complete games. As for veteran Jim Palmer, it was his best year yet. He led the major leagues with a 2.09 ERA, 10 shutouts, and tied Catfish Hunter in wins with 23. Palmer was voted the Cy Young Award for the second time.

Rick Dempsey guards home plate awaiting the throw with a runner bearing down. Dempsey, one of the few players to see action in four different decades, caught more games than any catcher in Oriole history.

Baseball's face would change forever after the 1975 season when arbiter Peter Seitz ruled that the reserve clause, which bound a player to a team forever, was unconstitutional. The original grievance had been filed by pitchers Andy Messersmith and former Oriole great Dave McNally. The ground rules changed drastically and nobody knew how drastic the changes would be.

Not counting the strike-shortened season of 1972, the Orioles had won 90 or more games every year since 1968. That string was broken in 1976 when the Orioles won 88 games, finishing 10½ behind the front-running Yankees. Hank Peters replaced Frank Cashen as general manager. Peters began his baseball career after World War II in the farm department of the St. Louis Browns, and later spent several years in player personnel with the Kansas City A's and the Cleveland Indians.

The first Nicaraguan-born player to reach the big leagues, Dennis Martinez won 14 games in his first full season in 1977. He would win 108 games with the Orioles before being traded to the Expos in 1986 where he would win 100 more.

Known as a conservative, Peters surprised everyone by engineering two "blockbuster" deals to totally transform the 1976 Orioles. In America's bicentennial year there were fireworks galore on the shores of the Chesapeake. Late in spring training, just a week before the season opener, Peters pulled off a stupendously controversial trade. He sent starter Don Baylor, the .282 hitting outfielder with 25 homers in 1975, along with 20-game winner Mike Torrez and top pitching prospect Paul Mitchell, to the Oakland A's. In return the Birds acquired slugger Reggie Jackson, left-handed pitcher Ken Holtzman, and minor-league pitcher Bill Van Bommell. The trade shocked Baylor. He broke into tears when he heard the

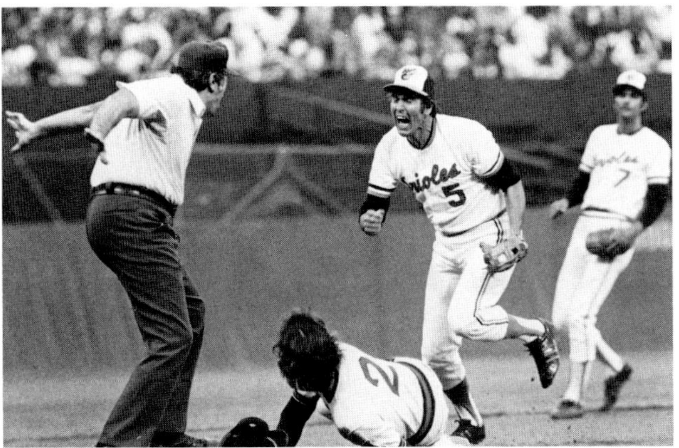

By the mid-1970s Brooks Robinson's long and distinguished career was winding down, but the competitive fire still burned. Brooks thought he had the out. Mark Belanger looks on from behind.

Brooks Robinson

What more can be said that already hasn't been said about Brooks Robinson? He went from humble beginnings to superstardom as the greatest third baseman in baseball history. Both Frank "Home Run" Baker and Casey Stengel, who spent over a half century in the game, agreed that Brooks was the best third baseman they ever saw, and they saw them all.

Little Rock, Arkansas, resident Lindsey Deal, an old minor league friend of Paul Richards, sent the Oriole skipper a letter about Brooks in 1955, calling him a natural third baseman with a lot of baseball savvy who was always cool when the chips were down.

That letter led to a $4,000 bonus and a career that culminated in his induction into the Baseball Hall of Fame. It didn't come easy. Brooks worked hard to perfect his skills and he ended up revolutionizing the third base position. Brooks combined quick reflexes, soft hands, an accurate throwing arm, and great baseball instincts.

He was also a gamer. Once, in Detroit, he crashed into a concrete ledge that tore open his lower jaw and chipped five teeth. Almost unconscious, Brooks refused to go to the hospital and stayed in the game. He remained the regular third baseman for 19 seasons, winning 16 Gold Gloves, and starting 15 straight All-Star games. His fielding in the 1970 World Series prompted one losing Red to remark, "He can field a ball with a pair of pliers." Said the late Pie Trayner, the third baseman he's most often compared to, "I once thought of giving him some tips, but dropped the idea. He's just the best there is."

Brooks was just as dazzling off the field as he was on. He was at the top of the fans' list for his politeness, friendliness, and down-home, easy-going manner. "Other stars had fans," said one observer. "Robby made friends." His patience and kindly nature with fans is legendary. Many Hall of Famers go into shells and retreat from the spotlight, only emerging when there's a chance for big bucks. Not Brooks. Brooks never changed from the moment he put on his first uniform to the day he took it off. The same holds true as a Hall of Famer in retirement. Never has a player meant more to a franchise and more to a city than Brooks has meant to the Orioles and the city of Baltimore. Brooks Robinson achieved greatness as a player and maybe even more important, as a human being.

Another Earl Weaver row, something Oriole fans never tired of. Before his first retirement after the 1982 season, Earl had been ejected from 89 games, including once in the World Series.

Earlier in spring training Jackson had dropped hints that he had grown weary of bumping heads with A's owner Charlie Finley and would welcome a trade. But when the trade was made, Jackson balked and refused to report. It took a full month, including three weeks of the regular season, before Reggie finally acquiesced and showed up. Meanwhile Oriole players separated into pro- and anti-Reggie factions. On the field Earl Weaver struggled to maintain order. The Orioles' record before Reggie reported was 6-9.

Blockbuster number two happened in mid-June with the Birds mired in fourth place with a 25-31 record. Peters sent Holtzman, whose surly attitude had caused friction with the other players, to the Yankees along with veterans Elrod Hendricks, Grant Jackson, and Doyle Alexander. In return the Orioles received pitchers Rudy May, Tippy Martinez, Dave Pagan, and minor-leaguers Scott McGregor and Rick Dempsey. The comings and goings were reminiscent of the Paul Richards era.

news. Raised in the Oriole system to be the heir-apparent to Frank Robinson, Don was blossoming into one of the most feared hitters in the league.

If 1976 was, in a sense, the revival of an era, it was also the end of one. Brooks Robinson, the greatest Oriole of all, second to only Ty Cobb in games played

Kenny Singleton played baseball with a quiet grace that embodied the Oriole philosophy of hustle and total dedication. Three times he batted over .300 as an Oriole with a high of .328 in 1977. Kenny spent nine seasons in Baltimore, from 1975-1984. A three-time winner of the Oriole MVP award, Ken won the prestigious Roberto Clemente Award in 1982.

in American League history, relinquished his starting job to the younger Doug DeCinces. Two other stalwarts from the glory days, Gold Glove centerfielder Paul Blair and four-time 20-game winner Mike Cuellar, were relegated to supporting roles.

Several players had big years in 1976. Most Valuable Oriole Lee May led the league in RBI with 109 to accompany his 25 homers. Despite a slow start, Jim Palmer won 22 to tie San Diego's Randy Jones for the most major-league wins. It was Palmer's sixth 20-win season in the last seven years. In June, young Wayne Garland jumped from the bullpen to a starter's role and went on to become the 17th Oriole 20-game winner since 1968. Garland won 12 of his first 13 decisions, lost only seven, pitched 14 complete games, and posted a brilliant 2.67 ERA.

Despite missing 28 games (including the first 16 when he didn't report), Reggie Jackson chalked up some impressive statistics. He led the Birds with 27 homers, driving in 91 to go with a .277 average. He also stole a career-high 28 bases and led the league in slugging percentage (.502). Until 1976, Reggie had hit only one grand slam. He hit three as an Oriole and all three were game winners. He missed several games with a sprained wrist and a few more after being beaned by New York's Dock Ellis on July 27. Returning to the lineup four nights later, he homered against Detroit.

For the second straight year the Orioles topped the million mark in attendance, but Peters was reluctant to open the purse strings and sign several of his top players. Jackson, Grich, and Garland all went through the new free agent re-entry draft after the 1976 season and ended up leaving Baltimore. The Orioles preferred to build from within while making trades and disdaining expensive free agents. Peters admitted that after 30 years in baseball, he was operating in the great unknown. "What greeted me was a chaotic adjustment to a new system. There was free agency and then in 1977 came expansion. It was a confusing period because nobody knew what we'd end up with."

Peters' big mistake was not signing Jackson to a new contract. Reggie became "Mr. October" with the Yankees and went on to spark them to World Series triumphs in 1977 and 1978. "Hank just didn't foresee what free agency would bring," remembers Reggie. "If it was a year later they wouldn't have let me go because they would have seen the kind of dollars involved. If I would have signed for five years and the $250,000-$300,000 I was asking for I'd have been an Oriole forever. There's so much tradition there. I got along with Earl Weaver and Hank Peters. I would have died a Bird and enjoyed it." Reggie firmly believes had he stayed it would have been the Orioles and not the Yankees in the 1977 and '78 World Series. His low point in 1976? "That's easy," says Reggie. "The last two weeks of the season when we were eliminated, because it showed that if I had played the whole year, we'd have won."

More than any Oriole, Lee May helped ease the transition for Eddie Murray to the big leagues. Murray eventually replaced him at first base. Obtained from Houston before the 1975 season, Lee belted 123 home runs in his six seasons in Baltimore.

The next season, 1977, was a historic one for the Orioles for several reasons. Reason one was their record.

Reggie Jackson spent one turbulent season in Baltimore in 1976. He reported late but once he made up his mind to play, he gave Earl Weaver, his teammates, and the fans everything he had. Reggie hit 27 homers and drove in 91 runs in 134 games in Baltimore before joining the Yankees as a free agent.

Rick Dempsey played 24 seasons, a remarkable achievement considering his modest hitting ability. Yet his hitting was good enough to cop World Series MVP honors in 1983. His strength was in handling pitchers.

Without Reggie or Bobby Grich or Wayne Garland—and picked by the experts to slip to the second division—the Orioles stunned the baseball world by winning 97 games, losing out to the Yankees by just 2½ games. They tied the Red Sox for second. With 10 days left in the season, they were only 1½ games out. The season marked Brooks Robinson's swansong and Eddie Murray's first in the majors. The 21-year-old Murray was rushed to the big leagues, and proved it wasn't too soon by setting an Oriole rookie record with 27 homers. He tied Lee May as club leader.

Mike Flanagan dubbed him "Stan the Man Unusual." Earl Weaver called him by another name, "Fullpack," which is what Earl would smoke every time he took the mound. Reliever Don Stanhouse was a premier shortman in the 1979 pennant year, but he never failed to elicit drama when he pitched. He would walk the bases loaded and then bail himself out with a big strikeout. Stanhouse saved 21 games in 1979.

His .283 average and 88 RBI earned Murray Rookie of the Year honors. Both May and Singleton drove in 99 runs with Singleton winning Oriole MVP honors with his 24 homers and .328 average, still the highest one-season average in Oriole history.

Brooks' last great moment took place on the night of April 19 when the Orioles trailed Cleveland by three runs in the bottom of the 10th at Memorial Stadium. Lee May singled in one run and then Brooks came up with two on to pinch hit for Larry Harlow. The count went to 3-2 and Robinson fouled off several pitches from Dave LaRoche, and then smashed a long home run to left to produce an instant 6-5 victory. The fans sprang to their feet, saluting Brooks with wild applause not only for the game-winning homer but for his 23 years of exemplary play. It was the 268th and last home run of Brooks' Hall of Fame career. It was also the first of 12 extra-inning wins pulled off by the Orioles in the 1977 season.

There were several moments worth recalling in 1977. The four-game series with the Yankees from July 8-11 ranks at the top. The Yankees won the first game but the Birds reeled off three straight wins over the World Champs, including two late-inning come-from-behind efforts. That series drew a record 154,835, gave the Orioles 10 wins in their last 11 games, and pulled them to within a half game of Boston.

Rick Dempsey races to the mound to congratulate Scott McGregor after he pitched a complete game 8-4 victory over the Pirates in game three of the 1979 World Series.

Catcher Rick Dempsey was hit on the wrist by a bone-breaking Don Gullett pitch in the first game of the Yankee showdown. Dave Skaggs took over behind the plate. To fill the void the Birds called up a journeyman backup named Dave Criscione. He was about to become an Oriole legend. Dave lined out in his only at-bat before the All-Star break. Then, during the break, his wife Marge gave birth to their first child. Three days later Criscione made his first start in the second game of a twin-bill with Milwaukee. He got his first base hit in the fourth, his second in the sixth, and in the eighth he laid down a perfect sacrifice to move the winning run to third. He received standing ovations for all three appearances. But that game was just a prelude. The next night he socked a dramatic 11th-inning pinch

One of the most popular players in Orioles history, Mike Flanagan spent 14 seasons in an Oriole uniform. Fourth on the club's all-time win list with 141, Flanny won the 1979 Cy Young Award with a 23-9 record.

Scott McGregor

hit homer to give the Birds a 4-3 win. Criscione was sent back to Rochester in early August, never to be heard from again. His big-league career consisted of three hits in nine at bats for a .333 average and one home run. "I had a higher home run ratio than Babe Ruth," jokes Dave, who now coaches college baseball in upstate New York at Fredonia State University.

While Criscione spent only two weeks in the major leagues, Brooks Robinson spent over 20 years. He retired as an active player on Sunday, August 21, to make room for Rick Dempsey's return. In 2,896 games, the Orioles' beloved third baseman had amassed 2,848 hits and 1,357 RBI. In 39 postseason games he had batted .303. His last hit was a seventh-inning single off Steve Mingori at Kansas City on June 3, an Oriole victory that saw the Birds pull off a triple play to end the game 7-5. Brooks Robinson rewrote the record book for fielding. Umpire Ed Hurley once said about Brooks, "He came down from a higher league." Handling 9,165 chances in 23 years, Brooks committed only 263 errors. He won an amazing 16 Gold Gloves.

Scott McGregor

When Scott McGregor was in his prime in the seven-year period from 1978 through 1984, the hitters would practically get themselves out. He tied them up in knots. From 1978 through 1985 he was the only major league pitcher over .500 in each of those eight seasons, capped by a 20–8 record in 1980. Yet to watch him pitch, you wondered how he did it. He wasn't that fast. He wasn't that big. And he threw in an unorthodox manner across his body that made his delivery seem even slower.

The Orioles' record book shows him as fifth all-time in wins with 138, fourth in innings pitched, seventh in strikeouts, and fifth in shutouts. Like left-hander Dave McNally before him, McGregor was a money pitcher who came through in the big games. In the championship year of 1983 he won 16 of his last 17 decisions on the road. He pitched the playoff clincher in Anaheim in 1979 and the World Series clincher in Philadelphia in 1983.

A former teammate of George Brett at El Segundo High School in California, Scotty was 51–5 in four years with an ERA of 0.29. At the plate he out-hit Brett.

His career as a Yankee was going nowhere. It took the big trade with New York in June of 1976 to bring him to Baltimore and give him a new lease on life. Developing a wicked changeup put Scotty into the pitching elite. "My pitching motion was very deceptive," said McGregor, who became a minister after his playing days. "My fastball was only 86 miles per hour and my changeup was 73 miles per hour. I slowed my curve to 63 miles per hour to give myself three pitches that were 10 mph different but yet were thrown from the same motion. So the hitters had no chance."

Scotty took the power away from the hitters because they had to stand flat-footed, wondering what was coming next. Most of the time they'd hit the ball on the ground or fly to Al Bumbry in center field.

Injuries began taking their toll on Scotty in 1987 when he developed a shoulder problem. It was all downhill after that and after an 0–3 start in 1988, he announced his retirement at the age of 34. "I lost my velocity and with it went my deception," he lamented. "There's only so many pitches in your arm and I was lucky to pitch 12 years and throw over 2,000 innings. But when you lose velocity off an 83 mph fastball, you're in trouble. My pitches were all coming in at the same speed practically and I was just beating my head against the wall."

Now he knew what he'd been doing to opposing hitters for eight years.

On Sunday afternoon September 18, 1977, a record regular-season crowd of 51,798 came out to pay tribute to Mr. Oriole on "Thanks Brooks Day." Brooks was driven around the stadium in the back of a 1955 Cadillac convertible to a lengthy and emotional standing ovation. Doug DeCinces ran out on the field,

Opponents' Home Runs

Hall of Fame slugger Harmon Killebrew hit more home runs than anybody against the Orioles. The Killer clouted 70 homers, including the longest ever hit at Memorial Stadium, some 471 feet from home plate, which he hit over the hedge in left-center in 1964 off Milt Pappas. Mickey Mantle is a far-back second with 44, followed by Reggie Jackson and Al Kaline with 40. Rocky Colavito slugged 39, Jim Rice 36 and Frank Howard 35.

ripped out the third-base bag, and gave it to Brooks. The tribute was a sincere and genuine outpouring of affection for a man who gave every ounce of himself on and off the field. As sportswriter Gordon Beard told the throng, in referring to the Reggie Jackson candy bar in New York, "In Baltimore we have a different set of values. We don't name candy bars after Brooks. Here, people name their children after Brooks."

Brooks Robinson rewrote the record book for his play at third base. Here he tags Red Sox shortstop Rick Burleson in a 1975 game with third base coach Don Zimmer looking on.

Atlanta sportswriter Furman Bisher wrote, "The baseball park was no place for his performances. He should have played at Carnegie Hall. No player of his time, and a rare few before him, have dominated their position as Robinson did. Aaron had his Clemente, Mays had his Mantle, Bench his Munson. But Brooks Robinson was third base to his generation. If third base has come up a bit shy as a cornerstone for greatness, it's probably because of the contradictory requirements that make a third baseman. He's supposed to have the indestructible qualities of a courthouse monument, a chest of iron, an arm like a deer rifle, yet play his ground with ballet delicateness and represent his place in the batting order with more than a trace of power. What Robinson did was bring a new kind of glory to the hot corner."

Brooks Robinson's 268th and last home run occurred in dramatic fashion. On April 19, 1977, with less than 5,000 fans in the stands, Brooks pinch hit in the 10th inning against Cleveland, with the Birds trailing 5-3. He worked the count to 3-2 before fouling off several pitches, then belted a pitch from lefty Dave LaRoche into the left field stands for a three-run homer and 6-5 Oriole win.

With Brooks gone, only Belanger and Jim Palmer remained from the World Series teams. Palmer won his last seven decisions in 1977 to finish with a 20-11 record, his seventh 20-win season in the last eight years. He had a remarkable 22 complete games and a sparkling 2.91 ERA. There was also the one big constant, Earl Weaver, who was voted Manager of the Year after the 1977 season. Earl did some of his best work during this transitional period. He even forfeited a game in Toronto when the umpires didn't order a tarp removed down the left-field line. He was rewarded with a new three-year contract, the first multi-year pact offered to an Oriole manager since Hank Bauer signed on for two years after the 1966 season. While Earl was solidly established in Baltimore, his coaches were coveted by other teams. Billy Hunter was lured away to manage the Rangers and George Bamberger took over the Milwaukee Brewers.

Many felt Weaver would have trouble adapting to a younger team but instead he gained even more respect for his ability to draw the most out of his players. In 1978, for the ninth time in 11 seasons, his team hit the 90-win level, although they fell to fourth place, nine games behind the Yankees. Another slow start (they were outscored 40-11 while losing three straight in Milwaukee to start the year) made it an uphill battle all year. Even a 26-7 spree in June couldn't bring them closer than 6½ from the top. They later lost eight straight and then won eight straight. The low point came in Toronto on June 26 when the Blue Jays bombed the Orioles 24-10 as the Birds set records for most runs and

A record crowd of 51,798 poured into Memorial Stadium on September 18, 1977, for Thanks Brooks Day. The Orioles all-time player was retiring after 23 seasons. The emotional ceremonies reached a peak when third baseman Doug DeCinces ripped the third base bag from its position and handed it to Brooks. He took a ceremonial drive around the park sitting on the back of a 1955 Cadillac.

hits allowed in one game, 24 each. During the game Weaver used catcher Ellie Hendricks and outfielder Larry Harlow as pitchers. The Orioles scored a season high 10 runs and still lost by 14.

Hendricks, who entered the game in the 5th with the Orioles down 24-6, said, "Weaver called the bullpen and was half laughing. He said, 'Can you throw strikes?' I said 'Yeah.' He said 'How long would it take you to get ready?' I said 'You're speaking to Elrod.' And he said, 'I know. How long would it take you to get ready?' I said, 'For what?' Earl said, 'Well, you're in the game.'"

Ellie's game plan was to throw the ball inside and hope the hitters would pull it and to throw it as slow as he could to mess up their timing. As it turned out, Ellie gave up only one hit and no runs in 2½ innings and struck out a batter.

Individually Eddie Murray won team MVP honors with 27 homers, 95 RBI, and a .285 average. Doug DeCinces had a banner year, banging out a team high 28 homers and setting a club record with a 21-game hitting streak. Lee May hit 20 or more homers for the 11th straight year to join only 14 others who had reached that level of long-ball consistency. In the field, Mark Belanger won his eighth Gold Glove with a .985 percentage, boosting his career mark to .977, tops in American League history. Second baseman Rich Dauer, in his second season, broke two major-league records for fielding excellence with 86 straight errorless games and 424 consecutive chances without an error.

On the mound, Mike Flanagan, Dennis Martinez and Scott McGregor all established themselves as future Oriole stars by winning 19, 16, and 15 respectively. On September 26, Flanagan had a no-hitter for 8⅔ innings against the Indians before Gary Alexander broke it up with a solo homer. For Jim Palmer, it was his last great season. A 21-12 record gave him eight 20-win campaigns, a feat that had gone unmatched in the American League since 1935 when Lefty Grove posted his last 20-win season, 43 years before. Palmer won his last seven decisions, pitched six shutouts, and finished with a 2.46 ERA. On May 28, 1978, against the Indians, he became the Orioles' first 200-

Succeeding Brooks wasn't easy, but Doug DeCinces performed solidly, hitting as many as 28 home runs in 1978.

20-Game Winners

Although the Orioles have not had a 20-game winner since 1984, Baltimore pitchers have produced 23 20-game winners over the past 25 years, substantially more than any other team. Oakland is next with 14. From 1968 through 1980, at least one Oriole cracked the 20-win barrier, a major-league record. The old standard was 12 consecutive years by John McGraw's New York Giants from 1903 through 1914, a mark single-handedly assured by Christy Mathewson, who won 20 or more every one of those years. The high-water mark was 1971 when the Orioles sported four 20-game winners, Dave McNally, Mike Cuellar, Jim Palmer, and Pat Dobson. Steve Stone was the earliest 20-game winner in Oriole history, winning his 20th game on August 19 en route to a club record 25 wins in 1980. Steve Barber (1963) was the first (and only) Oriole pitcher to win 20 games in the club's first 14 years in the league. Jim Palmer won 20 eight times, McNally four, and Cuellar four.

Called "The King of Swing" for his smooth batting stroke, Terry Crowley had two separate tours of duty with the Orioles, becoming one of the top pinch hitters in the game.

game winner, blanking the Tribe 3-0.

Oriole magic swooped down to 33rd Street in 1979. With dramatic home runs and Wild Bill Hagy's gang of crazies up in section 34, it was a season of excitement. Attendance exploded to 1,681,009, almost half a million fans more than any of the Orioles' previous 25 teams had drawn. Wild Bill Hagy, wearing a full red beard and a straw hat, had been coming to Orioles games for years but was suddenly "discovered" during the 1979 season as he spelled out O-R-I-O-L-E-S with his arms and legs, leading the entire stadium in unison. He disdained the yuppie crowds and wanted no part of any commercialization of his act. He was strictly a beer-drinking Oriole fan who became part of the atmosphere at Memorial Stadium. He faded away during the mid-1980s when Oriole fortunes plummeted. (Hagy resurfaced early in the 1994 season at Oriole Park, still driving his cab, performing an encore Oriole cheer at the urging of the crowd). The 1979 team was virtually the same as the year before. The only new additions were pitcher Steve Stone, a free agent affordable because of a so-so 67-72 career record, and outfielder John Lowenstein, picked up from Texas for the $20,000 waiver price.

After another typical slow start—a 3-8 stumble out of the gate—the tide began to turn on April 19 when Jim Palmer went the route to beat the Yankees 6-3. It marked the first of nine straight Oriole wins. The good times continued to roll as the Orioles won 15 out of 16, 26 out of 32, and 51 out of 67 through July 1. The Birds moved into first place on May 18, and except for one day, led the Division the rest of the season.

In June the catchphrase "Oriole Magic" was born. The Birds went 23-6 in June with 11 wins coming in the eighth inning or later. Probably the most dramatic series of the season happened on the weekend of June 22-24 when the Tigers came to town. Friday night, with more than 35,000 in the stands, the Birds entered the ninth down by two runs. Ken Singleton hit a solo homer to get one back. With two outs and Eddie Murray on first, Doug DeCinces came to the plate. "I hadn't played in seven weeks because of a bad back," he remembers. "And I'd only been back a few days. The fans were all there in the ninth. They were hoping. It wasn't a belief but the hope kept them at the park. And when I connected off Dave Tobik, they felt they were part of it." Doug's home run blast gave the Birds a dramatic 6-5 win and the fans stayed and stayed. "The fans were responsible for 'Oriole Magic,' not the players," continued Doug. "After the postgame celebration I was in the clubhouse and someone came and got me. We walked back to the field, a good 10 minutes after the game ended and everybody was still there, waiting for me to come back out. I couldn't believe it. It was a turning point in the history of Baltimore baseball."

As it turned out DeCinces' heroics were just the beginning. The very next night, this time with almost 49,000 on hand, the Orioles trailed by one run in the ninth in the first half of a twi-night doubleheader. After John Hiller walked two, Eddie Murray socked a dramatic three-run homer to end it. In the nightcap, Terry Crowley broke a 5-5 tie with an eighth-inning pinch RBI single to win it 6-5. The Great Houdini would have been proud of the Orioles.

The race that many thought would be a down-to-the-wire four-team free-for-all was over by September 22. The Orioles won the division by eight games over Milwaukee. Their 102 wins represented a total team

Armed with a bristling fastball and outstanding breaking ball, Tippy Martinez saved 105 games in 11 seasons in Baltimore. During the Orioles pennant drive of 1983, Tippy was 4-0 with 10 saves and a 1.87 ERA in 23 appearances. He saved two games of the 1983 World Series.

effort. "We were young and hungry to learn how to win," says catcher Rick Dempsey. "We were lucky to play for an organization that stressed fundamentals and had Earl Weaver as manager. He kicked our butts every day and we hated him for it. Now that we've all lived through it, and seen what happened to our careers because of it, to a man we say, 'He was the best I ever played for.' "

A mound conference during the seventh game of the 1979 World Series involving Mark Belanger, Earl Weaver, and Rick Dempsey.

Mike Flanagan replaced Palmer as the ace of the pitching staff, sporting a brilliant 23-9 record with 16 complete games, five shutouts, and a 3.08 ERA. Flanny was an easy winner of the Cy Young Award. The Oriole bullpen, anchored by Don Stanhouse, and supported by Tippy Martinez, Sammy Stewart, Tim Stoddard, and Dave Ford, rivaled the 1966 bullpen as the Orioles' best of all time.

Earl Weaver referred to his backup players as "Deep Depth." In left field, for instance, right-handed-batting Gary Roenicke and left-handed-hitting John Lowenstein combined for 36 homers and 98 RBI. Kenny Singleton had another banner year, hitting .295 with a career high 35 homers and 111 RBI. In 1977 there were no big stars. Palmer missed almost two months with an elbow ailment and slipped to a 10-6 record. Stone, who called the Orioles "A WE team, not an I team," won 11 to help take up some of the slack. Said Earl Weaver in comparing the two eras of pennant winners, one at the beginning of the decade and the other at the end: "In '69-'70 and '71 we had pitching, defense, power, and speed. Managing that team was easy. The same players were back each year. In spring training, when we went over fundamentals, it was a case of review rather than teaching. The 1979 team had to fight, scramble, and peck away."

The fans played a major role in the Birds' 55-24 home record. They buzzed and chattered and screeched—between batters, between innings, from the first out to the last. It was baseball played to rambunctious tunes. If Hagy wasn't stirring up the fans from the top of the dugout or up in the upper deck, then Dempsey was doing it from the dugout. "I was always doing something goofy to keep the fans involved," said Rick. "If we were down two or three runs, and I'd be sitting in the dugout, I knew I could communicate with any section of the ballpark by waving a towel. The fans would get rowdy and loud, and when all the fans got behind us, we were unbeatable." Dempsey, nicknamed "The Dipper," had a jocund manner that endeared him to the fans. After the last home game of the regular season, Dempsey led the cheers as the entire team came on the field to hail the fans for their support.

Lowenstein got the playoffs off to a winning start with a pinch three-run homer in the bottom of the 10th to lift the Birds to a 6-3 victory over the California Angels. The pinch homer was the first in the 11-year history of the major-league championship series. So euphoric was Earl Weaver that he jumped on Lowenstein as he rounded third base and ran with him all the way to home plate.

The 1979 Orioles, the makers of magic, reinvigorated the franchise with their never-say-die attitude and sincere work ethic. Veterans like Jim Palmer, Ken Singleton, Lee May, and Mark Belanger helped ease the way for Eddie Murray, Scott McGregor, Rich Dauer and Dennis Martinez.

The following day the Orioles scored nine runs in the first three innings, including a three-run Eddie Murray homer, and gave Mike Flanagan a 9-1 lead. The nine runs held up—just barely. The Angels rallied for seven runs before Don Stanhouse, who Earl Weaver called "Full-pack," retired the final batter. There were some scary moments when "Stan the Man Unusual," as Mike Flanagan dubbed him, took the mound. Weaver found himself reaching for his pack of cigarettes more than once. Thus the nickname "Full-pack."

In the third game the Angels rallied for two ninth-inning runs to win 4-3 in Anaheim.

Scotty McGregor nailed down the Orioles' fifth American League pennant with a sparkling six-hit shutout in game four, blanking the Angels 8-0. Pat Kelly hit a three-run homer. Kelly, who always saved his best for Sunday games, became a minister after his playing days. In the fifth inning DeCinces robbed the Angels of a potential game-tying three-run double by spearing a Jim Anderson smash, touching third, and throwing Anderson out at first to squelch the threat. Next up, the World Series, against the Pittsburgh Pirates. Calling themselves "Familee," the Bucs polished off the Reds in three straight to win the National League pennant.

After the final home game of the 1979 season, the players thanked the fans, who came out in record numbers, with an Oriole cheer. From left: coach Jim Frey, catcher Rick Dempsey, coach Frank Robinson, shortstop Kiko Garcia (no. 3), Dennis Martinez, and Doug DeCinces.

The start of the World Series was delayed a day by rain. The next morning there was snow on the ground, the earliest recorded snowfall in Baltimore history. The date was October 10. "I thought I had overslept and it was now December," said first-game starter Mike Flanagan. It was 41 degrees at game time when Flanagan took the mound at Memorial Stadium. "I'll never forget how honored I was to start the first game of the World Series," remembers Flanny. "Once you go through something like that, no matter what happens after it, no other game had the importance of that game to me personally."

The Orioles didn't let the weather affect them. They scored five first-inning runs, two coming on Doug DeCinces' homer in his first World Series at-bat (tying a record). The Pirates pecked away, scoring two runs in the sixth when DeCinces tied another series record with two errors in one inning. Willie Stargell's solo homer in the eighth cut the lead to 5-4. Flanagan pitched out of jams in both the eighth and ninth. "As fate would have it in the ninth, they had Dave Parker on third after his fourth hit and Stargell coming up again with two outs," recalled Flanagan. "I told myself to throw the ball as hard as I could and hope. Stargell popped to short left. I can still see Mark Belanger and his mincing steps going out and catching it for the last out."

Pittsburgh came back in game two to knot the series at one apiece when Manny Sanguillen's pinch ninth-inning single off Don Stanhouse gave the Bucs a 3-2 win before 53,739 at Memorial Stadium. Sanguillen had just four RBI all season. Eddie Murray, who homered in the second inning, was gunned out at the plate by Dave Parker in the sixth. It was shades of Roberto Clemente and the 1971 World Series.

The series resumed the next night in Pittsburgh. With the Orioles trailing 3-2, rain delayed the game in the third inning for 67 minutes. When play resumed the Birds scored five runs in the fifth inning, with the big blow a bases-loaded triple by shortstop Kiko Garcia. Scott McGregor toughened after the delay and retired the last 11 batters he faced. Kiko singled in Rick Dempsey for the final Oriole run in the seventh, giving him four hits and four RBI. The Orioles won, 8-4, to take a 2-1 lead in games. "Deep Depth" had saved the day again as Garcia backed up Mark Belanger at shortstop.

Down 4-0 after two innings in game four, "Deep Depth" bailed out the Birds again as they scored six runs in the eighth to pull out a 9-6 win and take a commanding 3-1 lead in games. The Orioles sent 11 men to the plate in the eighth. John Lowenstein's pinch double off Kent Tekulve scored two runs in the inning. Terry Crowley, batting for catcher Dave Skaggs, delivered a pinch double that scored DeCinces and Lowenstein for the go-ahead runs. It was the Birds' fourth pinch hit in five at-bats in the series. Weaver let reliever Tim Stoddard hit for himself and the 6-7 right-hander delivered his first hit as a professional, driving in the eighth Oriole run. Stoddard shut out the Pirates the rest of the way to get the win.

Maybe it was overconfidence. Maybe it was their inexperience in crucial situations. Whatever, the Orioles went into a shell after game four. After banging out 25 hits the previous two games at Three Rivers Stadium, they mustered only six hits in losing 7-1 in game five.

Even the change of venue back to Baltimore and the friendly confines of deafening Memorial Stadium couldn't arouse the Oriole bats. John Candelaria and Tekulve combined to pitch the first World Series shutout since 1975, winning 4-0. Jim Palmer matched Candelaria over the first six innings before the Pirates broke through with two runs in the seventh and two more in the eighth. The series had now come down to a seventh-game showdown. On the same day eight years before, Willie Stargell delivered an eighth-inning single to drive in the game winner for a 2-1 win and a Pittsburgh World Championship over Baltimore. Eight years later, Stargell repeated history.

Oriole fans did their best to fire up the Birds and disrupt the Pirates. Recollects Pirate outfielder Bill Robinson: "I remember my first at-bat in the seventh game in Baltimore. The fans let out a yell that I can still hear to this day. It was as loud as anything I've ever heard. It was almost frightening. I had to step out of the batters box, regain my composure, and get back in. I proceeded to pop one up to the catcher."

Rich Dauer gave Scott McGregor an early 1-0 lead with a solo homer off Jim Bibby in the third. But Stargell, the man they called "Pops," followed up on a Robinson single by walloping his third home run of the series to put the Bucs on top, 2-1. The Orioles' last threat was in the eighth. Still trailing 2-1 but with the bases loaded, Eddie Murray, hitless in his previous 20 at-bats, lined a shot to deep right. Dave Parker stumbled as he broke back but recovered in time to make the catch. Pittsburgh scored two more in the ninth to win, 4-1. Stargell, who went 4-for-5 in the seventh game, matched the Orioles' hit total. And with his three homers and seven RBI, Willie was the unanimous winner of the series MVP award. The Pirates had become just the fourth team in World Series history to come back from a 3-1 deficit and win. The Orioles had scored only two runs in the final three games.

In August of 1979 the Orioles were sold to prominent Washington attorney Edward Bennett Williams. Under the ownership of Jerry Hoffberger, which began with the 1966 World Series champs, the Orioles had won two World Championships, five American League pennants, and six Eastern Division flags. Hoffberger, like all the Oriole owners before him, had been from Baltimore. On a much smaller scale, he was the August Busch of Baltimore, having owned the National Brewing Company. Williams, the former owner of the Washington Redskins, was part of the Washington political inner circle. Right away rumors began that he would move the Orioles as soon as attendance slipped. The fans never gave Williams his chance.

1980–1983: Back to the Summit

The 1980 Orioles won an even 100 games and still lost the division title to the Yankees by three games. If ever there was an endorsement for the wild card in baseball this was it. No other club in baseball could match the Orioles' record—except the Yankees. Only the Royals, with 97 wins, came close. The Birds sizzled once the weather got warmer. On June 14, they were only 28-30. The rest of the way they went 72-32

The gleaming 1983 World Series trophy

Attendance ballooned to a club record 1,797,438 in 1980. In August during one five-day, five-game series with the Yankees, the Birds drew an amazing 249,605, the largest one-series turnout in major-league history.

Steve Stone signed with the Orioles as a free agent in 1979. Nothing in his eight-year career prior to coming to the Birds predicted the season he had in 1980. That year Stone dominated the American League, going 25-7 with a 3.23 ERA. Mixing his pitches well, Stone kept batters off balance all season and won the Cy Young. It was an extraordinary achievement for a pitcher who had never won more than 15 games in a season and had posted only three winning seasons in nine previous years. In 1981, be battled injuries all season and slumped to 4-7. He never pitcher again after that. The 25 wins still stands as an Oriole recored. One more note from this signal season: Stone reached 20 victories faster than any Oriole before or since.

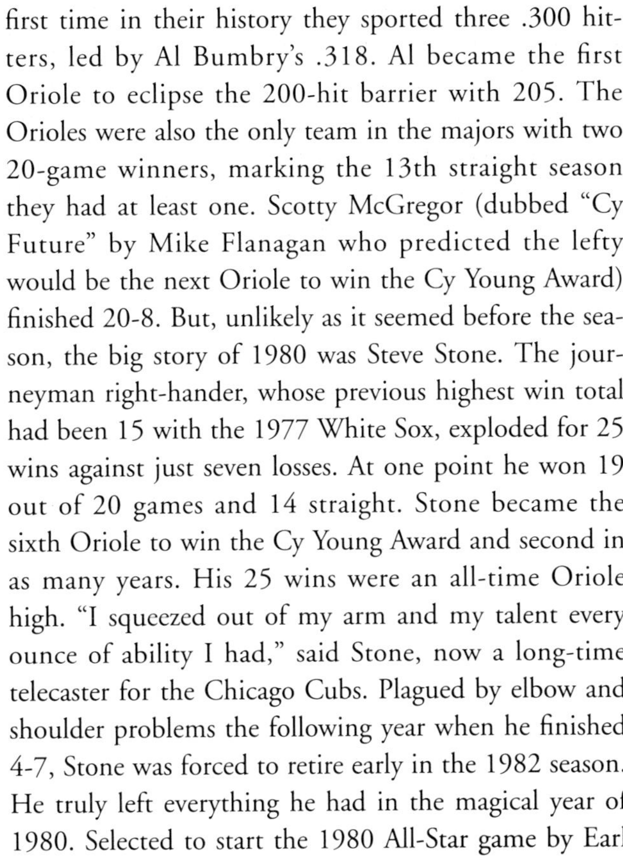

The reasons for the Birds' success were glaring. They set club records for runs, hits, and average (.273) while setting a new major-league fielding record with only 95 errors and a fielding percentage of .9849. For the first time in their history they sported three .300 hitters, led by Al Bumbry's .318. Al became the first Oriole to eclipse the 200-hit barrier with 205. The Orioles were also the only team in the majors with two 20-game winners, marking the 13th straight season they had at least one. Scotty McGregor (dubbed "Cy Future" by Mike Flanagan who predicted the lefty would be the next Oriole to win the Cy Young Award) finished 20-8. But, unlikely as it seemed before the season, the big story of 1980 was Steve Stone. The journeyman right-hander, whose previous highest win total had been 15 with the 1977 White Sox, exploded for 25 wins against just seven losses. At one point he won 19 out of 20 games and 14 straight. Stone became the sixth Oriole to win the Cy Young Award and second in as many years. His 25 wins were an all-time Oriole high. "I squeezed out of my arm and my talent every ounce of ability I had," said Stone, now a long-time telecaster for the Chicago Cubs. Plagued by elbow and shoulder problems the following year when he finished 4-7, Stone was forced to retire early in the 1982 season. He truly left everything he had in the magical year of 1980. Selected to start the 1980 All-Star game by Earl Weaver, Stone retired all nine batters he faced in his three-inning stint at Dodger Stadium, something no one had done since Denny McLain in 1966 in St. Louis.

In one lustrous 11-day stretch in August of 1980, the Orioles played 11 straight games against first-place clubs. For openers the Birds swept three from New York at Yankee Stadium. They then won the first game of a three-game series in Kansas City against the Western Division leaders. That gave the Orioles 10 straight wins and 17 of 19 over a three-week period. They dropped two straight before returning home to play the Yankees in a marathon five-game series. Stone got it going with a 6-1 win, but the Yankees rallied to win the next two. Then, on Sunday afternoon, McGregor tossed a brilliant six-hit shutout, throwing only 102 pitches in a 1-0 masterpiece. The Birds capped the series with a 6-5 win on Monday before another packed house. Despite going 24-10 over their last 34 games, the Orioles were eliminated on the next to last day of the season, the latest the Birds had ever been closed out of a pennant race.

A players' strike interrupted baseball in 1981, causing the season to be split into two separate sections. When play stopped on June 12, the Orioles had lost at Seattle and were sitting with a 31-23 record, two games behind the Yankees. They managed that record with their merriest month of May ever, going 21-8. Kenny Singleton was off to the best start ever for an Oriole batter, hitting .472 in April, including an incredible 10-

Shortstop Mark Belanger, nicknamed "The Blade," played 15 seasons in Baltimore, winning eight Gold Gloves, including six straight. His fielding percentage was the best in American League history. In this photo he completes the double play after forcing Minnesota's Roy Smalley at second.

Rick Dempsey

If ever a player got every ounce out of his ability, it was Rick Dempsey. "The Dipper" saw action in 24 major-league seasons and was one of just three catchers to play in four different decades. That's more than Brooks Robinson and more than Henry Aaron. Yet in all that time Rick barely topped the 1,000 hit mark, compiling a batting average in the low .230s. Ten of those seasons were spent in Baltimore where he caught some of the great pitchers in Orioles history and became one of the most beloved players in the history of the franchise.

Rick thrived in the post-season where he posted a .304 average in 19 games. His performance in the 1983 World Series stunned the Phillies and made him an immortal forever in Baltimore. Voted unanimously as series MVP, he had five hits, four doubles, and a homer, to post the five-game World Series record for extra-base hits. He batted .385 and tossed out Joe Morgan twice in three attempts on the bases. Morgan was the only Phillie who tried to run.

Besides his baseball performances, Rick's antics during rain delays were masterpieces. Rick inherited his show business talent from his parents, who worked in vaudeville and then on Broadway. He debuted his "Baseball Soliloquy in Pantomime" at Fenway Park during a rain delay, stuffing pillows in his belly to resemble Babe Ruth. He then added some Carlton Fisk into the act by mimicking Fisk's famous 1975 World Series home run trot. He performed in Milwaukee where he imitated Robin Yount, and in Baltimore, capping the routine off with a headfirst slide into home plate, sloshing up water all around him. He also performed as a singer, specializing in "Give Me That Old Time Rock 'N Roll," and led the O-R-I-O-L-E-S cheer from the dugout or the bullpen.

After leaving Baltimore in 1987, he played in Cleveland, Los Angeles, and Milwaukee, helping the Dodgers stun Oakland in the 1988 World Series. On the final weekend of the 1991 season, Rick got permission from the Brewers to come back to Baltimore to celebrate the last game at Memorial Stadium where he performed his theatrics one more time.

He was also around for the first year of Camden Yards in 1992, serving as an instructor and part-time player. He became the oldest player ever to play for the Orioles, beating out a bunt against the Red Sox for his only hit of the season.

In his own way, Rick Dempsey carved a niche in Baltimore baseball that will never be equalled.

Sammy Stewart was an imposing reliever and spot starter who struck out the first six batters he faced in his 1978 debut. He won nine games and saved seven in 1983 and tallied 42 saves and 55 wins in eight seasons with the Orioles.

for-10 over a 2½-game stretch to set a club record. A 3-9 tailspin to start the month of June dropped the Birds to second. Then baseball took an unprecedented 8½-week hiatus under the cloud of the longest strike in baseball history.

The season didn't resume until August 10, a day after the All-Star game in Cleveland, won by the National League, 5-4, despite a home run by Singleton. "Dr. Long Ball," a term coined by Earl Weaver in reference to Oriole home runs, almost saved the second part of the disjointed 1981 season. The Birds hit 49 homers in 51 games accounting for 99 of their 201 second-half runs. The 28-23 second-season finish was two games behind Milwaukee. Overall, the Orioles' 59-46 combined record was just one behind the Brewers. The playoff setup had the winners of each half playing each other. Thus the Yankees played the Brewers and the A's played the Royals. In the National League, the Reds had the best overall record by a four-game margin but didn't win either split-season and sat home.

Over the last 25 years, heading into 1982, no team in baseball had won more games than the Orioles. That record stretched to 26 years after an '82 season that saw the Birds come within a whisker of pulling off a final-

One-half of Earl Weaver's leftfield platoon with John Lowenstein, Gary Roenicke played eight years in Baltimore, hitting a high of 25 homers in the 1979 pennant year.

weekend miracle against the pennant-bound Milwaukee Brewers.

The year opened with a bang but then quickly fizzled. Eddie Murray hit a grand slam and rookie Cal Ripken Jr. went 3-for-5 with his first major-league homer (off Dennis Leonard) in a 13-5 opening-day win over the Royals in 1982. Then came a nine-game losing streak. Ripken went 4-for-55. By May 1, the young third baseman was hitting .117, 7-for-60. The turning point came against the Angels on May 2. Reggie Jackson was on third base and, never at a loss for words, offered some encouragement to Rip. "After he talked to me, I got a couple of flare hits and Reggie was on the bench laughing," recalls Cal. "He said, 'See, what did I tell you.' The next day I was beaned (by Seattle's Mike Moore) and everything fell into place after that." From May 6 until the end of the season Ripken hit .281, winning Rookie of the Year honors, leading all big-league rookies in doubles (32), homers (28), RBI (93), and total bases (284).

Cal began his rookie season as the Orioles' third baseman, but Weaver, a genius at appraising talent, was eager to try the 6-4, 200-pounder at shortstop. "I remember in 1981, the organization thought Cal should play third," said Weaver. "He had great potential, though, at shortstop. Great hands, a fantastic throwing arm. I walked out of a meeting saying, 'If you move this kid off shortstop, you're moving a potential Hall of Famer right out of his position.' In 1982, I started Cal at third with (highly touted prospect) Bobby Bonner at short and was dissatisfied and said, 'I don't care what happens to me, I'm moving the kid to shortstop where he belongs.' So I moved him to short on July 1 and he hasn't missed a game since."

The ultimate moment for Brooks Robinson, induction into baseball's Hall of Fame, the 14th player to enter on the first ballot. An emotional Brooks receives his plaque from commissioner Bowie Kuhn on July 31, 1983.

Every time he put on his uniform, Earl Weaver had only one thing in mind, to win that day's game. When he retired after 15 seasons in 1982, he ranked third on the all-time list in winning percentage. He won six division crowns, four American League pennants and one World Series. He was indisputably one of baseball's greatest managers.

Ripken had the added burden of making the majors on the same team that his father coached. Many felt Cal was in the big leagues because of his father, so he had to work harder to prove the doubters wrong. "I always said that if I'd have come to the big leagues as an overbearingly cocky kid, I'd have been better off in the early going because I'd have had more confidence in my own ability and wouldn't have been so in awe of being in the majors. I was timid and unsure at first."

Cal Ripken was only 21 when he debuted in 1981, winning Rookie of the Year in 1982 when he beat out the likes of Kent Hrbek and Wade Boggs. In 1982 he began his fabulous consecutive games streak that has him bearing down on Lou Gehrig's so-called unbreakable record.

The 1982 season was a rocky one most of the way. Stone retired with a sore arm. Palmer was ineffective and the bullpen was shaky. Just a few position players were having big years; Murray hit .316 with 32 homers and 110 RBI. The MVP award that year went to Robin Yount but it easily could have been Eddie. Veteran DH-

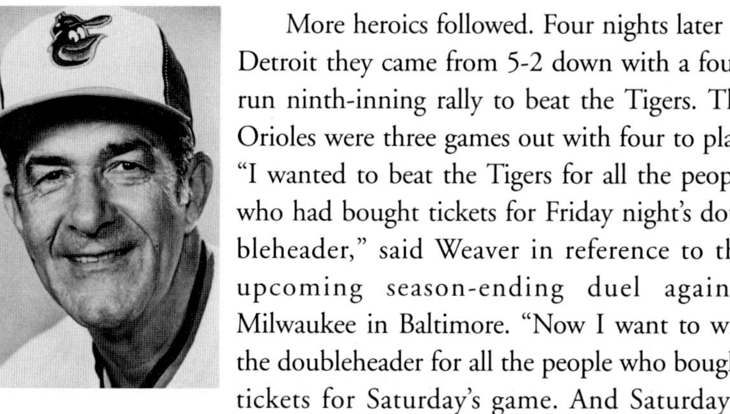

Joe Altobelli succeeded Earl Weaver as manager in 1983 and guided the Orioles to the World Championship. He certainly paid his dues, playing 20 seasons, mostly in the minor leagues, and managing 15 years, all but three in the minors.

pinch-hitter Terry Crowley said about Murray's year, "Eddie Murray owns this league. He just lets the rest of us play in it."

The left field conglomerate of Lowenstein, Roenicke, and Benny Ayala produced a total of 41 homers and 123 RBI. Cal Ripken won praise for his play at shortstop. Role-player Jim Dwyer got into the act by reaching base safely 13 straight times, three short of the all-time major-league record.

There were other bright spots. Tippy Martinez seized control of the bullpen in July and was named "pitcher of the month" in the American League. Palmer, banished to the bullpen in May, began pitching like the Palmer of old in June, reeling off 11 straight wins at one point, matching his longest win streak.

Weaver had announced earlier that 1982 would be his final season. One of the trademarks of his teams was their strong finishes. The 1982 Orioles were no exception. On August 19 they had lost 16 of 23 and things looked bleak but then came the turnaround. They won seven straight. They lost one, and then won 10 more in a row. By the next to last day of the season the Orioles had gone 33-10 in a six-week stretch and were tied for first place.

On September 19 a crowd of over 41,000 came out on "Thanks Earl Day," as the Orioles' legendary manager was honored with gifts and tributes. After 14 years, Earl's won-lost percentage of .596 ranked him third on the all-time list. After an emotional one-hour-and-15-minute ceremony, Rich Dauer capped the day with a 10th-inning homer to beat the Indians.

The Birds pulled off several dramatic wins down the stretch. One took place in Milwaukee on the Sunday before the final weekend. The Orioles were up 3-2 in the bottom of the eighth inning but the Brewers had runners on first and third. Cecil Cooper hit a fly ball to center that appeared deep enough to score Bob Skube from third. Centerfielder John Shelby caught the ball and fired a perfect strike to home plate, nailing the disbelieving Skube. Shelby's throw protected the lead and the Orioles scored two more in the ninth to win 5-2.

More heroics followed. Four nights later in Detroit they came from 5-2 down with a four-run ninth-inning rally to beat the Tigers. The Orioles were three games out with four to play. "I wanted to beat the Tigers for all the people who had bought tickets for Friday night's doubleheader," said Weaver in reference to the upcoming season-ending duel against Milwaukee in Baltimore. "Now I want to win the doubleheader for all the people who bought tickets for Saturday's game. And Saturday I want to win for all the people who bought tickets for Sunday. And Sunday I want to win for all of us."

They possessed only a slight pulse entering the four-game series against the Brewers. One loss and their pennant hopes stopped beating. The first order of business was a twi-night doubleheader on Friday night October 1 against Pete Vuckovich and Mike Caldwell, the Brewers' top pitchers. The Orioles won the opener, 8-3, behind Dennis Martinez. In the nightcap, 20-year-old rookie right-hander Storm Davis, nicknamed "Cy Clone" by Flanagan, tossed a six-hitter and won 7-1 as

The mix of youth and veterans that led the Birds to the 1983 pennant is represented here. Murray, a seven-year pro, cracked 33 homers and hit .306. Cal Ripken, in his second full season, was just ripening. His 27 homers and solid, if unspectacular defensive play established him as one of the top two shortstops in the American League.

the crowd of 51,883, the second largest in stadium history, chanted "sweep, sweep, sweep."

On Saturday afternoon the Birds unleashed an 18-hit attack and romped to an 11-3 victory as Scotty McGregor and Sammy Stewart combined on a six-hitter. The Orioles had outscored Harvey Kuenn's "Wallbangers" 26 runs to seven and had tied the Brewers for the division lead with one game to go. Only

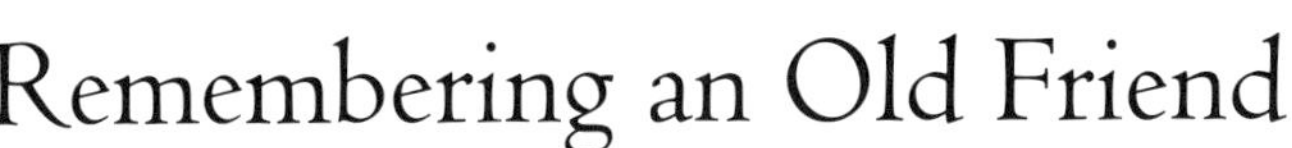

Remembering an Old Friend

Ben McDonald

Final game at Memorial Stadium

Oriole mascot

Oriole legends (from left) Jim Palmer, Earl Weaver, Brooks Robinson, and Frank Robinson

BALTIMORE Orioles
1966
AMERICAN LEAGUE
CHAMPIONS

THE SUN
BALTIMORE, MONDAY, OCTOBER 10, 1966
Complete 4-Game Sweep Of World Series
Sinking Dodgers, 1-0, On McNally's 4-Hit
WORLD'S CHAMPS
F. ROBINSON
PROVES POINT

WORLD SERIES
1966
AMERICAN LEAGUE CHAMPIONS
BALTIMORE
ORIOLES

Dist. by BALTIMORE JAYCEES
BALTIMORE
World Champion
HOME OF 1966
Orioles

BALTIMORE ORIOLES 1966 WORLD SERIES
SPIRIT OF '66
SOUVENIR PROGRAM $1.

1966 WORLD SERIES
BALTIMORE

1966 WORLD SERIES
NATIONAL LEAGUE CHAMPIONS
L.A. Dodgers
VS
Baltimore Orioles

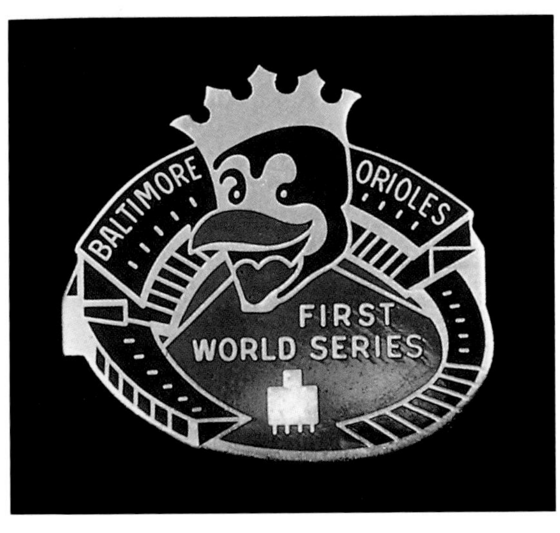
BALTIMORE
ORIOLES
FIRST
WORLD SERIES

1969
Baltimore
ORIOLES 1969
MEMORIAL STADIUM
WORLD SERIES CHAMPS

baltimore orioles 1969 world series souvenir program $1.00

1969 WORLD SERIES
Mets
REMEMBER ME ?
OFFICIAL PROGRAM AND SCORE CARD ONE DOLLAR
SHEA STADIUM, NEW YORK
100TH ANNIVERSARY

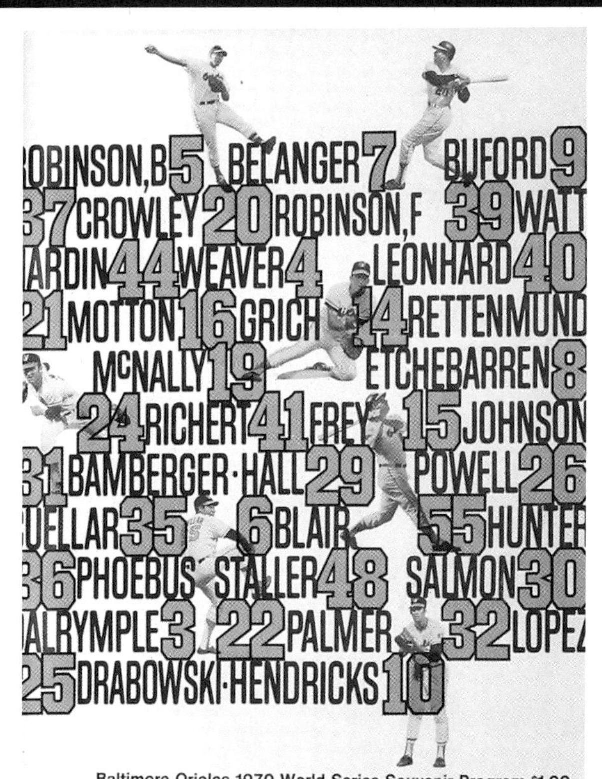

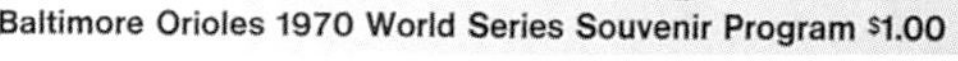
Baltimore Orioles 1970 World Series Souvenir Program $1.00

1971
Baltimore Orioles

1971 BALTIMORE ORIOLES
WORLD SERIES

E Herman
1971 WORLD SERIES $1.00

Orioles
FIFTH
WORLD SERIES

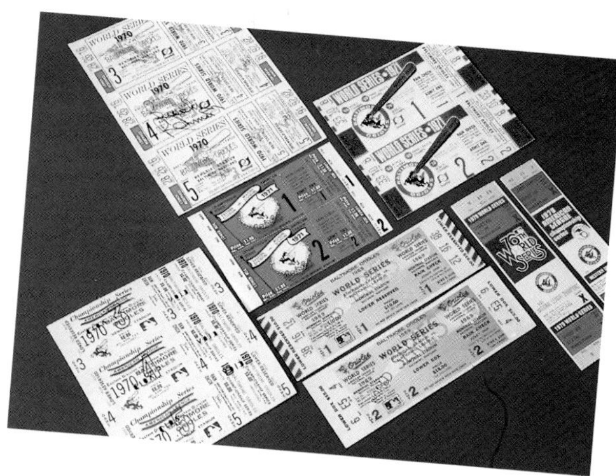

OFFICIAL PROGRAM
$2.00
World Series
1979

Baltimore Orioles
A.L. EASTERN DIVISION CHAMPS
1983

Boddicker
Davis
Flanagan
Martinez,D
Martinez,T
McGregor
Palmer
Stewart
Stoddard
Dempsey
Nolan
Cruz
Dauer
Murray
Ripken
Sakata
Ayala
Bumbry
Dwyer
Ford
Landrum
Lowenstein
Shelby
Roenicke
Singleton
MGR.
Altobelli
BALTIMORE ORIOLES
BALTIMORE
WORLD CHAMPS
ORIOLES
1983

BALTIMORE'S
SIXTH WORLD SERIES

Orioles
24

'83
HANG IN THERE
FANS. . .
WE'RE GONNA DO IT!

1993 MLB
BALTIMORE
Orioles
ALL-STAR GAME
ALL★STAR GAME
OFFICIAL MAJOR LEAGUE BASEBALL PROGRAM
BALTIMORE ORIOLES
STAR GAME
ADMIT ONE
WELCOME
All-Star Game Expanded Coverage
THE SUN

BALTIMORE ORIOLES
1993 ALL STAR GAME

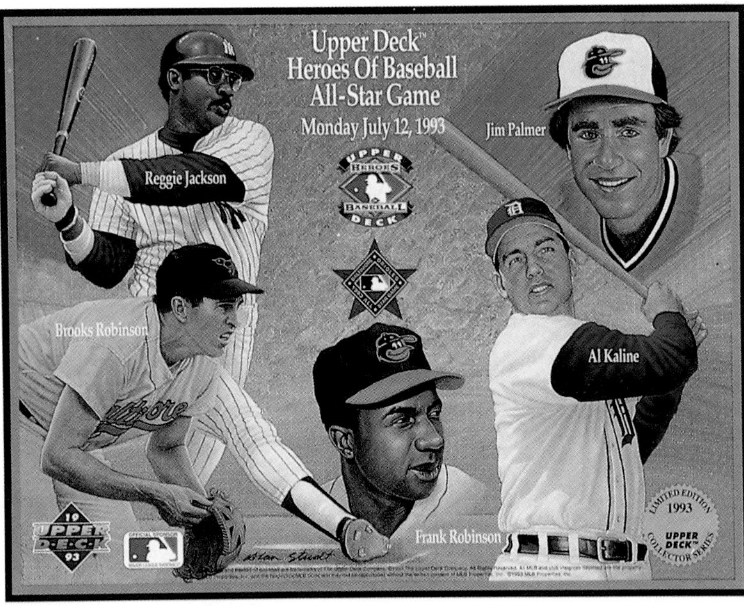

Upper Deck™
Heroes Of Baseball
All-Star Game
Monday July 12, 1993
Jim Palmer
Reggie Jackson
Brooks Robinson
Al Kaline
Frank Robinson
LIMITED EDITION 1993
UPPER DECK™ COLLECTOR SERIES

All-Star Week
1993

25th Silver Jubilee...
1958
All-Star GAME
ALL STAR
at Memorial Stadium Baltimore, Maryland July 8th, 1958
50¢
NATIONAL
AMERICAN
ALL★STAR
AMERICAN League
WILLIAMS
MANTLE
BERRA
FOX
TRIANDOS
TURLEY
SKOWRON
KUENN
PIERCE
KALINE
CERV
JENSEN
O'DELL
APARICIO
MALZONE
WYNN
BALTIMORE, MD. 1958
STENGEL, MGR.
American League
ALL STARS 1958

BALTIMORE ORIOLES
1993 ALL STAR GAME
UPPER DECK
ALL-STAR FANFEST
ADMIT ONE
1993
ALL-STAR GAME
OFFICIAL MAJOR LEAGUE BASEBALL PROGRAM
WELCOME

ALL-STAR
PREVIEW
Coca-Cola
CENTER
WEEK
ASK FOR YOUR COUPON COASTER FOR MAJOR LEAGUE VALUE!
ALL-STAR WEEK
JULY 8-14, 1993
Coca-Cola
CLASSIC

Cal Ripken

Orioles
22
22
PALMER
WHOLE GRAIN
WHEATIES
The Breakfast of Champions
INDUCTION DAY
August 5, 1990
Cooperstown, New York
FIFTY-FIRST ANNUAL PROGRAM
Sunday August 5, 1990
Monday August 6, 1990

Jim Palmer

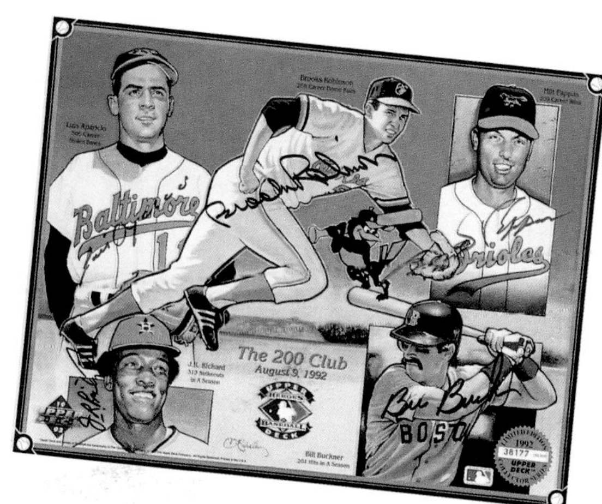

Brooks Robinson

three times in this century had a pennant race come down to the final day with the two teams tied for the lead playing each other. The first was in 1908, the second was in 1949, and the third would be on Sunday at Memorial Stadium.

Rich Dauer was a scrappy second baseman who teamed with Ripken to form an exceptional doubleplay combo in 1983.

The all-or-nothing Sunday afternoon showdown pitted two of the top right-handers in the game over the previous 15 years, Jim Palmer and Don Sutton. Palmer, who took a 15-4 record into the game, and had been magnificent down the stretch, didn't have it. He gave up three home runs, two to eventual American League MVP Robin Yount. He left trailing 4-1 in the sixth and the Brewers went on to win, 10-2. The day became known as Black Sunday in Baltimore. In looking back, Palmer called that loss the most memorable game he had ever pitched. "It was the last significant game I pitched, and I lost. I did win a game in the 1983 World Series, but I have a feeling the Orioles would have won without me that year."

An unforgettable emotional scene followed the last out of the game. While the Brewers celebrated near the mound, the crowd of 51,462 stayed in their seats, cheering their retiring manager and his players. After the curtain calls, a tearful Weaver and his players retreated to the clubhouse. The fans, however, refused to leave. Memories of past glories under Weaver kept them in their seats, and prodded them into screaming "We want Earl." Finally Weaver returned to the field for one last hurrah, leading the fans in a final O-R-I-O-L-E-S cheer. Commentator Howard Cosell, announcing the scene on national television, eloquently said, "The Baltimore fans showed that there's something bigger than winning. That losing can create its own very special treasure."

John Lowenstein had already played eight seasons in Cleveland and one in Texas when he joined the Orioles in 1979. John teamed with Gary Roenicke in left field for several seasons, hitting a high of .320 in 1982 with 24 home runs. He provided numerous clutch hits in the 1983 pennant drive.

The Oriole players wanted to win for Earl in 1982. The following year they would win for themselves.

Joe Altobelli, who spent only 166 games in the majors as a player and over 2,000 as a minor leaguer, was named the seventh Oriole manager in November. The 50-year-old Altobelli had spent 14 years in the Oriole system, his last six as manager of triple A Rochester, before heading to San Francisco as the Giants' skipper in 1977. Fired after three years, he joined the Yankees as a minor-league manager and eventually became their third base coach in the big leagues. Needless to say he had a tough act to follow in Baltimore. The coaching staff stayed the same and the team itself remained almost unchanged from the near-miss the year before. "The ship almost runs itself," said Jim Palmer. Altobelli, the favorite uncle type, was more subdued than Weaver, "although I'm not as calm as I appear," he said.

Despite a rare opening-day loss, the Orioles finished the first month with an 11-9 record, their first winning April in nine years. Hardships struck early, especially injuries to Palmer and Flanagan. Palmer, bothered by neck and back ailments, was held to only 76.2 innings, his lowest output in 17 years. He won only five games. Flanagan started 6-0 before tearing up a knee in mid-May. He would be lost for almost 12 weeks. Rookie right-hander Mike Boddicker, called up to replace Palmer, was counted on heavily. Boddicker, another product of the Orioles' renowned farm system, delivered big, posting a 16-8 record with a 2.77 ERA and five shutouts. Outfielder Dan Ford, leading the club in RBI and batting .314, hurt his knee in early June and missed the next seven weeks. Reliever Tippy Martinez rounded out the list by undergoing an emergency appendectomy in July which sidelined him three weeks.

Despite the injury bug, early omens suggested that this season would be special. On May 18, the

Oriole Families

There have been five families who have produced two players playing for the Orioles. The Ripkens of course provided Cal and Billy while there were also the Browns, the Bufords, the Kennedys, and the O'Donoghues. The late catcher Dick Brown (1963-1965) and his younger brother Larry (1973) are the only brothers other than the Ripkens to play for the Orioles. Third baseman Bob Kennedy (1954-1955) and his son Terry, who caught for the Birds in 1987 and 1988, are the first father-son duo to play for the Orioles. Two more father-son teams joined the list in 1993. Don Buford, former Orioles leadoff hitter who returned to the club as a coach in 1994, saw his son Damon make the team in 1993. John O'Donoghue Jr. pitched in 11 games in 1993. His dad, John O'Donoghue Sr., now an Oriole minor-league coach, relieved in 16 games in 1968.

Cal Ripken Sr. never played in the majors but managed and coached his two sons in Baltimore.

Birds mustered one hit off Chicago's Richard Dotson. That hit was a Ford homer that produced a 1-0 win. The following night against Toronto, Ford's two-run homer provided a 2-1 victory over the Blue Jays. In mid-June the Orioles trailed the Brewers 7-0 in the sixth inning and came back and won 11-7. After a stretch in which the Orioles lost 12 of 17, Boddicker blanked Seattle 2-0 on July 10 despite only two Oriole hits. From that point the Birds went 54-23 and clinched the pennant on September 25.

During that winning stretch, in early August, a huge crowd turned out to honor Brooks Robinson, who had been inducted into the baseball Hall of Fame the previous Sunday. The Orioles staged a Hall of Fame comeback. Trailing Chicago by two runs with two outs and nobody on in the ninth, the Birds strung together five hits, capped by Rich Dauer's RBI single, and won. Brooks knew the feeling.

Another incredible finish ocurred against the Toronto Blue Jays on August 24. Down 3-1 with two outs in the ninth, the Birds tied the score at Memorial Stadium but Cliff Johnson suddenly untied it with a 10th-inning homer off reliever Tim Stoddard. After Barry Bonnell followed with a single, Tippy was summoned. The defensive alignment had several players playing out of position. Lenn Sakata was catching for the first time since little league. Gary Roenicke was playing third for the first time in the majors, and John Lowenstein was playing second for the first time since 1975. "It was a freaky thing," said Tippy, "because the Blue Jays were trying to run on Lenny, and I didn't want to pitch the ball to Lenny because I wasn't sure he would catch it. He was sitting so far back in the box I couldn't see him. He wanted me to throw him the ball so he could throw somebody out. But I didn't want a loss and I decided to throw over to first every chance I got." Lowenstein said Tippy kept throwing to Eddie Murray at first because he was the only infielder he recognized. As it turned out, Tippy "picked off" the side. He picked off Bonnell, walked Jesse Barfield, picked off pinch runner Dave Collins, and nailed Willie Upshaw on a pickoff to retire the side. In the bottom of the 10th, Ripken, celebrating his 23rd birthday, homered to tie the score and Sakata ended it with a three-run home run.

On September 3 at the Metrodome in Minnesota, the Birds blanked the Twins, 13-0, behind Scotty McGregor. Cal Ripken banged out five hits, slugged his 22nd and 23rd homers to break Ron Hansen's club mark for shortstops, hit his 37th and 38th doubles to tie Brooks Robinson's club mark, and tied the team mark with 13 total bases.

Two "sudden death" singles by rookie catcher John Stefero on September 18 and 19 gave Milwaukee its 10th straight loss

Tito Landrum, acquired for spot duty during the 1983 pennant drive, hit one of the most memorable home runs in Oriole history, connecting off Chicago's Britt Burns in the 10th inning to break a scoreless tie and help clinch the 1983 pennant. The Orioles scored two more times after Tito's blast to win 3-0.

The Orioles mob Scott McGregor following his five-hit shutout of the Phillies in game five to clinch the 1983 World Series. It was the Orioles third World Championship in 14 years.

and eliminated the Brewers from contention. The Birds clinched the pennant against the Brewers on September 25 with a 5-1 win in Milwaukee. The following week back home, in the next-to-last game of the season, they drew a crowd of 38,000 and exceeded two million in attendance for the first time. The Orioles won 98 games and finished six games in front of Detroit.

Altobelli became the ninth manager in big-league history to win a pennant in his first year with that club. "I won't ever forget that we went about five weeks without losing two in a row," said Alto proudly. "I just tried to keep the club pointed in the same direction it has been going in the last 20 or 25 years."

"To play for this team, you almost have to set aside personal goals," said the veteran Ken Singleton. "It's been that way since day one. It's an attitude, a feeling. And it's passed on from the older players to the middle-years players to the younger players. When I came, Brooks Robinson was the role model. Now it's older guys like myself. The feeling was: We can win if we do it right. That's the way it's always been."

A few of the victorious Birds perch atop the steps of City Hall during the 1983 parade to honor the World Champions.

Ripken and Murray shared Oriole MVP honors: Rip batting .318 with 27 homers and 102 RBI and Eddie socking 33 homers and driving in 111 runs to go with a .306 average. The left field platoon of John Lowenstein and Gary Roenicke together belted 34 homers and drove in 124 runs, tops of any left field in baseball.

Said Mike Flanagan, who bounced back to win 12 and lose four, "It was a mature team. It was really the 1979 team, adding a couple of players like Cal. When the players got to spring training after losing on the last day in '82, you had a feeling we were destined to win. We were on a course, learning from 1979 and the frustration of '82, and we went wire to wire."

The White Sox, with one more win than the Orioles, were an easy winner in the West with a 20-game lead over second-place Kansas City. The starting trio of Lamarr Hoyt, Floyd Bannister, and Richard Dotson were a combined 42-5 after the All-Star break. Hoyt, the Cy Young winner, stayed hot in the opening game of the league championship series, winning his 14th straight, 2-1, over Scotty McGregor.

Mike Boddicker might have been a rookie but he pitched like a veteran, blanking the White Sox, 5-0, the following day to square the series at 1-1. Boddicker struck out a playoff record-tying 14 batters. Commentator Peter Gammons remembers game two of the playoffs as his top memory of the season. "Hoyt had won the day before and the Sox had the last three games at their place in the best-of-five. It didn't look good for the Orioles and when the team didn't come out for the National Anthem we speculated that they were nervous and rattled for the first time all year. Finally they came out and Boddicker pitched a great game to turn the momentum around. Later Mike Flanagan told me the reason they didn't come out was they were waiting for the decision on the "Peoples Court" television show. That was the personality of that

Determined to win without Earl Weaver the 1983 Orioles gave Joe Altobelli a World Championship in his first season as manager.

team," added Gammons. "They were iconoclastic, irreverent, and had a lot of fun. One of the truly last fun teams around."

Eddie Murray's first-inning three-run homer off Richard Dotson got the Orioles off and running to an 11-1 thumping of the White Sox in game three at Comiskey Park.

Rick Dempsey lines one in the 1983 World Series. Dempsey hit a home run and batted .385 in the Series.

Tito Landrum, an Oriole for only five weeks, carved his niche in Oriole lore in game four. Busting a long home run to left in the top of the 10th inning off Britt Burns, Tito broke open a scoreless game. The Orioles tallied two more to make it 3-0 as Tippy Martinez won it in relief of Storm Davis. "In my first couple at-bats I was pulling off the ball and uppercutting," said Tito, obtained from the Cardinal organization just before the post-season cutoff date. "I was just trying to put the ball up the middle." Landrum had spent most of the season in the minor leagues in Louisville before being added to the playoff roster at the last minute. He was playing in place of Dan Ford, who injured his foot in the first game. "That's the way the Orioles do it," said the soft-spoken Murray. "There's always somebody who comes along and does the job when we need it. We don't just depend on one or two people." "Tito Landrum," offered Lowenstein, "is what the Orioles are all about. Tito is a role player. The Orioles are a team of role players." Boddicker was named ALCS MVP as the White Sox mustered only three runs in the four-game playoff, and one of those was unearned.

The World Series featured the Orioles against the Phillies in the closest distance (86 miles) World Series since the Brooklyn Dodgers played the Yankees in 1956. It was the I-95 World Series. Paul Owens had taken over for Pat Corrales in mid-July and managed the Phillies to a 47-30 record and a six-game advantage over Pittsburgh. They were hoping to give the National League its fifth straight World Series winner. With Pete Rose, Joe Morgan, Tony Perez, Steve Carlton, and several other greybeards, the Phillies were dubbed "The Wheeze Kids," a take-off on the 1950 Whiz Kids. For the Orioles, World Series losers in both 1971 and 1979, it meant a chance for redemption.

Like the playoffs, the series didn't start well at Memorial Stadium. The Orioles and McGregor lost game one, 2-1, as John Denny won it with help from Al Holland. Homers by Morgan and Garry Maddox provided the only runs the Phillies would need.

It took Boddicker to pull a playoff encore and stun the Phillies in game two. The rookie pitched a three-hitter, giving up a lone unearned run, and squared the series with a complete game 4-1 win. Lowenstein homered and catcher Rick Dempsey doubled home the go-ahead run.

After a day off the series switched to Veterans Stadium on Friday night, October 14, when 300-career game winner Steve Carlton faced Mike Flanagan. The Phillies led 2-0 until the sixth. Rick Dempsey's second double off Carlton resulted in the tie run when Benny Ayala singled him home. Dan Ford's grounder to short, muffed by Ivan DeJesus, scored the game winner as relievers Jim Palmer, Sammy Stewart, and Tippy Martinez held the Phillies scoreless over the final five innings. Palmer, celebrating his 38th birthday the next day, became the first pitcher to win World Series games in three different decades.

Rich Dauer was the hero of game four with three hits and three RBIs. He also scored the winning run in the 5-4 win in Philadelphia that put the Birds up, three to one. Manager Joe Altobelli also had a big day, sending up four straight pinch hitters in the two-run sixth.

Joe Morgan is called out attempting to steal in the '83 Series. Dempsey shut down the Phillies running game, limiting them to only one stolen base

Unlike 1979 the Orioles weren't going to let this commanding lead slip away. McGregor went the distance and Eddie Murray clubbed two home runs in the 5-0 win that clinched the Orioles' third World Championship. One of the keys for Scotty was his mastery over Mike Schmidt. The Phillies' slugging third sacker went 0-8 off McGregor and 1-20 overall with no RBI in the series. Dempsey was the surprising

MVP, batting .385 in the five games with four doubles and a home run. The "Dipper" played a key role in three of the four Oriole wins and threw out Joe Morgan twice on the basepaths. "In 11 years, I've never been hot," said Dempsey, a .231 hitter in the regular season, who more than any other player epitomizes Oriole spirit. "I know it sounds like a cliche," said Jim Palmer, "but Rick has more will to win than any player I've ever seen."

The near-miss team of 1979 that led the Pirates 3-1 in the World Series, the team that won 100 games in 1980 and fell short, the team that came within a whisker of winning in the 1981 strike year, the team that lost on the last day in 1982, had finally kept its date with destiny. Once again the Baltimore Orioles were World Champions.

The Decline, Fall, and Rebirth

The Orioles declined steadily following the 1983 World Championship. The Tigers blazed to 16-1 start in 1984 and wiped away the field, winning by 15 games over second-place Toronto. The Orioles finished fifth, 19 games off the pace with an 85-77 record—their lowest finish in 17 years. Both Eddie Murray and Cal

Fred Lynn gave the team its best center field play since Paul Blair.

Ripken hit over .300, but the Birds fell to 12th in team batting, scoring 118 fewer runs than the year before. Mike Boddicker proved 1983 was no fluke, though, by becoming the league's only 20-game winner, registering a 2.79 ERA, lowest in the league.

Three all-time favorites played their final games in an Oriole uniform in 1984—veteran outfielders Al Bumbry and Ken Singleton and pitching immortal Jim Palmer. Although Singleton hit a career low .215, he achieved his 2,000th hit and finished with two grand slams and 16 RBI in his last 21 games. Bumbry hit .270 and batted .325 over the last six weeks of the season, but Al was 37 and didn't fit into the club's rebuilding plans.

An exceptional role player, Lenn Sakata played from 1980 through 1985 in Baltimore, popping up at second base, shortstop and even behind the plate on occasion. His clutch hits produced several "sudden death" wins over his six seasons in Baltimore.

Palmer barely dirtied his uniform in 1984 and was released after an 0-3 start on May 17. At 38, the eight-time 20-game winner felt he could still pitch and blamed his release on his age and the club's slow start. "We were 4-12 and the Tigers were off to a great start and Altobelli was worried about his job," reasoned Palmer. "He wasn't concerned about me, he was concerned about the whole club. The pitchers were all in the same boat, off to slow starts, but I was 38 so I was released. I hated to go out with a whimper. I worked to prove to myself and others that I could pitch and I didn't have a chance to do that." When he bowed out Palmer had won 268 games against only 152 losses. He was one of only three pitchers in American League history to win 20 or more games eight different times. His 2.86 ERA ranked fifth on the all-time list. He tossed 53 shutouts, and in 3,947 innings had never given up a grand slam homer. (Jim attempted a comeback in 1991, a year after his induction to baseball's Hall of Fame, but at 45 his body just wouldn't cooperate and he aborted the effort in spring training.)

Memorial Stadium filled to the brim. Several players, including Boston's Dwight Evans, called it their favorite park. Between the Orioles and Colts, it supplied the backdrop for some of the greatest moments in sports history.

Owner Edward Bennett Williams summed up the disppointment of 1984 thusly, "I will never again sit like a contented cow like I did after last season. I should have followed my instincts and made changes. Instead, because we were World Champs, I decided not to tinker. There were obvious changes that should have been made, especially on offense. I won't break up our strengths in some futile effort to bolster our weaknesses. Pitching is our strength and I won't break that up."

What Williams did before the 1985 season was to go against the basic foundation of the Oriole philosophy—always build from within the farm system and make smart, meaningful trades. General manager Hank Peters hated free agency because he believed it was not the cure-all many had predicted. Plus, the Birds' competitiveness during the turbulent early years of free agency was proof that the "Oriole Philosophy" worked.

But Williams was impatient and 85 wins just didn't pass muster, even if that was more than any American League West team. The famed lawyer went out and signed nine-time All-Star centerfielder Fred Lynn, 37-year-old outfielder Lee Lacy, who had hit .321 in Pittsburgh, and relief pitcher Don Aase, who had come back from an operation that had sidelined him for almost two full seasons.

The result was two less victories than the year before, an 83-78 fourth-place finish, 16 games behind the pennant-winning Toronto Blue Jays. The Birds clouted a club record 214 homers to top the majors, the seventh highest total by any team in baseball history. They socked seven grand slams. But the pitching, of all things, let the club down. The 4.38 team ERA was the highest in Oriole history. Injuries took their toll, beginning with Flanagan, who ruptured his achilles tendon in an off-season basketball game and won only four games. Tippy Martinez, Lacy, and Lynn all missed significant time, although the newcomers performed well overall. Aase led the relievers with 14 saves and sported a 10-6 record. Lacy hit .293 but played in only 121 games. Lynn also battled injuries, hitting 23 homers and batting .263 in 124 games. Lynn became "Mr. Clutch," hitting six ninth-inning homers and three extra-inning game winners.

Two future Hall of Famers, Cal Ripken and George Brett. Between them they've played in 24 All-Star games and recorded more than 5,000 hits.

Fred helped the Orioles to an 18-9 start in 1985, their best since 1970. His back-to-back ninth-inning homers off Minnesota's Ron Davis on May 10-11 set the tone. The next afternoon Lynn also homered in the ninth for the third game in a row, but the Birds lost, 7-3.

However, after the great start, the losses came often, as the Orioles went 65-69 the rest of the way. On June 12, after dropping their fifth straight game, 6-2, to the Tigers in Detroit, and sitting in fourth place with a 29-26 record, Altobelli was fired by owner Edward Bennett Williams. The well-meaning, low-profile Altobelli had never been a favorite of the flashy, omnipresent Williams, and with the team sinking fast, the owner acted. He turned to a familiar face: Earl Weaver. Earl had spent the previous three years playing golf in Florida and broadcasting network games. Williams asked. Earl waffled. Williams pleaded. Earl waffled. Williams sweetened the financial pot. Earl stopped waffling. His first game back was against the Brewers on June 14. The 38,783 fans greeted him with several ovations. The Orioles responded by winning 9-3 behind Storm Davis.

A week after Weaver returned, long-time pitching coach Ray Miller, disappointed that he wasn't named manager, left the Orioles to manage the Minnesota Twins.

Out of uniform for two years and eight months, Weaver guided the Orioles to a 53-52 record the rest of the way. The player turnover continued; after the 1985 season less than half the players who won the 1983 World Series were still around. Former mainstays Rich Dauer, Lenn Sakata, Gary Roenicke, and Sammy Stewart were either not re-signed or were traded.

The hoped-for-improvement in 1986 turned instead to disaster. The Orioles plunged to the East cellar as they suffered their first losing season in 18 years, winning only 73 games and losing 89, 22½ games behind the front-running Red Sox. Never had the Birds finished in last place. Only Boddicker among the starters posted a winning record (14-12) as the ERA was again high, a bloated 4.30. A hamstring injury contributed to the lowest home run output of Eddie Murray's career, 17. Ripken, Lynn, and Lacy all hit well but that wasn't enough to prevent a dreadful slump that gripped the Orioles over the last two months of the season.

The bottom fell out on August 6. After beating Texas the night before, the second-place Orioles pulled to within 2½ games of the first-place Red Sox. The Birds had gone 18-9 and were 13-6 since the All-Star break with a 59-47 record. Then on the night of August 6, despite two grand slams in one inning by Larry Sheets and Jim Dwyer for an 11-6 lead, the Birds lost 13-11 when the Rangers' Toby Harrah cranked his own grand slam. The three grand slams in one game was a big-league record. Harrah's grand slam did more than sink the Birds that night; it precipitated an Oriole free fall that ended only because the season did.

Weaver had suddenly lost the winning touch. "There wasn't just one malfunction," said Earl, shaking his head over the '86 collapse. "Everything broke down. The 0-for-4's, the left on base, the pitchers allowing all those home runs. It just all added up." The Birds went on to lose 42 of their last 56 games, including back-to-back doubleheader sweeps by Oakland in late August. Don Aase, the team's MVP with a club record 34 saves, lost both games in one of those doubleheader losses, a first in club history. The Birds ended the season eighth

Presidential Visits

So far the Orioles are 0-1 with President Bill Clinton on hand, losing 7-4 to Texas in the 1993 opener. They were 5-2 under George Bush, 4-2 at home. In 1991, the final year of baseball at Memorial Stadium, the President and Mrs. Bush hosted Queen Elizabeth II of England and Prince Philip, the Duke of Edinburgh, for a May 15 game. The Orioles lost to Oakland that night 6-3. The distinguished party greeted both teams in the Oriole dugout before watching several innings from the owner's box. Before President Bush, the Orioles' luck in playing before Presidents was all bad. They were 0-3 under President Reagan and 0-1 under Jimmy Carter. Carter was the first president to attend a game in Baltimore, watching a 1979 World Series game against Pittsburgh.

in batting and 10th in both pitching and fielding. The 14-42 finish sent Earl back to retirement, this time for good. The day after the season ended, Cal Ripken Sr. was named as the new manager for 1987.

Cal had spent 30 years in the Oriole system, beginning in 1957 as a player. He became a player-manager in the minors at the young age of 25 and managed 13 seasons in the Oriole system. After one year as a scout he joined the big-league coaching staff in 1976, replacing the retiring George Staller. When Billy Hunter left to manage the Rangers in 1978, Cal became third base coach, where he stayed for 9½ years. Rip was an organization man, the quintessential right-arm for any manager. He had devised and supervised the spring training regimen for years. Moreover, Rip was devoid of ego. He played down the fact that his two sons were playing for him, which was a major-league first. "They're all my sons, all 25 players, and I'll treat them all the same," he said. When someone asked him how Cal Jr. would react if his Dad were fired, Ripken Sr. just shrugged his shoulders, "He's a professional and I'm a professional," he answered. "He's been able to cope with a lot of situations. When you're hired to manage, you know someday you'll be fired. I know that when that day comes, Cal Jr. will handle the situation. It's nothing to be concerned about."

The player shake-ups continued after the 1986 season. Despite a career-high 13 homers, fan favorite Rick Dempsey was released after hitting only .208. Edward Bennett Williams continued to pressure general manager Hank Peters to make changes. To replace Dempsey, Peters traded pitcher Storm Davis to San Diego for catcher Terry Kennedy and pitcher Mark Williamson. Infielder Rick Burleson, who had played only 51 games from 1982 through 1985 because of shoulder problems, was signed as a free agent. Third baseman Ray Knight, the reigning World Series MVP with the Mets, was also signed as a free agent.

Although the hitting was respectable, the pitching caved in during 1987, as the team's ERA soared to 5.01. Not since Casey Stengel's lovable but inept 1962 Mets had a major-league team compiled an ERA over five. The Birds finished a notch ahead of 1986 in sixth place with a 67-95 record, but they were a distant 31 games behind the winning Detroit Tigers. In 78 games against Eastern Division opponents, the Orioles won only 18. They experienced their worst month ever in June, winning only five of 28 games. After losing 17 of 18 in September, the Orioles faced their earliest elimination in 31 years. The Birds bashed 211 homers but gave up a major-league record 226. Seven pitchers served time on the disabled list, with former mainstays Mike Flanagan and Scotty McGregor combining for only five wins against 13 losses. Flanagan didn't even make it through the season and was traded to Toronto in August for pitchers Jose Mesa and Ozzie Peraza. The

President Reagan attended the 1986 home opener against Cleveland, flanked by Oriole owner Edward Bennett Williams (left of Reagan) and Baseball Commissioner Peter Ueberroth (right).

high-water mark in wins was 10, achieved by three different pitchers. Homegrown product Larry Sheets emerged as the Orioles' MVP, leading the club in homers with 31 and batting average (.316). His 94 RBI ranked behind Cal Ripken's 98.

On April 15 history was made: The Brewers' Juan Nieves tossed the first no-hitter by an

Cal Ripken watching one of his 300 plus home runs leave the park. In 1993 Cal topped Ernie Banks of the Cubs as the top homer-hitting shortstop of all-time.

opponent in Memorial Stadium history. The first four Memorial Stadium no-hitters had all been thrown by Oriole pitchers. Nieves won 7-0. Robin Yount ended the game with a great play in right-center to snag Eddie Murray's sinking liner and save the no-hitter. "It was slicing away from me," said Yount afterwards. "You don't have time to think. I was going to do everything I could to catch it. I ran as far as I could, dove, and caught it." For Nieves, who soon developed arm troubles and drifted out of the majors, the no-hitter was his crowning moment. "I struggled the first few innings. My slider was awful and everything was hanging. Once I got a 3-0 lead, I decided to go right after the hitters. That's a tough lineup with Murray, Ripken, Lynn, and Knight. You earn a no-hitter against that lineup."

Time was now a factor for Edward Bennett Williams, who was beginning to show signs of losing a decade-long battle with cancer. His impatience peaked two days after the 1987 season when he fired respected general manager Hank Peters and farm director Tom

Cal Ripken

Besides Cal Ripken, only one other player did not miss a game during the 1993 season: Florida's Jeff Conine. Conine has the second-longest playing streak behind Cal with 162 straight. When you consider that Cal had not missed a game in any of the 10 previous seasons, you have one of the most impressive achievements in baseball history. Unlike Lou Gehrig, who played first base, Cal Ripken played shortstop, the most demanding position in the infield, and he's played it in Gold Glove style. Of a total of 17,271 innings during the streak, Cal had played in 17,135 (99.2 percent) going in to 1994.

Eclipsing Ernie Banks as the top home-run-hitting shortstop in baseball history, Ripken has become a power source at a position normally reserved for acrobatic, singles-type hitters. During Cal's first 12 full seasons, no player in baseball amassed more extra base hits than he did. His durability is now legendary. Since his consecutive games streak began in 1982, some 441 shortstops have taken the field on the other 27 clubs. A total of 3,072 major-league players had gone on the disabled list during Cal's streak and that doesn't include 1994.

Cal has played down the consecutive games streak and at times has almost apologized for his durability. "It's not something I set out to do. It's just the approach I bring to the ballpark every day," he says. "I want to be in the lineup and I want to play. I'm proud of the streak but it's not a conscious effort on my part. I don't come to the park and say, 'I'm going to add another game to my streak today.' I come, instead, to the park saying, 'This is the only game today and I want to play in it.' I fight the urge to look ahead. The mental part of the game can be a grind. The pressures and frustrations can buiild. It's a matter of how you handle it, and I think I've been good at dealing with the mental part of the game. I want to be remembered for what I did on the field, not for the streak."

No doubt, with two MVP seasons and some 15 big-league records, not to mention his consecutive games streak, Cal Ripken will be always remembered for his ability on the baseball field. He's set a standard that will be virtually impossible to top.

The Orioles last 20-game winner, Mike Boddicker (who accomplished the feat in 1984) became the first rookie to pitch a shutout in the ALCS, fanning 14 White Sox in the 1983 playoffs. He then beat the Phillies in the World Series.

Giordano. Williams hired former White Sox general manager Roland Hemond. Former Yankee exec Doug Melvin became the minor-league head. Frank Robinson was elevated from the coaching staff to become Mr. Williams' assistant on baseball matters. At the end of the day Williams announced ominously that, "This is neither the beginning nor the end of our re-organization. It's the end of the beginning."

Frank wasn't out of uniform long. After an 0-6 start in 1988, Cal Sr. was dumped as Oriole manager and replaced by Robinson, who promptly lost 15 more in a row. The 21 losses, in which the Orioles were outscored 129 runs to 44, set a major-league record for consecutive defeats to start a season. The season, to put it bluntly, was a disaster as exemplified by the 54-107 record, the worst in club history. The Birds finished in the Eastern cellar, 34½ games behind front-running Boston and 22½ games behind sixth-place Cleveland. The team average, .238, was a major-league low. Their 550 runs scored set a club record for fewest runs scored in a 162-game schedule. They hit only 137 homers, 74 fewer than the year before. They won only 20 games on the road. In the games where they scored one run or fewer they were 0-44. Only three pitchers were with the team from start to finish. The last two pitchers from the club's glory days departed the scene.

After an 0-3 start and an ERA of 8.83 Scott McGregor tearfully announced his retirement on May 2 at the age of 34. An injured shoulder had held him to two wins the year before. In 12 seasons McGregor had won 138 games, the fifth winningest pitcher in club history. Always tough in the clutch, Scotty had pitched a shutout over the Angels to sew up the 1979 pennant for the Orioles and clinched the 1983 World Series with a shutout over the Phillies. For five years (1979-1984) McGregor had the best winning percentage in the majors, at one point winning 17 of 18 on the road. In 1983 alone he was 14-1 on the road. "The change-up was my key pitch," said McGregor, who became a minister after his playing days. "Once I developed it in 1979 things really took off. I always had good control and could keep hitters off-balance, moving the ball around." His control was so sharp he once went 46 consecutive innings without issuing a base on balls. When McGregor was in his prime, the hitters got themselves out. He just started the process.

Mike Boddicker, another 1983 World Series hero, was traded to the Boston Red Sox on July 29 for outfielder Brady Anderson and pitcher Curt Schilling. Boddicker lost his first eight decisions with the Orioles in 1988, finishing 6-12. His 79 wins rank him in the Orioles' top-10 all-time.

The lone highlight of the 1988 season came on the night of May 2 when a crowd of 50,402 welcomed the team back from a 1-11 road trip. The Birds had limped back home 1-23, yet fan support was better than ever. One fan in the left-field corner raised a white banner that read: "139-23." Oriole fans demonstrated a

The most dominant switch-hitter of the last 15 years, Eddie Murray set a club record for homers (333), and banged out 2,021 hits while hitting .295 in his 12 seasons in Baltimore. The chants of EDDIE-EDDIE will be heard echoing from Memorial Stadium as long as the park stands.

tenacious spirit all season. They were rewarded on that "Fantastic Fans" night with a 9-4 win over the Texas Rangers. On that benchmark night Governor William Donald Schaefer electrified the crowd by announcing that owner Edward Bennett Williams and the Maryland Stadium Authority had agreed to a long-term lease for a new downtown ballpark to be built in the Camden railroad yards in time for the 1992 season. Mr.

Father and sons Ripken. Proud dad Cal Sr. managed his sons, Billy (left) and Cal (right,) in 1987, a first in baseball history.

Williams, gravely ill, waved to the crowd from his owner's box on the mezzanine level. Williams never attended another Oriole game.

Sadly, he never saw the new ballpark or even the team's turnaround on the field. The renowned lawyer and sportsman, who owned both the Washington Redskins and the Orioles and who based his life on "contest living," lost his battle against cancer and passed away on August 13, 1988, at the age of 68. Under his ownership the Orioles developed into one of the showcase franchises in major-league baseball. Even during the three disastrous seasons of 1985, 1986, and 1987, attendance averaged 1,823,203. Williams, considered an out-of-towner when he bought the team in 1979 amid rumors he would move the club to Washington, became enchanted by the city and its people. "We hold this franchise in trust for the people," he said a few years before his death. "And if you're a good trustee, you'll have no regrets. I told people in 1979 that we were staying in Baltimore. I regarded it as a permanent union. Nothing since then has changed my views."

Upon Williams' death the club was sold to a group headed by financier Eli Jacobs. Jacobs was a New Yorker with a flat personality who found it awkward being in the public eye. Winning and losing seemed inconsequential. He used the Orioles as a vehicle to entertain and impress high rollers in government, business, and entertainment. Fortunately the rebuilding of the club, thanks to Williams' efforts, was solidly under way.

Hemond stunned Baltimore that winter when he traded Eddie Murray, who had grown increasingly disgruntled as the losing seasons mounted and felt he was targeted as a scapegoat, to the Dodgers for pitchers Brian Holton and Ken Howell and infielder Juan Bell. Murray's number 33 became the fifth number retired in Oriole history, joining Brooks Robinson's number 5, Frank Robinson's number 20, Jim Palmer's number 22, and Earl Weaver's number 4. After 12 years in a Baltimore uniform, Eddie ranked first in homers (333) and total bases and was second to Brooks Robinson in every other category including hits, (2,021) and RBI (1,190). He missed only 61 games in 12 years, leaving with a .295 lifetime average and a reputation as one of the top clutch hitters ever. The chants of ED-DIE, ED-DIE will forever resound throughout Baltimore baseball.

Out of the rubble of 1988 came a remarkable rebirth. Improvement was expected in 1989. After all, up was the only direction to go. But a turnaround of 32½ games? That's what happened though, as the Orioles, bedecked in new uniforms and caps reminiscent of the 1954 style, won 87 games and pushed the pennant-winning Blue Jays to the final weekend of the season. The Birds were two wins shy of becoming the first team in this century to win a championship after finishing last the season before. Although Murray had departed, Cal Ripken Sr. had returned, by request from the man who replaced him as manager, Frank Robinson, to assume his old role as third base coach.

When the upstart Orioles, behind newscomers Randy Milligan, Mike Devereaux, Joe Orsulak, Mickey Tettleton, Jeff Ballard, Bob Milacki, and Gregg Olson, actually led the division by more than seven games in mid-July, "Why Not?" signs sprouted up at Memorial Stadium. The O's, with their youngest team since 1968 (average age, 27 years, two months) including six rookies

A grand-slam first occurred on the night of August 6, 1986, when the Orioles and Texas Rangers combined to hit three grand-slams in one game. Larry Sheets (left) and Jim Dwyer (right) both connected in the fourth inning. Toby Harrah hit Texas' slam in the 13-11 Ranger victory.

Fred Lynn made the spectacular look easy as he patrolled the Orioles' center field with skill and style for four seasons in the 1980s.

and others with less than two years' experience, aroused the nation and the home folks, who turned out in record numbers. Attendance jumped to 2,535,208. Only five writers out of 186 in *The Sporting News* preseason poll picked the Orioles to finish as high as fifth, yet they spent almost three months in first place before falling on the next-to-last day of the season following back-to-back one-run losses in Toronto.

Frank Robinson was deservedly named American League Manager of the Year. Highlights abounded. Local-boy-made-good Dave Johnson, a 29-year-old rookie, pitched a complete game, 6-1, win over the Twins in his Memorial Stadium debut on August 8. Rookies had either a win or a save in 50 of the Orioles 87 wins. Rookie reliever Gregg Olson saved 27 games, eight more than all other rookie relievers in the league combined. Blessed with an overpowering curve ball, he became the first rookie to win Oriole MVP honors. He was also voted Rookie of the Year in the American League. "This year was like lightning in a bottle," said manager Frank Robinson. "The key now is to not get complacent and forget about all the hard work that brought us back. Being in the race was a real bonus since we're a young ballclub that's still rebuilding. We've made a good start and now we have to improve on it."

His fears were realized when the Orioles slipped to fifth place in 1990 with a 76-85 record, 11½ games behind the winning Red Sox. The Birds entered the month of August only four games out of first, but a rash of injuries to Billy Ripken, Randy Milligan, and Dave Johnson (leading the team in wins with 13) led to a dismal 9-18 month that swept them out of the race.

The lack of depth proved costly, but hope for the future was renewed when the Orioles finished with 11 wins in their last 15 games. "Tall Cajun" Ben McDonald, the top draft pick of 1989 after a brilliant collegiate career at L.S.U., was a big part of that hope when he became the first Oriole to ever win his first five major-league starts and first six decisions. In his 15 starts he allowed two or fewer runs 11 times. The 6-7 right-hander tossed a shutout in his first big-league start on July 21, throwing only 85 pitches and giving up just four hits in a 2-0 win over Chicago.

Cal Ripken's consecutive game streak, which began in 1982, had reached 1,411 games by the end of the 1990 season. He vaulted past former Yankee and Red Sox shortstop Ev Scott, who played in 1,307 straight between 1918-1925, and into second place behind the Iron Horse, Lou Gehrig. Cal also established a new fielding standard for shortstops with just three errors and a .996 fielding average in 1990. The tallest shortstop in major-league history, Cal crafted streaks of 95 straight errorless games and 431 errorless chances. Yet, Cal was denied a Gold Glove, which went instead to Chicago shortstop Ozzie Guillen. In Ripken's season of streaks he hit 20 or more homers for the ninth straight year, a first for a shortstop.

Another incredible Ripken streak: He had played in 8,243 consecutive innings spanning 904 games from early 1982 to late 1987. Out of the 13,887 innings played during his streak of 1,411 games, Cal had played in 13,826 of them. "It's not something I set out to do," said Cal in referring to his iron man numbers. "It's just the approach I bring to the ballpark everyday. I want to be in the lineup and I want to play. I'm proud of the streak but it's not a conscious effort on my part. I don't come to the park and say, 'I'm going to add another game to my streak today.' Instead I come to the park saying, 'This is the only game today and I want to play in it and be a part of it.' I fight the urge to look ahead. My approach is one game at a time."

While Ripken was a rock of stability the rest of the Oriole cast was as settled as a

The 1989 Orioles shocked the baseball world by challenging Toronto for the Eastern pennant down to the final weekend. Lefty Jeff Ballard won 18 games in his first full season, more than any left-hander in the league.

Mike Flanagan

Maybe it's because both his father and his grandfather were professional ballplayers. They instilled in him a respect for not only the game itself, but also the special privilege of putting on a major league uniform. Mike Flanagan's dad and grandfather didn't make the major leagues. Mike did, however, and he treasured every hour and every day and every year that he spent in the game, over 16 years to be exact. All but three of them were in an Oriole uniform.

Flanagan came up to the Orioles when Mike Cuellar and Dave McNally were bowing out. Fortunately, Jim Palmer was still in his prime and the future Hall of Famer took Mike under his wing, just as Robin Roberts had with Jim some ten years earlier. Flanny didn't need much guidance, however. In many ways he reminded folks of Brooks Robinson, polite and humble. He also kept everybody loose with his clever sense of humor.

The New Hampshire native won 15 games at the age of 25 in 1977, and over the next eight years he started more games and pitched more innings than any pitcher in the American League. He won 122 games during that span, averaging 15 wins a season, topped by the Cy Young season of 1979 in which he posted a 23-9 record.

Always there with a ready quip, Mike's sense of humor became legendary. Take his player nicknames for instance. Twins infielder John Castino was dubbed "Clams" by Mike. Ruben Sierra became Ruben Scare-ya, and there was Jose "Don't Make a Mistake-O" Canseco. His Cy Young glossary from 1980 was equally clever. Since he had just won the award, Mike was Cy Young. Three-time winner Jim Palmer was Cy Old. Steve Stone, who won in 1980, was Cy Present, Scott McGregor Cy Future, and Storm Davis, a Palmer pitch-a-like, was Cy Clone. Cy Bex was a pitcher who had been hurt, and Cy-Anarah was a pitcher on his way out.

When Palmer's career ended in 1984, Mike assumed staff leadership and continued the tradition of being the father-figure for the young pitchers coming up. Traded to Toronto during the 1987 season, Flanny spent three-plus seasons with the Blue Jays before closing out his career in Baltimore. His career ended fittingly, as he pitched the final inning at Memorial Stadium and in the first season at Camden Yards. When he called it quits after the 1992 season he ranked fourth on the all-time club list in wins with 141, third in innings pitched with over 2300, and third in both games pitched and strikeouts. Now a roving instructor in the Oriole system and part-time telecaster at Camden Yards, Mike Flanagan came full circle in 1994 with his induction as the 25th member of the Orioles Hall of Fame.

granule of sand on a Tidewater beach. Three of the Birds' top young players, centerfielder Steve Finley, and right-handed pitchers Pete Harnisch and Curt Schilling, were dealt to Houston for power hitter first baseman Glenn Davis, who in a four-year stretch from '86 through '89 had averaged 31 homers in one of the toughest home run parks in the major leagues, the Astrodome. It's a deal the Orioles would like back. Davis had had a troubled youth and lived the bulk of his high school years with former Oriole Storm Davis (no relation) and his family. He played baseball and football for Storm's father in Jacksonville, Florida. Also coming aboard was 39-year-old Dwight Evans, who had spent more than 18 seasons in Boston as one of the premier rightfielders in the game. Also invited to spring training was former Oriole great Mike Flanagan who had been released by the Blue Jays in 1990.

The final season at Memorial Stadium, 1991, was not an artistic success on the field. But the 38th season of Oriole baseball at 33rd Street carried special meaning. Just as in 1954, the Vice President of the United States threw out the first ball. This time Dan Quayle did the honors. The starting pitchers from 1954, Bob Turley and Virgil Trucks, were brought back for a bow—and to toss out ceremonial first balls. The White Sox provided the opposition for the final opening day at the stadium, just as they did in the first opener in 1954. The result, however, wasn't as favorable. In a battle between former Stanford teammates Jack McDowell and Jeff Ballard, Chicago beat the Orioles 9-1. A Cal Ripken single, followed by a Glenn Davis double in his first Oriole at-bat, produced the only Baltimore run.

A "season to remember" was the catchphrase for the year, but there was little to remember on the field. On May 23, after a slow 13-24 start, Frank Robinson was replaced as manager by first base coach Johnny Oates, a former Oriole catcher who had managed in the Yankee and Oriole minor-league systems. While Frank accepted an offer to return to the front office, Oates went on to notch a 54-71 record as 14 different Oriole rookies saw action.

Another magic moment in Oriole history. Jim Palmer, one of the flashiest – and best – pitchers ever, is inducted into baseball's Hall of Fame in Cooperstown. Heavy rains moved the August 6, 1990, ceremony indoors, but that didn't dampen Palmer's spirits at all. Then commissioner Fay Vincent presents Jim with his plaque.

Despite the disappointing record several memories lingered from the Memorial Stadium swan song. At the top of the list was the visit of Her Majesty Queen Elizabeth II of England and her husband, Prince Philip, on May 15. President Bush and First Lady Barbara accompanied the Royal couple. The president tried to explain the basics of the game to the Royal couple who had greeted the players from the Orioles and the visiting A's in the dugout before the game.

The Orioles were involved in two no-hitters in '91, winning one and losing one. On July 13 in Oakland, four Oriole pitchers combined to no-hit the A's. Bob Milacki started and left after six innings when he was struck on the hand by a batted ball. Three relievers followed, each pitching an inning. Mike Flanagan, Mark Williamson, and Gregg Olson joined Milacki in hurling a rare multiple-pitcher no-hitter. On August 6, Chicago's young Wilson Alvarez tossed the sixth and last no-hitter at Memorial Stadium. The 21-year-old left-hander was making his first appearance on the year after being recalled by Double-A Birmingham. In his only previous big-league appearance Alvarez had failed to retire any of the five batters he faced.

The 1991 season will be remembered as the "Year of Cal." The 31-year-old All-Star enjoyed a season that rivaled Frank Robinson's 1966 Triple Crown year. The shortstop won about every post-season award, including MVP and Major League Player of the Year. He became the first Oriole to earn two MVP trophies. Batting .323, Cal led the Birds in 14 offensive categories and was at or near the top in most departments in the league. He socked 34 homers while striking out only 46 times. He drove in 144 runs and led the majors with 85 extra-base hits. His 210 hits ranked second in the majors, while his 368 total bases led the majors and set a club record. Ripken's .348 average at the All-Star break made him the first shortstop to lead both leagues in batting at the break since Cleveland's Lou Boudreau in 1948.

Ripken became the fourth Oriole to win All-Star MVP honors, singling and cracking a three-run homer to lead the American League to a 4-2 win over the Nationals. In the home-run-hitting contest the day before at the Skydome, Cal hit an amazing 12 homers in 22 swings to dominate the competition. Rip was at his peak all season and his consecutive-games streak climbed to 1,573. Lou Gehrig's insurmountable 2,130 was, incredulously, in sight.

Other positives from the '91 season were the 24 outfield assists turned in by hustling Joe Orsulak that led the majors and broke Chuck Diering's 37-year club record by seven. Underhanded reliever Todd Frowirth had an ERA of 1.87 in 51 appearances. Gregg Olson notched 31 saves and 1990's top draft choice, Mike Mussina, arrived from Rochester on July 31 and became the club's number one starter over the last two months of the season. Mussina's 2.87 ERA for 10 or more starts was tops among major league rookies as he held opponents to two or fewer runs in eight of his 12 starts.

As the 1991 season wound down, so did an era. In early September a spate of promotions was launched to honor great players or memorable games at the stadium. Doug DeCinces, Bobby Grich, and Tippy Martinez returned for various events. So too did the

October 6, 1991, was a day of great emotion in Baltimore. The final game at Memorial Stadium brought close to 100 former players back onto the field in uniform. In 38 seasons, more than 3,000 games were played there, 30 in the postseason. It was truly a House of Magic.

four 20-game winners of 1971, Dave McNally, Jim Palmer, Mike Cuellar, and Pat Dobson. There was even a tribute to the old Baltimore Colts with over 20 former players on hand, including the beloved Johnny Unitas, Art Donovan, Lenny Moore, and Jim Parker.

Without question, the toughest ticket since the 1983 World Series was for the final weekend at Memorial Stadium. The Tigers provided the opposition but the games themselves were anticlimactic. The place was awash in nostalgia. People who had criticized Memorial Stadium for its inadequacies were now filled with tears over its passing. Mickey Tettleton's homer on Friday gave Detroit the victory in the last night game at Memorial Stadium. The largest fireworks show in stadium history followed as the clock hit midnight.

On Saturday the Orioles' All-Time Team, a promotion of the *Baltimore Sun*, was introduced and several meaningful items of stadium memorabilia were given away: the bases, Frank Robinson's "Here" banner, the pitching rubber, and other treasures. Brady Anderson's bases-loaded triple and Chito Martinez' two-run homer, the last by a Bird in ballpark history, gave the Orioles their final Memorial Stadium win, 7-3.

No one who was on hand for the Sunday finale will ever forget it. It began with two Baltimore sports legends, Brooks Robinson and Johnny Unitas, throwing out first balls, Brooks a baseball and Johnny U. a football. The game itself was over early when the Tigers scored four first-inning runs off Bob Milacki and rolled to a 7-1 win. For the crowd of more than 50,000 the game highlight was watching Mike Flanagan, who had spent so many great years pitching at Memorial Stadium, come in to pitch to the final two batters. He fanned both Dave Bergman and Travis Fryman and received a thunderous standing ovation as he walked off the mound.

Just before the season began, Flanagan had torn a hamstring in one of the last exhibition games, but he still managed to pitch the ninth inning of the last Memorial Stadium opener. "I got them 1-2-3 with a couple of strike outs," said Mike. "At that time I felt whatever happens this year, pitching in the last stadium opener was something nobody could take away from me. Since I had been traded in 1987 during the pennant race, the fans had never had a chance to say goodbye. So to be brought in to pitch the last inning on the last game ever at Memorial Stadium was a perfect capper." Flanny asked coach Ellie Hendricks, who had been honored before the game for spending more time in an Oriole uniform than anybody, to warm him up since he had warmed him up over 300 times in the past. "I walked in slowly. I didn't want to rush the moment. I got myself together and treated every pitch with great importance. I felt that I wasn't just doing it for me but for all the guys I had played with. I had to back up and pause a couple of times because the moment was getting to me. I had the weight of all the generations who ever walked out the tunnel onto the field. All the guys who went before me. I didn't do it for me. I did it for them."

After Ripken bounced into a double-play to end the game, the magic began. First Frank Robinson trotted home from third to score the absolute last run at the stadium as home plate was dug up and taken by limo to the new park at Camden Yards. Then with background music from the movie, a living "Field of Dreams" began to appear. Brooks Robinson trotted out to third base as he had done thousands of times, standing alone and smoothing the dirt with his spikes. Then Frank Robinson trotted out to right field and Boog Powell to first and Jim Palmer to the pitcher's mound and Don Baylor to left, and Rick Dempsey behind the now empty plate and then Bobby Grich and Rich Dauer to second and Louis Aparicio and Mark Belanger to short, and Paul Blair and Al Bumbry to centerfield. The players just kept coming with the "Field of Dreams" melody playing. Dave McNally, Lee May, Jim Gentile, Pat Dobson, Mike Cuellar, George Zuverink, Chuck Diering, Billy O'Dell, Gene Woodling, Milt

ROAD TO BIRDLAND
ROAD TO BIRDLAND

"Baltimore knows Boh"
NATIONAL BOHEMIAN BEER
From the Land of Pleasant Living

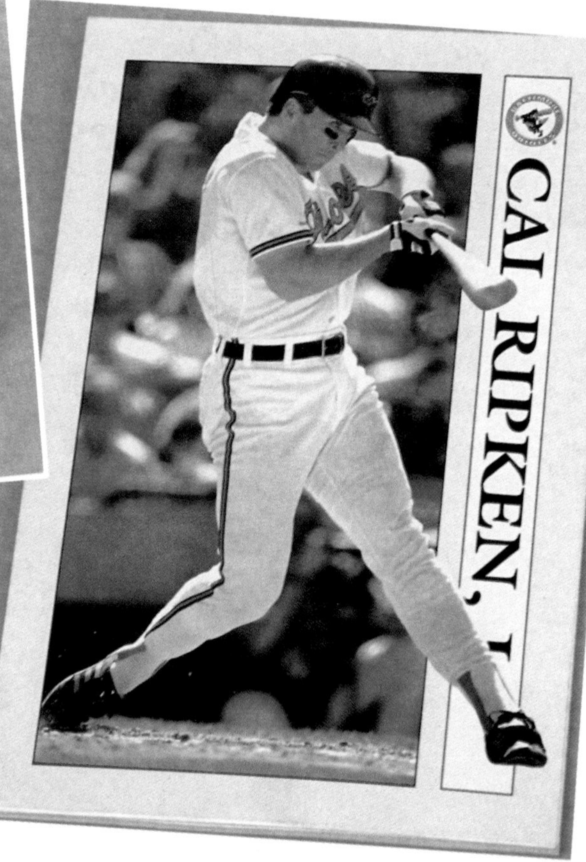
CAL RIPKEN, J

Boh's a Hit!
OFFICIAL
ORIOLE
Score Card and
REVIEW
15c
PLAY BALL!
1954
ORIOLES
The difference is satisfying flavor
NATIONAL
BOHEMIAN
"Oh boy-what a beer"
NATIONAL BOHEMIAN
PALE BEER

33 RPM
SPORTS RECORD
Jim Gentile

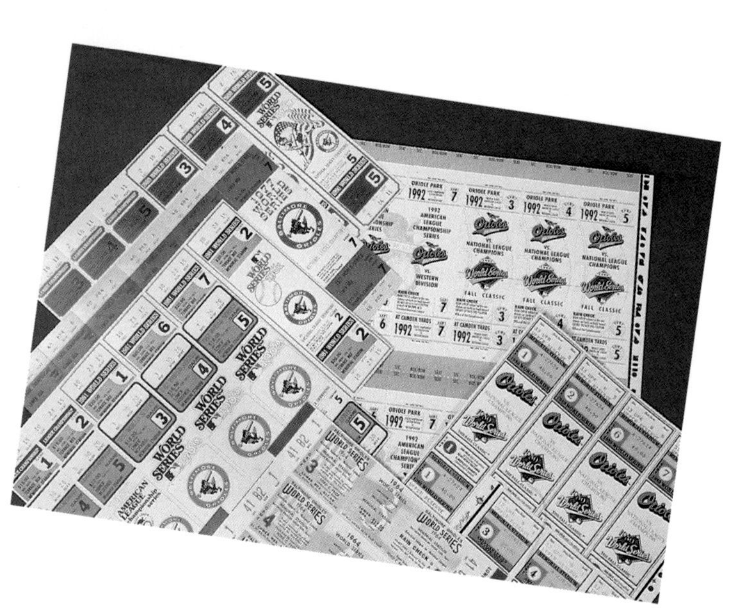

ORIOLE PARK
1992
AMERICAN LEAGUE CHAMPIONSHIP SERIES
WORLD SERIES

Bird Suits

1961 home, Jerry Walker

1954 original uniform and cap, manager Jimmie Dykes

1961 Barry Shetrone

1963 home, Steve Barber

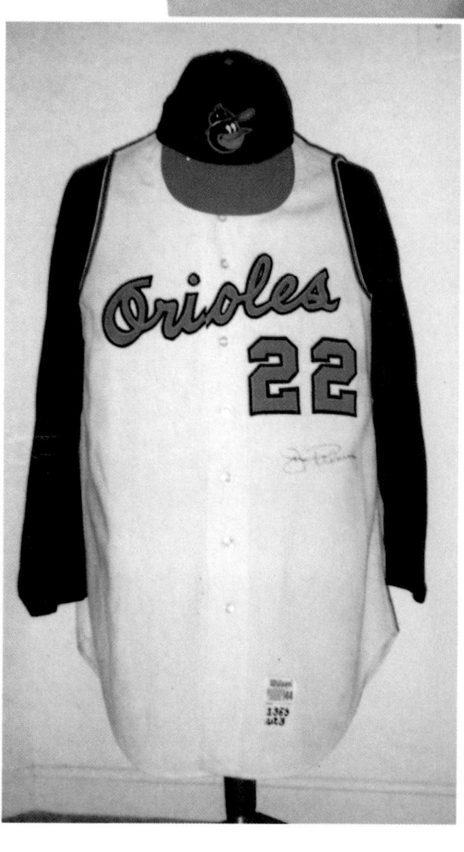

1969 sleeveless, worn only seven times before being scrapped because the pitchers disliked them.

1966 home, Dave McNally

1971 road, Dick Hall

1969 road, Frank Robinson

1971 home, 20-game winners Mike Cuellar, Pat Dobson, Dave McNally, and Jim Palmer. The all-orange shirts and pants were worn only twice then abandoned when someone cracked that Boog Powell resembled a giant pumpkin in his.

1973 road, Boog Powell

1975 home, Jim Palmer

1975, Brooks Robinson

1980 home, Mark Belanger

1980 home, Earl Weaver

1982, Cal Ripken Jr., rookie year

1985, Eddie Murray

1992, Mike Flanagan

Baltimore
5
22

1957
George Kell

LOUISVILLE SLUGGER
125
HILLERICH & BRADSBY Co
MADE IN U.S.A.
LOUISVILLE, KY.
Powerized
GENUINE
LOUISVILLE SLUGGER
Rawlings
ADIRONDACK
PRO
BIG STICK
REGGIE JACKSON
PROFESSIONAL MODEL
Sept 6.87
GENUINE
Frank Robinson
LOUISVILLE SLUGGER

Frank Robinson

Louisville Slugger
Powerized
BALTIMORE ORIOLES
AMERICAN LEAGUE
MARK BELANGER
SCOTT McGREGOR
JIM PALMER
HALL OF FAME INDUCTION
JULY 31, 1983
BALTIMORE ORIOLES
WORLD CHAMPIONS
1983
SCOTT McGREGOR
MIKE BODDICKER

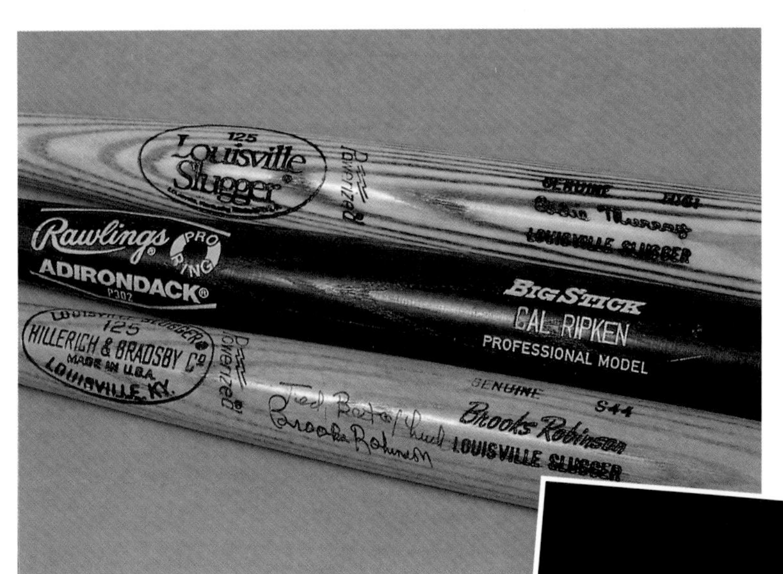
125
Louisville Slugger
GENUINE
LOUISVILLE SLUGGER
Rawlings
PRO RING
ADIRONDACK®
P302
BIG STICK
CAL RIPKEN
PROFESSIONAL MODEL
LOUISVILLE SLUGGER
125
HILLERICH & BRADSBY Co
MADE IN U.S.A.
LOUISVILLE, KY.
GENUINE S44
Brooks Robinson
LOUISVILLE SLUGGER

Johnny Oates
1991
THE LAST BASEBALL TEAM
TO PLAY AT
MEMORIAL STADIUM

Around

the Yards

Kirby Puckett, MVP of 1993 All-Star game at Camden Yards

1993 All-Star game player introductions

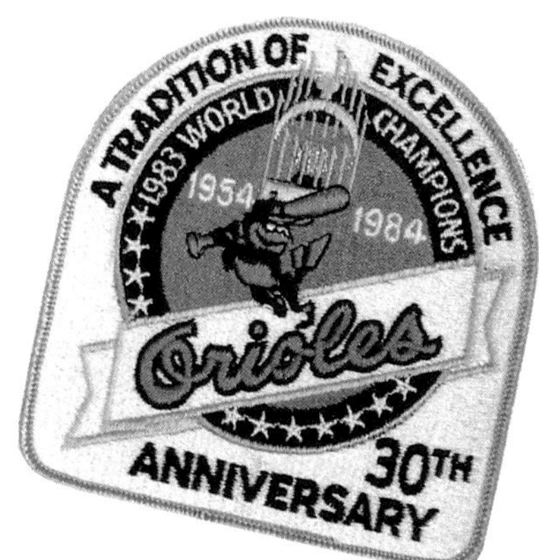

Orioles
HALL OF FAME

Orioles
'87
sun mon tue wed thurs fri sat
1
2
3
4
5
6 2:05 t/v TEX
7
8 4:05 TEX
9 7:35 t/v TEX
10 4:05 t/v CLE
11 1:35 CLE
12 1:35 t/v CLE
13 7:35 t/v MIL
14 7:35 t/v MIL
15 7:35 MIL
16 7:35 t/v CLE
17 8:05 CLE
18 7:35 t/v CLE
19 2:05 t/v CLE
20
21 8:35 t/v TEX
22 8:35 t/v TEX
23 8:35 t/v TEX
24 7:05 MIL
25 2:35 MIL
26 2:35 t/v MIL
27
28 8:35 t/v KC
29 8:35 t/v KC
30
HOME GAMES
AWAY GAMES
APRIL
THE BALTIMORE SUN

STARS OF THE FUTURE
29
Orioles
CROWN
Enjoy Coca-Cola CLASSIC

Papas, Gil Coan, Steve Barber. They kept coming, all regaled in the uniforms of their era. Jackie Brandt, Willy Miranda, Joe Durham, Ron Hansen, Dick Hall, Robin Roberts, Skinny Brown, Joe Ginsberg. Soon clusters of players formed at each position, 118 total, and finally out came the last one, number four Earl Weaver. They formed a giant "O" around the infield. "Auld Lang Syne" played in the background and 50,000 fans stood clapping, eyes moist, hearts heavy. Rick Dempsey led the fans in one last O-R-I-O-L-E-S cheer and trotted around the bases imitating Babe Ruth. Then it was over. The message board read, "Goodbye, Ole Friend." After 38 years, Camden Yards beckoned.

Frank Robinson spoke for most when he said: "I'll miss the old place. It had a great playing surface. You got used to it. It's like your wife. You've lived with her a long time. You got used to her and she gets used to you. You know how the ball plays and the odds and ends of playing the outfield. Memorial Stadium never got its just due."

Camden Yards: A Ballpark Jewel

The raves were streaming in before a pitch was thrown at Oriole Park at Camden Yards. *New York Times* columnist Dave Anderson called it "The Rookie of the Year." More than 3.5 million fans would pour through the turnstiles in the inaugural season of 1992, including sellouts for the last 59 dates. The park is a deft mixture of the old and new: red brick and painted green steel,

An aerial view of Oriole Park at Camden Yards, the Orioles' stunning new home in 1992.

nostalgic scoreboard, 1,000-foot warehouse housing the club offices, restaurants, and shops, modern amenities galore including skyboxes and unobstructed-view seats. It all adds up to a powerful baseball experience.

The historical aura isn't just the result of an architect's vision. Only two blocks away is Babe Ruth's birthplace. And 80 years ago Babe's dad ran a saloon that was situated where center field is now.

Several old parks influenced the design of Camden Yards. Looking down the right-field line evokes comparisons to Wrigley Field and Ebbets Field. Down the left-field line conjures up memories of Shibe Park and Comiskey Park. Despite natural grass, rainouts would be a rarity because of the elaborate drainage system underneath the surface. As one fan put it, "You sit here and feel like you're in the movie *The Natural* with Robert Redford about to step to the plate."

Rick Sutcliffe had the privilege of starting the first game at OPACY, opposing Cleveland's Charles Nagy on Monday, April 6, 1992. Paul Sorrento, the Indians' first baseman, collected the first hit in the top of the second inning. Glenn Davis led off the bottom of the second with the first Oriole hit. Sutcliffe, who at 35 was the oldest opening day starter in club history, pitched a five-hit shutout, winning 2-0. The bearded veteran went on to win 16 games and lead the major leagues in starts with 36. Both on and off the field he was a superb free agent acquisition. The first three games played at OPACY were shutouts, with the Birds winning two.

The Orioles thrived early in their new digs, going 13-8 in April for their best start since 1979. They were 10-1 at home, the best start ever for a team in a new park. From early May to early July, no more than a game separated the Orioles and Blue Jays. A seven-game West Coast winning streak in late August brought them to within a half game of the lead. Then, starting on September 5, they went on a 21-game streak where they scored no more than four runs a game. Their 8-13 finish dropped them to third place, 7½ games behind Toronto. Still the 89-73 record was the best since the championship year of 1983 and represented a 22-game improvement over 1991.

Rick Sutcliffe's debut as an Oriole coincided with the opening of Camden Yards. Sutcliffe launched the new ballpark with an auspicious 2-0 shutout of the Cleveland Indians. He steadied a young staff in his two years as an Oriole.

Home runs figured to jump out of the new park but, surprisingly, that was not the case. In fact the Orioles' total of 148 was 22 fewer than their last year at Memorial Stadium. Centerfielder Mike Devereaux led the way with 24 homers and 107 RBI and was voted Oriole MVP honors. Catcher Chris Hoiles drove in only 40 runs but socked 20 homers. The patience shown in leftfielder Brady Anderson finally paid off. Brady became the first player in American League history to hit 20 homers (21), steal 50 bases (53), and

Broadcasters

The Orioles have not only fielded a Hall of Fame lineup on the field over the years, but they've also distinguished themselves in the broadcast booth. Three former Oriole broadcasters have won the Ford Frick Award in Cooperstown, which is presented to a broadcaster for making major contributions to the game of baseball. The Orioles' first winner in 1981 was their first broadcaster, Ernie Harwell, who broadcast Oriole games from 1954 through 1959. Ernie then went on to broadcast for more than 30 years in Detroit. Chuck Thompson, who followed Harwell and is still active after 30 years with the Orioles, won the Frick Award in 1993. Bob Murphy, who spent a couple of seasons in Baltimore in the early 1960s before joining the Mets in 1962, is the 1994 winner of the Frick Award.

Other broadcasters who made important contributions in Baltimore include Herb Carneal, who assisted Harwell in the 1950s and has been with the Twins for over 30 years, the late Bill O'Donnell, who teamed with Thompson for over 15 years as their most memorable of all broadcast teams, Frank Messer, John Gordon, and current announcer Jon Miller.

drive in more than 75 runs (80) in the same season, remarkable—especially for a lead-off hitter. He hit a solid .271 after failing to hit over .231 in his previous four seasons in Baltimore and became the first Oriole outfielder to make the All-Star team since Ken Singleton in 1981. Mike Mussina pitched in the All-Star game and deservedly so. He compiled an 18-5 record and a glittering 2.54 ERA, the lowest by an Oriole since Jim Palmer's 2.46 in 1978. His best start was probably the one-hitter he tossed against Texas in his first start after the All-Star break. Mike won 8-0, striking out 10. At 23 Mussina became the Orioles' youngest 18-game winner since 19-year-old Wally Bunker won 19 in 1964.

Johnny Oates replaced Frank Robinson midway through the 1991 season. A former Oriole catcher, Oates was traded along with Davey Johnson to the Braves in 1973. Mostly a backup during his 11-year major-league career, Oates continues a tradition as old as Connie Mack: players with undistinguished careers who rise to become managers in the big leagues, often reaching undreamed of success. Johnny's 1992 and '93 Orioles finished above .500 and made pennant runs, perhaps signaling the beginning of a Connie Mack-like career.

Picked in the first round by the Orioles in the June 1988 amateur draft, Gregg Olson made a meteoric rise to the major leagues, reaching the "Show" shortly after signing with the Birds late in 1988. From 1989-1992, Olson was the best closer in the American League (this side of Oakland), saving 131 games in that span. He's the Orioles career leader in saves and reached 100 saves faster than anyone else in major-league history. An injury sidelined Gregg for most of 1993, and when his return for '94 looked doubtful, the Orioles reluctantly released him.

Cal Ripken completed his 10th straight season without missing a game as his streak reached 1,735 games. During the streak the Orioles played a total of 15,787 innings and Cal played in 15,659 of them (99.2 percent). A total of 2,708 players had gone on the disabled list since his streak began. By Cal's standards, however, 1992 was not a good year. His average plummeted 72 points from the year before and his home run output dropped to 14, 20 fewer than the year before. His 20-or-more homers streak ended at 10. Many felt the long, tedious negotiations to hammer out a new contract were taking their toll. Finally on August 24, on his 32nd birthday, he signed a five-year contract worth more than 30 million dollars. Winning the Roberto Clemente Award, presented annually to the player who best exemplifies the game both on and off the field, proved to be a major highlight of the season for Rip.

Extra excitement was building in 1993 because for the first time in 35 years the All-Star game was coming back to Baltimore. Only one current Oriole, Rick Sutcliffe, was even alive in 1958, the year the American League beat the Nationals 4-3. In just its second year, Oriole Park at Camden Yards would be on national display.

The Orioles opened slow, losing 13 of 18, and finished slow, losing 13 of 19. In between their 74-51 record was the best in the league. Their final tally of 85-77 put them in third place, 10 games behind the Blue Jays. The anticipated season-ending four-game clash with Toronto at Camden Yards turned out to be meaningless. The late-season slump ensured that. The Birds were dynamite again at the gate, drawing 3,644,965 in 80 dates, averaging 45,562 per game. Remarkably, they sold out their last 52 home games.

This was the streakiest Oriole club ever, once winning 10 straight and on two occasions winning eight straight. At one point they won eight straight series. In

Acquired in a trade with Boston prior to 1989, Brady Anderson blossomed in 1992 when he hit .271 and socked a professional high 21 homers. His play in center field evokes memories of Paul Blair, and his stolen base abilities make him an invaluable leadoff hitter.

August they won eight straight games and then promptly lost eight straight. In June they went 20-7 as David Segui (.402) became the first Oriole to hit .400 in one month since Eddie Murray in 1982. Fernando Valenzuela, a non-roster pitcher in spring training, was named American League pitcher of the month for July thanks to a 3-0 record and 1.56 ERA in five starts. Another non-roster invitee, left-hander Jamie Moyer, was called up May 20 and lost his first three starts before reeling off 12 wins against three losses over the next three months to top all big-league lefties in victories. Big Ben McDonald allowed three runs or less in 28 of his 34 starts, including 14 straight, yet could muster only a 13-14 record. McDonald, who never complained about the lack of support, allowed one run or less 15 times in 34 starts. Ben was the victim of shutouts five times and his teammates scored two or fewer runs for him eight other times.

Ben McDonald, the first pick of the 1989 amateur draft (and the first time the O's picked numero uno), enjoyed a breakthrough in 1993. Posting his best ERA in four full seasons, Ben established himself as one of the American League's rising stars. Winner of college baseball's most prestigious prize, the Golden Spike Award, McDonald throws in the 90s and should be a fixture in the Birds rotation for years to come.

Injuries to Mike Mussina and Gregg Olson dealt severe blows. Mussina, who finished 14-6 and became a *cause celeb* just by warming up in the bullpen during the All-Star game, missed six weeks with a shoulder and back strain. He did manage back-to-back complete-game shutouts against the Twins, a feat last accomplished by Jim Palmer in 1982.

Olson had 29 saves in 35 opportunities including a club record 11 in June, but missed 38 games with an elbow injury before facing one batter in September. After walking Albert Belle on September 20, Olson went back on the shelf. Electing to rehab his elbow rather than face surgery that could have sidelined him for more than a year, Olson accepted an offer to pitch with the Atlanta Braves in 1994.

At the plate, Brady Anderson led the club in eight offensive categories despite missing 15 games with the chicken pox. Playing on surgically repaired knees that limited him to 416 at-bats, Harold Baines, a native of Maryland's Eastern Shore, hit .313 with 20 home runs, batting .340 with men on base. Silent Hal tied Jim Dwyer's club record by reaching base 13 straight times and had eight consecutive hits. Baines collected his 2000th career hit off Minnesota's Scott Erickson on July 24, two weeks after Cal Ripken got his 2,000th off Chicago's Wilson (no-hit) Alvarez.

Catcher Chris Hoiles was voted Oriole MVP, just missing

Lifetime Winners and Losers

Hall of Famer Whitey Ford has the distinction of winning more games against the Orioles than any other pitcher. In 14 seasons, Whitey posted a 30-16 record against the Birds. Altogether, 13 pitchers have posted 20 or more wins over the Orioles in 39 seasons. Catfish Hunter (26-24), Billy Pierce (23-11), Early Wynn (21-8), and Frank Sullivan (21-8), head the list. Hunter, the second biggest winner, is also the biggest lifetime loser with 24. There have been four other 20-game losers, Luis Tiant and Jim Perry with 22 and Fritz Peterson and Jim Kaat with 21.

Not since Gus Triandos have the Orioles had a catcher so potent with the bat. Chris Hoiles has hit 61 homers in just over three seasons in Baltimore. He set the Oriole record for most RBI (82) in a season by a catcher in 1993 and fell one shy of tying Triandos for the Oriole home run record by a catcher. In 1993 he won the Most Valuable Oriole Award.

Best Start Ever

In 1992, the Orioles went 10-1 in their first 11 games at Oriole Park at Camden Yards, the best start ever by a team playing in a new ballpark. The previous best start by a team playing in a new park was shared by the 1953 Milwaukee Braves, who went 9-1 at County Stadium, and the Houston Astros, who also won nine of their first 10 games at the Astrodome in 1965.

becoming the first American League catcher ever to hit .300 with 30 home runs. As it was Chris batted .310, socked 29 homers, and surpassed Gus Triandos' club RBI record for a catcher by driving in 82, four more than Gus. He did all of this despite missing 21 games with a back injury.

Another non-roster invitee, Mark McLemore, became one of the big stories of '93. Not only did Mark learn a new position in right field and play it expertly, he hit a solid .284 in 581 at-bats, driving in 72 runs. His 49 multi-hit games put him among the club's best all-time. McLemore also emerged as a team leader, joining Sutcliffe as one of the few holler guys on the team.

Rookie Jack Voigt was nicknamed "Roy Hobbs" as in the movie *The Natural.* He hit .296 in 64 games, coming up with clutch hits just about everytime he was called on.

Cal Ripken improved his power totals (24 homers and 90 RBI) but once again his average was a disappointing .257. Still, he led major-league shortstops in homers and RBI. He hit .317 over his last 54 games to gain momentum heading into 1994. In this age of statistics, it's hard to imagine oversights, but that's what happened in the case of "most career homers by a shortstop." Cal went into the off-season thinking he needed four home runs to tie Ernie Banks for most home runs by a shortstop at 293. The Elias Sports Bureau discovered in 1990, however, that Banks was credited with 16 homers at shortstop that he actually hit while playing first base. Thus Mr. Cub hit only 277 of his 512 at short and Cal's 289 were more than enough to give him the all-time lead. The record breaker, which no one realized at the time, occurred on July 15 at Camden Yards when Cal connected off Minnesota's Scott Erickson.

Cal's consecutive games streak had reached 1,897 heading into the 1994 season. The next highest streak was 162 by Florida's Jeff Conine. A total of 3,072 players had gone on the disabled list since the streak began. Cal was almost one of them as he twisted his right knee in a Sunday afternoon melee against Seattle in June. His spikes caught in the grass and although he stayed in the game, the knee was swollen and painful the next day. Still, he didn't even miss infield practice. He said later, "It was the closest I've ever come to not playing."

Brady Anderson's outfield mate, Mike Devereaux socked 57 homers and drove in 241 runs from 1991- 1993. Devereaux's hallmark is his clutch hitting; he led the Orioles in game-tying or go-ahead RBI in 1992 and '93.

Baseball's all-time saves leader Lee Smith joined the Orioles in 1994 and saved 24 games in his first 26 opportunities.

Mike Mussina returned to form in 1994. Poised beyond his years, Mussina was called up halfway through 1991 and pitched like a veteran, finishing with a 2.87 ERA in 12 starts. His dominance in 1992 brought comparisons to past Oriole greats as he posted a stingy 2.54 ERA and an overpowering 18-5 record, the fourth best winning pct. in Oriole history. A control pitcher with a live fastball, Mussina started strong in '93 but stumbled in the second half of the season after suffering an arm injury. Healed, Mussina should reclaim his status as one of the game's deadliest pitchers.

(It was in that brush-back brawl with Seattle that Mike Mussina also was hurt.) Now Ripken is bearing down on Lou Gehrig's thought-to-be-invincible 2,130 straight. It could topple during the 1995 season.

On the down side of the 1993 season, the book was closed on the Glenn Davis trade as the hard-luck first baseman battled numerous injuries, including a broken jaw he received when he acted as a peacemaker in a brawl involving teammate Randy Ready outside a Norfolk, Virgina, billiards hall. Davis, rehabbing at the time, didn't return until late in the season. Then, sitting in the dugout a foul ball off the bat of Jeffrey Hammonds struck him flush on the head. The Orioles released him on September 8. In three seasons in Baltimore Davis averaged eight home runs and 28 RBI. Pete Harnisch and Steve Finley meanwhile flourished in Houston, while Curt Schilling, 3-5 with the 1991 Astros, became a big winner in Philadelphia, helping the Phillies to the 1993 National League pennant.

Signed during the 1993 offseason, Chris Sabo started slowly for the Birds, sustaining an early injury then losing his starting job to Leo Gomez. Chris was eventually moved to the outfield where he began winning games with both his bat and glove.

The July All-Star celebration in Baltimore lasted one sensational week. From the FanFest carnival at the Convention Center and Festival Hall to the home-run hitting contest and old-timers game, the All-Star break was three days of uninterrupted activity, truly a "FunFest." Brooks Robinson started two double plays and banged out two hits in the Heroes of Baseball game. Juan Gonzales and Ken Griffey Jr. put on a show in the home-run-hitting contest, turning Camden Yards into another Fort McHenry with an aerial bombardment that would have inspired Francis Scott Key. The sluggers tied with seven homers after the first round as Griffey became the first batter to hit

Rafael Palmeiro became an instant fan-favorite in Baltimore as he got off to a brilliant start in 1994, setting a new club consecutive game hitting streak and batting well over .300.

the warehouse on the fly, some eight feet up to be exact. Gonzales, batting from the right side, hit a ball off the facade of the second deck and then reached the third deck over 500 feet away. Juan capped his power display by hitting the center field wall on the fly, all Camden Yards firsts. In the end, Gonzales outhomered Griffey 12-11, and the fans went home the biggest winners of all.

The actual All-Star Game on July 13 was almost anticlimactic. The American League wallopped the National League, 9-3, for its sixth straight win. Kirby Puckett homered and doubled in another run to win MVP honors. Vice-President Al Gore was on hand. Al Kaline, Negro League great Leon Day, and Brooks

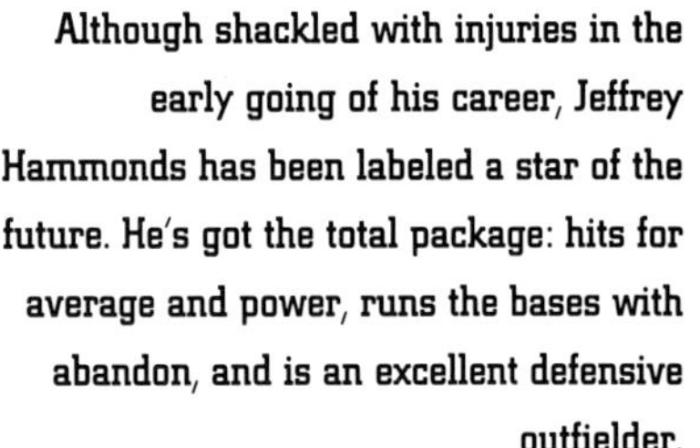

Although shackled with injuries in the early going of his career, Jeffrey Hammonds has been labeled a star of the future. He's got the total package: hits for average and power, runs the bases with abandon, and is an excellent defensive outfielder.

Hall of Famers

Eight modern Orioles have been elected to the Baseball Hall of Fame in Cooperstown, including four who made it in their first year of eligibility: Frank Robinson, Brooks Robinson, Jim Palmer, and Reggie Jackson, who played one season in Baltimore (1976). Others who played in Baltimore and are now enshrined at Cooperstown are Robin Roberts, Hoyt Wilhelm, George Kell, and Luis Aparicio.

Fifteen old-time Orioles, headed by Babe Ruth, saw action in an Oriole uniform. Ruth of course played for the minor-league Orioles. John McGraw, Joe Kelley, Wee Willie Keeler, Hughie Jennings, Wilbert Robinson, and Lefty Grove join the Babe at the head of the list.

Robinson tossed out first balls. Frank Robinson and Jim Palmer were honorary co-captains for the American League. The hometown fans booed Toronto manager Cito Gaston when he inserted his own pitcher, Duane Ward, instead of Oriole favorite Mike Mussina in the ninth. The drama heightened when Mussina started warming up on his own, but to no avail. Oriole fans, who hadn't hosted an All-Star game in 35 years, felt betrayed by the Blue Jays' manager. The fans were hoping for revenge when Toronto came back for the final four games of the season, but the race was over, defusing a potentially volatile situation.

Camden Yards adds an exclamation point to the rejuvenation of Baltimore.

In August Oriole baseball began a new era when beleaguered owner Eli Jacobs, awash in a sea of millions of dollars of debt, lost the team after being forced to declare bankruptcy. Rather than see the Orioles fall into the hands of an out-of-town owner, local attorney Peter Angelos, a Highlandtown native and self-made millionaire, became the principal owner of the Orioles. The price tag was a whopping 173 million dollars, the most ever paid for a pro sports franchise. Others in the ownership group included Cincinnati's Bill DeWitt (who at one point was the leading candidate to buy the club), local novelist Tom Clancy, comic-book king Steve Geppi, and local sports figures Jim McKay and Pam Shriver.

Where Jacobs was reclusive and invisible to the fans and media, Angelos was outgoing and available. His ownership, barely months old, brought back memories of the Jerry Hoffberger era in the 1960s. Unlike Jacobs, who was reluctant to spend money, Angelos wasn't shy about opening his pocketbook. Four high-priced free agents were signed for '94: first baseman Rafael Palmeiro who socked 37 homers and drove in 107 runs for Texas in '93; Chris Sabo who left the Reds to play third base in Baltimore (a position that has seen 40 different players since Brooks Robinson retired); Sid Fernandez, a solid left-handed pitcher with the Mets; and Lee Smith, an indomitable closer who held the record for career saves. (The newcomers made immediate impacts in '94. Palmeiro achieved something in his first two months as an Oriole that nobody had done in the first 40 years: a 24-game hitting streak, which broke the club record of 22 shared by Eddie Murray and Doug DeCinces. Smith set a big league record by saving 12 games in the month of April. Sabo made key contributions as an outfielder). Couple the newcomers with emerging stars like Mussina, McDonald, Hoiles, and young Jeffrey Hammonds, and the future in Baltimore looks bright.

Forty years. Think of it. Cleveland hasn't had a champion since 1948 and hasn't played in the World Series since the Orioles' first year in 1954. The White Sox haven't won since 1917, the Red Sox since 1918, and the Cubs since way back in 1908. In four decades, the Baltimore Orioles have won three World Championships, lost two World Series in seven games, and won six American League pennants. They are the franchise other franchises are measured against. The "Oriole Way" has been the right way. For the first 20 years they operated frugally with fan support a persistent concern. In the last 15 years, as attendance has soared, the Orioles have become the envy of many in baseball. May the magic of the first 40 years continue for 40 more—and then some.

TABLE 1
Season-by-Season Statistics

1954	Record	Finish	Games Behind	Manager
	W-54 L-100	7th	57	Jimmie Dykes

Leading Hitters (min. 300AB)		BA	HR	RBI	Leading Pitchers	W	ERA	SV	IP
RF	C. Abrams	.293	6	25	B. Turley	14	3.46	0	247
					J. Coleman	13	3.50	0	221
1B	E. Waitkus	.283	2	33	D. Pillette	10	3.12	0	179

1955	Record	Finish	Games Behind	Manager
	W-57 L-97	7th	39	Paul Richards

Leading Hitters (min. 300AB)		BA	HR	RBI	Leading Pitchers	W	ERA	SV	IP
LF	D. Philley	.299	6	41	J. Wilson	12	3.44	0	235
1B	G. Triandos	.277	12	65	R. Moore	10	3.92	6	152

1956	Record	Finish	Games Behind	Manager
	W-69 L-85	6th	28	Paul Richards

Leading Hitters (min. 300AB)		BA	HR	RBI	Leading Pitchers	W	ERA	SV	IP
LF	B. Nieman	.322	12	64	R. Moore	12	4.18	0	185
CF	D. Williams	.286	11	37	C. Johnson	9	3.43	0	184
					G. Zuverink	7	4.16	16	97

1957	Record	Finish	Games Behind	Manager
	W-76 L-76	5th	21	Paul Richards

Leading Hitters (min. 300AB)		BA	HR	RBI	Leading Pitchers	W	ERA	SV	IP
1B	B. Boyd	.318	4	34	C. Johnson	14	3.20	0	242
3B	G. Kell	.297	9	44	B. Loes	12	3.24	4	155
					R. Moore	11	3.72	0	227
					G. Zuverink	10	2.48	9	113

1958	Record	Finish	Games Behind	Manager
	W-74 L-79	6th	17.5	Paul Richards

Leading Hitters (min. 300AB)		BA	HR	RBI	Leading Pitchers	W	ERA	SV	IP
OF	B. Nieman	.325	16	60	B. O'Dell	14	2.97	8	221
1B	B. Boyd	.309	7	36	A. Portocarrero	15	3.25	2	205
					J. Harshman	12	2.89	4	236

1959	Record	Finish	Games Behind	Manager
	W-74 L-80	6th	20	Paul Richards

Leading Hitters (min. 300AB)		BA	HR	RBI	Leading Pitchers	W	ERA	SV	IP
RF	G. Woodling	.300	14	77	H. Wilhelm	15	2.19	0	226
3B	B. Robinson	.294	14	88	M. Pappas	15	3.27	3	209

1960	Record	Finish	Games Behind	Manager
	W-89 L-65	2nd	8	Paul Richards

Leading Hitters (min. 300AB)		BA	HR	RBI	Leading Pitchers	W	ERA	SV	IP
3B	B. Robinson	.294	14	88	C. Estrada	18	3.58	2	209
1B	J. Gentile	.292	21	98	M. Pappas	15	3.37	0	206

1961

Record	Finish	Games Behind	Manager	
W-95 L-67	3rd	14	Paul Richards	W-78 L-57
			Lum Harris	W-17 L-10

Leading Hitters (min. 300AB)		BA	HR	RBI
1B	J. Gentile	.302	46	141
CF	J. Brandt	.297	16	72

Leading Pitchers	W	ERA	SV	IP
S. Barber	18	3.33	1	248
C. Estrada	15	3.69	0	212
H. Wilhelm	9	2.30	18	110

1962

Record	Finish	Games Behind	Manager
W-77 L-85	7th	19	Billy Hitchcock

Leading Hitters (min. 300AB)		BA	HR	RBI
RF	R. Snyder	.305	9	40
3B	B. Robinson	.303	23	86

Leading Pitchers	W	ERA	SV	IP
M. Pappas	12	4.03	0	205
R. Roberts	10	2.78	0	191

1963

Record	Finish	Games Behind	Manager
W-86 L-76	4th	18.5	Billy Hitchcock

Leading Hitters (min. 300AB)		BA	HR	RBI
C	J. Orsino	.272	19	56
OF	A. Smith	.272	10	39

Leading Pitchers	W	ERA	SV	IP
S. Barber	20	2.75	0	259
M. Pappas	16	3.03	0	217
S. Miller	5	2.24	27	112

1964

Record	Finish	Games Behind	Manager
W-97 L-65	3rd	2	Hank Bauer

Leading Hitters (min. 300AB)		BA	HR	RBI
3B	B. Robinson	.317	28	118
LF	B. Powell	.290	39	99

Leading Pitchers	W	ERA	SV	IP
W. Bunker	19	2.69	0	214
M. Pappas	16	2.97	0	252
S. Miller	7	3.06	23	97

1965

Record	Finish	Games Behind	Manager
W-94 L-68	3rd	8	Hank Bauer

Leading Hitters (min. 300AB)		BA	HR	RBI
3B	B. Robinson	.297	18	80
RF	R. Snyder	.270	1	29

Leading Pitchers	W	ERA	SV	IP
S. Barber	15	2.69	0	221
M. Pappas	13	2.60	0	221
S. Miller	14	1.89	24	119

1966

Record	Finish	Games Behind	Manager
W-97 L-63	1st	0	Hank Bauer

Leading Hitters (min. 300AB)		BA	HR	RBI
3B	F. Robinson	.316	49	122
LF	R. Snyder	.306	3	41

Leading Pitchers	W	ERA	SV	IP
J. Palmer	15	3.46	0	208
D. McNally	13	3.17	0	213
S. Miller	9	2.25	18	92

1967

Record	Finish	Games Behind	Manager
W-76 L-85	6th	15.5	Hank Bauer

Leading Hitters (min. 300AB)		BA	HR	RBI
3B	F. Robinson	.311	30	94
CF	P. Blair	.293	11	64

Leading Pitcher	W	ERA	SV	IP
T. Phoebus	14	3.33	0	208

1968

Record	Finish	Games Behind	Manager	
W-91 L-71	2nd	12	Hank Bauer	W-43 L-37
			Earl Weaver	W-48 L-34

Leading Hitters (min. 300AB)		BA	HR	RBI
LF	D. Buford	.282	15	46
RF	F. Robinson	.268	15	52

Leading Pitchers	W	ERA	SV	IP
D. McNally	22	1.95	0	273
J. Hardin	18	2.51	0	244

1969

Record	Finish	Games Behind	Manager
W-109 L-53	1st	0	Earl Weaver

Leading Hitters (min. 300AB)		BA	HR	RBI
RF	F. Robinson	.308	32	100
1B	B. Powell	.304	37	121

Leading Pitchers	W	ERA	SV	IP
M. Cuellar	23	2.38	0	291
D. McNally	20	3.22	0	269

1970

Record	Finish	Games Behind	Manager
W-108 L-54	1st	0	Earl Weaver

Leading Hitters (min. 300AB)		BA	HR	RBI
RF	F. Robinson	.306	25	78
1B	B. Powell	.297	35	114

Leading Pitchers	W	ERA	SV	IP
D. McNally	24	3.22	0	296
M. Cuellar	24	3.47	0	298
J. Palmer	20	2.71	0	305

1971

Record	Finish	Games Behind	Manager
W-101 L-57	1st	0	Earl Weaver

Leading Hitters (min. 300AB)		BA	HR	RBI
RF	M. Rettenmund	.318	11	75
LF	D. Buford	.290	19	54

Leading Pitchers	W	ERA	SV	IP
M. Cuellar	20	3.08	0	292
J. Palmer	20	2.68	0	282
P. Dobson	20	2.90	0	282
D. McNally	21	2.89	0	224

1972

Record	Finish	Games Behind	Manager
W-80 L-74	3rd	5	Earl Weaver

Leading Hitters (min. 300AB)		BA	HR	RBI
UT	B. Grich	.278	12	50
C	J. Oates	.261	4	21

Leading Pitchers	W	ERA	SV	IP
J. Palmer	21	2.07	0	274.1
C. Cuellar	18	2.58	0	248.1

1973

Record	Finish	Games Behind	Manager
W-97 L-65	1st	0	Earl Weaver

Leading Hitters (min. 300AB)		BA	HR	RBI
OF	A. Bumbry	.337	7	34
RF	R. Coggins	.319	7	41

Leading Pitcher	W	ERA	SV	IP
J. Palmer	22	2.40	1	296

1974

Record	Finish	Games Behind	Manager
W-91 L-71	1st	0	Earl Weaver

Leading Hitters (min. 300AB)		BA	HR	RBI
DH	T. Davis	.289	11	84
3B	B. Robinson	.288	7	59

Leading Pitchers	W	ERA	SV	IP
M. Cuellar	22	3.11	0	269
R. Grimsley	18	3.07	1	296

1975

Record	Finish	Games Behind	Manager
W-90 L-69	2nd	4.5	Earl Weaver

Leading Hitters (min. 300AB)		BA	HR	RBI	Leading Pitchers	W	ERA	SV	IP
RF	K. Singleton	.300	15	55	J. Palmer	23	2.09	1	323
DH	T. Davis	.283	6	57	M. Torrez	20	3.06	0	271

1976

Record	Finish	Games Behind	Manager
W-88 L-74	2nd	10.5	Earl Weaver

Leading Hitters (min. 300AB)		BA	HR	RBI	Leading Pitchers	W	ERA	SV	IP
LF	K. Singleton	.278	13	70	J. Palmer	22	2.51	0	315
RF	R. Jackson	.277	27	91	W. Garland	20	2.68	1	232

1977

Record	Finish	Games Behind	Manager
W 97 L 64	2nd	2.5	Earl Weaver

Leading Hitters (min. 300AB)		BA	HR	RBI	Leading Pitchers	W	ERA	SV	IP
RF	K. Singleton	.328	24	99	J. Palmer	20	2.91	0	319
CF	A. Bumbry	.317	4	41	R. May	18	3.61	0	252

1978

Record	Finish	Games Behind	Manager
W-90 L-71	4th	9	Earl Weaver

Leading Hitters (min. 300AB)		BA	HR	RBI	Leading Pitchers	W	ERA	SV	IP
RF	K. Singleton	.293	20	81	J. Palmer	21	2.46	0	296
3B	D. DeCinces	.286	28	80	M. Flanagan	19	4.03	0	281

1979

Record	Finish	Games Behind	Manager
W-102 L-57	1st	0	Earl Weaver

Leading Hitters (min. 300AB)		BA	HR	RBI	Leading Pitchers	W	ERA	SV	IP
1B	E. Murray	.295	25	99	M. Flanagan	23	3.08	0	266
RF	K. Singleton	.295	35	111	D. Martinez	15	3.67	0	292

1980

Record	Finish	Games Behind	Manager
W-100 L-62	2nd	3	Earl Weaver

Leading Hitters (min. 300AB)		BA	HR	RBI	Leading Pitchers	W	ERA	SV	IP
CF	A. Bumbry	.318	9	53	S. Stone	25	3.23	0	251
RF	K. Singleton	.304	24	104	S. McGregor	20	3.32	0	252

1981

Record	Finish	Games Behind	Manager
W-59 L-46	2nd	1	Earl Weaver

Leading Hitters (min. 300AB)		BA	HR	RBI	Leading Pitchers	W	ERA	SV	IP
1B	E. Murray	.294	22	78	D. Martinez	14	3.32	0	179
RF	K. Singleton	.278	13	49	S. McGregor	13	3.26	0	160

1982

Record	Finish	Games Behind	Manager
W-94 L-68	2nd	1	Earl Weaver

Leading Hitters (min. 300AB)		BA	HR	RBI	Leading Pitchers	W	ERA	SV	IP
LF	J. Lowenstein	.320	24	66	D. Martinez	16	4.21	0	252
1B	E. Murray	.316	32	110	J. Palmer	15	3.13	1	227
					M. Flanagan	15	3.97	0	236

1983

Record	Finish	Games Behind	Manager
W-98 L-64	1st	0	Joe Altobelli

Leading Hitters (min. 300AB)		BA	HR	RBI
SS	C. Ripken	.318	27	102
1B	E. Murray	.306	33	111

Leading Pitchers	W	ERA	SV	IP
S. McGregor	18	3.18	0	260
M. Boddicker	16	2.77	0	179

1984

Record	Finish	Games Behind	Manager
W-85 L-77	5th	19	Joe Altobelli

Leading Hitters (min. 300AB)		BA	HR	RBI
1B	E. Murray	.306	29	110
SS	C. Ripken	.304	27	86

Leading Pitcher	W	ERA	SV	IP
M. Boddicker	20	2.79	0	261

1985

Record	Finish	Games Behind	Manager	
W-83 L-78	4th	16	Joe Altobelli	W-29 L-26
			Cal Ripken	W-1 L-0
			Earl Weaver	W-53 L-52

Leading Hitters (min. 300AB)		BA	HR	RBI
1B	E. Murray	.297	31	124
RF	L. Lacy	.293	9	48

Leading Pitcher	W	ERA	SV	IP
S. McGregor	14	4.81	0	204

1986

Record	Finish	Games Behind	Manager
W-73 L-89	7th	22.5	Earl Weaver

Leading Hitters (min. 300AB)		BA	HR	RBI
1B	E. Murray	.305	17	84
UT	J. Beniquez	.300	6	36

Leading Pitcher	W	ERA	SV	IP
M. Boddicker	14	4.70	0	218

1987

Record	Finish	Games Behind	Manager
W-67 L-95	6th	31	Cal Ripken

Leading Hitters (min. 300AB)		BA	HR	RBI
LF	L. Sheets	.316	31	94
2B	B. Ripken	.308	2	20

Leading Pitchers	W	ERA	SV	IP
M. Boddicker	10	4.18	0	226
E. Bell	10	5.45	0	165
D. Schmidt	10	3.77	1	124

1988

Record	Finish	Games Behind	Manager	
W-54 L-107	7th	34.5	Cal Ripken	W-0 L-6
			F. Robinson	W-54 L-101

Leading Hitters (min. 300AB)		BA	HR	RBI
RF	J. Orsulak	.288	8	27
1B	E. Murray	.284	28	84

Leading Pitchers	W	ERA	SV	IP
J. Ballard	8	4.40	0	153
D. Schmidt	8	3.40	2	130

1989

Record	Finish	Games Behind	Manager
W-87 L-75	2nd	2	Frank Robinson

Leading Hitters (min. 300AB)		BA	HR	RBI
RF	J. Orsulak	.285	7	55
LF	P. Bradley	.277	11	55

Leading Pitchers	W	ERA	SV	IP
J. Ballard	18	3.43	0	215
B. Milacki	14	3.74	0	243

1990

Record	Finish	Games Behind	Manager
W-76 L-85	4th	11.5	Frank Robinson

Leading Hitters (min. 300AB)		BA	HR	RBI
2B	B. Ripken	.291	3	38
LF	P. Bradley	.270	4	26

Leading Pitcher	W	ERA	SV	IP
D. Johnson	13	4.10	0	180

1991

Record	Finish	Games Behind	Manager	
W-67 L-95	6th	24	Frank Robinson	W-13 L-24
			Johnny Oates	W-54 L-71

Leading Hitters (min. 300AB)		BA	HR	RBI
SS	C. Ripken	.323	34	114
LF	J. Orsulak	.278	5	43
1B	D. Segui	.278	2	22

Leading Pitcher	W	ERA	SV	IP
B. Milacki	10	4.01	0	184

1992

Record	Finish	Games Behind	Manager
W-89 L-73	3rd	7	Johnny Oates

Leading Hitters (min. 300AB)		BA	HR	RBI
RF	J. Orsulak	.289	4	39
CF	M. Devereaux	.276	24	107
DH	G. Davis	.276	13	48

Leading Pitchers	W	ERA	SV	IP
M. Mussina	18	2.54	0	241
R. Sutcliffe	16	4.47	0	237

1993

Record	Finish	Games Behind	Manager
W-85 L-77	3rd	10	Johnny Oates

Leading Hitters (min. 300AB)		BA	HR	RBI
DH	H. Baines	.313	20	78
C	C. Hoiles	.310	29	82

Leading Pitchers	W	ERA	SV	IP
B. McDonald	13	3.39	0	220
M. Mussina	14	4.46	0	167.2

TABLE 2
Manager's Records

	Regular Season			League Championship Series		World Series		
	W	L	T	W	L	W	L	T
Jimmie Dykes	54	100	0					
Paul Richards	517	539	7					
Billy Hitchcock	163	161	0					
Hank Bauer	407	318	1			4	4	0
Earl Weaver	1480	1060	0	15	7	11	13	0
Joe Altobelli	212	167	0	3	1	4	1	1
Cal Ripken	68	101	0					
Frank Robinson	230	285	0					
Johnny Oates	143	144	0					

TABLE 3
World Series & Divisional Playoffs

World Series 1966
Baltimore defeats Los Angeles 4 games to 0

Leading Hitters		BA	HR	RBI	Leading Pitchers	W	ERA	IP
1B	B. Powell	.357	0	1	D. McNally	1	1.59	11.1
					W. Bunker	1	0.00	9
OF	F. Robinson	.286	2	3	J. Palmer	1	0.00	9
2B	D. Johnson	.286	0	1				

Divisional Playoffs 1969
Baltimore defeats Minnesota 3 games to 0

Leading Hitters		BA	HR	RBI	Leading Pitchers	W	ERA	IP
3B	B. Robinson	.500	0	0	D. McNally	1	0.00	11
OF	P. Blair	.400	1	6	J. Palmer	1	2.00	9

World Series 1969
New York defeats Baltimore 4 games to 1

Leading Hitters		BA	HR	RBI	Leading Pitcher	W	ERA	IP
1B	B. Powell	.263	0	0	M. Cuellar	1	1.13	16
SS	M. Belanger	.200	0	1				

Divisional Playoffs 1970
Baltimore defeats Minnesota 3 games to 0

Leading Hitters		BA	HR	RBI	Leading Pitchers	W	ERA	IP
3B	B. Robinson	.583	0	1	J. Palmer	1	1.00	9
1B	B. Powell	.429	1	6	D. McNally	1	3.00	9

World Series 1970
Baltimore defeats Cincinnati 4 games to 1

Leading Hitters		BA	HR	RBI	Leading Pitchers	W	ERA	IP
OF	P. Blair	.474	0	3	J. Palmer	1	4.60	15.2
3B	B. Robinson	.429	2	6	M. Cuellar	1	3.18	11.1
					D. McNally	1	3.00	9

Divisional Playoffs 1971
Baltimore defeats Oakland 3 games to 0

Leading Hitters		BA	HR	RBI	Leading Pitchers	W	ERA	IP
3B	B. Robinson	.364	1	3	M. Cuellar	1	1.00	9
2B	D. Johnson	.300	0	0	J. Palmer	1	3.00	9
1B	B. Powell	.300	2	3				

World Series 1971
Pittsburgh defeats Baltimore 4 games to 3

Leading Hitters		BA	HR	RBI	Leading Pitchers	W	ERA	IP
SS	M. Belanger	.318	0	5	D. McNally	2	1.98	13.2
OF	F. Robinson	.280	2	2	J. Palmer	1	2.65	17

Divisional Playoffs 1973
Oakland defeats Baltimore 3 games to 2

Leading Hitters		BA	HR	RBI	Leading Pitcher	W	ERA	IP
					J. Palmer	1	1.84	14.2
C	A. Etchebarren	.357	1	4				
DH	T. Davis	.286	0	2				

Divisional Playoffs 1974
Oakland defeats Baltimore 3 games to 1

Leading Hitters		BA	HR	RBI	Leading Pitcher	W	ERA	IP
OF	P. Blair	.286	1	2	M. Cuellar	1	2.84	12.2
OF	D. Baylor	.267	0	0				
DH	T. Davis	.267	0	1				

Divisional Playoffs 1979
Baltimore defeats California 3 games to 1

Leading Hitters		BA	HR	RBI	Leading Pitcher	W	ERA	IP
1B	E. Murray	.417	1	5	S. McGregor	1	0.00	9
C	R. Dempsey	.400	0	2				

World Series 1979
Pittsburgh defeats Baltimore 4 games to 3

Leading Hitters		BA	HR	RBI	Leading Pitchers	W	ERA	IP
SS	K. Garcia	.400	0	6	S. McGregor	1	3.18	17
OF	K. Singleton	.357	0	2	M. Flanagan	1	3.00	15

Divisional Playoffs 1983
Baltimore defeats Chicago 3 games to 1

Leading Hitters		BA	HR	RBI	Leading Pitcher	W	ERA	IP
SS	C. Ripken	.400	0	1	M. Boddicker	1	0.00	9
1B	E. Murray	.267	1	3				

World Series 1983
Baltimore defeats Philadelphia 4 games to 1

Leading Hitters		BA	HR	RBI	Leading Pitchers	W	ERA	IP
C	R. Dempsey	.385	1	2	S. McGregor	1	1.06	17
OF	J. Lowenstein	.385	1	1	M. Boddicker	1	0.00	9

ORIOLES CAREER PITCHING LEADERS

ERA (500 or more Innings)

Player	ERA
S. Miller	2.37
Wilhelm	2.42
Watt	2.73
Dobson	2.78
Palmer	2.86
O'Dell	2.86
Hall	2.89
Hardin	2.95
Phoebus	3.06
Roberts	3.09

STRIKEOUTS

Player	Strikeouts
Palmer	2,212
McNally	1,476
Flanagan	1,297
Cuellar	1,011
Pappas	944
Barber	918
McGregor	904
D. Martinez	858
Boddicker	836
T. Martinez	584

GAMES

Player	Games
Palmer	558
T. Martinez	499
Flanagan	450
McNally	424
Watt	363
McGregor	356
Hall	342
Williamson	337
Olson	320
D. Martinez	319

WINS

Player	Wins
Palmer	268
McNally	181
Cuellar	143
Flanagan	141
McGregor	138
Pappas	110
D. Martinez	108
Barber	95
Boddicker	79
Hall	65

INNINGS

Player	Innings
Palmer	3,947.2
McNally	2,653.0
Flanagan	2,317.2
McGregor	2,141.1
Cuellar	2,028.0
D. Martinez	1,775.1
Pappas	1,632.0
Barber	1,415.0
Boddicker	1,273.2
H. Brown	1,032.0

SHUTOUTS

Player	Shutouts
Palmer	53
McNally	33
Cuellar	30
Papas	26
McGregor	23
Barber	19
Flanagan	17
Boddicker	13
Phoebus	11
D. Martinez	10

LOSSES

Player	Losses
Palmer	152
Flanagan	116
McNally	113
McGregor	108
D. Martinez	93
Cuellar	88
Barber	75
Pappas	74
Boddicker	73
Ballard	51

SAVES

Player	Saves
Olson	160
T. Martinez	105
S. Miller	92
Watt	72
Stoddard	57
Hall	51
Aase	50
Stanhouse	45
Stewart	42
Wilhelm	40

WON-LOST PCT (Minimum 50 dec)

Player	Pct	Record
Mussina	692	(36-16)
Stone	656	(40-21)
Palmer	638	(268-152)
Bunker	620	(44-27)
Cuellar	619	(143-88)
Hall	619	(65-40)
McNally	616	(181-113)
Pappas	598	(110-74)
Davis	586	(61-43)
Dobson	581	(36-26)

ORIOLES CAREER BATTING LEADERS

GAMES

Player	Games
B. Robinson	2,986
Belanger	1,962
C. Ripken, Jr.	1,962
Murray	1,820
Powell	1,763
Blair	1,700
Singleton	1,446
Bumbry	1,428
Dempsey	1,245
Dauer	1,140

AT BATS

Player	At Bats
B. Robinson	10,654
C. Ripken, Jr.	7,583
Murray	6,845
Powell	5,912
Belanger	5,734
Blair	5,606
Singleton	5,115
Bumbry	4,958
Dauer	3,829
Dempsey	3,585

RUNS

Player	Runs
B. Robinson	1,232
C. Ripken, Jr.	1,130
Murray	1,048
Powell	796
Bumbry	772
Blair	737
Singleton	684
Belanger	670
F. Robinson	555
Dauer	448

ORIOLES CAREER BATTING LEADERS (CONTINUED)

HITS		DOUBLES		TRIPLES	
B. Robinson	2,848	B. Robinson	482	B. Robinson	68
C. Ripken, Jr.	2,087	C. Ripken, Jr.	395	Bumbry	52
Murray	2,021	Murray	351	Blair	51
Powell	1,574	Blair	269	C. Ripken, Jr.	37
Singleton	1,455	Powell	243	Aparicio	34
Blair	1,426	Singleton	235	Belanger	33
Bumbry	1,403	Bumbry	217	Devereaux	28
Belanger	1,304	Dauer	193	Grich	27
Dauer	984	D.Johnson	186	Anderson	26
D. Johnson	904	Belanger	174	Murray	25

HOME RUNS		TOTAL BASES		RUNS BATTED IN	
Murray	333	B. Robinson	4,270	B. Robinson	1,357
Powell	303	C. Ripken, Jr.	3,447	Murray	1,190
C. Ripken, Jr.	297	Murray	3,421	C. Ripken, Jr.	1,104
B. Robinson	268	Powell	2,748	Powell	1,063
Singleton	182	Singleton	2,274	Singleton	767
F. Robinson	179	Blair	2,175	Blair	567
Triandos	142	Bumbry	1,883	F. Robinson	545
Blair	126	Belanger	1,604	Triandos	517
Gentile	124	F. Robinson	1,598	L. May	487
L. May	123	Triandos	1,351	Gentile	398

EXTRA-BASE HITS		BATTING AVERAGE (Minimum 1,200 ab's)		STOLEN BASES	
B. Robinson	818	Nieman	.303	Bumbry	252
C. Ripken, Jr.	729	Boyd	.301	Blair	167
Murray	709	F. Robinson	.300	Aparicio	166
Powell	557	Murray	.295	Belanger	166
Blair	446	T. Davis	.291	Anderson	126
Singleton	436	Rettenmund	.284	Baylor	118
F. Robinson	340	Singleton	.284	Buford	85
Bumbry	322	Bumbry	.283	Grich	77
DeCinces	282	Orsulak	.281	Wiggins	71
D. Johnson	268	Lacy	.280	Devereaux	64

WALKS

Powell 889; Singleton 885; B. Robinson 860; Murray 856; C. Ripken, Jr. 817; Belanger 571; Bumbry 464; F. Robinson 460; Grich 457; Dempsey 424; Blair 420

GWRBI

B. Robinson 184; Murray 166; C. Ripken, Jr. 146; Powell 140; Singleton 95; F. Robinson 83; L. May 77; Blair 67; Gentile 58; D. Johnson 57

ORIOLES RECORDS

1954 thru 1993

BATTING

Individual (By Game)

Most Hits — 5 Accomplished 31 times: 3 times—**Luis Aparicio** (all in '66); **Cal Ripken, Jr.** [(8/22/82) vs. Tex (A), 9/3/83 vs. Min (A), 5/5/85 vs. Min (A)]... *Twice*—**Don Baylor, Bob Boyd, Al Bumbry, Tommy Davis, Brooks Robinson**... *Once*—**Jerry Adair, Mark Belanger, Paul Blair** ('69 ALCS), **Phil Bradley, Rich Coggins, Clint Courtney, Rich Dauer, Mike Devereaux** [7/3/92 vs. Min (A)], **Billy Goodman, Mark McLemore** [6/9/93 vs. Oak (H)] , **Bob Melvin, Eddie Murray, Joe Orsulak, Russ Snyder, Gene Woodling.**

Most Hits Home Games	5	Accomplished 5 times: **Jerry Adair** [8/24/62—vs. NY] **Bob Boyd§** [9/15/57 vs. Cle] **Rich Dauer** [6/2/8O]—vs. Mil], **Billy Goodman§** [9/15/57], **Mark McLemore** [6/9/93—vs. Oak].
Most Runs	4	Accomplished 30 times: 3times by **Merv Rettenmund,** and most recently by **David Segui** [8/3/93 vs. Mil (H)].
Most RBI	9	**Jim Gentile**—May 9, '61 vs. Minnesota (A) **Eddie Murray**—Aug 26, '85 vs. California (A)
Most RBI, Home Game	7	**Boog Powell**—July 6, '66 vs. KC A's **Eddie Murray**—May 18, '86 vs. Oakland
Most RBI, Opp	8	**Danny Tartabull**—Sep 8, '92, New York (H)
Most RBI, D-header	11	**Boog Powell**—July 6, '66 vs. KC A's (H)
Most Doubles	4	**Charlie Lau**—July 13, '62 vs. Cleveland (H) **Dave Duncan**—June 30, '75 vs. Boston (A)
Most Triples	3	**Al Bumbry**—Sep 22, '73 vs. Milwaukee (A)
Most Home Runs	3	See Home Run Section on page 214
Most Total Bases	13	**Eddie Murray** (twice)—Sep 14, '80 vs. Toronto (A) & Aug 26, '85 vs. Califomia (A). **Boog Powell**—Aug 15, '66 vs. Boston (A) **Cal Ripken Jr.**—Sep 3, '83 vs. Minnesota (A) **Dan Ford**—July 20, '83 vs. Seattle A) **Lee Lacy**—June 8, '86 vs. New York (A)
Most Total Bases, Home Game	12	**Bobby Grich**—June 18, '74 vs. Minnesota **Juan Beniquez**—June 12, '86 vs. New York **Randy Milligan**—June 9, '90 vs. New York
Most Total Bases, Opp	16	**Rocky Colavito**—June 10, '59, Cleveland (H)
Most Stolen Bases	3	Accomplished 14 times: 5 times—**Luis Aparicio;** 3 times—**Don Baylor;** Once—**Paul Blair, Don Buford, Al Bumbry, Mike Devereaux** [5/17/91 vs. Califomia (H)], **Steve Finley, Larry Harlow.**
Most Stolen Bases, Opp.	4	**Rickey Henderson**—June 26, '85, New York (A) **Dave Collins**—Aug 5, '84, Toronto (H) **John Jaha**—Sep 12, '92 vs. Milwaukee (H) **Chad Curtis**—Apr 17, '93, vs. California (H)
Most Bases on Balls	5	**Bobby Grich**—Aug 9, '75 vs. Chicago (A) [9 inn, consecutive] **Phil Bradley**—Sep 7, '89 vs. Texas (A)
Most Strikeouts, Extra Inning Game	5§§	**Sam Horn**—July 17, '91 vs. Kansas City (A) [15 inn, consecutive]
Most Consecutive Hits 2 or more games	10	**Ken Singleton**—Aug 26-28, '81
Most Consecutive Times, Reached Safely	13	**Jim Dwyer**—Sep 29 thru Oct 2, '82 [5 walks/8 hits] **Harold Baines**—Apr 30 thru May 4, '93 [5 walks/8 hits]
Most Times Reaching Base on Error	3§§	**Phil Bradley**—Aug 4, '89 vs. Texas (H)

§— Boyd & Goodman were the first two of only 4 O's to get 5 hits in one game in 38 seasons at Memorial Stadium, and they did it in the same game, Sep 15, '57 *—American League Record §§—Ties Major League Record

Club (Season)

Highest Average	.273	'80	Most Extra Base Hits	478	'83
Lowest Average	.225	'68	Most GIDP	159	'86
Highest Slugging Pct	.430	'85	Most Sacrifice Hits	110	'57
Most Runs	818	'85	Most Sacrifice Flies	59	'69, '92
Most Hits	1523	'80	Most Stolen Bases	150	'76
Most Total Bases	2370	'85	Most Walks	717	'70
Most Doubles	287	'93	Most Intentional Walks	69	'71
Most Triples	49	'54	Most Strikeouts	1019	'64, '68
Most Home Runs	214	'85	Most Hit by Pitch	58	'74

*—Ties American League Record
§—Major League Record

MOST HOME RUNS

Individual (Game & Season)

Most Consecutive		4§§	Don Baylor—July 1-2, '75—vs. Bos (A)—1 vs. Det (A)—3
Most, Game		3	Accomplished 14 times
3 Times:	Eddie Murray—		Aug 29, '79—vs. Minnesota (A-Metro)
			Sep 14, '80—vs Minnesota (A-Exhib Stadium)
			Aug 26, '85—vs. California (A)
	Boog Powell—		Aug 10, '63—vs. Washington (A-RFK)
			June 27, '64—vs. Washington (A-RFK)
			Aug 15, '66—vs. Boston (A)
Once:	Don Baylor—		July 2, '75—vs. Detroit (A)
	Juan Beniquez—		June 12, '86—vs. New York (H)
	Paul Blair—		Apr 29, '70—vs. Chicago (A)
	Curt Blefary—		June 16, '67—vs. California (A)
	Dan Ford—		July 20, '83—vs. Seattle (A)
	Bobby Grich—		June 18, '74—vs. Minnesota (H)
	Lee Lacy—		June 8, '86—vs. New York (A)
	Randy Milligan—		June 9, '90—vs. New York (H)
Most, Home Game		3	Bobby Grich—June 18, '74 vs. Minnesota
			Juan Beniquez—June 12, '86 vs. New York
			Randy Milligan—June 9, '90 vs. New York
Most, Home Game, by Opp		4§§	Rocky Colavito—June 10, '59, Cleveland
		3	Manny Jimenez—July 4, '64, K.C. A's
			Lee Stanton—July 10, '73, California
Most, Road Game, by Opp		3	Preston Ward—Sep 9, '58, K.C. A's
			Bill Madlock—June 28, '87, Detroit
			Ernie Whitt—Sep 14, '87, Toronto
			Harold Baines—May 7, '91, Oakland
			Juan Gonzalez—Aug 28, '93, Texas
Most, Season		49	Frank Robinson—'66
Most, Season, MS		27	Frank Robinson—'66
Most, Season, OPCY		15	Brady Anderson—'92
Most, Season, Rookie		28	Cal Ripken Jr.—'82
Most, Season, Pitcher		6	Jack Harshman—'58

Most, Lifetime, Oriole	333	Eddie Murray—'77-'88
	303	Boog Powell—'61-'74
	297	Cal Ripken Jr.—'81-'92
	268	Brooks Robinson—'55-'77
Most, Lifetime, MS	160	Eddie Murray—'77-'88
	138	Brooks Robinson—'55-'77
	133	Boog Powell—'61-'74
Most, Lifetime, OPCY	24	Chris Hoiles—'92-'93
Most Multi-Homer Games, Season	7	Frank Robinson—'66
Most Multi-Homer Games, Career	20	Eddie Murray—'77-'88
		Boog Powell—'61-'74
Most Grand Slams, Season	5	Jim Gentile—'61
Most Grand Slams, Game	2§§	Jim Gentile—May 9, '61—vs. Minnesota (A)
		Frank Robinson—June 26, '70—vs. Washington (A)
Most Grand Slams, Lifetime	14	Eddie Murray—'77-'88
Most, Season vs. One Opponent	11	Frank Robinson—vs. Detroit, '66
Most, Season, by One Opponent	9	Frank Howard—Washington, '68
Most, Season, by Opponent, MS	5	Rocky Colavito—Detroit, '59
		Tony Perez—Boston, '80
		Jim Sundberg—Texas, '80
Most, Season, by Opponent, OPCY	6	Dean Palmer—Texas, '93
Most, Lifetime, by Opponent	70	Harmon Killebrew—Wash, Min '55-'75
Most, Lifetime, by Opponent, M.S.	30	Harmon Killebrew—Wash, Min '55-'75
Most, Lifetime, by Opponent, OPCY	7	Dean Palmer—Texas '92-'93
Most, Pinch-Hit, Season	3	Whitey Herzog—'62
		Sam Bowens—'67
		Pat Kelly—'79
		Jim Dwyer—'86
		Sam Horn—'91
Most, Lifetime, Pinch-Hit, O's.	9	Jim Dwyer—'80-'88
Most Consecutive Games, Hit HR	6	Reggie Jackson—July 18-23, '76
Most Extra Innings HRs Game	2§§	Mike Young—May 28, '87 vs. California (H)
Most Times Career, Hitting HRs Left & Righthanded Same Game	8	Eddie Murray—'77-'87
Most Times Season, Hitting HRs Left & Righthanded, Same Game	2§§	Eddie Murray (twice); '82—Apr 24 vs. Chicago (A) & Aug 26 vs. Toronto (H); '87—May 8-9 vs. Chicago (A)
Most Consecutive Games Hitting HRs Left & Righthanded	2§	Eddie Murray—'87—May 8-9 vs. Chicago (A)

Club (Game & Inning)

Most, Game	7	**May 17, '67**—vs. Boston (A) [Blair, B. Robinson, F. Robinson, Etchebarren, Bowens, Powell, D. Johnson]
		Aug 26, '85—vs. California (A) [Murray—3, Shelby Rayford, Roenicke, Dempsey]
Most, Home Game, MS	6	**May 28, '87**—vs. California
Most, Home Game, OPCY	5	**May 1, '92**—vs. Seattle; **Aug 26, '92**—vs. California
Most, Game, Opponent	10§	**Sep 14, '87**—by Toronto (A)
Most, Home Game, MS, Opponent	6	**June 10, '59**—Cleveland [Colavito, Martin, Minosa]
Most, Home Game, OPCY, Opponent	4	On several Occasions

Most, Home Game, MS Both Clubs	8	May 28, '87—Baltimore-6, California-2
Most, Home Game, OPCY, Both Clubs	7	Sep 12, '93—Baltimore-4, Oakland-3
Most, Inning	4	May 17, '67—vs. Boston (A) [Etchebarren, Bowens, Powell, D. Johnson]
Most Succession	3	Apr 30, '61—Detroit (A) [Gentile, Triandos, Hansen] Sep 10, '65—vs. KC (H) [B. Robinson, Blefary, Adair] Sep 4, '69—vs. Detroit (A) [F. Robinson, Powell, B. Robinson] May 8, '79—vs. Oakland (H) [Murray, L. May, Roenicke] Sep 16, '65—vs. Detroit (A) [Ripken, Murray, Lynn]
Most, 11 consec games	32§	May 8-18, '87
Most, 12 consec games	35§	May 8-19, '87
Most, 13 consec games	36§	May 8-20, '87
Most, 14 consec games	38§	May 8-22, '87
Most, consec games, 2 or more	9§§	May 8-16, '87

Club (Season)

Most, Season	214	'85	Most, Opp, Home	125	'87
Most, Season, Home	110	'87	Most, O's & Opp, Home	235	'87
Most, Season, Opp	226§	'87	Most, Pinch-Hit	11**	'82
Most, Season, O's & Opp	437§	'87	Most, Grand Slams	8	'70, '79, '82, '83, '84
Most Pinch Hit Grand Slams	3§	'82	Most, Month	58§	May, '87
Most, vs. One Club	32		(vs. Detroit, 18 games)		'66
	26		(vs. Cleveland & Detroit, 13 games		'85

§§Ties Major League Record **American League Record §Major League Record

PITCHING

Individual (Game & Season)

Most Strikeouts, Game	14*	**Bob Turley**—Apr 21, '54 vs. Cle (H) **Connie Johnson**—Sep 2, '57 vs. NY (H) **Mike Boddicker**—Oct 6, '83 vs. Chi—ALCS#2 (H) **Mike Mussina**—May 16, '93 vs. Det (A)
Most Bases on Balls, Game	12**	**Jack Fisher**—Aug 30, '61§ vs. L.A. (A), 9 inn
Most Inn., Pitched, Game	16	**Jerry Walker**—Sep 11, '59 vs. Chi (H)
Fewest Batters Faced, 9 Inning Game	27	**Bob Milacki**—Apr 23, '89 vs. Minn (H) **Jim Palmer**—May 12, '67 vs. NY (A) **Mike Flanagan**—May 3, '82 vs. Sea (H)
Most Consec. Shutout, Inn.	41*	**Gregg Olson**—Aug 4, '89 to May 4, '90
Most Consec. Shutout Inn., Season	36	**Hal Brown**—July 7 to Aug 4, '90
Most Consec. Shutouts	3	**Jack Fisher**—1960; **Hal Brown**—1961; **Milt Pappas**—1964, **Tom Phoebus**—1967; **Jim Palmer**—1978

Most Consecutive Scoreless Appearances	29	Gregg Olson—Aug 4, '89—May 4, '90
Most Consecutive Wins	17	Dave McNally—Sep 22, '68 to Aug 3, '69
Most Consecutive Losses	13	Mike Boddicker—('87-'88)
Most Consecutive Wins, One Season	15	Dave McNally—Apr 12 to Aug 3, '69
Most Consecutive Losses, One Season	10	Jay Tibbs ('88)
Most Consecutive Games Won, Reliever		
3 Consecutive Games	3§§	Grant Jackson—Sep 29, 30, Oct 1, '74, 5.1 innings
Most Wins, One Day	2§§	Wes Stock—May 26, '63 vs. Cle (A)
Most Losses, One Day	2§§	Don Aase—Aug 28, '86 vs. Oak (A)
Most Wins vs. One Club, Season	6	Wally Bunker—vs. KC, '64
Most Losses vs. One Club Season	5	Don Larsen—1954 vs. Chi
		Joe Coleman—1954 vs. NY
		Jim Wilson—1955 vs. Cle
Most Wins by Opp, Season	6	Bud Daley, K.C.—1959
Most Wins by Opp, Season, (Since '61 Expansion)	5	Joe Coleman, Jr., Det—1973
		Pat Dobson, Cle—1976
Most Losses by Opponent, Season	5	Ned Garver, KC—1957
		Dick Stigman, Min—1963
		Stan Williams, Cle—1969
		"Catfish" Hunter, NY—1976

*Club record is 21 set by 5 pitchers [Steve Barber, Wally Bunker, Eddie Watt, Eddie Fisher & Stu Miller] on June 4, '67 vs. Wash (H)—19 innings. Club record for 9 innings is 17 by 3 pitchers [Nelson—13, Drabowsky—3, Beene—1] on Sep 18, '68 vs. Bos (A).

**Club record is 14 set by 3 pitchers [Bruce Howard—6, Gene Brabender—5, & Eddie Watt—3] on Apr 30, '68 vs. NY (H).

§Paul Richards' last game as O's manager...Ed Hurley was plate umpire

§§Ties major league record

• M.L. record for a relief pitcher

Individual Pitching by Season

Most Games	76	Tippy Martinez	1982
Most Games, Rookie	64	Gregg Olson	1989
Most Games Started	40	Dave McNally	1969-1970
		Mike Cuellar	1970
		Mike Flanagan	1978
Most Games Started, Rookie	36	Bob Milacki	1989
Most Complete Games	25	Jim Palmer	1975
Most Games Finished	62	Gregg Olson	1991
Most Wins	25	Steve Stone	1980
Most Wins, Rookie	19	Wally Bunker	1964
Most Losses	21	Don Larsen (W-3)	1954
Best Won-Lost Pct. 808	(21-5)	Dave McNally	1971
Most Bases on Balls	181	Bob Turley	1954
Most Hit Batsmen	15	Chuck Estrada	1960
Most Strikeouts	202	Dave McNally	1968
Most Innings Pitched	323	Jim Palmer	1975
Most Innings Pitched, Rookie	243	Bob Milacki	1989
Most Shutouts	10	Jim Palmer	1975
Most Home Runs Allowed	35	Robin Roberts	1963
		Scott McGregor	1986
Fewest Home Runs Allowed (by qualifier)	8	Milt Pappas (209 ip)	1959
		Billy Loes (155 ip)	
Lowest ERA (by qualifier)	1.95	Dave McNally	1968
Highest ERA (by qualifier)	5.75	Rick Sutcliffe	1993

Most Saves	37	Gregg Olson	1990
Most Saves, Rookie	27*	Greg Olson	1989
Most Wins, Reliever	14	Stu Miller	1965
Most Relief Points (win + saves) (6+37)	43	Gregg Olson	1990
Most Innings Pitched by Reliever	140.1	Sammy Stewart	1983

Club (Season)

Most Consecutive Shutouts	5*	Sep 2 thru 6, '74 (Grimsley, Cuellar, Palmer, McNally, Cuellar)
Most Consecutive Shutout Innings	54*	Sep 1 (from 9th inn.) to 7 (thru 8th inn.),'74
Most Complete Games, Season	71	1971
Most Consecutive Complete Games	7	May 1 thru 7, '68
Most Shutouts, Season	21	1961
Most Strikeouts, Season	1070	1966
Most Bases on Balls, Season	395	1972
Lowest ERA, Season	2.53	1972
Highest ERA, Season	5.01	1987
Most Hits Allowed, Season	1,555	1987
Most Runs Allowed, Season	880	1987
Most Home Runs Allowed, Season	226§	1987
Fewest Home Runs Allowed, Full Season	78	1954
Most Grand Slams Allowed, Season	7	1988

*American League Record
§Major League Record

ALL-TIME ORIOLES ROSTER
1954 Thru 1993 (40 Seasons)

Managers	DOB	Birthplace	Residence
Altobelli, Joe ('83-'85)	5/26/32	Detroit, MI	Rochester, NY
Bauer, Hank ('64-'68)	7/31/22	E. St. Louis, IL	Shawnee Mission, KS
Dykes, Jimmy ('54)	11/10/96	Philadelphia, PA	Died 6/15/76 (79)
Harris, Luman ('61)	1/17/15	New Castle, AL	Vincent, AL
Hitchcock, Billy ('62-'63)	7/31/16	Inverness, AL	Opelika, AL
Oates, Johnny ('91-)	1/21/46	Sylva, NC	Colonial Heights, VA
Richards, Paul ('55-'61)	11/21/08	Waxahachie, TX	Died 5/4/86 (77)
Ripken, Cal Sr ('87-'88)	12/17/35	Aberdeen, MD	Aberdeen, MD
Robinson, Frank ('88-'91)	8/31/35	Beaumont, TX	Bel Air, CA
Weaver, Earl ('68-'82, '85-'86)	8/14/30	St. Louis, MO	Pembroke Pines, FL

Coaches	DOB	Birthplace	Residence
Adair, Jimmy ('57-'61)	1/25/07	Waxahachie, TX	Died 12/9/82 (75)
Appling, Luke ('63)	4/2/09	High Point, NC	Died 1/3/91 (81)
Bamberger, George ('68-'77)	8/1/25	Staten Island, NY	Redington Beach, FL
Bauer, Hank ('63)	7/31/22	E. St Louis, IL	Shawnee Mission, KS
Biagini, Greg ('92-)	3/12/52	Chicago, IL	Greenville, NC
Bosman, Dick ('92-)	2/17/44	Kenosha, WI	Palm Harbor, FL
Brecheen, Harry ('54-'67)	10/14/14	Broken Bow, OK	Ada, OK
Buford, Don ('88, '94)	2/2/37	Linden, TX	Sherman Oaks, CA

Busby, Jim ('61)	1/8/27	Kenedy , TX	Millen, GA
Crowley, Terry ('85-'88)	2/16/47	Staten Island, NY	Cockeysville, MD
Ermer, Cal ('62)	11/10/23	Baltimore, MD	Chattanooga, TN
Ferraro, Mike ('93)	8/18/44	Kingston, TX	Coral Springs, FL
Frey, Jim ('70-'79)	5/26/31	Cleveland, OH	Timonium, MD
Harris, Luman ('55-'61)	1/17/15	New Castle, AL	Vincent, AL
Hart, John ('88)	7/21/48	Tampa, FL	Fairview Park, OH
Hendricks, Elrod ('78-)	12/22/40	St Thomas, VI	Randallstown, MD
Hoscheit, Vern ('68)	4/1/22	Brunswick, NE	Plainview, NE
Hunter, Billy ('64-'77)	6/4/28	Punxsutawney, PA	Lutherville, MD
Jackson, Al ('89-'91)	12/25/35	Waco, TX	Dix Hills, NJ
Johnson, Darrell ('62)	8/25/28	Horace, NE	Ord, NE
Lau, Charlie ('69)	4/12/33	Romulus, MI	Died 3/18/84 (50)
Lollar, Sherman ('64-'67)	8/23/24	Durham, AR	Died 9/24/77 (53)
Lopes, Davey ('92-)	5/3/46	East Providence, RI	Providence, RI
McCraw, Tom ('89-'91)	11/21/40	Malvern, AR	Huddleston, VA
Mendoza, Minnie ('88)	11/16/33	Havana, CUBA	Charlotte, NC
Miller, Ray ('78-'85)	4/30/45	Takoma Park, MD	New Athens, OH
Motton, Curt ('89-'91)	9/24/40	Darnell, LA	Cockeysville, MD
Narron, Jerry ('93)	1/5/56	Goldsboro, NC	Goldsboro, NC
Oates, Johnny ('89-'91)	1/21/46	Sylva, NC	Colonial Heights, VA
Oliver, Tom ('54)	1/15/03	Montgomery, AL	Died 2/26/88 (85)
Ripkin, Cal Sr ('76-'86, '89-'92)	12/17/35	Aberdeen, MD	Aberdeen, MD
Robinson, Brooks ('77)	5/18/37	Little Rock, AR	Baltimore, MD & So. California
Robinson, Eddie ('57-'59)	12/15/20	Paris, TX	Ft Worth, TX
Robinson, Frank ('78-'80, '85-'87)	8/31/35	Beaumont, TX	Bel Air, CA
Rowe, Ken ('85-'86)	12/21/33	Ferndale, MI	Norcross, GA
Rowe, Ralph ('81-'84)	7/14/24	Newberry, SC	Newberry, SC
Scarborough, Ray ('68)	7/23/17	Mt Gilead, NC	Died 7/1/82 (64)
Skaff, Frank ('54)	9/30/13	LaCrosse, WI	Died 4/12/88 (74)
Staller, George ('62, '68-'75)	4/1/16	Rutherford Hghts, PA	Died 7/31/92 (76)
Starrette, Herm ('88)	11/20/38	Statesville, NC	Statesville, NC
Vincent, Al ('55-'59)	12/23/06	Birmingham, AL	Beaumont, TX
Weaver, Earl ('68)	8/14/30	St Louis, MO	Pembroke Pines, FL
Wiley, Mark ('87)	2/28/48	National City, CA	Miami Springs, FL
Williams, Jimmy ('81-'87)	5/15/26	Toronto, ONT	Joppa, MD
Woodling, Gene ('64-'67)	8/16/22	Akron, OH	Medina, OH

Players	**DOB**	**Birthplace**	**Residence**
Aase, Don ('85-'88), RHP	9/8/54	Orange, CA	Yorba Linda, CA
Abrams, Cal ('54-'55), OF, L-L	3/2/24	Philadelphia, PA	Tamarac, FL
Adair, Jerry ('58-'66), 2B, R-R	12/17/36	Sand Springs, OK	Died 5/31/87 (50)
Adams, Bobby ('56), IF, R-R	12/14/21	Tuolumne, CA	Scottsdale, AZ
Adamson, Mike ('67-'69), RHP	9/13/47	San Diego, CA	Moorpark, CA
Aldrich, Jay ('90), RHP	4/14/61	Alexandra, LA	Pine Brook, NJ
Alexander, Bob ('55), RHP	8/7/22	Vancouver, BC	Died 4/7/93 (70)
Alexander, Doyle ('72-'76), RHP	9/4/50	Cordova, AL	Arlington, TX
Alexander, Manny ('92-), IF, R-R	3/20/71	SP de Macoris, DR	SP de Macoris, DR
Anderson, Brady ('88-), OF, L-L	1/18/64	Silver Spring, MD	Newport Beach, CA
Anderson, John ('60), RHP	11/23/32	St Paul, MN	
Anderson, Mike ('78), OF, R-R	6/22/51	Florence, SC	Florence, SC
Aparicio, Luis ('63-'67), SS, R-R	4/29/34	Maracaibo, VEN	Barquisimento, VEN
Arnold, Tony ('86-'87), RHP	5/3/59	El Paso, TX	Palm City, FL
Avila, Bobby ('59), 2B, R-R	4/2/24	Veracruz, MEX	Veracruz, MEX
Ayala, Benny, ('79-'84), OF, R_R	2/7/51	Yauco, PR	Toa Baja, PR
Bailor, Bob ('75-'76), IF, R-R	7/10/51	Connellsville, PA	Palm Harbor, FL
Baines, Harold ('93-), DH, L-L	3/15/59	St. Michaels, MD	St. Michaels, MD
Baker, Frank ('73-'74), IF, L-R	10/29/46	Moridian, MS	Meridian, MS
Ballard, Jeff ('87-'91), LHP	8/13/63	Billings, MT	Billings, MT
Bamberger, George ('59), RHP	8/1/25	Staten Island, NY	Redington Beach, FL
Barber, Steve ('60-'67), LHP	2/22/39	Takoma Park, MD	Las Vegas, NV
Barker, Ray Buddy ('60), 1B, L-R	3/12/36	Martinsburg, WV	Martinsburg, WV
Barnowski, Ed ('65-'66), RHP	8/23/43	Scranton, PA	Webster, NY
Bautista, Jose ('88-'91), RHP	7/24/64	Bani, DR	Cooper City, FL
Baylor, Don ('70-'75), OF, R-R	6/28/49	Austin, TX	La Quinta, CA

Beamon, Charlie ('56-'58), RHP	12/15/34	Oakland, CA	Palo Alto, CA
Beene, Fred ('68-'70), RHP	11/24/42	Angleton, TX	Oakhurst, TX
Belanger, Mark ('65-'81), SS, R-R	6/8/44	Pittsfield, MA	Timonium, MD
Bell, Eric ('85-'87), LHP	10/27/63	Modesto, CA	Modesto, CA
Bell, Juan ('89-'91), SS, S-R	3/29/68	SP de Macoris, DR	SP de Macoris, DR
Beniquez, Juan ('86), OF, R-R	5/13/50	San Sebastian, PR	Carolina, PR
Bertaina, Frank ('64-'67, '69), LHP	4/14/44	San Francisco, CA	Santa Rosa, CA
Besana, Fred ('56), LHP	4/5/31	Lincoln, CA	Roseville, CA
Bickford, Vern ('54), RHP	8/17/20	Hellier, KY	Died 5/6/60 (39)
Birrer, Werner Babe ('56), RHP	7/4/28	Buffalo, NY	Williamsville, NY
Blair, Paul ('64-'76), OF, R-R	2/1/44	Cushing, OK	Owings, Mills, MD
Blefary, Curt ('65-'68), OF, L-R	7/5/43	Brooklyn, NY	Ft Lauderdale, FL
Blyzka, Mike ('54), RHP	12/25/28	Hamtramck, MI	Cheyenne, WY
Boddicker, Mike ('80-'88), RHP	8/23/57	Cedar Rapids, IA	Overland Park, KS
Bonilla, Juan ('86), 2B, R-R	2/12/56	Santurce, PR	Quincy, FL
Bonner, Bob ('80-'83), IF, R-R	8/12/56	Uvalde, TX	Corpus Christi, TX
Boone, Dan ('90), LHP	1/14/54	Long Beach, CA	El Cajon, CA
Bordi, Rich ('86), RHP	4/18/59	San Francisco, CA	Carmel Valley, CA
Boswell, Dave ('71), RHP	1/20/45	Baltimore, MD	Joppa, MD
Bowens, Sam ('63-'67), OF, R-R	3/23/39	Wilmington, NC	Leland, NC
Boyd, Bob ('56-'60), 1B, L-L	10/1/26	Potts Camp, MS	Wichita, KS
Brabender, Gene ('66-'68), RHP	8/16/41	Madison, WI	Black Earth, WI
Bradley, Phil ('89-'90), OF, R-R	3/11/59	Bloomington, IN	Columbia, OH
Brandt, Jackie ('60-'65), OF, R-R	4/28/34	Omaha, NE	Papillion, NE
Breeding, Marv ('60-'62)	3/8/34	Decatur, AL	Decatur, AL
Brideweser, Jim ('54, '57), IF, R-R	2/13/27	Lancaster, OH	Died 8/25/89 (62)
Briles, Nellie ('77-'78), RHP	8/5/43	Dorris, CA	Greensburg, PA
Brown, Dick ('63-'65), C, R-R	1/17/35	Shinnston, WV	Died 4/12/70 (35)
Brown, Hal Skinny, ('55-'62), RHP	12/11/24	Greensboro, NC	Greensboro, NC
Brown, Larry ('73), IF, R-R	3/1/40	Shinnston, WV	West Palm Beach, FL
Brown, Mark ('84), RHP	7/13/59	Bellows Falls, VT	N. Walpole, NH
Brown, Marty ('90), IF, R-R	1/23/63	Lawton, OK	Antioch, TN
Brunet, George ('63), LHP	6/8/35	Houghton, MI	Died 10/25/91 (56)
Buford, Damon ('93-), OF, R-R	6/12/70	Baltimore, MD	Sherman Oaks, CA
Buford, Don ('68-'72), OF, S-R	2/2/37	Linden, TX	Sherman Oaks, CA
Bumbry, Al ('72-'84), OF, L-R	4/21/47	Fredericksburg, VA	Lutherville, MD
Bunker, Wally ('63-'68), RHP	1/25/45	Seattle, WA	Coeur d'Alene, ID
Burke, Leo ('58-'59), IF-OF, R-R	5/6/34	Hagerstown, MD	Hagerstown, MD
Burleson, Rick ('87), IF, R-R	4/29/51	Lynwood, CA	La Habra Hgts, CA
Burnside, Pete ('63), LHP	7/2/30	Evanston, IL	Wilmette, IL
Busby, Jim ('57-'58, '60-'61) OF, R-R	1/8/27	Kenedy, TX	Millen, GA
Buzhardt, John ('67), RHP	8/17/36	Prosperity, SC	Prosperity, SC
Byrd, Harry ('55), RHP	2/3/25	Darlington, SC	Died 5/14/85 (60)
Cabell, Enos ('72-'74), IF, R-R	10/8/49	Ft Riley, KS	Sugar Land, TX
Carey, Paul ('93-), 1B, L-R	1/8/68	Boston, MA	Weymouth, MA
Carrasquel, A. Chico ('59), SS, R-R	1/23/26	Caracas, VEN	Chicago, IL
Carreon, Camilo ('66), C, R-R	8/6/37	Colton, CA	Died 9/2/87 (50)
Castleman, Foster ('58), IF, R-R	1/1/31	Nashville, TX	Cincinnati, OH
Causey, Wayne ('55-'57), IF, L-R	12/26/36	Ruston, LA	Ruston, LA
Ceccarelli, Art ('57), LHP	4/2/30	New Haven, CT	Orange, CT
Chakales, Bob ('54), RHP	8/10/27	Asheville, NC	Richmond, VA
Chevez, Tony ('77), RHP	6/20/54	Telica, NIC	Telica, NIC
Chism, Tom ('79), 1B, L-L	5/9/55	Chester, PA	Chester, PA
Cimoli, Gino ('64), OF, R-R	12/18/29	San Francisco, CA	Tiburon, CA
Clements, Pat ('92), LHP	2/2/62	McCloud, CA	Chico, CA
Coan, Gil ('54-'55), OF, L-R	5/18/22	Monroe, NC	Brevard, NC
Coggins, Richie ('72-'74), OF, L-L	12/7/50	Indianapolis, IN	New York, NY
Coleman, Joe ('54-'55), RHP	7/30/22	Medford, MA	Redmond, MA
Coleman, Walter Rip ('59-'60), LHP	7/31/31	Troy, NY	Troy, NY
Connally, Fritz ('85), 3B, R-R	5/19/58	Bryan, TX	Arlington, TX
Consuegra, Sandy ('56-'57), RHP	9/3/20	Potrerillos, CUBA	Miami, FL
Cook, Michael ('93-), RHP	8/14/63	Charleston, SC	Charleston, SC
Corbett, Doug ('87), RHP	11/4/52	Sarasota, FL	Jacksonville, FL
Corey, Mark ('79-'81), OF, R-R	11/3/55	Tucumcari, NM	Aurora, CA
Courtney, Clint ('54, '60-'61), C, L-R	3/16/27	Hall Summit, LA	Died 6/16/75 (48)
Cox, Billy ('55), 3B, R-R	8/29/19	Newport, PA	Died 3/30/78 (58)

Criscione, Dave ('77), C, R-R	9/21/51	Dunkirk, NY	Fredonia, NY
Crowley, Terry ('69-'73, '76-'82), 1B-OF, L-L	2/16/47	Staten Island, NY	Cockeysville, MD
Cruz, Todd ('83-'84), 3B, R-R	11/23/55	Highland Park, MI	San Bernardino, CA
Cuellar, Mike ('69-'76), LHP	5/8/37	Las Villas, CUBA	Almonte Spr, FL
Dagres, Angelo ('55), OF, L-L	8/22/34	Newburyport, MA	Byfield, MA
Dalrymple, Cly ('69-'71), C, L-R	12/3/36	Chico, CA	Chico, CA
Dauer, Rich ('76-'85), 2B, R-R	7/27/52	San Bernardino, CA	Hinckley, OH
DaVanon, Jerry ('71), IF, R-R	8/21/45	Oceanside, CA	Houston, TX
Davis, George Storm ('82-'86, '92), RHP	12/26/61	Dallas, TX	Cockeysville, MD
Davis, Glenn ('91-'93), 1B, R-R	3/28/61	Jacksonville, FL	Columbus, GA
Davis, Tommy ('72-'75),DH, R-R	3/21/39	Brooklyn, NY	Alta Loma, CA
Davis, Wallace Butch ('88-'89), OF, R-R	6/19/58	Williamston, NC	Williamston, NC
DeCinces, Doug ('73-'81), 3B, R-R	8/29/50	Burbank, CA	Newport Beach, CA
de la Rosa, Francisco ('91), RHP	3/3/66	La Roma, DR	La Roma, DR
DeLeon, Luis ('87), RHP	8/19/57	Ponce, PR	Ponce, PR
Delock, Ike ('63), RHP	11/11/29	Highland Park, MI	E. Naples, FL
Dempsey, Rick ('76-'86, '92), C, R-R	9/13/49	Fayetteville, TN	West Lake Villiage, CA
Devereaux, Mike ('89-), OF, R-R	4/10/63	Casper, WY	Tampa, FL
Diering, Chuck ('54-'56), OF, R-R	2/5/23	St Louis, MO	St Louis, MO
Dillard, Gordon ('88), LHP	5/20/64	Salinas, CA	Salinas, CA
Dillman, Bill ('67), RHP	5/25/45	Trenton, NJ	Winter Park, FL
Dimmel, Mike ('77-'78), OF, R-R	10/18/54	Albert Lea, MN	Carrollton, TX
Dixon, Ken ('84-'87), RHP	10/17/60	Monroe, VA	Baltimore, MD
Dobson, Pat ('71-'72), RHP	2/12/42	Depew, NY	Cape Coral, FL
Dodd, Tom ('86), DH-PH, R-R	8/15/58	Portland, OR	Decatur, AL
Dorish, Harry ('55-'56), RHP	7/13/21	Swoyersville, PA	Kingston, PA
Drabowsky, Moe ('66-'68, '70), RHP	7/21/35	Ozanna, POLAND	Highland Park, IL
Drago, Dick ('77), RHP	6/25/45	Toledo, OH	Brooksville, FL
Dropo, Walt ('59-'61), 1B, R-R	1/30/23	Moosup, CT	Boston, MA
Dukes, Tom ('71), RHP	8/31/42	Knoxville, TN	Arcadia, Ca
Duncan, Dave ('75-'76), C, R-R	9/26/45	Dallas, TX	Tucson, AZ
Duren, Ryne ('54), RHP	2/22/29	Cazenovia, WI	Middleton, WI
Durham, Joe ('54, '57), OF, R-R	7/31/31	Newport News, VA	Randallston, MD
Dwyer, Jim ('81-'88), OF, L-L	1/3/50	Evergreen Park, IL	Evergreen Park, IL
Dyck, Jim ('55-'56), OF, R-R	2/3/22	Omaha, NE	Cheyney, WA
Epstein, Mike ('66-'67), 1B, L-L	4/4/43	Bronx, NY	Dana Point, CA
Essegian, Chuck ('61), OF-PH, R-R	8/9/31	Boston, MA	Los Angeles, CA
Estrada, Chuck ('60-'64), RHP	2/15/38	San Luis Obispo, CA	San Luis Obispo, CA
Etchebarren, Andy ('62, '65-'75), C, R-R	6/20/43	Whittier, CA	Walnut, CA
Evans, Dwight ('91), OF, R-R	11/3/51	Santa Monica, CA	Lynnfield, MA
Evers, Walter Hoot ('55-'56), OF, R-R	2/8/21	St Louis, MO	Died 1/25/91 (69)
Farmer, Ed ('77), RHP	10/18/49	Evergreen Park, IL	Calabasas, CA
Fernandez, L. Chico ('68), IF, R-R	4/23/39	Havana, CUBA	Miami, FL
Ferrarese, Don ('55-'57), LHP	6/19/29	Oakland, CA	Apple Valley, CA
Finigan, Jim ('59), 3B, R-R	8/19/28	Quincy, IL	Died 5/16/81 (52)
Finley, Steve ('89-'90), OF, L-L	5/12/65	Union City, TN	Paducah, KY
Fiore, Mike ('68), 1B L-L	10/11/44	Brooklyn, NY	Malverne, NY
Fisher, Eddie ('66-'67), RHP	7/16/36	Shreveport, LA	Altus, OK
Fisher, Jack ('59-'62), RHP	3/4/39	Frostburg, MD	Easton, PA
Fisher, Tom ('67), RHP	4/4/42	Cleveland, OH	Indianapolis, IN
Flanagan, Mike ('75-'87, '91-'92), LHP	12/16/51	Manchester, NH	Parkton, MD
Flinn, John ('78-'79, '82), RHP	9/2/54	Merced, CA	Long Beach, CA
Floyd, Bobby ('68-'70), IF, R-R	10/20/43	Hawthorne, CA	Port St Lucie, FL
Foiles, Hank ('61), C, R-R	6/10/29	Richmond, VA	Virginia Beach, VA
Ford, Dan ('82-'85), OF, R-R	5/19/52	Los Angeles, CA	Anaheim, CA
Ford, Dave ('78-'81), RHP	12/29/56	Cleveland, OH	North Olmstead, OH
Fornieles, Mike ('56-'57), RHP	1/18/32	Havana, CUBA	New Brighton, MA
Fox, Howie ('54), RHP	3/1/21	Coburg, OR	Died 10/9/55 (34)
Francona, Tito ('56-'57), OF-1B, L-L	11/4/33	Aliquippa, PA	New Brighton, PA
Frazier, Joe ('56), OF, L-R	10/6/22	Liberty, NC	Tulsa, OK
Freed, Roger ('70), 1B-OF, R-R	6/2/46	Los Angeles, CA	Chino, CA
Fridley, Jim ('54), OF, R-R	9/6/24	Phillippi, WV	Port Charlotte, FL
Frohwirth, Todd ('91-'93), RHP	9/28/62	Milwaukee, WI	Milwaukee, WI
Fuller, Jim ('73-'74), OF, R-R	11/28/50	Bethesda, MD	Pasadena, TX

Gaines, Joe ('63-'64), OF, R-R	11/22/36	Bryan, TX	Oakland, CA
Gallagher, Dave ('90), OF, R-R	9/20/60	Trenton, NJ	Bel Air, MD
Garcia, Alfonso Kiko ('76-'80), IF, R-R	10/14/53	Martinez, CA	Concord, CA
Garcia, Vinicio Chico ('54), 2B, R-R	12/24/24	Veracruz, MEX	Monterrey, MEX
Gardner, Billy ('56-'59), 2B, R-R	7/19/27	Waterford, CT	Waterford, CT
Garland, Wayne ('73-'76), RHP	10/26/50	Nashville, TN	Nashville, TN
Gastall, Tom ('55-'56), C, R-R	6/13/32	Fall River, MA	Died 9/20/56 (24)
Gentile, Jim ('60-'63), 1B, L-L	6/3/34	San Francisco, CA	Edmond, OK
Gerhart, Ken ('86-'88), OF, R-R	5/19/61	Charleston, SC	Murfreesboro, TN
Gilliford, Paul ('67), LHP	1/12/45	Bryn Mawr, PA	Malvern, PA
Ginsberg, Myron Joe ('56-'60), C, L-R	10/11/26	New York, NY	Punta Gorda, FL
Gomez, Leo ('90-), IF, R-R	3/2/67	Canovanas, PR	Canovanas, PR
Gonzales, Rene Gonzo ('87-'90), IF, R-R	9/23/62	Austin, TX	Newport Beach, CA
Goodman, Billy ('57), IF-OF, L-R	3/22/26	Concord, NC	Died 10/1/84 (58)
Graham, Dan ('80-'81), C-3B, L-R	7/19/54	Ray, AZ	Malmee, OH
Gray, Ted ('55), LHP	12/31/24	Detroit, MI	Clarkston, MI
Green, Gene ('60), OF-C, R-R	6/26/33	Los Angeles, CA	Died 5/23/81 (47)
Green, Lenny ('57-'59, '64), OF, L-L	1/6/33	Detroit, MI	Detroit, MI
Grich, Bob ('70-'76), 2B, R-R	1/15/49	Muskegon, MI	Long Beach, CA
Griffin, Mike ('87), RHP	6/26/57	Colusa, CA	Hawthorne, NJ
Grimsley, Ross ('74-'77, '82), LHP	1/7/50	Topeka, KS	Towson, MD
Gross, Wayne ('84-'85), 3B, L-R	1/14/52	Riverside, CA	Danville, CA
Gulliver, Glenn ('82-'83), 3B, L-R	10/15/54	Detroit, MI	Allen Park, MI
Gutierrez, Jackie ('86-'87), IF, R-R	6/27/60	Cartagena, COL	Miami, FL
Habyan, John ('85-'88), RHP	1/29/63	Bay Shore, NY	Bel Air, MD
Haddix, Harvey ('64-'65), LHP	9/18/25	Medway, OH	Died 1/10/94 (68)
Hale, Bob ('55-'59), 1B, L-L	11/7/33	Sarasota, FL	Park Ridge, IL
Hall, Dick ('61-'66, '69-'71), RHP	9/27/30	St Louis, Mo	Timonium, MD
Hammonds, Jeffrey ('93-), OF, R-R	3/5/71	Plainfield, NJ	Scotch Plains, NJ
Hamric, Bert ('58), OF-PH, L-R	3/1/28	Clarksburg, WV	Died 8/8/84 (56)
Haney, Larry ('66-'68), C, R-R	11/19/42	Charlottesville, VA	Barboursville, VA
Hansen, Ron ('58-'62), SS, R-R	4/5/38	Oxford, NE	Baldwin, MD
Hardin, Jim ('67-'71), RHP	8/6/43	Morris Chapel, TN	Died 3/9/91 (47)
Harlow, Larry ('75, '77-'79), OF, L-L	11/13/51	Colorado Springs, CO	Norco, CA
Harnisch, Pete ('88-'90), RHP	9/23/66	Commack, NY	Commack, NY
Harper, Tommy ('76), DH, R-R	10/14/40	Oak Grove, LA	Sharon, MA
Harrison, Bob ('55-'56), RHP	9/22/30	St Louis, Mo	
Harrison, Roric ('72), RHP	9/20/46	Los Angeles, CA	Mission Viejo, C(
Harshman, Jack ('58-'59), LHP	7/12/27	San Diego, CA	San Diego, CA
Hart, Mike L. ('87), OF. L-L	2/17/58	Milwaukee, WI	West Allis, WI
Hartzell, Paul ('80), RHP	11/2/53	Bloomsburg, PA	Houston, TX
Hatton, Grady ('56). IF, L-R	10/7/22	Beaumont, TX	Warren, TX
Havens, Brad ('85-'86), LHP	11/17/59	Highland Park, MI	Royal Oak, MI
Hazewood, Drungo ('80), OF, R-R	9/1/59	Mobile, AL	Sacramento, CA
Heard, Jehosie ('54), LHP	1/17/20	Atlanta, GA	Birmingham, AL
Held, Mel ('56), RHP	4/12/29	Edon, OH	Edon, OH
Held, Woodie ('66-'67), IF-OF, R-R	3/25/32	Sacramento, CA	Dubois, WY
Hendricks, Elrod ('68-'72, '73-'76, '78-'79), C, L-R	12/22/40	St Thomas, VI	Randallstown, MD
Hernandez, Leo ('82-'83, '85), 3B, R-R	11/6/59	Santa Lucia, VEN	Edo. Mirando, VEN
Herzog, Whitey ('61-'62), OF, L-L	11/9/31	New Athens, IL	Blue Springs, MO
Hickey, Kevin ('89-'91), LHP	2/25/56	Chicago, IL	Sparks, MD
Hoeft, Billy ('59-'62), LHP	5/17/32	Oshkosh, WI	Anne Arbor, MI
Hoiles, Chris ('89-), C, R-R	3/20/65	Bowling Green, OH	Cockeysville, MD
Holdsworth, Fred ('76-'77), RHP	5/29/52	Detroit, MI	Chelsea, MI
Holton, Brian ('89-'90), RHP	11/29/59	McKeesport, PA	Hunt Valley, MD
Holtzman, Ken ('76), LHP	11/3/45	St Louis, MO	Buffalo Grove, IL
Hood, Don ('73-'74), LHP	10/16/49	Florence, SC	Estero, FL
Horn, Sam ('90-'92), 1B-DH, L-L	11/2/63	Dallas, TX	Birmingham, AL
Houttemen, Art ('57), RHP	8/7/27	Detroit, MI	Lake Orion, MI
Howard, Brucc ('68), RHP	3/23/43	Sallsbury, MD	Sarasota, FL
Hudler, Rex ('86), IF, R-R	9/2/60	Tempe, AZ	Fresno, CA
Huffman, Phil ('85), RHP	6/20/58	Freeport, TX	Lake Jackson, TX
Hughes, Keith ('88), OF, L-L	9/12/63	Bryn Mawr, PA	Paoli, PA
Huismann, Mark ('89), RHP	5/11/58	Lincoln, NE	Blue Springs, MO

Hulett, Tim ('89-), IF, R-R	1/12/60	Springfield, IL	Springfield, IL
Hunter, Billy ('54), SS, R-R	6/4/28	Punxsutawney, PA	Lutherville, MD
Huppert, Dave ('83), C, R-R	4/1/57	Southgate, CA	Zephyr Hill, FL
Hutto, Jim ('75), C, R-R	10/17/47	Norfolk, VA	Pensacola, FL
Hyde, Dick ('61), RHP	8/3/28	Hindsboro, IL	Champaign, IL
Jackson, Grant ('71-'76), LHP	9/28/42	Fostoria, OH	Pittsburgh, PA
Jackson, Lou ('64), OF, L-R	7/26/35	Riverton, LA	Died 5/27/69 (33)
Jackson, Reggie ('76), OF, L-L	5/18/46	Wyncote, PA	Oakland, CA
Jackson, Ron ('84) 3B, R-R	5/9/53	Birmingham, AL	Fullerton, CA
Jefferson, Jesse ('73-'75), RHP	3/3/49	Midlothian, VA	Midlothian, VA
Jefferson, Stan ('89-'90), OF, S-R	12/4/62	New York, NY	Bronx, NY
Johnson, Bob ('63-'67), IF, R-R	3/4/36	Omaha, NE	St Paul, MN
Johnson, Connie ('56-'58), RHP	12/27/22	Stone Mountain, GA	Kansas City, MO
Johnson, Darrell ('62), C, R-R	8/25/28	Horace, NE	Ord, NE
Johnson, Dave ('65-'72), 2B, R-R	1/30/43	Orlando, FL	Winter Park, FL
Johnson, Dave ('89-'91), RHP	10/24/59	Baltimore, MD	Baltimore, MD
Johnson, David ('74-'75), RHP	10/4/48	Abilene, TX	Abilene, TX
Johnson, Don ('55), RHP	11/12/26	Portland, OR	Portland, OR
Johnson, Ernie ('59), RHP	6/16/24	Brattleboro, VT	Atlanta, GA
Jones, Gordon ('60-'61), RHP	4/2/30	Portland, OR	Sacramento, CA
Jones, O'Dell ('86), RHP	1/13/53	Tulare, CA	Beaverton, OR
Jones, Ricky ('86), IF, R-R	6/4/58	Tupelo, MS	Athens, GA
Jones, Sad Sam ('64), RHP	12/14/25	Stewartsville, OH	Died 11/5/71 (45)
Jones, Stacy ('91), RHP	5/26/67	Gadsden, AL	Attalla, AL
Kell, George ('56-'57), 3B, R-R	8/23/22	Swifton, AR	Swifton, AR
Kellert, Frank ('54), 1B, R-R	7/6/24	Oklahoma City, OK	Died 11/19/76 (52)
Kelly, Pat ('77-'80), OF, L-L	7/30/44	Philadelphia, PA	Timonium, MD
Kennedy, Bob ('54-'55), 3B, R-R	8/18/20	Chicago, IL	Mesa, AZ
Kennedy, Terry ('87-'88), C, L-R	6/4/56	Euclid, OH	Escondido, CA
Kerrigan, Joe ('78, '80), RHP	11/30/54	Philadelphia, PA	Daly City, CA
Kilgus, Paul ('91), LHP	2/2/62	Bowling Green, KY	Bowling Green, KY
Kinnunen, Mike ('86-'87), LHP	4/1/58	Seattle, WA	Seattle, WA
Kirkland, Willie ('64), OF, L-R	2/17/34	Siluria, Al	Detroit, MI
Kittle, Ron ('90), 1B-DH, R-R	1/5/58	Gary, IN	Valparasio, IN
Klaus, Billy ('59-'60), IF, L-R	12/9/28	Fox Lake, IL	Valley Crucie, NC
Knight, Ray ('87), 3B, R-R	12/28/52	Albany, GA	Albany, GA
Knowles, Darold ('65), LHP	12/9/41	Brunswick, MO	St Petersburg, FL
Kokos, Dick ('54), OF, L-L	2/28/28	Chicago, IL	Died 4/9/86 (58)
Komminsk, Brad ('90), OF, R-R	4/4/61	Lima, OH	Lima, OH
Koslo, George Dave ('54), LHP	3/31/20	Menasha, WI	Died 12/1/75 (55)
Krenchicki, Wayne ('79-'81), IF, L-R	9/17/54	Trenton, NJ	Palm Harbor, FL
Kretlow, Lou ('54-'55), RHP	6/27/23	Apache, OK	Enid, OK
Kryhoski, Dick ('54), 1B, L-L	3/24/25	Leonia, NJ	Birmingham, MI
Kuzava, Bob ('54-'55), LHP	5/28/53	Wyandotte, MI	Wyandotte, MI
Lacy, Lee ('85-'87), OF, R-R	4/10/48	Longview, TX	Agoura Hills, CA
Landrith, Hobert Hobie ('62-'63), C, L-R	3/16/30	Decatur, IL	Bloomfield Hills, MI
Landrum Terry Tito ('83, '88), OF, R-R	10/25/54	Joplin, MO	New York, NY
Larsen, Don ('54, '65), RHP	8/7/29	Michigan City, IN	Morgan Hill, CA
Lau, Charlie ('61-'63, '64-'67), C, L-R	4/12/33	Romulus, MI	Died 3/18/54 (50)
Lefferts, Craig ('92), LHP	9/29/57	Munich, W. GER	Poway, CA
Lehew, Jim ('61-'62), RHP	8/19/37	Baltimore, MD	Baltimore, MD
Lehman, Ken ('57-'58), LHP	6/10/28	Seattle, WA	Sedro Wooley, WA
Lenhardt, Don ('54), OF, R-R	10/4/22	Alton, IL	St Louis, MO
Leonard, Mark ('93), 1B, L-R	8/14/64	MountainView, CA	San Jose, CA
Leonhard, Dave ('67-'72), RHP	1/22/42	Arlington, VA	Beverly, MA
Leppert, Don E. ('55), 2B, L-R	11/20/30	Memphis, TN	Memphis, TN
Lewis, Richie ('92), RHP	1/25/66	Muncie, IN	Losantville, IN
Littlefield, Dick ('54), LHP	3/18/26	Detroit, MI	Detroit, MI
Locke, Charlise ('55), RHP	5/5/32	Malden, MO	Poplar Bluff, MO
Lockman, Carroll Whitey ('59), 1B, L-R	7/25/26	Lowell, NC	Scottsdale, AR
Loes, Billy ('56-'59), RHP	12/13/29	Long Island City, NY	Astoria, NY
Lopat, Eddie ('55), LHP	6/21/18	New York, NY	Hillsdale, NY
Lopez, Carlos ('78), OF, R-R	9/27/50	Mazatlan, MEX	Mexico City, MEX
Lopez, Marcelino ('67, '69-'70), LHP	9/23/43	Havana, CUBA	Miami, FL

Lowenstein, John ('79-'85), OF, L-R	1/17/47	Wolf Point, MT	Las Vegas, NV
Luebber, Steve ('81), RHP	7/9/49	Clinton, MO	Carl Junction, MO
Luebke, Dick ('62), LHP	4/8/35	Chicago, IL	Died 12/4/74 (39)
Lynn, Fred ('85-'88), OF, L-L	2/3/52	Chicago, IL	LaCosta, CA
Mabe, Bobbie ('60), RHP	10/8/29	Danville, VA	Danville, VA
Maddox, Elliott ('77), OF-3B, R-R	12/21/47	E. Orange, NJ	Guttenberg, NJ
Majeski, Hank ('55), 3B, R-R	12/13/16	Staten Island, NY	Died 8/9/91 (74)
Marquis, Roger ('55) OF, L-L	4/5/37	Holyoke, MA	Holyoke, MA
Marsh, Fred ('55-'56), IF, R-R	1/5/24	Valley Falls, KS	Corry, PA
Marshall, Jim ('58), 1B, L-L	5/25/32	Danville, IL	Scottsdale, AZ
Martin, Morrie ('56), LHP	9/23/22	Dixon, MO	Washington, MO
Martinez, Dennis ('76-'86), RHP	5/14/55	Granada, NIC	Miami, FL
Martinez, Felix Tippy ('76-'86), LHP	5/31/50	LaJunta, CO	Towson, MD
Martinez, Reyenaldo Chito ('91-'93), OF, L-L	12/19/65	Belize City, BELIZE	Metairie, LA
Matchick, Tom ('72), 3B, L-R	9/7/43	Hazelton, PA	Maunee, OH
Maxwell, Charlie ('55), OF, L-L	4/8/27	Lawton, MI	Paw Paw, MI
May, Dave ('67-'70), OF, L-R	12/23/43	New Castle, DE	New Castle, DE
May, Lee ('75-'80), 1B, R-R	3/23/43	Birmingham, AL	Cincinnati, OH
May, Rudy ('76-'77), LHP	7/18/44	Coffeyville, KS	North Fork, CA
McCormick, Mike ('63-'64), LHP	9/29/38	Pasadena, CA	Cupertino, CA
McDonald, Ben ('89-), RHP	11/24/67	Baton Rouge, LA	Denham Springs, LA
McDonald, Jim ('55), RHP	5/17/27	Grants Pass, OR	Downey, CA
McGehee, Kevin ('93-) RHP	1/19/69	Alexandria, LA	Pineville, LA
McGregor, Scott ('76-'88), LHP	1/18/54	Inglewood, CA	Towson, CA
McGuire, Mickey ('62, '67), IF, R-R	1/18/41	Dayton, OH	Dayton, OH
McKnight, Jeff ('90-'91), IF-OF, S-R	2/18/63	Conway, AR	Bee Branch, AR
McLemore, Mark ('92-), IF, S-R	10/4/64	San Diego, CA	Gilbert, AZ
McNally, Dave ('62-'74), LHP	10/31/42	Billings, MT	Billings, MT
Mele, Sam ('54), OF, R-R	1/21/23	Astoria, NY	Quincy, MA
Melendez, Francisco ('89), 1B, L-L	1/25/64	Rio Piedras, PR	Juana Diaz, PR
Melvin, Bob ('89-'91), C, R-R	10/28/61	Palo Alto, CA	Germantown, TN
Mercedes, Luis ('91-'93), OF, R-R	2/20/68	SP de Macoris, DR	SP de Macoris, DR
Mesa, Jose ('87, '90-'92), RHP	5/22/66	Pueblo Viejo, DR	Rochester, NY
Miksis, Eddie ('57-'58), IF, R-R	9/11/26	Burlington, NJ	Huntingdon Valley, PA
Milacki, Bob ('88-'92), RHP	7/28/64	Trenton, NJ	Lake Havasu City, AZ
Miller, Bill ('55), LHP	7/26/26	Minersville, PA	Hatboro, PA
Miller, Dyar ('75-'72), RHP	5/29/46	Batesville, IN	Sarasota, FL
Miller, John ('62-'63, "65-'67), RHP	5/30/41	Baltimore, MD	Baltimore, MD
Miller, Randy ('77), RHP	3/18/53	Oxnard, CA	
Miller, Stu ('63-'67), RHP	12/26/27	Northhampton, MA	Cameran Park, CA
Milligan, Randy ('89-'92), 1B, R-R	11/27/61	San Diego, CA	Virginia Beach, VA
Mills, Alan ('92-), RHP	10/18/66	Lakeland, FL	Lakeland, FL
Mirabella, Paul ('83), LHP	3/20/54	Belleville, NJ	Bannton Manor, NJ
Miranda, Willy ('55-'59), SS, S-R	5/24/26	Velasco, CUBA	Baltimore, MD
Mitchell, John ('90), RHP	8/11/65	Dickson, TN	Nashville, TN
Mitchell, Paul ('75), RHP	8/19/49	Worcester, MA	Berlin, MA
Moeller, Ron ('56, '58), LHP	10/13/38	Cincinnati, OH	Cincinnati, OH
Molinaro, Bob ('79), OF, L-R	5/21/50	Newark, NJ	Del Ray Beach, FL
Moore, Ray ('55-'57), RHP	6/1/26	Meadows, MD	Upper Marlboro, MD
Mora, Andres ('76-'78), OF, R-R	5/25/55	Rio Bravo, MEX	
Morales, Jose ('81-'82), C-PH, R-R	12/30/44	Frederiksted, VI	Orlando, FL
Moreland, Keith ('89), DH, R-R	5/2/54	Dallas, TX	Deerfield, IL
Morgan, Mike ('88), RHP	10/8/59	Tulare, CA	Ogden, UT
Morogiello, Dan ('83), LHP	3/26/55	Brooklyn, NY	Brooklyn, NY
Morris, John ('68), LHP	8/23/41	Lewes, DE	Scottsdale, NE
Moss, Les ('54-'55), C, R-R	5/14/25	Tulsa, OK	Longwood, FL
Moyer, Jamie ('93-), LHP	11/18/62	Sellersville, PA	Granger, IL
Motton, Curt ('67-'71, '73-'74), OF, R-R	9/24/40	Darnell, LA	Cockeysville, MD
Murray, Eddie ('77-'88), 1B, S-R	2/24/56	Los Angeles, CA	Los Angeles, CA
Murray, Ray ('54), C, R-R	10/12/17	Spring Hope, NC	Ft Worth, TX
Muser, Tony ('75-'77), 1B, L-L	8/1/47	Van Nuys, CA	Los Alamitos, CA
Mussina, Mike ('91-), RHP	12/8/68	Montoursville, PA	Montoursville, PA
Narum Leslie Buster ('63), RHP	11/16/40	Philadelphia, PA	Clearwater, FL

Nelson, Bob ('55-'57), OF	8/7/36	Dallas, TX	Dallas, TX
Nelson, Roger ('68), RHP	6/7/44	Altadena, CA	Shawnee, KS
Nichols, Carl ('86-'88), C, R-R	10/14/62	Los Angeles, CA	Modesto, CA
Nicholson, Dave ('60, '62), OF, R-R	8/29/39	St Louis, MO	Schaumburg, IL
Niedenfuer, Tom ('87-'88), RHP	8/13/59	St Louis Park, MN	Beverly Hills, CA
Nieman, Bob ('56-'59), OF, R-R	1/26/27	Cincinnati, OH	Died 3/10/85 (58)
Nixon, Donell ('90), OF, R-R	12/31/61	Evergreen, NC	Evergreen, NC
Nolan, Joe ('82-'85), C, L-R	5/12/51	St Louis, MO	St Louis, MO
Noles, Dickie ('88), RHP	11/19/56	Charlotte, NC	Aston, PA
Nordbrook, Tim ('74-'76), IF, R-R	7/7/49	Baltimore, MD	Baltimore, MD
Northrup, Jim ('74-'75), OF, L-R	11/24/39	Breckenridge, MI	Pontiac, MI
Oates, Johnny ('70, '72), C, L-R	1/21/46	Sylva, NC	Colonial Heights, VA
Obando, Sherman ('93-), OF, R-R	1/23/70	Bocas del Tor, PANAMA	Changuinola, PANAMA
O'Connor, Jack ('87), LHP	6/2/58	29 Palms, CA	Yucca Valley, CA
O'Dell, Billy ('54, '56-'59), LHP	2/10/33	Whitmire, SC	Newberry, SC
O'Donoghue, John, Jr. ('93-), LHP	5/26/69	Wilmington, DE	Elkton, MD
O'Donoghue, John ('68), LHP	10/7/39	Kansas City, MO	Elkton, MD
Oertel, Chuck ('58), OF, L-R	3/12/31	Coffeyville, KS	Naubinway, MI
Oliver, Bob ('74), OF-1B, R-R	2/28/43	Shreveport, LA	Linda, CA
Olson, Gregg ('88-'93), RHP	10/11/66	Scribner, NE	Reisterstown, MD
O'Malley, Tom ('85-'86), 3B, L-R	12/25/60	Orange, NJ	Montoursville, PA
Oquist, Mike ('93-), RHP	5/30/68	LaJunta, CO	LaJunta, CO
Orsino, John ('63-'65), C, R-R	4/22/38	Teaneck, NJ	Bonyton Beach, FL
Orsulak, Joe ('88-'92), OF, L-L	5/31/62	Glen Ridge, NJ	Cockeysville, MD
Pacella, John ('84), RHP	9/15/56	Brooklyn, NY	Westerville, OH
Pagan, Dave ('76), RHP	9/15/49	Nipawin, SASK	Nipawin, Sask, CAN
Paglioarulo, Mike ('93), 3B, L-R	3/15/60	Medford, MA	Winchester, MA
Palica, Erv ('55-'56), RHP	2/9/28	Lomita, CA	Died 5/29/82 (54)
Palmer, Jim ('65-'67, '69-'84), RHP	10/15/45	New York, NY	Brooklandville, MD
Papa, John ('61-'62), RHP	12/5/40	Bridgeport, CT	Huntington, CT
Pappas, Milt ('57-'65), RHP	5/11/39	Detroit, MI	Beecher, IL
Pardo, Al ('85-'86), C, S-R	9/8/62	Oviedo, SPAIN	Lutz, FL
Parent, Mark ('92-'93), C, R-R	9/16/61	Ashland, OR	San Diego, CA
Paris, Kelly ('85-'86), IF, S-R	10/17/57	Encindo, CA	Westlake Village, CA
Parrott, Mike ('77), RHP	12/6/54	Oxnard, CA	Lyons, CO
Patton, Tom ('57), C, R-R	9/5/35	Honey Brook, PA	Honey Brook, PA
Pearson, Albie ('59-'60), OF, L-L	9/12/34	Alhambra, CA	LaQuinta, CA
Pena, Orlando ('71, '73), RHP	11/17/33	Victoria de las Tunas, CUBA	Miami, FL
Pennington, Brad ('93-), LHP	4/14/69	Salem, IN	Salem, IN
Peraza, Oswald ('88), RHP	10/19/62	Puerto Cabello, VEN	Puerto Cabello, VEN
Peterson, Carl Buddy ('57), IF, R-R	4/23/25	Portland, OR	Sacramento, CA
Philley, Dave ('55-'56, '60-'61), OF, 1B, S-R	5/16/20	Paris, TX	Paris, TX
Phoebus, Tom ('66-'70), RHP	4/7/42	Baltimore, MD	Stuart, FL
Pilarcik, Al ('57-'60), OF, L-L	7/3/30	Whiting, IN	Scherrville, IN
Pillette, Duane ('54-'55), RHP	7/4/22	Detroit, MI	San Jose, CA
Piniella, Lou ('64), OF, R-R	8/28/43	Tampa, FL	Allendale, NJ
Poole, Jim ('91-), LHP	4/28/66	Rochester, NY	Ellicott City, MD
Pope, Dave ('55-'56), OF, L-R	6/17/25	Talladega, AL	Cleveland, OH
Portocarrero, Arnie ('58-'60), RHP	7/5/31	New York, NY	Died 7/21/86 (55)
Powell, John Boog ('61-'74), 1B, L-R	8/17/41	Lakeland, FL	Key West, FL
Powers, John ('60), OF, L-R	7/8/29	Birmingham, AL	Birmingham, AL
Powis, Carl ('57), OF, R-R	1/11/28	Philadelphia, PA	Crosby, TX
Price, Joe ('90), LHP	11/29/56	Inglewood, CA	Poway, CA
Pyburn, Jim ('55-'57), OF, R-R	11/1/32	Fairfield, AL	Jasper, AL
Quirk, Art ('62), LHP	4/11/38	Providence, RI	Glastonbury, CT
Quirk, Jamie ('89), C, L-R	10/22/54	Whittier, CA	Overland Park, KS
Ramirez, Allan ('83), RHP	5/1/57	Victoria, TX	Victoria, TX
Rayford, Floyd ('80, '82, '84-'87), 3B-C, R-R	1/27/57	Memphis, TN	Columbia, MD
Reinbach, Mike ('74), OF, L-R	8/6/49	San Diego, CA	Died 5/20/89 (39)
Rettenmund, Merv ('68-'73), OF, R-R	6/6/43	Flint, MI	Poway, CA

Reynolds, Bob ('72-'75), RHP	1/21/47	Seattle, WA	Beverley Hills, CA
Reynolds, Harold ('93), 2B, S-R	11/26/64	Eugene, OR	Corvallis, OR
Rhodes, Arthur ('91-), LHP	10/24/69	Waco, TX	Sarasota, FL
Rice, Del ('60), C, R-R	10/27/22	Portsmouth, OH	Died 1/26/83 (60)
Richert, Pete ('67-'71), LHP	10/29/39	Floral Park, NY	Palm Springs, CA
Rineer, Jeff ('79), LHP	7/3/55	Lancaster, PA	Nottingham, PA
Ripken, Bill ('87-'92), 2B, R-R	12/16/64	Havre de Grace, MD	Fallston, MD
Ripken, Cal Jr ('81-), SS, R-R	8/24/60	Havre de Grace, MD	Reisterstown, MD
Roberts, Robin ('62-'65), RHP	9/30/26	Springfield, IL	Temple Terrace, FL
Robinson, Brooks ('55-'77), 3B, R-R	5/18/37	Little Rock, AR	Baltimore, MD & So. California
Robinson, Earl ('61-'62, '64), OF, R-R	11/3/36	New Orleans, LA	Oakland, CA
Robinson, Eddie ('57), 1B, L-R	12/15/20	Paris, TX	Ft Worth, TX
Robinson, Frank ('66-'71), OF, R-R	8/31/35	Beaumont, TX	Bel Air, CA
Robinson, Jeff M. ('91), RHP	12/14/61	Ventura, CA	San Diego, CA
Robles, Sergio ('72-'73), C, R-R	4/16/46	Magdalena, MEX	Magdalena, MEX
Rodriguez, Auerlio ('83), 3B, R-R	12/28/47	Cananea, MEX	Los Mochis, MEX
Rodriguez, Vic ('84), 2B, R-R	7/14/61	New York, NY	Carolina, PR
Roenicke, Gary ('78-'85), OF, R-R	12/5/54	Covina, CA	Nevada City, CA
Rogovin, Saul ('55), RHP	10/10/23	Brooklyn, NY	New York, NY
Rowdon, Wade ('88), 3B, R-R	9/7/60	Riverhead, NY	Orlando, FL
Rowe, Ken ('64-'65), RHP	12/31/33	Ferndale, MI	Norcross, GA
Royster, Willie ('81), C, R-R	4/11/54	Clarksville, VA	Washington, DC
Roznovsky, Vic ('66-'67), C, L-R	10/19/38	Shiner, TX	Fresno, CA
Rudolph, Ken ('77), C, R-R	12/29/46	Rockford, IL	Mesa, AZ
Sakata, Lenn ('80-'85), IF, R-R	6/8/54	Honolulu, HI	Merced, CA
Salmon, Rutherford Chico ('69-'72), IF, R-R	12/2/38	Colon, PANAMA	Panama City, PANAMA
Sanchez, Orlando ('84), C, L-R	9/7/56	Canovanas, PR	Canovanas, PR
Saverine, Bob ('59, '62-'64), IF-OF, S-R	6/2/41	Norwalk, CT	Stamford, CT
Scarsone, Steve ('92-'93), IF, R-R	4/11/66	Anaheim, CA	Anaheim, CA
Schallock, Art ('55), LHP	4/25/24	Mill Valley, CA	Novato, CA
Scherrer, Bill ('88), LHP	1/20/58	Tonawanda, NY	Tampa, Fl
Schilling, Curt ('88-'90), RHP	11/14/66	Anchorage, AK	Phoenix, AZ
Schmidt, Dave ('87-'89), RHP	4/22/57	Niles, MI	Agoura, CA
Schmitz, Johnny ('56), LHP	11/27/20	Wausau, WI	Wausau, WI
Schneider, Jeff ('81), LHP	12/6/52	Bremerton, WA	Geneseo, IL
Schu, Rick ('88-'89), 3B, R-R	1/26/62	Philadelphia, PA	Carmichael, CA
Scott, Ralph Mickey ('72-'73), LHP	7/25/47	Weimar, GER	Binghamton, NY
Segrist, Kal ('55), IF, R-R	4/14/31	Greenville, TX	Lubbock, TX
Segui, David ('90-), 1B-OF, S-L	7/19/66	Kansas City, KS	Kansas City, KS
Severinsen, Al ('69), RHP	11/9/44	Brooklyn, NY	Baldwin, NY
Sheets, Larry ('84-'89), OF-DH, L-R	12/6/59	Staunton, VA	Lutherville, MD
Shelby, John ('81-'87), OF, S-R	2/23/58	Lexington, KY	Lexington, KY
Shetrone, Barry ('59-'62), OF, L-R	7/6/38	Baltimore, MD	Towson, MD
Shields, Tommy ('92), IF, L-R	8/14/64	Fairfax, VA	Devon, PA
Shopay, Tom ('71-'72, '75-'77), OF, L-R	2/21/45	Bristol, CT	Miami, FL
Short, Billy ('62, '66), LHP	11/27/37	Kingston, NY	Sarasota, FL
Siebern, Norm ('64-'65), 1B, L-R	7/26/33	St Louis, MO	Naples, FL
Simmons, Nelson ('87), OF, S-R	6/27/63	Washington, DC	San Diego, CA
Singleton, Ken ('75-'84), OF, S-R	6/10/47	New York, NY	Lutherville, MD
Sisk, Doug ('88), RHP	9/26/57	Renton, WA	Tacoma, WA
Skaggs, Dave ('77-'80), C, R-R	6/12/51	Santa Monica, CA	Norco, CA
Sleater, Lou ('58), LHP	9/8/26	St Louis, MO	Towson, MD
Smith, Al ('63), OF, R-R	2/7/28	Kirkwood, MO	Chicago, IL
Smith, Billy ('77-'79), 2B, S-R	7/14/53	Hodge, LA	Austin, TX
Smith, Hal ('55-'56), C, R-R	12/7/30	West Frankfort, IL	Houston, TX
Smith, Lonnie ('93), OF, R-R	12/22/55	Chicago, IL	Atlanta, GA
Smith, Texas Mike ('89-'90), RHP	10/31/63	San Antonio, TX	San Antonio, TX
Smith, Nate ('62), C, R-R	4/26/35	Chicago, IL	
Smith, Roy ('91), RHP	9/6/61	Mt. Vernon, NY	Mt. Vernon, NY
Snell, Nate ('84-'86), RHP	9/2/52	Orangeburg, SC	Vance, SC
Snyder, Russ ('61-'67), OF, L-R	6/22/34	Oak, NE	Nelson, NE
Stanhouse, Don ('78-'79, '82), RHP	2/12/51	DuQuoin, IL	Dallas, TX
Stanicek, Pete ('87-'88), IF-OF, S-R	4/18/63	Harvey, IL	Park Forest, IL
Starrette, Herm ('63-'65), RHP	11/20/38	Statesville, NC	Statesville, NC
Stefero, John ('83, '86), C, L-R	9/22/59	Sumter, SC	Pasadena, MD

Stephens, Gene ('60-'61), OF, L-R	1/20/33	Gravette, AR	Oklahoma City, OK
Stephens,Vern ('54-'55), 3B, R-R	10/23/20	McAlister, NM	Died 11/3/68 (48)
Stephenson, Earl ('77-'78), LHP	7/31/47	Benson, NC	Tampa, FL
Stewart, Sammy ('78-'85), RHP	10/28/54	Asheville, NC	Swannanoa, NC
Stillman, Royle ('75-'76), 1B-DH, L-L	1/2/51	Santa Monica, CA	
Stock, Wes ('59-'64), RHP	4/10/34	Longview, WA	Tacoma, WA
Stoddard, Tim ('78-'83), RHP	1/24/53	East Chicago, IN	Barrington, IL
Stone, Dean ('63), LHP	9/1/30	Moline, IL	Silvis, IL
Stone, Jeff ('88), OF, L-R	12/26/60	Kennett, MO	Lindenwold, NJ
Stone, Steve ('79-'81), RHP	7/14/47	Euclid, OH	Scottsdale, AZ
Stuart, Marlin ('54), RHP	8/8/18	Paragould, AR	Paragould, AR
Sundin, Gordon ('56), RHP	10/10/37	Minneapolis, MN	Estero, FL
Sutcliffe, Rick ('92-'93), RHP	6/21/56	Independence, MO	Lee's Summit, MO
Swaggerty, Bill ('83-'86), RHP	12/5/56	Sanford, FL	Westminster, MD
Tackett, Jeff ('91-), C, R-R	12/1/65	Fresno, CA	Cockeysville, MD
Tasby, Willie ('58-'60), OF, R-R	1/8/33	Shreveport, LA	Plant City, FL
Taylor, Dom (('90), RHP	8/11/58	Abington, PA	Bensalem, PA
Taylor, Joe ('58-'59), OF, L-L	3/2/26	Alhambra, CA	Pittsburgh, PA
Telford, Anthony ('90-'93), RHP	3/6/66	San Jose, CA	San Jose, CA
Temple, Johnny ('62), 2B, R-R	8/8/28	Lexington, NC	Died 1/12/94 (66)
Tettleton, Mickey ('88-'90), C, S-R	9/16/60	Oklahoma City, OK	Scottsdale, AZ
Thomas, Valmy ('60), C, R-R	10/21/28	Santurce, PR	Santurce, PR
Thomson, Bobby ('60), OF, R-R	10/25/23	Glasgow, SCOTLAND	Watchung, NJ
Throneberry, Marv ('61-'62), 1B, L-L	9/2/33	Collierville, TN	Collierville, TN
Thurmond, Mark ('88-'89), LHP	9/12/56	Houston, TX	Katy, TX
Tibbs, Jay ('88-'90), RHP	1/4/62	Birmingham, AL	Trussville, AL
Torrez, Mike ('75), RHP	8/28/46	Topeka, KS	White Plains, NY
Traber, Jim ('84, '86, '88-'89), 1B, L-L	12/26/61	Columbus, OH	Tulsa, OK
Triandos, Gus ('55-'62), C, R-R	7/30/30	San Francisco, CA	San Jose, CA
Trout, Paul Dizzy ('57), RHP	6/29/15	Sandcut, IN	Died 2/28/72 (56)
Turley, Bob ('54), RHP	9/19/30	Troy, IL	Marco Island, FL
Turner, Shane ('91), IF, L-R	1/8/63	Los Angeles, CA	Chino Hills, CA
Underwood, Tom ('84), LHP	12/22/53	Kokomo, IN	Lauderhill, FL
Valentine, Fred ('59, '63, '68), S-R	1/19/35	Clarksdale, MS	Washington, DC
Valenzuela, Fernando ('93), LHP	11/1/60	Navojoa, Sonora, MEX	Los Angeles, CA
Van Gorder, Dave ('87), C, R-R	3/27/57	Los Angeles, CA	Tucson, AZ
Vineyard, Dave ('64), RHP	2/25/41	Clay, WV	Left Hand, WV
Virgil, Ozzie ('62), 3B, R-R	5/17/33	Montecristi, PR	Glendale, AZ
Voigt, Jack ('92-), OF, R-R	5/17/66	Sarasota, FL	Venice, FL
Waitkus, Eddie ('54-'55), 1B, L-L	9/4/19	Cambridge, MA	Died 9/15/72 (53)
Walker, Greg ('90), 1B, L-R	10/6/59	Douglas, GA	Douglas, GA
Walker, Jerry ('57-'60), RHP	2/12/39	Ada, OK	Ada, OK
Ward, Pete ('62), OF, L-R	7/26/39	Montreal, Que, CAN	Lake Oswego, OR
Warwick, Carl ('65), OF, R-L	2/27/37	Dallas, TX	Houston, TX
Washington, Ron ('87), IF, R-R	4/29/52	New Orleans, LA	New Orleans, LA
Watt, Eddie ('66-'73), RHP	4/4/42	Lamonie, IA	North Bend, NE

MAJOR ORIOLES AWARD WINNERS

Most Valuable Player, AL (BBWAA): Brooks Robinson ('64), Frank Robinson ('66), Boog Powell ('70), Cal Ripken Jr. ('83 and '91).

Cy Young Award, AL (BBWAA): Mike Cuellar ('69 tied with Denny McLain), Jim Palmer ('73, '75, '76); Mike Flanagan ('79), Steve Stone ('80).

Manager of the Year (BBWAA): Frank Robinson ('89).

Manager of the Year, Major League (TSN): Hank Bauer ('66), Earl Weaver ('77, '79), Frank Robinson ('89), Johnny Oates ('93).

Manager of the Year, AL (AP): Paul Richards ('60), Hank Bauer ('64, '66), Earl Weaver ('73, '77, '79), Frank Robinson ('89).

Manager of the Year, AL (UPI): Earl Weaver ('79), Joe Altobelli ('83), Frank Robinson ('89).

Rookie of the Year, AL (BBWAA): Ron Hansen ('60), Curt Blefary ('65), Al Bumbry ('73), Eddie Murray ('77), Cal Ripken Jr. ('82), Gregg Olson ('89).

Rookie of the Year, AL (TSN): Ron Hansen ('60), Curt Blefary ('65), Al Bumbry ('73), Cal Ripken Jr. ('82), Craig Worthington ('89).

Rookie Pitcher of the Year, AL (TSN): Wally Bunker ('64), Tom Phoebus ('67), Mike Boddicker ('83).

Player of the Year, AL (TSN): Brooks Robinson ('64), Frank Robinson ('66), Cal Ripken Jr. ('83 and '89).

Player of the Year, AL (*Baseball America*): Cal Ripken Jr. ('83 and '91).

Pitcher of the Year, AL (TSN): Chuck Estrada ('60), Jim Palmer ('73, '75, '76), Mike Flanagan ('79), Steve Stone ('80).

Player of the Year, Major League (TSN): Frank Robinson ('66), Cal Ripken Jr. ('83 and '89).

Executive of the Year, Major League (TSN): Harry Dalton ('70), Hank Peters ('79), Roland Hemond ('89).

Executive of the Year, Major League (UPI): Hank Peters ('79), Roland Hemond ('89).

Roberto Clemente Award (Commissioner's Office): Presented annually to player who best typifies the game of baseball, both on and off the field—Brooks Robinson ('72), Ken Singleton ('82), Cal Ripken Jr. ('92).

Joe Cronin Award (AL Office): Presented annually to an AL player for significant achievement—Jim Palmer ('76), Brooks Robinson ('77).

Bart Giamatti Caring Award (Baseball Alumni Team): For exceptional devotion and contribution to both Baseball and the Community—Cal Ripken Jr. ('90)...it was the first time presented.

Most Valuable Player, World Series: Frank Robinson ('66), Brooks Robinson ('70), Rick Dempsey ('83).

Most Valuable Player, ALCS (Leland S. MacPhail Jr. Award): Mike Boddicker ('83).

Most Valuable Player, All-Star Game (Commissioner's Office): Now known as Arch Ward Memorial Trophy—Billy O'Dell ('58), Brooks Robinson ('66), Frank Robinson ('71), Cal Ripken Jr. ('91).

Jack Dunn Memorial Community Service Award: Elrod Hendricks ('87), Ken Singleton ('88), Brooks Robinson ('89), Jim Palmer ('91).

MOST VALUABLE ORIOLES, '54-'93

1954-Chuck Diering (OF)
1955-Dave Philley (OF)
1956-Bob Nieman (OF)
1957-Billy Gardner (2B)
1958-Gus Triandos (C)
1959-Gene Woodling (OF)
1960-Brooks Robinson (3B)
1961-Jim Gentile (1B)
1962-Brooks Robinson (3B)
1963-Stu Miller (RHP)
1964-Brooks Robinson (3B)
1965-Stu Miller (RHP)
1966-Frank Robinson (OF)
1967-Frank Robinson (OF)
1968-Dave McNally (LHP)
1969-Boog Powell (1B)
1970-Boog Powell (1B)
1971-B. Robby (3B)/F. Robby (OF)
1972-Jim Palmer (RHP)
1973-Jim Palmer (RHP)
1974-Paul Blair (OF)/Mike Cuellar (LHP)
1975-Ken Singleton (OF)
1976-Lee May (1B)
1977-Ken Singleton (OF)
1978-Eddie Murray (1B)
1979-Kan Singleton (OF)
1980-Al Bumbry (OF)
1981-Eddie Murray (1B)
1982-Eddie Murray (1B)
1983-E. Murray (1B)/C. Ripken Jr. (SS)
1984-Eddie Murray (1B)
1985-Eddie Murray (1B)
1986-Don Aase (RHP)
1987-Larry Sheets (OF)
1988-E. Murray (1B)/C. Ripken Jr. (SS)
1989-Gregg Olson (RHP)
1990-Cal Ripken Jr. (SS)
1991-Cal Ripken Jr. (SS)
1992-Mike Devereaux (OF)
1993-Chris Hoiles (C)

ORIOLES GOLD GLOVE AWARD WINNERS

Year	Winner (pos)
1960	B. Rohinson (3b)
1961	B. Robinson
1962	B. Robinson
1963	B. Robinson
1964	B. Robinson (3b) Aparicio (ss)
1965	B. Robinson (3b)
1966	B. Robinson (3b) Aparicio (ss)
1967	B. Robinson (3b) Blair (of)
1968	B. Robinson (3b)
1969	B. Robinson (3b) Belanger (ss)
	D. Johnson (2b)
	Blair (of)
1970	B. Robinson (3b)
	D.Johnson (2b)
	Blair (of)
1971	B. Robinson (3b)
	Belanger (ss)
	D. Johnson (2b)
	Blair (of)

Year	Winner (pos)
1972	B. Robinson (3b)
	Blair (of)
1973	B. Robinson (3b)
	Belanger (ss)
	Grich (2b)
	Blair (of)
1974	B. Robinson (3b)
	Belanger (ss)
	Grich (2b)
	Blair (of)
1975	B. Robinson (3b)
	Belanger (ss)
	Grich (2b)
	Blair (of)
1976	Belanger (ss)
	Grich (2b)
	Palmer (p)
1977	Belanger (ss)
	Palmer (p)

Year	Winner (pos)
1978	Belanger (ss)
	Palmer (p)
1979	Palmer (p)
1980	None
1981	None
1982	Murray (1b)
1983	Murray (1b)
1984	Murray (1b)
1985	None
1986	None
1987	None
1988	None
1989	None
1990	None
1991	C. Ripken Jr. (ss)
1992	C. Ripken Jr. (ss)
1993	None

ORIOLES ALL-STAR GAME SELECTEES

1954
Bob Turley (DNP)

1955
Jim Wilson (DNP)

1956
George Kell (ST)

1957
George Kell (ST)
Billy Loes
Gus Triandos (DNP)

1958
Billy O'Dell
Gus Triandos (ST)

1959
Billy O'Dell[2]
Gus Triandos (ST)
Jerry Walker (ST)+[2]
Hoyt Wilhelm (DNP 1st)
Gene Woodling[2]

1960
Chuck Estrada (DNP 2nd)
Jim Gentile (DNP 2nd)
Ron Hansen (ST both)
Brooks Robinson

1961
Jack Brandt (DNP 2nd)
Jim Gentile (DNP 2nd)
Brooks Robinson (ST both)
Hoyt Wilhelm (DNP 2nd)

1962
Jim Gentile (ST both)
Milt Pappas (both)
Brooks Robinson (both)
Hoyt Wilhelm*

1963
Luis Aparicio
Brooks Robinson
Steve Barber*

1964
Luis Aparicio*
Brooks Robinson (ST)
Norm Siebern

1965
Milt Pappas (ST)+
Brooks Robinson (ST)

1966
Steve Barber (DNP)
Andy Etchebarren (DNP)
Brooks Robinson (ST)
Frank Robinson (ST)

1967
Andy Etchebarren (DNP)
Brooks Robinson (ST)
Frank Robinson (DNP)

1968
Dave Johnson
Boog Powell
Brooks Robinson (ST)

1969
Paul Blair
Dave Johnson *
Dave McNally
Boog Powell (ST)
Brooks Robinson
Frank Robinson (ST)

1970
Mike Cuellar (DNP)
Dave Johnson (ST)+
Dave McNally (DNP)
Jim Palmer (ST)+
Boog Powell (ST)
Brooks Robinson
Frank Robinson (ST)

1971
Don Buford
Mike Cuellar
Jim Palmer
Boog Powell *
Brooks Robinson (ST)
Frank Robinson (ST)

Managers: Paul Richards, '61**; Hank Bauer, '67; Earl Weaver, '70, '71, '72, '74++, '80; Joe Altobelli, '84.
* Selected but did not attend due to injury.
+ Started but not elected.
++ Honorary Manager
[1] Selected for 1st game only.
** Replaced Casey Stengel
[2] Selected for 2nd game only.

1972
Pat Dobson (DNP)
Bobby Grich (ST)+
Dave McNally
Jim Palmer (ST)+
Brooks Robinson (ST)

1973
Paul Blair
Brooks Robinson (ST)

1974
Mike Cuellar (DNP)
Bobby Grich
Brooks Robinson (ST)

1975
Jim Palmer (DNP)

1976
Mark Belanger
Bobby Grich (ST)

1977
Jim Palmer (ST)+
Ken Singleton

1978
Jim Palmer (ST)+
Mike Flanagan (DNP)
Eddie Murray (DNP)

1979
Ken Singleton
Don Stanhouse (DNP)

1980
Al Bumbry
Steve Stone (ST)+

1981
Scoff McGregor (DNP)
Eddie Murray
Ken Singleton (ST)

1982
Ken Singleton (ST)

1983
Tippy Martinez (DNP)
Eddie Murray
Cal Ripken Jr.

1984
Mike Boddicker (DNP)
Eddie Murray
Cal Ripken Jr. (ST)

1985
Eddie Murray (ST)
Cal Ripken Jr. (ST)

1986
Don Aase
Eddie Murray (ST)
Cal Ripken Jr. (ST)

1987
Terry Kennedy (ST)
Cal Ripken Jr. (ST)

1988
Cal Ripken Jr. (ST)+

1989
Mickey Tettleton
Cal Ripken Jr. (ST)

1990
Gregg Olson (DNP)
Cal Ripken Jr. (ST)

1991
Cal Ripken Jr. (ST)

1992
Brady Anderson
Mike Mussina
Cal Ripken Jr. (ST)

1993
Mike Mussina
Cal Ripken Jr. (ST)

Managers: Paul Richards, '61**; Hank Bauer, '67; Earl Weaver, '70, '71, '72, '74++, '80; Joe Altobelli, '84.
* Selected but did not attend due to injury.
+ Started but not elected. [1] Selected for 1st game only. [2] Selected for 2nd game only.
++ Honorary Manager ** Replaced Casey Stengel

ORIOLES HALL OF FAME MEMBERS (24)

Brooks Robinson, 3b ('77)
Frank Robinson, of ('77)
Dave McNally, 1hp ('78)
Boog Powell, 1b ('79)
Gus Triandos, c ('81)
Luis Aparicio, ss ('82)
Mike Cuellar, 1hp ('82)
Mark Belanger, ss ('83)
Earl Weaver, mgr ('83)
Paul Blair, of ('84)
Paul Richards, mgr ('84)
Milt Pappas, rhp ('85)
Jim Palmer, rhp ('86)
Ken Singleton, of ('86)
Al Bumbry, of ('87)
Steve Barber, lhp ('88)
Jim Gentile, 1b ('89)
Stu Miller, rhp ('89)
Dick Hall, rhp ('89)
Hank Bauer, mgr ('90)
Scott McGregor, lhp ('90)
Hal Brown, rhp ('91)
Gene Woodling, of ('92)
Don Buford ('93)